THE LIFE AND DEATH OF TROTSKY

THE LIFE AND DEATH OF TROTSKY

ROBERT PAYNE

McGRAW-HILL BOOK COMPANY

NEW YORK
ST. LOUIS
SAN FRANCISCO
DÜSSELDORF
MEXICO
TORONTO

Book design by Judith Michael.

1234567890DODO783210987

Library of Congress Cataloging in Publication Data

Payne, Pierre Stephen Robert, 1911
  The life and death of Trotsky.
  Bibliography: p.
  Includes index.
  1. Trotskii, Lev, 1879–1940.   2. Revolutionists—
Russia—Biography.   3. Communists—Russia—Biography.
I. Title.
DK254.T6P35   947.084'092'4 [B]   77-7523
ISBN 0-07-048940-8

Maps of the second escape journey and the Fortress at Coyoacan appear
on the rear endpapers.

For PATRICIA
always

CONTENTS

He who establishes a dictatorship and does not kill Brutus, or he who founds a republic and does not kill the sons of Brutus, will only reign a short time.

Machiavelli, *Discorsi*

EARLY YEARS

PART ONE

A curse upon all Marxists, and upon those who want to bring dryness and hardness into all the relations of life.

INTRODUCTION

He was the man who changed the world, for he was responsible for the triumph of the Russian Revolution and for its survival when sixteen armies attempted to strangle the infant Soviet republic at birth. For good or evil we live now, and will continue to live for generations to come, under the shadow of the revolution he brought about. In his time he was a towering figure, giving orders that were heard from Vladivostok to the gates of Warsaw and beyond, commanding armies, spinning theories, shaping and organizing the republic until there was scarcely any corner of it that did not bear the stamp of his intelligence. He was Lenin's close comrade in arms and Lenin's designated successor. He was revolutionary, statesman, supreme commander of the Red Army, a political strategist of a high order, the author of twenty books and a myriad articles, a man whose brilliance shone out with remarkable clarity. All those who heard him remember his extraordinary skill as an orator, and how he would marshal his arguments with an almost mechanical precision and yet pour so much emotion into them that every speech became a call to arms. He possessed all the revolutionary virtues: impatience, audacity, courage, fanaticism. He was the heir of Danton and Robespierre and suffered their fate. Of all the Russian revolutionaries, he was the one with the most clear-cut intelligence and the most philosophical turn of mind. He was in love with ideas and liked to think out his thoughts to their inevitable conclusions. Above all, he possessed an instinctive sense of action, and the drama of action. Archimedes said that if a man could find the right lever and the right place to insert it, he could move the world. Trotsky moved it.

Today in the Soviet Union he has become a forgotten man. There are no statues in his honor, no biographies of him are permitted to be written, and on the rare occasions when he is remembered he is reviled as a Judas figure, a betrayer and a traitor. History has been rewritten to avoid any mention of his name. By Stalin's orders he became that most pathetic of creatures—a nonperson, someone who never had any existence but whose books and documents might nevertheless be examined by a few select scholars in the closed section of the Lenin Library in Moscow. He exists in limbo, the ghost of a ghost. Nevertheless, there are many people still living who remember him, and nearly everything he wrote has found its way to the West. The more the Soviet government attempted to silence him, the louder became his voice.

In Russia the Revolution had scarcely begun before it changed its course. The people demanded peace, bread, and freedom, and for a few weeks or days all these seemed to be within their grasp. At Brest-Litovsk, Trotsky confronted the German military machine, defied it, invented a state of affairs that was neither peace nor war, and waited for the German people to rise up against their military masters. But the peace that seemed so close at hand proved to be elusive. There was no German revolution, the German military forces swept deeper into Russia, Allied armies attempted to strangle the infant republic, and the Russian Revolution nearly drowned in blood during three years of invasions and civil wars. Under Trotsky, in supreme command of the Russian armies, the invaders were thrown back to their own countries and the White armies were destroyed. When the wars were over, the Russian people were utterly exhausted in a land of famine. There were only a handful of locomotives on the broken-down railroads, and supplies were running so short that half the factories had to be shut down. There was no peace, there was no bread; there was only exhaustion.

This was the moment, very early in 1921, when the Revolution might have been saved, when those who brought it about might have encouraged the people to participate in their own affairs. What Lenin called the dictatorship of the proletariat was a tragic misnomer for the dictatorship of a small group of men dominated by Lenin and Trotsky, who issued decrees which were carried out mercilessly by Dzerzhinsky, a Pole who had been appointed head of the secret police. When Karl Marx invoked the dictatorship of the proletariat, he meant the dictatorship of the working class; he did not mean the dictatorship of a small, self-chosen revolutionary élite. The power would be spread around; it would not be concentrated in the hands of the few. With the blindness born of arrogance, the rulers of Russia continued to rule by decree and to reinforce their decrees with the aid of punitive expeditions, assassinations, executions, prison camps, slave labor, torture, and long terms of imprisonment. Dzerzhinsky's Tcheka, the punitive arm of the government, became almost a separate government ruling independently over vast areas of Russia, wherever there were prison camps and canals to be dug with human hands. All parties except the Communist Party were destroyed, all discussion was prohibited, all books were censored. Trotsky had thought of putting the entire population to work in labor armies at the direction of the government, with the Tcheka standing by to see that the work was carried out, but this extreme solution was abandoned because it proved to be inefficient. The small group continued to rule by decree; then Stalin came and one man ruled, and instead of the dictatorship of the working class there was the dictatorship of Stalin. He reigned for nearly thirty years. Never in the history of mankind have so many injustices been committed as during his long reign. Instead of the millennium promised by the Marxists, there was absolute tyranny in a land of ten thousand labor camps, of dead hopes, of a people terrified into submission to the whims of a psychotic dictator.

All this was very far from the intentions of the people who fought for the revolution—the workers, sailors, and soldiers of Petrograd. They had hoped for an egalitarian society where the privileges of the ancient feudal regime would be obliterated, where there would be no masters and no slaves, where the fruits of the land and of industry would be shared by all. They had not worked for an iron-heeled dictatorship, for one-man rule, for congresses compelled to rubber-stamp the decisions of the dictator. They had not worked for the police state and its torture chambers, or for the privileged minority that lived in great wealth. They had not fought in the streets to ensure the continued existence of a bureaucracy insensitive to the needs of the people. Lenin had sworn to destroy the stranglehold of the bureaucracy, but the bureaucracy continued to flourish. Soviet bureaucracy was another form of feudalism, just as the Tcheka was another form of the secret police that had existed in Russia long before the time of Ivan the Terrible.

Trotsky contributed weightily to the corruption of the Russian Revolution. His authoritarian temper and his sardonic view of human nature permitted him to become a brilliant secretary of foreign affairs and a formidable commissar of war, but in matters of government he was dangerously ignorant and incompetent. He demanded freedom for himself, not for others. He was cold, hard, reserved, without human sympathies outside his immediate family. In all his life he made exactly one close friend: Christian Rakovsky, the Rumanian Bolshevik, whom he met while a war correspondent during the Balkan Wars of 1912–1913. Lenin, too, made only one close friend: Julius Martov, a Men-

shevik, whose childlike laughter and bohemian habits
suggested a character at the opposite pole to Lenin, the
incorrigible scholastic who believed that all men must
conform to the laws of Marx. Martov, who possessed a
deep respect for Marx, believed that nothing was to be
gained by killing men in Marx's name.

In their attitude toward killing, Lenin, Trotsky, and
Stalin, distinguished themselves by an unerring ruthlessness. Banana-republic dictators could not have
been more bloodthirsty. They killed methodically, ab-
stractly, ordering executions on a large scale as a
warning to others or simply because they felt that an
occasional massacre was good for the nation. They did
not themselves do the killing: other men did their dirty
work for them. Lenin, Trotsky, and Stalin never watched
an execution and may never have seen a man being
killed, but between them they were responsible for at
least twenty million deaths. They were experts in the
art of "liquidation." Whole classes were wiped out at
their orders. No one dared to protest the waste of
human lives and human resources. The moral law
meant nothing to them, for they were outside the law
and contemptuous of humanistic tradition. They regarded themselves as the "new men" who would
introduce the just society whose coming was prophesied by Marx, and they therefore permitted themselves
every kind of excess in order to achieve their goal,
justifying their acts by pretending that the end justifies
the means. But the chief lesson of history is that the end
never justifies the means; and if the means is terror,
then the end is terror. In Trotsky's Russia, inhumanity
was built into the system from the beginning, and a
government that thought of people as cattle inevitably
treated them like cattle and butchered them at its
pleasure. The secret police—the butchers—were self-
perpetuating. Their power increased until they formed
a government within a government. The oppressed
people, unable to express their grievances, were reduced to humiliation and silence.

Lenin and Trotsky were both brilliant improvisers in
the art of revolution, they were men of clear intelli-

gence and great daring, and they both betrayed the Revolution by assuming dictatorial powers and by annihilating problems instead of solving them. They knew what they were doing; they did not always know what the secret police were doing, and they did not care.

For the betrayal of the Revolution, Trotsky was as much to blame as Lenin. Of the two, he had the sharper intelligence, the greater learning, the wider knowledge of affairs. He was a Jew, a Russian, a European, a cosmopolitan. He was well-read, at ease in any society, able to make himself understood in five or six languages. He did not, like Lenin, carry with him a heavy burden of private obsessions. To the end of his life he remained the questing student, seeking, probing, attempting to come to grips with insoluble problems. Pride was his fatal flaw. Sometimes he had the decency to doubt his own omniscience, but this did not happen often. Half of him lived in the brightness of his intelligence, while the other half lived in the shadow of a phenomenal will to power that led him to the conquest of Petrograd and of the armies invading Russia, and during the last weeks of his life it flared up again as he made plans for an insurrection in the United States with a handful of his followers.

Handsome, eloquent, possessing physical courage and grace of manner, he strode across the world as though it belonged to him. There was no limit to his daring. Like Napoleon he dared to do impossible things, and like Napoleon he was deeply troubled when he learned that not everyone admired him and that there were many who wanted to destroy him. So he became one of the tragic giants of our time, and not the least of them.

ROBERT PAYNE

AN IDYLLIC CHILDHOOD 1

Trotsky was born on November 7, 1879, on the two-hundred-and-fifty-acre estate of his father, a rich farmer in the Ukraine. His father's name was David Leontievich Bronstein, and the son was given the name Lev Davidovich Bronstein. When he became a revolutionary, the son abandoned the Germanic Bronstein for the Russian and rather aristocratic sounding name of Trotsky. This name had in fact been borne by a family belonging to the minor nobility in the reign of Ivan the Terrible.

Lev Bronstein was born in Yanovka, a small Ukrainian village which is not marked on any map. The village acquired its name from a certain Colonel Yanovsky who rose from the ranks to become a favorite of Tsar Alexander II and who was rewarded for his services by a land grant of a thousand acres. The colonel proved to be an indifferent farmer and sold a quarter of his estate to David Bronstein and leased him another four hundred acres, together with his house and all the outbuildings. Not long after the sale he died, and his widow would sometimes come and visit with the Bronsteins.

David Bronstein was a tall, handsome, wiry man with a broad, high forehead, deep-set eyes, finely modeled features, large sweeping mustaches and a heavy bristling beard. In a photograph taken in old age, when the beard and mustaches had turned white, he gives an impression of great dignity and distinction, and could be taken for a retired high official, a judge, or the governor of a province. It is a face teeming with intelligence and forthrightness, and everything we know about him suggests that he knew exactly what he was doing and why he was doing it at every moment of his life. Trotsky, who liked his father but was a little afraid of him, says he could not read and spoke a curious mixture of Ukrainian and Russian. It is unlikely that he was illiterate—it may have been that he was impatient of books and newspapers and expended nearly all his energies on managing his estate, and therefore was rarely seen reading. And since he was a Jew who conversed with Jews, it is likely that he spoke Yiddish, which was their common language all over Russia.

There is some mystery about David Leontievich Bronstein's father's name. Leontievich means "son of Leonty": but Leonty is the name of a Christian saint and was generally used only by Christians. There is at least the suggestion that two generations before him there had been in the family a falling away from the Jewish faith. Although David Bronstein was not a particularly devout Jew, he attended services in the synagogue at Gromokley on high holy days. His wife, Anna, was more devout and attended services regularly. Gromokley was only a short distance away, and she would make the journey in one of the farm-carts, accompanied by her children.

David Bronstein did not belong to the class later known as *kulaks*, the hard-fisted rich peasants. He was a landed proprietor working his own land and striving to extend it. He owned the only mechanical thresher for miles around, and received as his fee one-tenth of the grain threshed. If he was not inordinately rich, he was rich enough to afford all kinds of luxuries, but since he despised luxuries—his greatest luxury was the sight of his acres of golden wheat, which stretched as far as the eye could see—he was content to live frugally and to work zestfully. He had a commanding presence, enjoyed giving orders to his workmen, and was out in the fields or the barns all day. Yanovka was his whole world, and a very satisfying one.

For Anna Bronstein it was probably far less satisfying. She had a rather broad, heavy, and not very intelligent face, if we can trust a photograph taken in middle age, where she looks simultaneously energetic and somnolent. She was town bred, had received some education, and liked to spend the long winters reading novels beside the window while the snow drifted outside. She liked to read aloud, and did not always understand what she was reading. It was not that she was slow witted; it was simply that she could not possibly understand some of the romantic novels, which she borrowed from the library in the small town of Bobrinetz a few miles away.

David Bronstein had zest and stood out against the landscape. His wife, worn out by many pregnancies, fades into the landscape, almost vanishes. She gave her husband eight children, of whom four survived. Of those who lived, the eldest was Alexander, then came Elizavetta, then Lev, then Olga, The children liked each other, played together, and were completely different in character. Not one of them became a farmer. In later life Alexander owned a brewery, Elizavetta married a doctor in Odessa, Lev became a revolutionary, and Olga in her small way also became a revolutionary, for she married Leon Rosenfeld, better known as Kamenev, who became a Bolshevik leader. Olga served as his secretary and was given various minor posts in the Bolshevik government. What was extraordinary about the family was its very ordinariness: there was nothing to suggest that the family of the landed proprietor would produce one of the arch-revolutionaries of modern times.

There was one other person on the farm who deeply influenced Trotsky. This was Ivan Vasilyevich Greben, who was in charge of the machine shop. He had thick red mustaches and a beard which he wore in "the French way," which meant that he wore it like Napoleon III. He was handsome, well set, indispensable, and sat down at meals with the family. He represented the world of mechanics and industry breaking into the age-old life of the farm, for he could rebuild an engine, repair a boiler, turn a metal ball, make a spring carriage, mend a clock, upholster furniture, and if someone provided the tires, he could make a bicycle. On one famous occasion he put together a broken-down spinet, bought by David Bronstein for sixteen rubles sometime in the past, and completely refashioned it. He cleaned it, glued it, polished it, replaced the ivory keys and the strings, and played on it to the satisfaction of everyone who gathered round him in the living room. Out of an old spinet which was found to contain a pair of dead mice when taken to the machine shop, Ivan Greben had made something wholly new and memorable. And just as David Bronstein represented intelligent command over the land and the men who worked on it, so Ivan Greben represented mechanical inventiveness, the Prometheus-like power of man to bend the physical world to his will.

Out of old junk Ivan Greben made farm machinery, and people came from miles around to have their farming implements repaired by him. Binders and seed-drills in various stages of disrepair were brought to him, dismantled, the pieces laid out on the benches of the machine shop, the missing parts replaced, and then the machines were reassembled, polished, and returned to the owner as good as new. The neighboring German settlers came to Yanovka to seek his advice on the purchase of threshing machines and steam engines. The machine shop was almost a factory, for Ivan Greben had many assistants and was training many apprentices.

Although Trotsky feared his father a little, he had no fear at all of this master mechanic, who could put life into an old spinet as easily as he could make a gun or cut threads for nuts and bolts. It was not only that he was prodigiously inventive, kindly and unassuming in spite of all the power he wielded on the farm, but he was also immensely brave. The story was told that one day—it happened to be the day when Trotsky was born—he very nearly cut off his thumb with an ax, so that it hung almost by the skin. David Bronstein was in the machine shop when it happened. Very calmly, with the blood pouring out of the wound, Ivan Greben placed what was left of the thumb on a board and raised the ax, ready to get rid of it altogether. Just in time David Bronstein shouted: "Stop! The thumb will grow again!" So it did, although it could never be bent back and there was always a deep scar where the ax had fallen.

Trotsky admired the man this side of adoration. He was a constant visitor to the machine shop, where, as a child, he was sometimes allowed to cut the threads of nuts and bolts and perform small mechanical tasks. In a rather feminine way he was in love with the man. Forty-five years later he could remember entering the machine shop to find Ivan Greben sitting in a corner with a tool in his hand, smoking, deep in contemplation or perhaps thinking about nothing at all. "At such times," he wrote, "I used to sit down beside him and gently curl his thick auburn mustache around my finger, or examine those hands, the unmistakable hands of an artisan." He remembered every detail of those hands: the little black spots that came from grinding millstones, the broadness at the tips, their suppleness and tenacity, and their softness and self-consciousness, for each finger seemed to be living and acting independently while the whole hand acted with wonderful efficiency. It was a woman's way of looking at a man's hands.

From time to time all the laborers and artisans working on the farm would make their way to the machine shop. Almost it was a club where people came to talk to pass the time away, while Ivan Greben hammered on sheet metal or turned a croquet ball on a lathe. Many of these men were "characters": they could have stepped out of Chekhov's stories. There was the surly, red-haired Yashka, the fireman, who passionately loved hunting and sold his gun for a drink; he would vanish for long intervals to hunt or to go on a drinking spree, and no one much cared whether he came or went. There was "our Ignat," who was distinguished from "humpback Ignat," who was drafted into the army and somehow escaped to become a factory worker, returning to Yanovka in new clothes and in full possession of a watch, which he displayed to everyone. He had been engaged to a girl on the farm, but it appeared that he had found a new girl in the city. Anna Bronstein was outraged and sent him packing.

But these were all minor characters. One man dominated the farm, and this was Ivan Greben, Orthodox Christian, master of machinery, chief adviser on all things under the sun. It was Greben who spoke to the young Lev about the afterlife, pointing to the heavens and speaking about the paradise of the dead; and as the boy remembered it, they both laughed and thought it somehow absurd that people should make their way to the sky. Lev was about seven years old when this happened, and he had already developed a certain critical ability. What happened to people after they were dead was not, he thought, a serious matter.

A more serious matter was hunting—especially the hunting of tarantulas. This, too, he learned from Ivan Greben, who kept tarantulas in a jar filled with sunflower-seed oil. The way to catch them was to fasten a piece of wax on a thread and then drop the thread into a burrow. Tarantulas loved wax, clung to it, and could be pulled out. Then it was easy to put them in empty matchboxes. Later they joined the other tarantulas in Ivan Greben's jar of sunflower-seed oil, considered to be the best antidote to a tarantula bite.

Like David Bronstein, Ivan Greben belonged to a family that had immigrated from Germany, probably at the time of Catherine the Great. He had the German virtues: efficiency, mechanical ability, good humor. David Bronstein, on the other hand, had the temperament of the Russian *barin*, one of those landlords who rule over vast estates—at one time he controlled over 3,000 acres—as though they were born to it. He was morose, kindly, generous, impatient of accounts, and stubborn as a mule whenever his interests were affected. The money side of things did not interest him overmuch, but he was well aware that he was the sole owner of his fields, his mill, his cattle, his Merino sheep, and everything else that grew on the land or fed off it. Trotsky remembered his father suddenly exclaiming at supper: "Come, write this down! I have received thirteen hundred rubles from the commission merchant. I gave the Colonel's widow six hundred, and four hundred to Dembovsky. Put down, too, that I gave Theodosia Antonovna one hundred rubles when I was in Elizavetgrad last spring."

He had to be a very rich man indeed to be so cavalier about his income and expenditures.

Yet there were no outward signs of riches. They lived in the house built by Colonel Yanovsky, plastered with clay and whitewashed, with a straw roof. The deep cracks in the walls were the breeding place of snakes which seemed, like salamanders, to resist intense heat, for whenever snakes were believed to be burrowing in the cracks, boiling hot water from the samovar was poured on them, but without effect. The rooms were small and dark, the floors were stamped clay, fleas flourished, water leaked through the low ceilings after heavy rain, and buckets and basins were placed under the places where the roof leaked. But the rain was the least of their worries, soon the sun shone, and once more they were basking in the scent-filled countryside, in the land that the Greeks knew as the Golden Chersonese.

In summer the house almost vanished under the climbing vines, and the red and white roses. Acacias grew nearby. Not far away stood the famous machine shop where Ivan Greben presided, with its tile roof, and here too were the main kitchen, the servants' quarters, and three reed-thatched barns. These barns were raised on stones so that the damp earth would not harm the grain. Underneath the barns the farm dogs, pigs, and chickens took refuge from the summer heat and winter cold; and sometimes the hens laid their eggs there, and the boy would slither over the rough stones on his belly to find them and bring them triumphantly to the house. On the roof of the big barn the storks nested every year, and one of the boy's earliest memories was the sight of the storks raising their red bills to heaven as they swallowed snakes and frogs; he was fascinated by the strange heavings and coilings of the storks' long necks as they gorged themselves.

But the real wealth of the farm lay not so much in the barns as in the great storage sheds, hundreds of feet long, which lay some distance beyond the barns. Here, under a roof like an inverted V, was stored the fresh grain waiting to be winnowed, pure and sweet-smelling, and beyond these sheds lay the cow pen.

The center of this empire, the command post, was David Bronstein's dining room. This was also the office, where he kept his few records; here he met his guests, the grain merchants and local farmers, and held court. The implements of his office rested on a bare rafter that stretched across the low ceiling. On the rafter he kept his account books, pens, ink bottles, pieces of string, and nails. Plates of food were placed there out of reach of the cat. The rafter was so low that the children instinctively cried out to all visitors: "Mind your head!"

Here the boy sat curled up on the sofa with the large holes in the cushions which his father never bothered to mend, dreaming his long dreams or copying pictures of horses out of magazines or writing execrable poems at night in the light of a charcoal fire. When the door was closed and the window sealed, the fumes from the charcoal fire sometimes made him lightheaded; and on winter evenings he would sometimes find himself alone in this room and he would be overcome by a terrifying sense of loneliness and then he would run out of the house and scream into the darkness: "Mashka! Mashka! Come into the dining room!" over and over again. Mashka was a servant girl, still busy with the work of the farm, which went on until late in the evening.

In spite of the sudden spells of loneliness, it was an idyllic childhood. The worst that happened was an occasional cutting word from his father or a reprimand from his mother if he acted too boisterously. It is clear that he was a chatterbox, mischievous, and highly strung. He was easily hurt and was often in tears, and sometimes he cried for no reason at all. One day a peasant's horse strayed into a wheat field and did some damage. David Bronstein knew what to do on such occasions. He took the horse away and locked it up in the stable, then marched back to his house, followed by the peasant who was wailing that it was not his fault that his horse had strayed. Young Lev heard the peasant's cries, ran into his mother's bedroom, threw himself on the bed, wept unrestrainedly for half an hour, and only came out into the dining room when his father told him that he had not punished the peasant, the horse had been returned to him, there was nothing in the least to be disturbed about. Shamefaced, pouting, pretending that he had been communing with a private sorrow, he took his accustomed place on the sofa, his mother facing him across the table and his father on the high-backed chair beside him.

Looking back on his childhood, Trotsky was a little puzzled by it. He sometimes asked himself what motivated a privileged boy on a farm to become a revolutionary. Delving into his memories he could discover very few occasions when he was moved by a sense of social protest. Once, when he was appointed paymaster for a day, sitting over an account book and writing out the names of the seasonal workers and the amounts due to them less whatever amounts were docked for misbehavior or damage of property, he suddenly announced that a worker would have to be paid more because "it was not enough to get along on." The boy made a speech, emphasizing the man's needs, which were far greater than the wages he was receiving. His father told him to shut up, the man received the wages due to him and no more, and the single act of protest was quickly forgotten.

He remembered with sympathy the hopeless lives of the seasonal workers. Two or three hundred thousand seasonal workers came to the province of Kherson at harvest time. They received a pittance for four months' work; they lived in the open fields; at midday they were fed on vegetable soup and porridge and in the evening they were given millet soup. The food was inadequate, and they sometimes protested by gathering outside the clay house, lying face downward on the ground, and waving their bare, cracked legs in the air. At such times the boy's father issued extra rations—curdled milk, watermelons, half a sack of dried fish. Having received these gifts, they went away singing. Old reapers known to have worked on the farm for many years would receive a glass of vodka from the hands of the lord of the manor, who remembered them from the previous year and knew they were efficient and well trained and would serve as examples to the others; these old reapers would receive a few more rubles than the others. During one summer the food was so bad that there was an epidemic of night blindness, and newspaper articles were written about laborers who were seen moving about the fields with their hands stretched out in front of them. A government inspector arrived at Yanovka. He concluded that night blindness was caused by a lack of animal fats, and thereafter a small portion of fat was included in the laborers' rations.

This was the land once occupied by the Scythians, whose royal mounds rose above the plains, concealing treasures of gold testifying to the formidable art of those ancient craftsmen. Now the land was occupied by dedicated farmers like David Bronstein or by landowners who mortgaged their farms over and over again, lived in style in their columned mansions, kept horses and went out hunting, accompanied by their servants and white wolfhounds, spent vast amounts of money on entertainment, and were in debt to their stewards. David Bronstein, who was never in debt, accumulated their properties, their lands, and their wolfhounds. His empire was continually expanding until it seemed that it would eventually stretch out all over the entire province of Kherson.

The luxury of the country houses left the boy wide-eyed with wonder and excitement. Those columned mansions sometimes resembled palaces with more rooms and more servants than you could count, with billiard tables and picture galleries and grand pianos, with stables, parks, and artificial lakes. There were gilded chairs and carpets as thick as cushions. Somewhere, in a little room under the roof, there was always a steward practicing double-entry bookkeeping.

This was one kind of luxury. He was about seven when he was taken for the first time to Elizavetgrad. He was thunderstruck: a large town, house after house, with sidewalks, green-tiled roofs, balconies, shops, policemen, and red balloons. Where was the end of it? Neither Paris nor New York, which he visited many years later, made such an impression on him as Elizavetgrad, founded in 1754 by the Tsaritsa Elizabeth, the daughter of Peter the Great, but looking as new as though it was built yesterday.

Then, in the same year, came a luxury so great that it drove him nearly mad with happiness, though at first it drove him nearly mad with fear. In Christmas week, while the family was sitting in the dining room, a troop of mummers came running in and began to act out a drama called "Tsar Maximilian." The boy had never seen actors before, did not know they existed. He was so terrified when they entered that he fell off the sofa from sheer fright. Afterward, summoning his courage, he began to look at them and was wholly transported into the realm of splendor they were creating around him. In those moments he was in a state of rapture. Tsar Maximilian's great speech was so dazzling and the impersonation of the Tsar was so complete that he could scarcely believe that he was not in the presence of a fabulous monarch with power of life and death over a vast empire. When he learned that the Tsar was really a former soldier called Prokhor he still found it difficult to believe. When the play was over, he ran after the soldier and begged him to dictate the speech slowly so that he could write it down. Prokhor was a servant on the estate. The boy had to cling to him and plead with him before he assented. On the following day, in the dining room, Prokhor began to recite the rhymed verses, while the boy wrote them down, using the windowsill as a desk. He had only recited a few lines when David Bronstein erupted into the room, saw what was happening, and ordered the servant back to work. The boy was inconsolable and wept for the rest of the afternoon.

The seeds of drama had at last been planted in his life. A few years later, when he saw his first play in Odessa, he could scarcely bear the excitement and remained in his seat during the intermission for fear of missing anything. The pleasure was so intense that he likened it to torture. Once he encountered a boy who had actually performed in amateur theatricals. This was a godsent opportunity. He had read Pushkin's play *The Covetous Knight* and admired it, and with the help of the boy he hoped to stage it. He was still dreaming of being an actor and a stage manager when the boy was found to be suffering from tuberculosis and was sent away. Once more he was inconsolable. Still later, he attempted to write a long play on a revolutionary subject with the help of another friend, but nothing came of it. Meanwhile, at Yanovka, smitten by poetic fury, he wrote verses. Many of his verses had already been written by other poets but he enjoyed their sound. He attempted to conceal his verses from his sister and was unsuccessful. His sister told his mother who told his father, and on the next occasion when visitors came to the house he was peremptorily ordered to present himself and recite his verses to the company. Seized with terror and confusion, he did as he was told and many years later he could still feel the anguish of stepping in front of an audience and reading his own compositions.

Gromokley, the small town about a mile and a half from Yanovka, was divided by a ravine into two separate parts, the German part and the Jewish part. The German part looked neat and clean with fine houses, tiled roofs, sleek horses, and fat cattle. By contrast the Jewish part was poverty stricken and run down, the roofs falling apart, the cattle thin and scrawny. Here lived his Aunt Rachel and a schoolteacher called

Shufer, a lean, mild-mannered man with an obsequious smile, who offered to teach him Russian grammar, arithmetic, and the Old Testament in Hebrew. Accordingly his father drove him to Gromokley one day when he was about seven and a half and arranged that he should live with Aunt Rachel and attend school every day. Payment was made by barter. Aunt Rachel received wheat flour, barley flour, buckwheat, and millet, and the teacher received some sacks of wheat and a few rubles. Gromokley made little impression on the boy, who felt that he had been wrenched away from home and the rich life of the farm into a dark, unwholesome *shtetl* where everything inevitably went wrong. Here there was no Ivan Greben to instruct and entertain him with machinery, and there was no one to play with. Happily, he could walk to Yanovka whenever he pleased and he did not feel that he was hopelessly entangled. Of Aunt Rachel's husband Abraham he could remember only that on a few occasions the old man gave him a bone with marrow, remarking: "I wouldn't take ten rubles for this bone."

He learned some Hebrew, reciting the words in chorus with the other pupils, and he learned to write Russian in a very clear and well-rounded hand. He showed little enthusiasm for his teacher, who was very thin and married to a well-fleshed wife. On one memorable occasion the wife entered the classroom, showed her husband a handful of flour, and complained that it smelled bad. The teacher bent his sharp nose to smell the flour and she promptly pushed it into his face. He stood there in the classroom among the laughing children with flour all over his face.

His few memories of this period were of the same kind. It was as though he blotted Gromokley out of his memory by an act of will: the misery, the horror, the scrawny cattle, and the poverty-stricken houses. Gromokley was a dark enclosed space, a prison, from which he could escape whenever he wanted to.

In the summer of 1888, when he was eight and a half, a visitor came to stay on the farm at Yanovka. His name: Moissey Shpentzer, he was Anna Bronstein's nephew, and he held himself with a certain air of distinction. He was staying on the farm because he was recovering from a bout of tuberculosis and needed fresh air, plentiful supplies of milk, and plain food. They called him "Monya," and this affectionate name served him well. What was immediately apparent was that he was totally unlike the people on the farm and at Gromokley; he had the voice, the manners, and the bearing of a man of the city.

The boy became attached to Shpentzer, who was about twenty-eight years old, knew everything, had traveled everywhere, had been a part-time journalist, and had studied statistics, a mysterious science apparently beyond the comprehension of nearly everyone, and in addition he was an excellent teacher. He offered to teach the boy Russian grammar and mathematics, and the boy became his happy pupil. He also taught other things: how to hold a glass, how to wash, how to behave. He paid particular attention to the correct pronunciation of words, as befitted a man who had attended a university. He was a humanist and a humanitarian, a cultivated man. He felt the inadequacy of life on the farm: it was too raw, too bitter. Once he saw an overseer strike a shepherd with a knout, and said: "How shameful," while hissing through his teeth. For the first time the boy understood that it was shameful and remembered it.

David Bronstein had been wondering for some time what to do about his son's education. Now an answer presented itself: Lev would go to Odessa, stay with Moissey Shpentzer, and attend the gymnasium. In this way he would remain within the family, and since Shpentzer would soon be marrying a woman who was a principal in a school for Jewish girls, there was little doubt that he would be well cared for.

In the spring of 1889, wearing a new uniform, with a large trunk containing gifts for his relatives in the city, the nine-year-old boy set out for Odessa. There was a long drive across the steppe, then a train journey to Nikolayev, and then a ride by steamer to Odessa, where for the first time he saw the open sea. When he left Yanovka his mother and sisters wept, and he wept with them. When he reached Odessa, Moissey fussed over him and asked him about Yanovka and the cows. He fell in love with Odessa the moment he set eyes on it, and he said the cows were not worth talking about.

2 THE YOUNG PEACOCK

Odessa was a little more than a hundred years old when Lev Bronstein went to live there. Here the boy who had enjoyed an idyllic childhood spent seven years of unalloyed happiness with the Shpentzers, who were kindly, intelligent, and understanding of his foibles. They doted on him; he doted on them. He lived very much as he pleased, and the Shpentzers marveled at their good fortune in having him. They found only two faults in him: he was obsessively neat and he was a little too self-admiring.

The city, too, was self-admiring. Founded by French aristocrats who fled from the French Revolution, it was perfectly aware of its aristocratic charm, its beauty, and its power. It stood on a cliff overlooking the Black Sea, and was wealthy because it controlled the trade from the Golden Chersonese. The first governor-general was Armand du Plessis, Duc de Richelieu, who watched it grow from a small village to a full-fledged city in a period of eleven years. Hard-headed, unscrupulous, and mild-mannered on ordinary occasions, he exerted an immense influence on southern Russia before returning to France and occupying many high positions. He left behind him a taste for aristocratic splendor and sumptuous living which the people of Odessa never forgot.

After his death they erected in his honor a bronze statue of him in a public square. It was no ordinary statue, for he is seen wearing the costume of a Roman, and it was no ordinary square: he stands on the main square and looks down on two hundred granite steps leading to the sea. He was the model for all the young schoolboys of Odessa: the peaceful conqueror, the superb administrator, the aristocratic adventurer.

He was one of those who helped to design the city with its long, straight, tree-shaded boulevards, parks, gardens, elegant townhouses, and public squares filled with flowers. The best houses looked out on the Black Sea, which was black for only a few days in winter and for the rest of the year was a heavenly blue. Odessa was the newest city in Russia and gleamed like new paint.

Lev Bronstein arrived in Odessa three weeks after the Shpentzers had their first baby, a girl, and promptly took charge of her. He rocked the cradle, watched for the first smile, and later taught her to walk and to read. He poured affection on her—perhaps too much, for the Shpentzers were afraid he might rock the baby to death. He was curly haired and mischievous and very appealing with his bright blue eyes and quick eager smiles. In those days the Shpentzers were still poor—later Moissey Shpentzer would become the head of a small publishing empire—and the boy slept at night behind a curtain drawn across the small living room. But the poverty was only relative. Shpentzer himself had no employment: he was not permitted to teach because he had been expelled from the university for expressing some mild socialist ideas. His wife, who was the headmistress of a school for Jewish girls, brought in money. Their first task was to teach the boy to speak Russian rather than the Ukrainian dialect spoken in Yanovka. They also taught him politeness and good manners, lessons which he never forgot. They opened up their library to him and in the evenings they read aloud to him—Pushkin and Lermontov especially. Shpentzer possessed a sensitive and disciplined mind, and in his quiet way was determined that the boy should follow in his footsteps. His wife, Fanny, took life less seriously and sometimes teased the boy. His perpetual neatness sometimes provoked her into reminding him that it was not the most important thing in life to appear to be wearing a new suit; he continued to remove every speck of lint from his clothing. He was becoming urbanized.

Sometimes, of course, he felt a longing for Yanovka, the smells of the farm, the happy disorder of his parents' cluttered house, Greben's beautiful machine shop. At such times he would sob into his pillow or trace out on a frosty windowpane a message to his mother, whom he loved dearly. Yanovka was the lost paradise, but Odessa was paradise regained. How does one choose between paradises?

In 1887 the Russian government instituted the *numerus clausus*, which severely restricted the number of Jews entering secondary schools. Bronstein had not even gone to primary school, and his chances of being admitted to secondary school after a stiff competitive examination were all the weaker. In fact, he failed the first time he took the examination. Shpentzer arranged that the boy should go into a preparatory class at St. Paul's School, and tutored him, while Fanny, who was wise in the affairs of the Odessa school boards, was able to help in various ways. The combination of Moissey and Fanny Shpentzer was a formidable one, for they were both deeply respected in the community.

St. Paul's School in Odessa was founded by German Lutherans to serve the numerous German residents. It was gradually being Russified. By the time Bronstein entered it, only half the teachers were German in origin and all the teaching was conducted in Russian. It was a *realschule* as distinguished from a *gymnasium*, that is, it concentrated on mathematics, science, and modern languages, especially French and German, rather than supplying a classical education. When he finally entered the school, Bronstein proved to be an unusually brilliant pupil, winning high marks. 5 was the highest mark, 1 was the lowest. There was a teacher who liked to say that only God gets 5, yet he gave Bronstein 5. When another boy complained that his own work deserved 5, the teacher said: "I don't give 5's."

"But you gave Bronstein 5!"

"That's Bronstein," the teacher answered.

This was a phrase that accompanied the boy throughout his school years. He took no interest in sports or girls; he lived with the high purpose of always being top of the class. Years afterward Fanny Shpentzer remembered: "He was only ten years old, but he was self-contained and self-confident. And he had an extraordinary sense of duty that must have been instinctive. No one had to take charge of his training, no one had to worry about his lessons. He always did more than was expected of him."

The desire to excel had become a passion which threatened to devour him. It was not a modest passion; he flaunted it; and though he says in his autobiography that he was popular with the other students, it is not necessary to believe that he was popular with all of them at all times. His perpetual neatness, his reserve, his sense of innate superiority could be exasperating, and he appears to have delighted precisely in this exasperating quality that kept the other students at a distance from him. Sometimes he appalled the teachers by asking them impossible questions, knowing that they did not know the answer, and after watching them floundering for some time, he would politely and gently give the right, the accurate, the irreproachable answer.

Boys like this sometimes come to bad ends: they become teachers who despise their pupils.

Even the Shpentzers found his neatness nearly insufferable. On the day when he entered the preparatory school, he was inordinately proud of his brand-new uniform and all the appurtenances that went with it. He imagined that the passers-by were looking at him with amazement and envy. He wore a new cap with yellow braid and a metal badge bearing the complicated insignia of St. Paul's School, and on his back a fresh leather schoolbag filled with textbooks in brightly colored bindings together with a handsome pencil case, all the pencils newly sharpened, with a penholder and an eraser. He made his regal progress along Uspenskaya Street, one of the main thoroughfares of Odessa, deeply aware that he was covered with glittering brass buttons, wore a cap with a blue peak, and was the proud possessor of the emblem of St. Paul's School enclosed in crossed golden palm-leaves. "Those golden buttons afforded me an indescribable delight," he said later, "and in general it seemed to me that upon my shoulders, or at least in my knapsack, rested the dignity of the whole school whose threshold I was about to cross for the first time."

To his surprise no one paid any attention to him. Suddenly he saw a shabby, thirteen-year-old streetboy wearing a tattered shirt and broken boots standing in his way. The boy threw back his head, cleared his throat, and spat. Then he ran away. In total confusion Bronstein looked down at the spittle on his sleeve. There was nothing to be done except to wipe it away with some chestnut leaves and continue his journey to school. There he was met with another outrageous alteration in the proper management of his affairs. He was told that he had no right to wear the baubles on his uniform. As a pupil of the preparatory school, he must wear ordinary buttons; the yellow braid on his cap and the crossed golden palm-leaves were reserved for those who had passed the examination. Happily there was no school that day. Instead he was led into the school chapel where the organ played and Pastor Binneman addressed the new pupils from the pulpit, urging them to be good, to study hard, and to behave kindly to one another. The torrential waves of sound from the organ terrified the boy, who had never before heard these sounds, and the Lutheran pastor with the white facings on his clerical uniform spoke with such a heavy German accent that it was impossible to understand him. School was only another name for a prolonged reign of terror.

The next day he attended his first classes, and the

terror was dissipated. He did well in arithmetic, receiving two 5's, and another 5 for accurately copying out a passage in German on the blackboard. He ran home in triumph, no longer oppressed by the fact that preparatory schoolboys must wear dark buttons, not the golden buttons stamped with the imperial eagle.

He was not always a paragon of virtues. Fanny Shpentzer remembered one nasty and inexplicable incident when he stole some of her husband's best books and sold them to buy candy. One of the boy's most vivid recollections in later years was of himself standing in a doorway, quickly and laboriously gobbling up the candy. Was it defiance? Self-assertion? An act of revenge? He must have known that Moissey Shpentzer loved books only a little less than he loved his wife. He must have known, too, that the act would involve the harshest punishment even if that punishment consisted of nothing more than a silent rebuke. Something had gone profoundly wrong. Max Eastman, who wrote a short book on the early life of Trotsky, heard the story from Fanny Shpentzer and then confronted Trotsky with it. His impression was that the boy did not want the candy; instead, he just wanted to steal the books and this gave him a great feeling of independence. It is an unlikely solution to the problem. It is much more likely that the stealing of the books was his boyhood way to punish and obliterate the father-figure who was dominating his life. In this sense it was a calculated act of rebellion, a deliberate effort to smash the relationship. Why? The boy probably did not know. It was something in his character, like his obsessive neatness. Suddenly the fatal knife falls and the thread is cut. Moissey Shpentzer was all-forgiving, for he bore no grudge and continued to love and help the boy through the rest of his career in the school.

Teachers in provincial schools tend to assume the roles of caricatures, and the teachers at St. Paul's School were no exception. Many were grotesquely unhappy: one hanged himself from a window frame, another cut his throat with a razor. In his autobiography Trotsky drew a whole gallery of portraits of his teachers. Here for example is his description of Gustave Burnande, the teacher of French, called "the Frenchman," though he was a Swiss:

> He was a lean man with a profile so flat that it seemed to have just been squeezed in a press. He had a small bald spot, thin, blue, unkindly lips, a sharp nose, and a mysterious large scar in the form of the letter X on his forehead. Burnande was disliked unanimously, and with reason. A sufferer from indigestion, he kept swallowing tablets during classroom hours, and regarded every pupil as a personal enemy. The scar on his forehead was a constant source of conjecture and theory. It was said that Gustave in his youth had fought a duel, and that his opponent succeeded in tracing a twisted cross on his forehead with a rapier. This was denied several months later. It was then asserted that there had been no duel but instead a surgical operation, in the course of which part of his forehead was employed to repair his nose. The boys carefully scrutinized his nose, and the more venturesome ones affirmed that they could see the stitches.

It was an unkind portrait, deliberately so. It was sharply drawn; there is enough detail to permit us to see him in the round, and sufficient venom to color it vitriol-green. If there are any compensating features, we are not told of them. The intensity of the venom tends to spoil the picture.

As a bright student, always at the top of his class, a little too conscious of the power of his intelligence and a little distant with his fellow students, who did not always like him, the boy held fast to the proposition that high marks were an absolute desideratum and nothing else mattered very much. The company of his school fellows did not interest him, though he tolerated them. He did not play with them, rarely saw them after school hours, and never went boating or fishing with them on the Black Sea. The supreme moment came when some odious teacher singled him out in the class and congratulated him on the excellence of his work, giving him 5+. Since God only received 5, this was sufficient to keep him happy for many days. "Anton

Krizhanovsky singled me out for my knowledge of Russian grammar and my love of the language," he wrote later. "He made it a fixed rule to read my written works aloud to the class, giving me a mark of 5$^+$." The information would be received a little more generously if we had not been previously told that Krizhanovsky was a crafty, red-bearded, former theological student, a man who constantly took bribes and concealed his cunning nature behind an appearance of benevolence.

Bronstein's character was being formed, but one essential element of it has not yet been discussed. Although he appeared to be stronger than most children of his age, and during the summer vacations at Yanovka demonstrated that he was a good horseman, he was in fact unwell, suffering from what the doctors called "chronic catarrh of the digestive tract," which was another way of saying that they did not know what was the matter with him. They gave him medicines, but the medicines had little or no effect, and they put him on a diet, but the diet evidently was quite useless, for the digestive tract worked no better than before. Nervous shocks nearly always affected his digestion. He had a nervous stomach which interfered with his studies to such an extent that the doctors concluded that he should work less and avoid the excitements of Odessa. He was in the fourth grade when it was decided that he should spend some time at Yanovka to recover his health; to avoid falling behind in his studies, it was arranged that he should have a private tutor.

"Chronic catarrh of the digestive tract," whatever it was, gave him considerable pain and misery, and it seems to have lasted throughout his entire life. It also seems to be connected with his frequent fainting spells and fits of nausea. Outwardly he would appear in good health; inwardly he was an invalid very conscious of a continuing and inexplicable infirmity. He was always going to see doctors, hoping for a cure. To some limited extent his ferocious desire to excel served as compensation for his infirmity; his intellectual pride masked his physical weakness.

Bronstein's tutor, chosen for him by Moissey

Shpentzer, appears to have been a rather insignificant man who talked too much and demanded more respect than the boy was willing to give him. The description of him follows the same pattern as the description of the luckless Burnande. First, the odd appearance, then the advance column of slighting adjectives (vain, fantastic, talkative, lacking in character), followed by a battering ram composed of selected anecdotes that effectively reduce him to zero. In the end the poor tutor was dismissed during a violent quarrel. Bronstein returned to school after two or three unhappy months in the country.

Moissey Shpentzer's fortunes were beginning to advance: he now had his own small publishing house and no longer eked out a living by translating Greek classics into Russian, or writing occasional articles, or auditing accounts. The smell of printer's ink invaded the small apartment. For the first time the boy observed how books were made, how proofs were corrected, and how the bindings were stitched on. The acid smell of ink delighted him, he came to love the texture of good bindings, and authorship fascinated him. A certain Sergey Sychevsky, a writer, an authority on Shakespeare, and a veteran journalist, sometimes came to dinner at the apartment. He liked to joke and tell stories, drank huge amounts of vodka, and enjoyed the careful study of poetry. One day it occurred to him to ask Bronstein to compare two poems, Pushkin's "Poet and Bookseller" and Nekrasov's "Poet and Citizen." He was not content until Bronstein settled down with the works of Pushkin and Nekrasov in front of him and composed an essay on the two poems. The boy was frightened, not so much by the difficulty of the task, but by the fact that he was being judged by an author, a real author, someone whose works had been published. At last he finished the essay and presented it to Sychevsky, who read it aloud and then advanced upon the bewildered essayist, saying: "Wherever did you learn to put it so well? Really, I must give you a kiss!" It was the supreme benediction. A few words from the essay has survived. It reads: "The poet lived with his beloved nature, whose every sound, both gay and sad, echoed in the poet's heart." This is the earliest known of his writings. Some years earlier he had composed his first poem. It was called "The Pure Little Drop" and was intended to introduce a magazine composed by the schoolboys in the second grade. The magazine was called *The Drop*, and the title was suggested by Moissey Shpentzer, who felt that the entire contents of the magazine might be described as a "drop" in the ocean of literature.

It is clear that Shpentzer was a sentimentalist, kindly, urbane, permissive, without fixed principles. It is equally clear that the boy could twist him round his fingers, which was something he could not do with Fanny Shpentzer or his own parents. The young peacock was spreading his brilliant feathers and exerting his will on his teachers. He was riding for a fall.

The first heavy fall came when he was in the second grade. The cause of the fall was an absurd schoolboy plot directed at Gustave Burnande, the French teacher with the strange cross marked on his forehead. Burnande had been giving low marks to a German boy called Vakker, whom he obviously detested. It was true that the boy was stupid, but Burnande was insisting that he was more stupid than in fact he was, thus arousing the schoolboys' sense of fair play. Vakker was in despair; he would be forced to remain in the class for another year, to be tormented still further by Burnande with his thin, flattened face and skimpy beard. Bronstein organized the appropriate punishment which consisted of "giving Burnande a concert." The class came to an end, Burnande turned to leave the room, and simultaneously from all the boys there came a howl of disapproval. The howl was well rehearsed and was accomplished with closed mouths. When Burnande looked back at the class he saw row upon row of boys in attitudes of perfect innocence. They gazed back at him politely and respectfully. He turned into the corridor and the howl of disapproval followed him.

There was worse to come. Bronstein, deciding that the school must be rid of the insufferable Burnande once and for all, proposed that the boys in the class should write a letter of protest to the President of the State Board of Education, asking for his removal. There was no danger. "We will each write one letter of each word," Bronstein explained, "and they won't be able to say who did it. They can't expel all of us." They were in fact in grave danger. In the midst of this plotting Burnande and the principal appeared in the doorway. They were looking for the boy responsible for the unearthly howling. Vakker, the miserable Vakker, the cause of all the trouble, was sobbing in a corner of the classroom. It was a simple matter to get the truth out of him. "It wasn't me," he sobbed. "It was Lev." And to ensure that there should be no doubt about the real culprit, he pointed at Lev Bronstein, who was thereupon sent to wait outside the principal's study until in due course he was cross-examined by a commission of enquiry consisting of all his teachers, and one by one all the other boys were cross-examined, until it emerged without the slightest possibility of doubt that Lev Bronstein was responsible both for the howling and for the proposed letter to the President of the State Board of Education. Before being sent home, he was told to ask his parents to come to the school to hear their verdict.

"My parents are far away in the country."

"Then send your guardians."

Before leaving for the Shpentzers' apartment, the boy encountered Burnande outside the principal's office. He made the obligatory deep bow which all Russian schoolboys made to their teachers. The triumphant Burnande was saying coldly: "You are the *top* boy in my class and you are a moral monster."

The next morning Fanny Shpentzer put on her coat and made her way to the principal's office to hear the verdict. She was told that he was incorrigible and would be expelled. Herself the principal of a school, and therefore with considerable authority in these matters, she argued that it was absurd to expel a promising student for a peccadillo. Told that it was not a peccadillo but a question of the moral standards that a school must keep if it is to remain alive, she sensibly went to all his teachers to learn from them that he was probably the most brilliant student the school had ever had. Then she returned to the attack, but to no avail. Burnande convinced the teachers that remorseless punishment must be meted out—nothing less than expulsion. Accordingly Bronstein was expelled.

Expulsion, however, was not necessarily final: there were degrees of expulsion. There was absolute expulsion, by which the student was not only expelled from St. Paul's School but was not permitted to enter any other school. Then there was a restricted form of expulsion: he would not be permitted to reenter St. Paul's School but could enter another school. Finally, there was temporary expulsion, by which he would be permitted to return in a few months.

Lev Bronstein was not a hero. Prostrated by anxiety and nervous exhaustion, he took to his bed and waited for Moissey Shpentzer to announce the final verdict handed down some days later. "Temporarily expelled," Moissey Shpentzer said in a strained voice. His wife remembered that the boy turned green with fright.

There remained the problem of how to break the news to the boy's parents. There were long discussions: the Shpentzers were protective and wrote a letter to Lev's elder sister, with instructions on how best the news might be broken. The letter was not sent. Instead, Lev remained in Odessa until the summer vacation and went home as though nothing had happened. There was an elaborate cover-up: everyone knew except the parents, who must be protected from knowing the worst about their son, and then quite suddenly Lev vanished from Yanovka to stay for a few days with a young friend. In that interval the parents were told what had been concealed for so long. They took it well. His father was especially indulgent. "Show me how you whistled at the headmaster!" he exclaimed. "Like this? With two fingers in the mouth?" He was roaring with laughter. In vain the boy attempted to explain how to howl through a closed mouth. "Show me—show me how you whistled!" his father insisted. Everything was forgiven. The dreadful affair was at last seen to be an absurdity.

At the end of the summer vacation the boy returned to

Odessa, the little book-lined apartment on Pokrovsky Lane, the protective arms of the Shpentzers, the lonely bed behind the curtain drawn every evening across the living room. At school he was a little more subdued but he was still the most brilliant pupil. In his class he found the boys who had shamelessly offered evidence against him when the principal held a commission of enquiry. In his eyes they had betrayed him. Not all had betrayed him, for some had been neutral and others had stoutly defended him, and to these last he showed devotion and friendship. In later years he would become a close student of all possible acts of betrayal until he understood their most exquisite refinements. In his eyes it was the ultimate sin, and he was betrayed again and again.

Unwell, excitable, controlling himself with difficulty, without any real interest in his lessons, he remained a student, but the center of his world was already shifting. He had no interest in politics or religion, but there exists an area of ideas peripheral to them which may be called "philosophy of life" or "attitudes toward life" which he began to cultivate. Moissey Shpentzer took him on long walks, told him the story of *Faust*, which set his head on fire, and attempted to imbue the boy who was almost his foster-son with the feeling that literature and poetry were worthy of a lifetime's devotion. About this time, following his father's wish to have a son who could read the Bible in Hebrew, the boy began to study Hebrew with an old scholar after school hours. In his autobiography we are told that these studies "lasted only a few months and did little to confirm me in my ancestral faith." But an intelligent boy can learn a lot of Hebrew "in a few months." With Shpentzer, too, he studied the Bible "as history." He had no belief in God, but his arguments against God are on an elementary level: "Who made the world? God. Who made God? No one. Therefore there is no God." He had no feeling for faith or ritual, or the human need for them. In later years he would say: "It is obvious that there is no God—it is not a matter that can possibly be discussed." This, too, like so much else, he derived from Moissey Shpentzer, who did more to shape his character than all his teachers.

Odessa, too, although he walked about the city blindly, helped to shape him. The white city with its provincial magnificence seethed with drama. What could be more dramatic than the immense granite stairway leading down to the Black Sea and the waiting ships? The stairway, which is arranged in many tiers, gives an impression of leaning back from the sea and rejoicing in its own luxuriance. There was drama, too, in the faces of the people, for many races were gathered there: Great Russians, Ukrainians, Jews, Poles, Germans, Greeks, Armenians, Turks, Tatars, and all the peoples of Central Asia. It was a city where cosmopolitanism flourished, where it was impossible to be fiercely nationalistic because so many nations were living together, on top of one another. About a third of the population was Jewish and about a fifth were descendants of German settlers, and there was no quarrel between them.

The arts flourished, especially the performing arts. Italian opera was the rage, and Bronstein was one of its most dedicated devotees. He attended the opera regularly, sometimes doing some tutoring to afford the price of a seat. For a while he believed himself hopelessly in love with a coloratura soprano called Giuseppina Uget who sang in the huge ornate opera house on Theater Square and who seemed to have descended straight from heaven in order to ravish his senses. All these things fed his feeling for dramatic style.

Meanwhile he attended to the drudgery of school: Krizhanovsky's approval, Burnande's bitter silences, Gamov's curious indifference. Anton Gamov despised his students so much that he could scarcely bring himself to look at their work. He was young, fair-haired, plump, short-sighted. He was lazy, unpunctual, and careless. He apparently lost some class papers; the students asked for them back; he told them to shut up. One student, called Yablonovsky, who was particularly proud of his compositions, announced firmly in class that this was an impossible situation and must be remedied. Bronstein, though normally cautious, took Yablonovsky's part. "Yablonovsky is right," he said in his loud voice, "and we all support him!" This was repeated by some of the other boys. Gamov flew into a rage and ordered Yablonovsky out of the room. Then there was uproar. Later Yablonovsky and Bronstein were both punished with twenty-four hours in solitary confinement. It was Bronstein's first taste of imprisonment; it was a punishment he would suffer many times in the future.

In St. Paul's School there was no seventh grade; to complete his secondary education he must go elsewhere. The choice fell on Nikolayev, a river port with large shipbuilding yards closer to Yanovka. The town, which had been founded by Prince Potemkin, the lover of Catherine the Great, was almost as cosmopolitan as Odessa; there was a large population of Jews and Germans. Bronstein spent a restless summer at Yanovka and was still more restless when he entered his new *realschule* in a strange town, alone, without the helping hands of the Shpentzers. His father gave him an allowance; he lodged in the house of a woman whose older children professed socialist ideas, but he said he had not the slightest interest in "utopias." What did he intend to do with his life? He did not know, and seemed not to care. His schoolwork deteriorated; he played truant; the school inspector came to his lodging to discover why he was not attending classes and went away after receiving a promise that he would improve his attendance. He was not punished, because he was evidently a brilliant student living in a respectable house, and there was hope for him. What the school inspector did not know was that Bronstein was drowning, clutching at straws, in a state of frustration and despair, suffering in his adolescent turmoil as he had never suffered before and would perhaps never suffer again.

THE NURSERY GARDEN 3

In the life of Trotsky there were many chance encounters that profoundly affected the course of his
life but if he ever asked himself which was the single
encounter that produced the greatest impact on him he
would have to answer that it was his meeting with a
poor nursery gardener who lived on the outskirts of
Nikolayev. His name was Franz Shvigovsky, he was
Czech by origin, and he was possessed of a fanatical
determination to solve all the problems of the universe
in general and of society in particular. Like many
Czechs, he was both gentle and strong-minded. He
accepted his poverty willingly; gardening gave him
time to think and read; he loved books passionately
and he especially liked to discourse on them with the
young friends who flocked to his samovar set up under
an apple tree in an open arbor outside his small house.
Sometimes he would invite them to meals in the comfortable dining room, where they would be served with
vegetables from the garden.

Shvigovsky was a character out of Turgenev's novels:
sweet-tempered, noble, generous, earthy, but with
ideas sharpened to a razor's edge. He read in many

languages, was devoted to the classics, subscribed to many foreign newspapers, feared no one, and kept his temper even under extreme provocation. He was the pure scholar who believed that scholarship was concerned with life. He had a broad forehead and a huge beard and he was, apparently, one of those people who inspire affection at the first meeting. He was in his late twenties but seemed as old and as young as the ages.

With Shvigovsky, endlessly pouring tea from his samovar or presenting his guests with apples from his small orchard, life became joy, entertainment, and argument. There were no compulsions; everyone did as he pleased, or rather everyone imagined he was doing as he pleased. In fact, in many subtle ways Shvigovsky proved himself to be the master and the young students who flocked to him were his pupils. He was also an organizer and arranged that each of the students who came to the nursery garden provided books and magazines to the general fund of literature. The garden gradually became a center for communal living with his five or six friends contributing eleven rubles a month for the pleasure of eating his vegetables.

The original Czech name of Shvigovsky was probably Schweik, as in the Czech novel *The Good Soldier Schweik*, but he was always known by his first name Franz, pronounced "Frants" in Russian. To the Russians Franz was a rather sentimental name associated with Schubert and German romanticism.

Lev Bronstein first met Franz Shvigovsky in the fall of 1896 shortly after he arrived in Nikolayev. He had known Shvigovsky's younger brother at school, and so passed into the orbit of the older brother in the most natural way possible. Proud, opinionated, and handsome, Bronstein showed impressive powers of argument, and there was nothing Shvigovsky liked better than a good argument. But it soon became evident that Lev knew very little about social conditions, politics, the wages of industrial workers, and the iniquities of the Russian government. He needed to be harnessed to an idea. Shvigovsky took him in hand and gave him books on the Narodniks, the students and middle-aged men

who in the seventies and eighties went out among the
peasants to teach them to read and write and to stir up
in them a spirit of rebellion. *Narod* means "people,"
and the movement, which was led by the sociologist
Nikolay Mikhailovsky, was nothing less than an attempt to bring the educated classes and the poor
together. The movement was still in existence, but the
Tsarist police were busily stamping it out. A few exiled
Narodniks were living in Nikolayev, and the police
were keeping a close watch on them.

The police were also keeping a close watch on the
nursery garden, where it appeared that subversive
ideas were being discussed. Shvigovsky, in their eyes,
was obviously a potential revolutionary, for he was
known to have read the works of Jeremy Bentham and
John Stuart Mill. He sometimes employed laborers to
help him in his garden; from time to time the police
were able to learn through the reports of the laborers
how many times he had poured tea from the samovar,
how many times he had opened a newspaper, and more
importantly the names of the people who visited him
under the apple tree.

It was probably in the winter of 1896 that the
seventeen-year-old Lev Bronstein first met his future
wife, Alexandra Sokolovskaya, under this apple tree.
She was the daughter of a Narodnik, but she had gone
further—she was a Marxist, the first he had ever met.
Brought up in great poverty, with a mind of her own, not
pretty but attractive, much loved by the group around
Shvigovsky, she brought to their conversations in the
garden a certain decisiveness and idealism, which
pleased them, and a dry dogmatism, which sometimes
infuriated them and was especially infuriating to Lev
Bronstein. Alexandra had two brothers, Grigory and
Ilya, and a younger sister Maria. All of them regarded
themselves as revolutionaries even though their revolutionary activity consisted largely of arguing in the
nursery garden.

At the end of the year there occurred an event that
Lev Bronstein sometimes remembered with bewilderment and shame. He took part in a plot designed to "put

down" Alexandra and to punish her for her dedication to Marxism. There had been some severe arguments in the garden with Alexandra asserting the infallible truth of the *Communist Manifesto*, while Lev, in his free-wheeling way, asserted the opposite—that it was full of lies and totally meaningless and irrelevant to the present situation in Russia. They were both skilled debaters and argued vehemently. Shvigovsky appears to have been amused by their vehemence and was probably the originator of the plot, which began when he invited her to a New Year's party in the garden and gave her as a New Year's present the information that Lev Bronstein had become a convinced Marxist.

"Don't tell me that!" she laughed. "If you want to fool me, tell me something I can believe."

Shvigovsky said it was quite true. The boy had been doing a good deal of reading and had "turned round completely."

Alexandra was suspicious, talked to some of the other habitués of the garden, asked pointed questions, and learned to her joy and amazement that there had been a real conversion. When at the appropriate time she reached the garden she found everyone in high spirits, laughing and joking merrily—a little too merrily. She advanced on Lev and said: "What is this they are saying about you?" and he answered: "Yes, yes—absolutely—you don't believe it?" She half believed him. At midnight, while they were sitting at table, Lev raised his glass and made the speech he had lovingly and carefully prepared: "A curse upon all Marxists, and upon those who want to bring dryness and hardness into all the relations of life!"

There was a good deal more of it. Alexandra was incensed by what in her eyes was a gratuitous insult, pushed back her chair and began to walk out of the room. Shvigovsky, seeing that the joke had gone too far, ran after her.

"You know it was only a little joke," he pleaded with her.

Alexandra turned on him in fury.

"A joke!" she exclaimed. "You would sell your friend

and your father for a joke! There are some things too important to make jokes about. And you can tell Bronstein that he needn't speak to me again! I don't want to have anything more to do with him again!"

She made good on her promise. For several weeks she was not seen in the garden. She was trying to raise the fare to St. Petersburg, where she hoped to work with a Marxist group, but the money for the fare was not available. She remained in Nikolayev.

The small group that called itself the "nursery gardeners" (*razsadniki*) had acquired a uniform. They wore the blue blouses of workmen, round straw hats, and carried black, gnarled walking sticks. They had also acquired a program: to enliven the intellectual life in Nikolayev. They were a small chartered company intent on going public, and their first task was to offer a series of public lectures as the first step toward the founding of the University of Nikolayev. This appears to have been Lev Bronstein's idea, and the arrangements for the lectures were left largely in his hands.

As Alexandra well knew, he was a clever debater on subjects he knew nothing about. By cunning, by misdirection, by an entire series of debater's tricks, he could drive his opponent's arguments into the ground. He gave an impression of great earnestness and possessed an astonishing volubility. In fact he knew very little. He was still the young peacock relying on his charm and quick brain to overcome all obstacles. Nothing, he thought, would be easier than to give a series of lectures on sociology and the philosophy of history. There was only one hitch: he knew nothing about either subject.

There arose the Universal Knowledge Association, director Franz Shvigovsky, secretary Lev Bronstein. They distributed handbills, hired a hall, filled it with a nonpaying audience, and Lev Bronstein delivered the first public speech he ever delivered in his life. To say that it was not a success is to exaggerate the real situation; it was not so much a failure as a shambles. No one understood what he was saying, and the speaker himself was completely confused. He used all the long words he knew, quoted Gumplowitz and John Stuart Mill, lost himself in the foothills, soared improbably to the high mountains, and all the time the audience was begging him silently to stop, because he was making an exhibition of himself. Finally he crashed to an abrupt halt, someone asked whether there were any questions, and none was forthcoming, because it is impossible to ask questions about something that is incomprehensible. Lev Bronstein was exhausted and soaking with sweat. His shoulders shaking, he walked off the platform and threw himself face downward on a convenient sofa, hiding his shame.

This was the end of the Universal Knowledge Association, but it was not the end of the "nursery gardeners." When they learned that the local library association had raised its fee from five to six rubles a year, they went into action, circulated petitions, harassed the library directors, arranged by an appeal for funds so that a lot of new readers should be admitted into the library, and set up a war committee under the presidency of Alexandra Sokolovskaya, who saw no objection to having Lev Bronstein on the board, particularly since he had offered to advance part of his earnings as a private tutor to the cause. An unremitting attack on the library association's board of directors led to their downfall at the annual meeting. Outnumbered and outmaneuvered, they were forced out of office, and a new board of directors headed by Franz Shvigovsky took its place. Another member of the board was a novelist called Osipovich, a Narodnik who had once been exiled to Siberia. Lev Bronstein, who still detested Marxism, took this occasion to demand from the floor that the magazine *Novoye Slovo*, formerly owned by the Narodniks but recently captured by the Marxists, should henceforth not be circulated in the library.

Their success in taking over the library whetted their appetite for more reforms, and various harebrained schemes were discussed in the garden. None of them came to anything, but Lev Bronstein for the first time began to see the advantages of direct action among the workers. Here again there was a hitch: he did not know any workers. One of the most revealing passages in his autobiography describes how he and one of Alexandra's brothers went in search of a worker:

> I was walking along the street with a younger member of our commune, Grigory Sokolovsky, a boy about my age. "It's about time we started," I said.
> "Yes, it's about time," he answered.
> "But how?"
> "That's it, how?"
> "We must find workers, not wait for anybody or ask anybody, but just find workers, and set to it."
> "I think we can find them," said Sokolovsky. "I used to know a watchman who worked on the boulevard. He belonged to the Bible sect. I think I'll look him up."
> The same day Sokolovsky went to the boulevard to see the sectist. He was no longer there. But he found there a woman who had a friend who also belonged to some religious sect. Through this friend of the woman he did not know, Sokolovsky, on that very day, made the acquaintance of several workers, among them an electrician, Ivan Andreyevich Mukl.in, who soon became the most prominent figure in our organization. Sokolovsky returned from his search all on fire. "Such men! They are the real thing!"

In this chance way, seeking among members of the Bible sect, Sokolovsky found his first workmen and solemnly presented them to Bronstein who, perhaps characteristically, had himself not gone in search of them. That evening Bronstein, Sokolovsky, and Mukhin met in a tavern where an automatic organ played so noisily that their voices were not likely to be heard. Mukhin was already something of a revolutionary and had already worked out a very simple and satisfying philosophy of revolution. He was a thin man with a pointed beard and the shrewd, crafty look of a seasoned workman. He had a habit of half-closing his left eye, which gave him a quizzical expression. He spread some imaginary beans on the table, He said:

> "It's very simple. I put a bean on the table and say, 'This is the Tsar.' Around it I place more beans. 'These are

ministers, bishops, generals, and over there the gentry and merchants. And in this other heap the plain people.' Now, I ask, 'Where is the Tsar?' They point to the center. 'Where are the ministers?' They point to those around. Just as I have told them, they answer. Now, wait," and at this point Mukhin completely closed his left eye and paused. "Then I scramble all the beans together," he went on. "I say, 'Now tell me where is the Tsar? The ministers?' And they answer me, 'Who can? You can't spot them now.' . . .'Just what I say. You can't spot them now.' And so I say, 'All beans should be scrambled.'"

Bronstein was so deeply moved by the argument that he broke out in a sweat. Here was revolution explained in its simplest possible terms: *All beans should be scrambled*. That this was ultimately illogical and silly did not disturb the beauty of the argument. One bean represented the army, another the police, a third the revolutionaries. It was as purposeless and as aimless as a game of musical chairs. Also, as Mukhin hinted, it was extremely difficult. "Only how to scramble them, damn them, that's the problem!" he said, looking Bronstein sternly in the eyes.

At this precise moment, in a tavern in Nikolayev, with the music of an automatic organ blaring in his ears, Bronstein began to think seriously about a revolutionary career.

For the moment, however, there were other matters to attend to. His father, seeing that he was spending most of his time in the nursery garden and not attending to his studies, had cut off his allowance. This was not a very serious matter, for he could always make a small income by tutoring. All the father's horror over his son's misconduct was dissipated when he learned that the boy with his usual brilliance had completed the seventh grade at the Nikolayev *realschule* with honors. He had done well—in spite of everything. The question of his future employment was discussed. What did he want to do? He did not know or would not say. An uncle from Odessa providentially arrived in Yanovka with a suggestion that sounded inviting because it would give him further time to think. Why not attend lectures at the

University as he pleased, so that he could make his choice among the subjects worth studying? The uncle's house in Odessa was open to him. Money was no problem: the uncle owned a fairly large boiler factory. He was kindly, generous, well-meaning, "sympathizing with the aspirations of the workingman." Bronstein accepted the offer, attended classes at the university, and even discussed with the professor of mathematics a career in mathematics, in which he had shown outstanding talent. In the evenings, returning from his lectures, he engaged in long discussions with his long-suffering uncle about Julius Caesar, Napoleon, and Tolstoy, and went on to discuss the nature of wealth and wages as they applied to boiler factories. The uncle showed himself to be "advanced," he possessed "enlightened views," and he was "all for improving the lot of the workingman." His nephew thought he was not sufficiently advanced, that he was not sufficiently enlightened, and that he could improve the lot of the workingman by giving him the boiler factory. Another relative, who had made a fortune in Minsk, commented that Lev would change his ideas when he grew older and offered to bet a kopeck that in ten years time he would be laughing at the ideas he held now.

"I refuse to bring my ideas into relation to your kopecks," Bronstein said drily.

The experiment was not succeeding, and after a few months Bronstein went to live again with the Shpentzers. He continued to attend the university and look a job as an instructor in a tutorial academy, from which he was dismissed for wearing his hair too long and for dressing in a manner unworthy of a member of a tutorial academy. He was in communication with the self-styled revolutionaries in Nikolayev and had attempted to organize the workers in the boiler factory without much success. He was evidently feeling his way toward a solution of an overriding problem: should he, a natural pedagogue, devote his life to the pure study of mathematics or one of the sciences, later becoming a teacher or a professor, or should he embark on a career as a revolutionary? Of one thing he was certain: the time had come to make a decision. He was weighing Odessa against Nikolayev, prosperity against poverty, the bourgeoisie against the lower classes, Shpentzer against Shvigovsky, the hunter against the hunted. It was evidently not an easy choice, for he delayed making it for a long time, and the stay in Odessa provided him with a long breathing space. Finally he returned to Nikolayev, rejoined the group around Shvigovsky, and declared himself a member of an as yet unnamed revolutionary party, which eventually came to be called the South Russian Workers' Union. In the beginning, it was a large name for a very small group of men.

The chief assets of the revolutionary party were a constitution, which Bronstein drew up himself, a hectograph, and a hideout in the house of a blind worker at Nikolayev. The man had lost his sight in a factory accident. He said: "Everywhere is prison for a blind man," meaning that he had nothing to lose if he was arrested. Two young workmen guarded the house at night, while Bronstein wrote out in longhand, in clear and crisp handwriting, the political tracts and proclamations which were later reproduced on the hectograph. It was a messy business: a shallow tin tray, gelatine, glycerin, purple ink, each page pressed down with exquisite care on the jellylike surface. The government regarded hectographs as severely as they regarded secret printing presses, and so there was a can of kerosene within reach in order to destroy the evidence if there was a police raid.

Bronstein was hugely enjoying his conspiratorial activity: the secret meetings, the passwords, the organization of new revolutionary groups, the news from the factories ceaselessly flowing into his headquarters and then flowing out again in the form of hectographed sheets distributed secretly in Nikolayev and Odessa. Sometimes he took the night boat down the Bug River to Odessa, sleeping on deck, and the next morning he would be in a factory in Odessa handing out his purple-inked political tracts and receiving information from the workmen which would go into the next tract. Bronstein seemed to be simultaneously in Nikolayev and Odessa; he was everywhere and nowhere. There were scarcely two hundred dues-paying members of the South Russian Workers' Union enrolled in centers of twenty-five members, each center being virtually independent and in contact with Bronstein only through its leader. Like all conspiratorial organizations, it was hierarchical. Alexandra Sokolovskaya headed one center, while her brothers headed other centers. Theoretically the leaders were all equal; in fact Bronstein was the commander-in-chief, and he did the most work.

The political tracts were well written, succinct, concrete. Workmen who complained about conditions in a factory or a shipyard would be surprised to see the complaint written up in a tract twenty-four or forty-eight hours later. The tracts inevitably fell into the hands of the employers, who called meetings to denounce the new revolutionary organization and paid informers to divulge the names of its members, but the members had many names. A few copies of these tracts have survived. Here Bronstein attacks an engineer who appealed to the workmen not to be influenced by this mischievous propaganda:

> Neumann climbed up to the top story of the electric-dynamo shop, assembled the workers and made a speech in which there were more lies than words. It was not Neumann but his salary that made the speech. "You are a mere handful," cried the salary of Neumann, "and you dare to revolt against a terrible power!" Ask Neumann, comrades, whether he reads the newspapers and knows what is happening in this world. Does he know that 46,000 workers in St. Petersburg alone, by means of two strikes, compelled that same terrible power to give them the law of July 2 concerning the length of the working day? . . . "You will suffer in prison," said this engineer, "and your wives and children will die of hunger and cold." You understand how he is worried about your welfare? About you and about your wives and children? Answer Neumann, who

knows no other joy but a fat meal and a luxurious dwelling, that there is a joy both higher and more glorious—a struggle for the great cause of freedom and justice!

This was good propaganda for a wage increase and better conditions in the engineering shops. The style was simple and clear; the details are precisely stated; he takes care to introduce the facts known to the workers, as for example that the engineer addressed them in the top story of the electric-dynamo shop. Propaganda inevitably met counter-propaganda. The police and the factory owners soon became aware that the South Russian Workers' Union was being directed by students who were obviously out for trouble and had never done a day's work in a factory. This counterpropaganda was sufficiently effective for Bronstein to write out a tract in self-defense:

> Do not believe anyone who says that we are some kind of dangerous persons, some students desiring only to stir up the people. No, comrades, we are workers just like all other workers. Only we want once for all to get out of our poverty and live a human life. We want this not for ourselves only, but for all the workers. . . . Let our first commandment be "All for one and one for all." Then we shall soon win our right to assemble and openly discuss the workers' cause. Comrades, for our sacred cause we are ready to lay down our lives!

There is no doubt that Bronstein was prepared to lay down his life for the cause or to suffer atrociously in prison at the hands of the police. Idealistic Russian students all over the country were prepared to do the same, but few of them were capable of building up a revolutionary organization from scratch and writing out revolutionary propaganda as though they were born to it. From tracts and one-page proclamations he went on to produce almost single-handed a revolutionary magazine called *Our Cause*, which was also reproduced on the hectograph machine. He spent whole nights at his desk writing out the contents of the magazine and whole days working on the hectograph. There were evening conferences with his groups, conferences with the workers in the shipyards, more journeys on the night boat to Odessa with the illegal literature in a knapsack serving as a pillow, and all the time he was earning a meager living as a tutor, composing poetry, drawing cartoons, settling disputes, organizing new circles, smelling out informers, reaching out across Russia to join hands with other similar groups. He was eighteen years old, and looked younger. He was buoyed up by what his friend Ziv called "chronic enthusiasm," and this enthusiasm was shared by nearly all the students and workers who were members of the South Russian Workers' Union. Ziv describes the euphoria of those times convincingly; they were all elated by the new-found cause. At last, instead of conducting interminable discussions and arguments in the nursery garden, they were doing something. In memory of those times Bronstein wrote on a group photograph the words "Faith without works is death."

The photograph, made by a Nikolayev photographer, shows them in the innocence and deadly seriousness of youth. The photographer has formed a pyramid with Alexandra Sokolovskaya at the apex, standing up, with her hand on the shoulder of Bronstein, who is sitting on one side of her, her brother Ilya on the other side. Hers is a severe face, the dark hair drawn back straight from her forehead. She is dressed in a white pleated blouse and a black shirt, and could be taken for a woman of thirty, though she was about twenty-four. Her brother Ilya looks like a young workman, wearing a coat over his Russian blouse. He is rugged, decisive, careworn. Bronstein, round-faced under a helmet of thick, black curly hair, has the curiously empty look of short-sighted people who have put aside their spectacles, and he too wears a Russian blouse. Ziv, sitting on a low stool in the foreground, leaning one arm negligently on Ilya's knee, is the only one who shows any animation. He is well groomed, wears Western clothes with a coat and tie, as befitted a young man soon to complete his final year in medical school in Kiev, and gazes at the camera as though he were entranced by all its mysterious mechanisms. He has a neat beard, and evidently possesses a quick brain and considerable charm. Bronstein, moon-faced and disinterested, with his hands lying limply on his lap, seems to be the least forceful person in the photograph.

It was stupid of them to have their photographs taken, for eventually this photograph, and others, would fall into the hands of the police. They were also capable of other stupidities, for even when they knew or should have known that the police were watching them closely and were deliberately delaying to arrest them only because they could not bring themselves to believe that a handful of students were in charge of the organization, suspecting that there were more powerful figures in the background, the students remained at their posts and refused to go underground. They were also too trusting, and allowed too many informers into their ranks. One of them, a certain Shrentsel, was unmasked. Invited to Mukhin's apartment, he heard his life story recounted by Bronstein as though it had happened to someone else: his visits to the police, the names of men he had incriminated, his travels, his jobs, until at last it dawned on him that he was on trial in a revolutionary court and was in danger of being tied up in a sack and thrown into the river. Finally, when he saw that they were talking about him and no one else, he groveled for mercy, promising never again to be an informer. Bronstein waved a revolver in his face, threatening to kill him if he should change his mind, and let him go. This was a mistake: he went straight to the police.

Another informer, a Ukrainian carpenter called Nestorenko, famous for his red hair, his singing voice, and his skill as a composer of songs—he wrote a ballad on Karl Marx—was liked and trusted by everyone. The ballad began with the words "Lo, a great prophet comes," and the young revolutionaries liked to sing it softly on the sand dunes while watching the ships go past.

One day in the winter of 1897, Nestorenko told Bronstein that he would wait for him in a cemetery to

receive a packet of illegal literature. It was dark; the
snow lay heavy on the ground; Nestorenko was in the
appointed place. Bronstein was giving him the packet
when he observed a figure detaching himself from the
cemetery wall, then walking past them, touching Nestorenko with his elbow.

"Who is he?" Bronstein asked.

"I don't know," Nestorenko replied.

Even then, in his innocence, Bronstein did not suspect
him.

Earlier in the year Shvigovsky had abandoned the
nursery garden and worked as a gardener on the estate
of a wealthy landowner somewhere between Yanovka
and Nikolayev. With a briefcase full of illegal material,
Bronstein went to visit him on January 27, 1898. As a
precaution the briefcase was hidden for the night in a
hole dug in a cabbage patch. In the morning, just after
the briefcase was dug out of the cabbage patch, the
police raided the estate. It was a concerted raid which
netted altogether two hundred members of the South
Russian Workers' Union in Nikolayev and Odessa and
was carried out like clockwork. There was just time for
Shvigovsky to drop the incriminating briefcase behind
a water barrel. Placed under arrest, the young revolutionaries were allowed to enjoy their last breakfast in
freedom under the eyes of the police. At breakfast
Shvigovsky was able to whisper to his old housekeeper
to hide the briefcase. Then, in chains, the prisoners
were driven off to the jail in Nikolayev.

The old housekeeper obeyed her instructions and
threw the briefcase into a snowdrift.

THE FERMENT RISES

PART TWO

The well-defined concept of the class struggle and
the clear, unequivocal propositions of Marxist
thought—all these are being drowned by you in a
squalid sea of vague and uncompleted thinking.

THE DARK OF PRISON

4

When the door of his cell in the old prison of Nikolayev clanged shut, Lev Bronstein found himself in a room such as he had never expected to find in a prison. He had thought a cell would be quite small, perhaps dark, with barred windows, a bed, and a pail, with perhaps a three-legged chair in the corner and a coat hook on the wall. Instead he found himself in a room large enough to hold thirty people without a stick of furniture and with a big square opening in the door that looked out on an open corridor leading into the courtyard. There was one window under the ceiling and a white-brick stove in the wall, which gave off very little heat. It was probably a storeroom, and its nakedness and emptiness were terrifying.

Prisoners have a habit of remembering their first prisons, and this one left an indelible impression on him. He had been arrested in the depth of winter, and it was now freezing cold. The prison authorities may have hoped he would die of pneumonia: the heat from the stove was barely enough to keep him alive. He was not alone. As he entered the enormous cell, he saw another prisoner crouching beside the stove, wearing an overcoat and a hat. He could make nothing of this man whom he suspected of being a common criminal, a murderer or a thief, and for a while there was no conversation between them. Who he was, who Lev Bronstein was, were matters to be discovered through secret signs and hinted questions, by whispered statements that said one thing and meant another, and by the study of half-smiles and inclinations of the head. Finally they learned each others' names and discovered that they were both revolutionaries. The other man was a young bookbinder called Misha Yavich, and he must have belonged to one of the still active groups of Narodniks, for Bronstein had never met him before.

Misha Yavich was a pleasant and earnest young man with little schooling. Later Bronstein pronounced him to be "a very good comrade," which was the highest tribute he could pay to anyone. His pedagogical instinct was aroused and soon he was teaching the bookbinder some science.

In prison they were like brothers very close to each other. Indeed, they were forced to be close to each other to keep alive in the desperately cold weather, huddled together by the stove, and in this position they might remain for two hours without either of them making any movement. Then they would spring up and begin running from the stove to the opposite wall and back again to keep their circulations going. The police paid no attention to them; there were no cross-examinations; evidently they had been forgotten except by the prison "trusties" who brought them food and by the guard who every night spread a straw mattress on the floor and promptly at six o'clock the next morning rolled it up and took it away. If they were still asleep, he simply yanked the mattress from under them.

Through the "trusties" they learned what was happening in the outside world. They had no pencils, no paper. Somehow they acquired pins and sent messages by pricking out letters in newspapers which would be read by other prisoners. They also received pricked-out messages. In this way Bronstein learned that his entire revolutionary organization with the exception of a few

minor figures was under arrest. Alexandra Sokolovskaya was also under arrest. She had found a hiding
place in Ekaterinoslav, where she was quite safe. One
day she learned through the underground that the
incriminating evidence had not been found; she went
in search of it and fell into a police trap. Nor did the
police find it until many months later, for after the snow
melted around it, the summer grass grew over it, and it
grew so high that the mowers were summoned in the
autumn to cut it down. Just before the coming of the
snow, the evidence was found by the children of the
landowner when they were playing in the grass.

The main reason why none of the revolutionaries
were cross-examined or put on trial for many months
can now be explained: the police were searching for
the evidence.

For three weeks Bronstein remained in the bitterly
cold cell in Nikoleyev, and then without warning he
was transferred to Kherson. He was driven in a mail-
carriage thirty-five miles across country to Kherson in
the company of two powerfully built gendarmes. Probably the newspapers that served as his medium of
communication had been discovered. At all costs the
police were determined to prevent the revolutionaries
from communicating with one another. Of the twenty-
eight they had arrested, only the six leaders really
interested them. The rest—steam fitters, cutters, join-
ers, boilermakers, blacksmiths, bookbinders, a seam-
stress, and a soldier—could expect severe punishment,
but a still more severe punishment would fall on
Shvigovsky, Bronstein, Alexandra Sokolovskaya, and
three others. The police were not stupid and knew what
they were doing.

The cell at Kherson was designed to break his spirit.
It was very dark, very cold, very gloomy. The only light
came from a narrow, slitlike window which was never
opened, and the only advantage came from the fact that
the closed window kept out the cold air. His isolation
was absolute. There was no one to talk to, no messages
could be delivered on pricked newspapers, there were
no books, he was not given a pencil or paper, he had no

clean linen, he spent most of his time picking out his own lice and walking mechanically from one corner of his cell to the other. For breakfast and supper there was some rye bread and salt; for lunch there was prison stew. He engaged in interminable colloquies with himself about when, and on what conditions, he should be permitted to have more rye bread or more salt; should he have a big breakfast and a small supper or a small breakfast and a big supper? He felt hungry all the time and very dirty, for there was no soap. The air of the cell was foul, and the filth of his own body filled him with perpetual nausea. He was kept in many prisons—by his own count nearly twenty prisons—and thirty years later he could still summon up the horror of the dark, fetid, airless prison at Kherson, remembering it as the worst of all.

He was sick with loneliness and misery, paced the cell, counted out one thousand one hundred and eleven paces, and then began over again, and sometimes while walking from one side of the cell to the other he attempted to write poems. On his own confession they were appallingly bad. One has survived to prove that he was a good critic of his own verses. There had survived a violent revolutionary song supposed to have been sung by Volga boatmen:

> Oh, little oak club, heave-ho!
> Oh, the little green one,
> She rises by herself.
> Give her a little push and—ho!

Bronstein's adaptation came about by transforming the skull-cracking club into a machine:

> Oh, dear little machine, lightly!
> Oh, the little steel one,
> She runs by herself.
> Give her a little oil and—ho!

The poem at least has the merit of prophecy: the revolution, when it came, would not be waged with clubs but with machine guns and machines of all kinds. For a few years the poem appeared in a Bolshevik songbook.

One morning, after nearly six months in prison, the guard brought him evidence that the outside world existed. His mother had at last found out where he was. She hurried to Kherson, bought many things outside the prison gates, and somehow convinced the warden that her son should receive all of these gifts at once and without fail. It was a princely treasure consisting of a pillow, a blanket, fresh linen, white bread, tea, sugar, ham, canned foods, apples, oranges, and a jar of jam. In addition there was soap—the gift he wanted above all others—and a comb, which he wanted only slightly less, for he was very vain of his thick, black, curly hair. "Your mother sent them," said the guard, smiling. The smile was one of those reckless smiles bestowed on the poor by the rich, for a heavy bribe had evidently been paid to the warden who in turn had paid off the guard. Anna Bronstein had spent ten gold rubles on her purchases for her son and probably another ten gold rubles on the bribes.

On or about May 1, 1898, Bronstein was led out of his cell in Kherson, thrown into a patrol wagon, taken to the riverside docks, and he spent the night on the boat sailing for Odessa, where there was a new and formidable prison. The solitude was over, for the Odessa prison, though scientifically designed, permitted the prisoners to communicate with one another by tapping, by shouting through the window, by means of "the telephone," which was a form of speaking along water pipes, and by bribing the guards. The worst prison was followed by the best. In Bronstein's eyes it was "the perfect prison," and he spent his days reciting verses to his fellow prisoners, learning what had happened to the Nikolayev group, and entertaining himself, no longer crushed by his environment. After silence there was noise—the noise of the beds, which were attached to the walls, being folded up and let down again at night, the noise made by the keys of the prison guards rattling along the rails, loud footsteps in the galleries where the floor was made of iron sheeting, and always the rustling noise of mysterious conversations. Sometimes, too, there was the sound of blows. "Uninterrupted noise and clangor of brick, cement and iron," he wrote with relief and contentment. Yet he was still in solitary confinement, and though he could converse with the other prisoners, he could not see them.

Because the prisoners sometimes called across to each other and because it was necessary that the guards should not know who was talking, he was given the name of "May" by the other prisoners. He accepted the name gratefully but rarely engaged in these calling matches. He felt that it was possible to gain very little information from them, and the shouting made him nervous.

His nerves had been ruined by the ten weeks of solitary confinement at Kherson. Now more than ever he needed books in order to restore his mental health, and these were available in large quantities from the prison library. A noncommissioned police officer called Usov ruled over the political prisoners. He was a firm, intelligent, clever man, not altogether lacking in goodwill, and Bronstein regarded him with respect, while having no respect for his assistant, who was effeminate and sang hymns through his nose. Officer Usov brought the books and magazines, in this way becoming the messenger of learning and the proof that the outside world existed. The assistant, whose name was Miklin, was a caricature and proved nothing. Greedy, insolent, lying, eternally singing hymns and rattling keys, he appeared to have stepped straight out of the pages of Gogol. Once Bronstein suggested that the poor prisoners in the Odessa jail were being treated just as badly as the early Christians by the Roman soldiers. In answer Miklin explained that the heretic Arius exploded alive because he called the Mother of God simply the Mother of Christ. The answer, which appears to be a *non sequitur*, was in fact precise and to the point. It said: "May you explode alive!" Miklin was one of those prison guards who enjoy their jobs.

Bronstein threw himself into reading like a man who

has been starved too long of the sight of the printed page. Now at long last he was receiving a proper education.

He received bound volumes of the *Historical Messenger*, a journal noted for its authoritative historical and political articles. He also relished religious magazines like *The Orthodox Review* and *The Pilgrim*, remembering vividly the absurdities of religious argument as practiced in Russia in the nineteenth century. He was an insatiable collector of religious curiosities and of strange sects and heresies. He remembered many years afterward a passage in *The Orthodox Review* which began by stating that there could be no quarrel between science and the Christian consciousness and gave as an example the miracle of Balaam's ass entering into a dispute with a prophet. The miracle was supported by modern science, for it was a scientific fact that parrots and canaries can talk. He relished too the learned arguments by which ecclesiastics demolished the ideas of Voltaire, Kant, and Darwin. Sometimes in his reading he came upon the little dots or prick marks under the letters which recorded a prisoner's attempt to communicate with other prisoners, giving his name, why he was arrested, and how long he had been in prison, and whatever other details might be of interest.

Bronstein had been desperate to communicate at Nikolayev and Kherson, but at Odessa he at first felt little need. He was absorbed in his books. Weeks passed before he began to pay attention to the problem. His neighbor on the right began to tap on the wall, but it was not in the accepted prison code. He was an amateur who tapped twenty-six times to reach the letter Z. Bronstein was bored, refused to listen, went on reading, telling himself that the incessant tapping was monotonous and unintelligible, not worth his attention. One day he listened. Nineteen taps on the wall—S. Fifteen—O. Eleven—K. It was, as he had half expected after hearing the first letter, one of the Sokolovsky brothers. He, too, had spent a miserable period in Kherson jail. Thereafter, until he was moved to another cell, Bronstein was in constant communication with his friend, and it was not long before he discovered that he could communicate without the need of tapping. The drainpipe of the toilets of the two cells entered the ventilator shaft, and the lower portion of the shaft was walled with only one brick. When the brick was removed, they could peer at each other face to face. Bronstein had been too busy reading to turn his attention to the possibility that he might be able to see the man in the next cell. Nearly all the other prisoners had discovered it long ago.

About this time there occurred a shattering event— his first meeting with his parents since his imprisonment. He was led into a cell like a cage and suddenly he saw his parents standing outside it. His father went pale and had to support himself by leaning heavily against the wall. His expression scarcely changed. His mother, on the contrary, showed only too well that she was horrified to see her son in a cage like a wild beast. She spoke vehemently but not accusingly, in horror and pity. The son spoke little. He was proud and detached, having discovered that he belonged to another family. He now believed himself to be a Marxist.

Exactly how he came to this conclusion is unclear, and perhaps it was unclear to himself. He had not read Marx's *Das Kapital*. In prison he read the novels of Vladimir Korolenko, full of bitter sympathy for the poor and the humiliated, and much of Darwin and the entire works of the populist Nikolay Mikhailovsky. He had also read Georgy Plekhanov's *Toward the Development of the Monistic View of History* and a work by an Italian Marxist, Antonio Labriola, who wrote in a lively style omitting altogether the dry-as-dust arguments of the regular Marxists. For Labriola history was drama, and the appearance of Marx was one of the high points of the drama. And it was Labriola who convinced him that history was progressing inexorably toward the dictatorship of the proletariat, though he could not have said exactly what the dictatorship of the proletariat was. That he had suffered an act of conversion was clear to himself but not to others. He conveyed his new discovery to Shvigovsky, who was also in the prison.

Shvigovsky remained an unbeliever, neither believing in Marxism nor in Bronstein's true conversion. It was easier to convince Sokolovsky, who had gone out in search of workers, one worker, any worker, for he was young and impressionable. Ziv was already a declared Marxist, and was not particularly surprised when he heard the news, but he thought he knew Bronstein well enough to know that it was more a deliberately assumed attitude of mind than a real conversion. He thought Marxism was something Bronstein cultivated for dramatic effect.

Ziv's memoir on his friend, published in New York in 1921, is one of the prime sources for these early revolutionary days. It has been described as "one long stricture," but in fact it is a sober and penetrating account of the shaping of a revolutionary personality written with affection and sometimes with bewilderment, and if he had reservations about his friend's character, they are such as anyone might have from knowing too much about him. They were often together; they knew each other well; they argued interminably and knew each other's strengths and weaknesses. Here in somewhat shortened form is Ziv's account of his encounters with Bronstein in the Odessa prison:

In March 1898 I was arrested and in the following month I found myself in the same prison as Bronstein and all the others involved in the case. The security was tight but we were able to communicate by knocking on the walls or by talking illegally through the windows.

Soon I learned that he had been converted to Marxism. This pleased me, but I was anxious to discuss this with him in order to determine whether there had in fact been a fundamental change in his attitude. I could not imagine how this man, who so strongly condemned Marxism in the past, could bring himself to accept it wholly and unreservedly, for he had previously called it a doctrine fit only for shopkeepers and tradesmen.

I learned something from the discussions we had through the windows, but I did not learn enough to come to any definite conclusion, for our talks were brief and hurried and often they were broken short, and this usually happened through the intervention of the police at the most interesting point. Also, I must observe that in these short interrupted arguments Bronstein often used underhand methods, a fact observed by others who were listening. He had studied Schopenhauer's "science of argument," and even in prison he was more concerned with winning the argument than with the truth, he liked to defeat his adversary in front of an audience, and he was quite capable of treacherously employing logic to trip up his opponent.

His attitude toward his opponents disturbed me, as it disturbed many others, and I attempted to explain it by his consciousness of his own intellectual superiority, and because he was always certain of winning an argument he would use any means that came to hand and he was always in a hurry to rid himself of a weak adversary, who in any case was doomed to be defeated.

On this subject we had many quarrels and there were occasions when we did not speak to one another for long periods. Like all converts, he showed a strong desire to express himself and possessed no other outlet for his tumultuous energy. And this explains, too, why he was always the first to stretch out the hand of reconciliation. I was always touched by this, because it was so contrary to everything in his autocratic nature.

One morning I was wakened by a familiar knocking on the wall. Someone was telling me that when I went to the bathroom I would find a matchbox on the floor. In it there would be a note from Bronstein.

During this time we were not being allowed to receive books from outside. Newspapers and writing materials were also forbidden. Sometimes, by means of extraordinary ingenuity, we were able to acquire a small scrap of paper and a bit of pencil. Then, very laboriously, we would compose a letter in a microscopic hand (to economize on paper) and enormous ingenuity would be displayed in sending the letter, even if it was only to the next cell. Sometimes, of course, the message never reached its destination and was lost on the way.

Imagine my pleasure when I opened the matchbox and found a long message, an entire letter, written in his small, familiar and precise hand. It was a literary masterpiece and all the more valuable to me because it was a long time since I had read any literature at all, apart from the "Lives of the Saints," or those letters from relatives that had passed the strictest censorship of the police.

Bronstein possessed an extremely active nature, thirsted for power and loved giving orders, and he therefore suffered more than any of us through his enforced inactivity behind the four walls of a small cell. Therefore he was delighted to discover a way to vent his feelings in a literary work expressing his hatred and outrage against those who had put a halt to the activity that promised so bright a future. The problem was formidable. He wrote out the entire story of his arrest and how it occurred and all the statements he made to the police when he was being questioned, and in writing this in order to give me as complete a picture as possible, he had to conceal everything that indicated he had written it, in case the letter was intercepted. He accomplished this in a masterly fashion. It was a brilliant letter filled with well-aimed sarcasm and malicious satire.

In this way I received his messages every day, but the correspondence was one-sided. His cell was closer to the bathroom than mine, he was always the first to go to the bathroom, and it was impossible for me to leave messages there and expect that he would receive them the next day, for many others would have been there in the interval. Naturally this irritated him. After his conversion to Marxism he was bursting with ideas and wanted to communicate them.

"For God's sake think of a way of answering me," he wrote. I, too, wanted to answer him. Finally we were able to discover a method which permitted us to communicate regularly, and he immediately suggested that we should discuss subjects like "the place of the individual in history." To his statements I replied very carefully—too carefully. One day I received full punishment. He wrote: "The well-defined concept of the class struggle and the clear, unequivocal propositions of Marxist thought—all these are being drowned by you in a squalid sea of vague and uncompleted thinking." Bronstein was talking like an iron-clad Marxist.

Ziv's account of Bronstein in the Odessa prison is illuminating because it allows us to see Bronstein's mind at work: its ingenuity, its courage, and its intolerance of opposition. Bronstein was never more himself than when he was in prison. Ziv was appalled by the emergence of the doctrinaire pedagogue. It was not very long ago that Bronstein had been saying that Marxism was worthy only of shopkeepers.

Yet they continued to enjoy an uneasy friendship and they continued to exchange messages. Although Ziv was a Marxist, he rebelled against doctrinaire Marxism: he rejected the iron jacket. In the course of time Bronstein too would reject it or half-reject it, wearing it when he felt in a mood to wear it and slipping out of it whenever it pleased him. Sometimes he regarded himself as "the philosopher who comes after Marx."

Later, when the police had completed their inquiries and all the prisoners were convicted, some of their restrictions were lifted. They were permitted to take walks together for fifteen or thirty minutes. Previously each prisoner was allowed an exercise period, alone, with a guard following him. Then an even greater privilege was offered them. They were allowed to go to the prison *banya*, the bath house, together. For all of them the visit to the bath house was the purest and most intense pleasure. Suddenly the other prisoners observed through the steam that Bronstein was behaving strangely. He seemed to be suffering from a fit. He fainted but recovered quickly. The incident alarmed many of the prisoners. Ziv was especially alarmed because he was a medical student and realized that a fainting spell of this kind might indicate an organic sickness. These fainting spells did in fact continue at intervals throughout Bronstein's life, especially in periods of nervous excitement. During a speech he would sometimes pause abruptly and inexplicably; there would be silence for one or two minutes, and then with some difficulty, with the air of a man who is not quite sure what has happened to him, he would somehow continue the speech. Ziv came to the conclusion that Bronstein suffered from *petit mal*, a mild form of epilepsy.

Meanwhile the arguments concerning the exact interpretation of Marxism came to an end, for Bronstein was engaged in other work. It was nothing less than a history and interpretation of Freemasonry, a subject that fascinated him. The prison library had three or four books on the subject. He devoured them, copied out long extracts in a huge notebook—the notebook had a thousand numbered pages—and completed the study before he left the prison. Since the book seemed to have nothing to do with current political affairs and was mostly concerned with the medieval guilds and social and historical developments in the seventeenth and eighteenth centuries, the prison authorities permitted him to keep it.

Freemasonry in Russia formed a powerful political force, beginning about 1780 and surviving until the time of the October Revolution. The initiation rite described by Tolstoy in *War and Peace* was deliberately made terrifying in order to test the ardor of the postulant—Pierre Bezhukov is blindfolded, led through corridors until he loses his sense of direction, and suddenly the blindfold is whipped off him and he is confronted with knives leveled at his bare chest and a man wearing a bloodstained shirt—but the elaborate rituals were designed with a serious purpose. The aim of the Freemasons in Russia was to hammer out a new social order, and the Decembrist revolution in the early nineteenth century was largely commanded by idealistic and aristocratic Freemasons. After the failure of the Decembrists, Freemasonry was banned by order of the Tsar; nevertheless it continued. Bronstein was not studying Freemasonry in the spirit of a man attracted by an exotic subject. It was a conspiratorial movement with its own secret codes and secret hierarchy, profoundly antimonarchical while professing loyalty to the monarchy. A revolutionary studying the history of Russian Freemasonry could derive many lessons from his studies.

Ziv, who had no interest in Freemasonry, was puzzled by Bronstein's interest in a subject that seemed so remote from Marxism. He reported accurately that Bronstein undertook "to write about Freemasonry from the point of view of the materialistic understanding of history." Less accurately, he reported that "understandably nothing came of it and he dropped it."

The truth was that he did not drop it. He completed the immensely long manuscript, was permitted to take it with him into exile after he was sentenced, and for some years carried it about with him, hoping to see it in print. Finally he lost all trace of it and concluded that a Swiss landlady to whom he had entrusted his papers had lit the fires with it.

The prisoners in the Odessa prison were easily managed, unprotesting. There were no revolts, no attempts to escape. Once, at the time of the Dreyfus case, when the students sensibly sided with Dreyfus, someone spread the rumor that the French government had been overthrown and the monarchy had been restored. The prisoners, who considered themselves the heirs of the French Revolution, were overwhelmed by the news and began banging and shouting in their cells. The prison guards were running up and down the iron stairways, attempting to quiet the prisoners. They could not imagine what had gone wrong and at first they thought it was a protest against bad food. As it happened, they were protesting against something in another country thousands of miles away that had not happened and could not possibly happen.

On one occasion some of the political prisoners went on hunger strike. The police had picked up some youths whose only crime was that they knew some of the revolutionaries. They had been kept in prison for many months. There came a rumor that the police had offered to release a boy on condition that his father administered suitable punishment in the form of a beating. Bronstein was incensed. Why should an innocent boy be punished? He began to campaign for a hunger strike, and some of the younger revolutionaries, afraid to be thought cowardly and lacking in revolutionary fervor, agreed with him. It was necessary to let the prison authorities know that the prisoners considered it was barbaric to release a boy and then to have him punished. A hunger strike was the only answer.

Ziv disagreed. He thought Bronstein was being hopelessly wrongheaded. But the hunger strike did take
place, with about half the prisoners participating. Then
they rebelled at the absurdity and misery of it, and on
the third day the hunger strike collapsed. The prison
officials were solicitous and asked what they could do
to satisfy the prisoners. They would not release the boy,
but they were anxious to have contented prisoners.
Bronstein was one of the members of the ad hoc
committee to improve the lot of the prisoners. He made
two demands. The prisoners should be allowed to
choose their cells and to communicate with their neighbors through holes bored through the cell walls. This
was done, and Ziv found himself in the cell next to
Bronstein.

"You were wrong about the hunger strike," Ziv said.
"We haven't been able to do anything to help the boy
who was completely innocent."

"No, I am not wrong," Bronstein said. "We have won
a great victory. In the first place all Europe knows what
we have done and in the second place we have the cells
we wanted."

It was an astonishing answer, for it was beyond
belief that all Europe knew or cared about what was
happening in the Odessa prison.

Ziv was disturbed. It seemed to him that the gap
between himself and Bronstein was widening, and
there were, or there seemed to be, structural faults in
the character of the young Jewish revolutionary who
was so appealing, so brilliant, so demanding, and so
lacking in common sense. He was showing signs of an
incipient *folie de grandeur*, imagining himself in the
limelight of Europe when he was in fact in a small cell,
and there was his extremism and his dangerous power
to make others do what he wanted them to do.

In later years Ziv would find himself wondering why
Bronstein eventually assumed the name Trotsky. In
Russian the name has a vigorous, explosive sound
well-suited to a revolutionary. He remembered the
heavyset chief guard of the Odessa prison, which was
shaped like a cross, and the chief guard stood at his

post where the lines of the cross intersected. In this way the guard could look down all the corridors of cells and if there was the slightest disturbance he would summon the junior guards and indicate where the disturbance was taking place.

His will dominated the prison, and nothing happened but he was aware of it. He accepted bribes, but only within reasonable limits. The junior guards also accepted bribes, but first they would have to consult the chief guard, whom they feared more than they feared the governor of the prison. He stood there like a statue, like a monument, majestic in his power and insolence as he leaned on his long sword and surveyed his empire.

His name was Trotsky.

ESCAPE TO LONDON 5

There was no trial, nothing that could be called a trial. The police collected evidence, interrogated prisoners, compiled dossiers, summarized their conclusions, and in due course all the paperwork would be sent to the Ministry of Justice in St. Petersburg, where after many months and sometimes many years an administrative order would be issued, releasing the prisoner or consigning him to a certain prison or a certain place of exile. The bureaucrats took their time. On the whole they were civilized men who sought to find extenuating circumstances and rarely inflicted the full punishment according to the statutes and the codes of law.

Bronstein could have been sentenced to twenty years of hard labor, and the same punishment could have been inflicted on many of the other members of the revolutionary organization. Instead, in the late autumn of 1899, almost two years after his arrest and a year and a half since his imprisonment in Odessa, he was sentenced to four years exile in eastern Siberia. The same punishment was given to Ziv, Shvigovsky, Alexandra Sokolovskaya, her sister and her two brothers, and Mukhin, the electrician, who dreamed about scrambling all the classes of Russia and wondered how it could be done.

The journey to Siberia was a long one, with many halts on the way. The first halt was in the transfer prison in Moscow, where they spent the winter. Here Bronstein married Alexandra Sokolovskaya, thus ensuring that they would spend their term of exile in the same Siberian village. They had planned to be married in the prison at Odessa. Somehow David Bronstein heard of their intentions, sent off a telegram to the Ministry of Justice in St. Petersburg saying that his son was obviously being coerced into marriage by an older woman, and he refused his parental permission. But in Moscow the marriage came about very simply with the help of a rabbi and a ring loaned for a few minutes by a prison guard. It was a marriage of convenience based on respect rather than on deeply felt affection.

They were lodged in the Butyrky Prison in the famous Pugachevsky Tower where, a little more than a hundred years before, Emelian Pugachev was imprisoned by Catherine the Great for his generalship in many uprisings. The prisoners slept on boards set against the curving wall. They were happy to be together, continued their debates on Marxist theory, read Lenin's *The Development of Capitalism in Russia*, and played *lapta*, a form of tennis, in the prison courtyard. There one day they encountered a huge, uniformed bureaucrat with bright brass buttons down the length of his overcoat who advanced with a roar and ordered Bronstein to remove his hat.

"Don't yell at me—I am not your soldier!" Bronstein said.

The alarm was sounded; guards hurried up; the uniformed bureaucrat ordered all the other prisoners to remove their hats in his own imposing presence, but none did. Bronstein was evidently the ringleader and at the bureaucrat's orders he was carried off by the burly guards to another tower, where he lived off bread and water until he had paid for his impudence, while various punishments were meted out to other prisoners. Such was Bronstein's account of the affair. Ziv, who was present, tells it somewhat differently. He said that Bronstein knew that the important bureaucrat was coming and he insisted that they should all wear their hats, knowing that the bureaucrat would be enraged. And when the bureaucrat, who was probably the governor of the prison, ordered them to remove their hats in his presence, Bronstein said proudly: "Why don't you remove yours?"

Rarely the detached observer, but always accurate, Ziv can usually be relied upon when he describes a person, an incident, or an atmosphere. He describes the prisoners in the Butyrky Prison as though they were living in a paradise of perfect comradeship. If anyone was in trouble, Bronstein would hear of it, and somehow the trouble would vanish. He went among them all with healing hands. He was absolutely fearless, and very gentle. He had a habit of caressing his friends, embracing them and kissing them, and he was especially chivalrous toward women. When relatives came, they usually took away the prisoners' washing and brought it back on the next visit. Bronstein announced that this was an intolerable abuse practiced only by the bourgeois, who habitually gave the dirty work to women, for after all it was the womenfolk who would have to wash the clothes. He therefore washed and repaired his own clothes and counseled others to do the same. There was something in him of the young nobleman who was only happy when those around him were happy, and Ziv remembered especially his gaiety and courtesy.

On May 3, 1900, at the beginning of summer, the prisoners at last set out under guard on the journey to Siberia. It was a slow journey with many short stops in the transfer prisons along the way. Nearly four months later, at the end of August, the prisoners were taken from the prison at Irkutsk and given their marching orders, the authorities having at last decided the most suitable places where they should spend their terms of exile. Bronstein and his wife were sent down the Lena on a large river barge with a crowd of common criminals and white-clothed *skoptsy*, members of a strange sect who castrated themselves in honor of God, having found in both the Old and New Testaments texts that fortified their beliefs. The barge floated downriver in the most leisurely fashion, and at every village it paused to let off a few convicts. Finally, at the small village of Ust-Kut, once a staging area for workers in the Lena goldmines further north, they were ordered to walk off the barge. This village of about ninety huts was to be their home for the following year.

Bronstein liked the village as much as he could like any village. The peasants drank to drown their misery, the cockroaches flourished, sometimes carpeting the floor and always making a strange rustling sound, and in the summer the air was crowded with midges and gnats. It was said that a cow wandering in the nearby woods was bitten to death by midges. In spring and autumn the whole village swam in mud. But the village scarcely had any interest for Bronstein: for him it was a place like any other place where he could think, write, and continue his studies. He received nineteen rubles a month from the Russian government and supplemented his income by writing articles in the magazine *Eastern Review*, published in Irkutsk, at the rate of two kopecks a line, later increased to four kopecks.

He enjoyed the household chores, washed dishes, chopped down trees for firewood, swept the floors, and was particularly adept at keeping the cook from getting drunk before he had prepared the dinner. The cook was also an exile. His name was Miksha, and in his native Poland he had been a shoemaker. Now, having been arrested for some long-forgotten political crime, he survived with nothing except "his charming good humor and a terrible thirst."

The hut stood at the end of the village near the woods and was owned by a peasant who was moderately well off, generous, kindly, and spirited. He was a man of character; his wife was a woman of character. Bronstein liked them and regretted only their constant drunkenness and violent quarrels, chiefly because they became so noisy that they interfered with his work. Under the signature Antid Oto—while searching for a pseudonym he opened an Italian dictionary and *antidoto* was the first word that met his eye—he wrote about an imaginary village called Urgutsk which was merely Ust-Kut slightly disguised. He even described his landlord's family in one of their recurrent bouts of drunkenness: the landlord roaring and pushing his wife out of the hut, and the old grandmother following after them, leaning on her long thin cane, and all of them cursing, until suddenly the wife who has fallen to the ground grabs the old lady's hand and brings her down. As she falls the old lady screams: "They are killing me. The brigands are after me!"

> I run out and lift up the old lady, who steadily continues to assert that they are killing her. My presence embarrasses the landlord. He stands tall and disheveled with hands spread out helplessly, and after I have set the old lady on the bench begins to repeat:
> "We dropped gra'mother. . . . Mister, lift gra'mother up. . . . Please, mister, lift up. . . . We dropped the old lady. You, please, mister, lift her up!"
> After that the landlord disappears, to come back in about an hour completely drunk again. His wife employs this intermediate time by running to me in my room, putting in my hand a twenty-five ruble note—probably one of those stolen from the landlord. Intoxicated, bruised, her skirt torn and her breast naked, she begins to beseech me in a wailing, tearful-drunken voice:
> "Be my own father! Go out, for the love of God, and buy me a little bottle."
> All Urgutsk seems to me at this moment a drunken pit without exit, a prison surrounded with that stockade of jungle trees.

Such things however did not happen every day, and life in Ust-Kut had many compensations. The village was more or less civilized, more or less orderly. There was time to write articles on all manner of subjects for the *Eastern Review*, which was delighted to pay for them. He wrote about the plays of Ibsen and Hauptmann, the novels of Maupassant, Andreyev, and Gorky, and the philosophy of Nietzsche. He had always dreamed of seeing himself in print, and the writing of the articles during the long silent night while the landlord was asleep gave him immense pleasure. Here too he was able to read Marx's *Das Kapital*, "brushing the cockroaches off the pages."

Then, briefly, tiring of Ust-Kut, they went to live in another remote village about a hundred miles to the east where he was offered a job as a clerk to an enormously rich fur merchant. It was comparatively easy to obtain transfers, but it was difficult to concentrate on clerking. The fur merchant bought furs cheaply from the Tunguses and sold them at a vast profit at the annual fair at Nijni Novgorod. For the first time in his life Bronstein was seeing capitalism at close quarters. The fur merchant dealt in all kinds of commodities as well as furs. One day Bronstein made the mistake of sending to one of his stores a bill for one *pood* (forty pounds) of red lead when he should have written one pound. Fired, he returned to Ust-Kut in the depth of winter while the temperature fell to 55 degrees Fahrenheit below zero, and the coachman had to break the icicles forming on the horses' heads. Soon he went to a slightly warmer place in the south called Verkholensk, and it was there that he began to receive, inside the covers and the spines of books, folded among the sheets of newspapers, or hidden in boxes of food, the revolutionary literature printed on very thin paper which was then being distributed throughout Russia by Lenin, Plekhanov, and Martov.

Verkholensk was a forcing ground for revolutionaries, for it was largely inhabited by Poles deported there following the Polish uprising in January 1863 to spend the rest of their lives at hard labor, and since the hard labor consisted of building roads, they had become experts in communication. The Poles were adept at bringing forbidden books into the town and distributing them all over Siberia and were very helpful to exiles who wanted to escape. They were proud and bitter, and ruthlessly determined to wrest Poland away from the Russian autocracy. Among those Polish exiles was the young Felix Dzerzhinsky with the burning eyes, soft

beard, and sculptured features of a Polish aristocrat.
Bronstein took a great liking to him and one night,
sitting beside a bonfire in the open air, he listened to
his friend reciting his own verses in Polish. Later
Dzerzhinsky would become the most feared man in all
of Russia, for he would head the Tcheka, the Extraordinary Commission brought into existence to punish the
real or imagined adversaries of the revolution.

While there was no sign of revolution in Verkholensk,
theories of revolution flourished. Anarchists, Social
Democrats, and moderate socialists were arguing and
disputing, making speeches, writing books and pamphlets, planning every imaginable form of revolution,
while the police looked away. A certain Makhaisky,
possessing a fine style and an absolute hatred of
dictatorship, wrote a series of hectographed essays
which were widely distributed. The pamphlets attacked the Social Democratic followers of Marx for their
opportunism and insidious reasoning. He attempted to
show that the dictatorship of the proletariat would
inevitably become the dictatorship of a few determined
revolutionaries over the proletariat and over everyone
else; instead of a free society they would produce a
prison as wide as the entire nation. The workers would
find themselves exploited even more atrociously under
the dictatorship of the proletariat than they had ever
been exploited before, and Makhaisky concluded that
only by the rejection of all political struggle could the
workers benefit themselves. In effect he advocated a
primitive anarchism. Bronstein thought these pamphlets were weak stuff and he attacked them vigorously. The statement that the dictatorship of the proletariat
was really the dictatorship *over* the proletariat he
described as "an amazing conclusion," and all
Makhaisky's beliefs were denounced as "lifeless and
cowardly."

But these pamphlets were being widely read and
eagerly discussed. Bronstein spoke against them, not
always with complete conviction. Early in 1902 Lenin
wrote his famous hundred-page pamphlet *What is to be
done?* which called for a revolutionary elite to take

charge of the revolution, while the workers were rele-
gated to an inferior position, obedient to the profession-
als. A small, close-knit, conspiratorial group would
sieze power in Russia and once it had established its
rule in one country, it would go on to extend the
revolution throughout the whole world. Implicit in
Lenin's argument was the fact that the revolutionaries
would rule by terror. It is a strangely disorganized little
book, but it is a seminal work for the understanding of
the history of our century. Here, finally, Lenin hammered out his preliminary blueprint for the world socialist revolution.

Bronstein was intrigued by the pamphlet and detect-
ed in it, as others had done, a ferocious pride and a
willingness to go to any extreme in order to acquire
power. Dogmatism thunders through the little book like
the thunder of horses' hooves, and there are passages
that are borrowed from Nechayev's *Catechism of a
Revolutionary*, with its bleak prophecies of merciless
and annihilating destruction. The Social Revolutionary
Party had also embarked on a program of violence, and
the assassinations of Bogolyepov, the Minister of Education, by a student, and of Sipyagin, the Minister of the
Interior, by another student, testified to the increasing
willingness of the revolutionaries to resort to violence.
And while Bronstein had reservations about *What is to
be done?* and the first issues of *Iskra* (The Spark),
Lenin's inflammatory newspaper printed in Munich
and now circulating illegally in Russia, he had no
reservations about the uses of violence. Neither for him
nor for Lenin was violence an abstraction, for they were
both realists. Their differences were in matters of style:
Lenin hammering dogmas into the readers' skulls,
Bronstein attempting always to put some semblance of
logic and order into the argument.

Makhaisky's pamphlets and *What is to be done?* had
the effect of rousing Bronstein from the intellectual
torpor that had settled on him at Ust-Kut. The articles
for the *Eastern Review* were easy to write, but they did
not advance him an inch along the revolutionary road
and served only to make him known as one more

journalist from the region around Irkutsk. Life in exile was reasonably pleasant, the greatest danger coming from boredom. A surprisingly large number of exiled revolutionaries became apathetic and indifferent to the revolution, and some went mad and others committed suicide. Bronstein was determined to be in the thick of the excitement, and it was clear to him that Lenin was emerging as a practical revolutionary leader, that things would happen where Lenin was, and nothing of any importance was happening at Verkholensk. He consulted his wife, now the mother of two daughters, one of them only four months old, and she agreed that it was time for him to escape, make contact with Lenin, and resume the life of an active revolutionary which he had last practiced in Nikolayev and Odessa. In retrospect, he imagined that his wife was the first to broach the subject.

It was not difficult to escape from a place like Verkholensk. A carefully planned escape had about an 8 to 1 chance of being successful: failure meant hard labor for life. His method was a simple and well-tried one. Toward the end of the summer of 1902 he pretended to fall ill, and when the police visited the house in Verkholensk they saw him lying in bed with his face turned toward the wall. One day, when they visited the house, they saw instead of a man a dummy. By this time he was hundreds of miles away in the direction of Irkutsk, having made the journey under the hay in a peasant's cart. Friends in Irkutsk provided him with a traveling bag filled with new clothes, including starched shirts and neckties which gave him a suitable bourgeois appearance, and a passport with the name left vacant. He decided that for the purposes of the journey he would call himself "Trotsky" and wrote later that he chose the name at random, little thinking that it would continue to be his name for the rest of his life. There are however excellent reasons for believing that he adopted this name with some care. "Antid Oto" was an amusing name for a journalist, and we can well believe that he found it in an Italian dictionary when turning the pages at random. "Trotsky" is something else altogether. It has weight and dignity, and is memorable. It is an acceptable Russian name but derives from the German *Trotz*, meaning boldness, intrepidity, defiance, confidence, insolence, disdain. Bronstein knew German well enough to read it with the help of a dictionary and was well aware of the meaning of the word. He may also have remembered, as Ziv suggests, the portly, heavyset guard who leaned on his long sword as he commanded the fate of all the prisoners in the Odessa prison. Henceforth we shall call him by the name he called himself.

There was living at this time at 30 Holford Square, Pentonville, London, not far from one of England's most famous prisons, a certain Dr. Jacob Richter, who described himself in an application to use the British Museum Reading Room as "a student of the land question." The land he was studying was Russia; the question was how to bring about the overthrow of the monarchy and to establish a new social order. He lived with his wife in two small rooms where there were a kitchen, a bed, a shelf for books, a table, three chairs, and little else. Richter was not his real name. It means "judge, magistrate, director," and like Trotsky he appears to have chosen his *nom de guerre* because it suitably described him. His real name was Vladimir Ilyich Ulyanov, and he is known to history as Lenin.

One day at the end of October 1902 there came three sharp knocks on Lenin's door. It was still very early in the morning, Lenin was sound asleep, and his wife Nadezhda finally opened the door, peered into the cold pre-dawn air, saw a remarkably handsome young Jew standing impatiently outside, and exclaimed: "The Pen has come!" "The Pen" was a name given to Trotsky by a certain Anton Krizhanovsky, an engineer in Samara who was also the head of the local *Iskra* group. He had written to Lenin some weeks earlier to say that the Pen was on his way to London. This name had been given to him because Krizhanovsky was impressed by his skill as a writer. With these words Trotsky was ushered into the apartment to meet Lenin who was hurriedly putting on his clothes.

For Nadezhda the arrival of Trotsky was an exciting event, for she was in charge of all the secret correspondence with Russia and was largely responsible for finding the secret couriers to distribute *Iskra*. Recently the secret correspondence had been going astray, and there were few reliable "drops" in Russia. She wanted urgently to know what the real situation was.

These were important matters to Lenin, but he was more interested in his studies in the British Museum Reading Room, his theories and his writings. Still half-asleep, sitting at the breakfast table, he attempted to size up this young man who had so immensely impressed his friend Krizhanovsky. Lenin was thirty-two but looked much older; Trotsky, a veteran of more than four and a half years of prison and exile, was twenty-three and looked much younger. Trotsky told how he had escaped from Verkholensk, met Krizhanovsky in Samara, visited the party groups at Kiev, Kharkov, and Poltava, and had some difficulty crossing the Austrian border near Kamenets-Podolsk because the smugglers who generally helped party members across the border had turned or been turned against the party. The organization was patchy and much needed to be done to improve communications. Trotsky talked endlessly, Lenin listened. Lenin could find very few faults in the newcomer who was quite obviously passionately devoted to the revolution. Either on this day or another day Trotsky mentioned that he had studied Lenin's book on the development of capitalism in Russia while in the transfer prison in Moscow, being especially impressed by the vast amount of statistical data which had been critically examined, weighed, and clearly presented, and Lenin nodded and said with the faintest hint of embarrassment: "Well, it was not done all at once."

On the following day Lenin and Trotsky went for a long walk around London. They stood on Westminster Bridge and gazed at the Houses of Parliament, and Lenin said: "This is *their* Westminster," and Trotsky was under no illusions about the meaning of *their*. Lenin detested all parliaments, believing that they were wholly in the hands of the ruling classes; and in this, as in so many other things, he differed from Marx, who had a certain respect for parliamentary procedures.

The purpose of the walk was to discover in greater depth the workings of Trotsky's mind. At any normal time Trotsky would have intensely disliked this subtle form of cross-examination, but this was not a normal time. His philosophical views, his reading of *Das Kapital*—he had not yet gone beyond the second volume—and his attitude toward the works of the Polish socialist-anarchist Makhaisky who had influenced so many exiles on the banks of the Lena River, all these were discussed at length, pondered, commented upon. Above all, Lenin was concerned with the young man's aptitude for revolutionary work and his knowledge of its dangers. He wrote a few months later: "Trotsky—strictly conspiratorial comprehension of the party." This was the highest form of compliment. Trotsky in his eyes had come to most of the right conclusions philosophically, but his chief usefulness lay in revolutionary leadership in the field.

It was necessary to find lodgings for the newcomer, who soon found himself living in the same house as two other remarkable revolutionaries, Julius Martov and Vera Zasulich. Martov was twenty-nine, excitable, talkative, reasonable, hating all excesses while at the same time very close to Lenin, whose mind moved among excesses as though they were the only real things in the world. Vera Zasulich was fifty-one, abrupt, volatile, endlessly smoking cigarettes and spraying the ashes on her blouse, her skirt, and even her face. In February 1878 she shot and wounded General Trepov, the governor of St. Petersburg, and was acquitted after a sensational trial. She had known the archrevolutionary Sergey Nechayev and possessed a clear and precise brain in spite of her bohemian manner. Lenin, Zasulich, and Martov formed half the staff of *Iskra*. The others were Plekhanov, the founder of Russian Marxism, a courtly man who enjoyed bourgeois comforts and possessed a quick wit, and Axelrod, a Jew from southern Russia, who made a living selling buttermilk and resembled with his kindly eyes and spreading beard the pastor of an earthly church, and a certain Potresov, whom Trotsky rarely saw and who was usually traveling in Europe. Plekhanov and Axelrod lived in Switzerland, and their absence from England was both a convenience for Lenin and a source of confusion to Zasulich and Martov. *Iskra* was the spark that eventually set a large part on the world on fire, but the beginnings were very amateurish.

Inevitably, even in this small group, cliques were being formed. Zasulich felt close to Plekhanov; the "soft" Martov seemed to be attempting to pull away from the "hard" Lenin; Axelrod was losing his revolutionary fervor. The editorial board was divided neatly between the old (Plekhanov, Zasulich, Axelrod) and the young (Lenin, Martov, Potresov). There were cracks in the side of the building.

Trotsky soon came to learn about the strains in the organization. He wrote articles for *Iskra* which were blue-penciled by Lenin whenever Trotsky indulged in flowers of speech. He wrote an article to celebrate the two-hundredth anniversary of the capture of Schlüsselburg Fortress by Peter the Great, and since he had been reading the *Iliad* it occurred to him to use the Homeric phrase "invincible arms" when he was describing how in time the revolutionaries would pull down that prison fortress with their bare arms. Out came "invincible arms"! Trotsky was not in the least annoyed and was well aware of the temptations of a flowery style. Meanwhile, he was being sent out to make speeches to the Russian workers in Whitechapel, hoping to convert them to the cause of the Social Democratic Party. A good speaker, he won the arguments but made few converts among these exiles who preferred the Narodniks and the anarchists to the Social Democrats who had not yet produced a coherent policy. Then, again at Lenin's insistence, he went abroad on a speaking tour through France, Switzerland, and Belgium, spending as much time as possible in Paris with Natalie Sedova, a young woman of considerable beauty who had been expelled from a school for young ladies of noble birth at Kharkov and was studying the history of art at the Sorbonne. She became his common-law wife, and he lived with her for the rest of his life.

The speaking tour was to enable him to test out his newly discovered oratorical skill and to gauge the party's following in western Europe. He lived among Russians and spoke only to Russians. Natalie was able to coax him into the Louvre, he peered at the paintings, enjoyed Natalie's enthusiasm, and was not profoundly interested. In Paris he received a telegram recalling him to London. There was a plan to send him to Russia to organize party work, but nothing came of it. More important issues were being discussed. The party was still in its infancy, and it was necessary that it should acquire legitimacy. The first Congress had been held in 1898 at Minsk, attended by only eight persons, who had time to publish a manifesto before they were arrested. This Congress was scarcely more than a gesture of revolt, a clenching of the fists. It was decided to hold the second Congress in Brussels in July 1903. The site was a warehouse full of bales of wool and consequently full of fleas. Some forty-four delegates were invited, but they stayed only a few days in Brussels because the Belgian police, having received from the Russian and German police advance notice of the meeting, decided to ban the Congress. The delegates moved on to London, where the first true meeting of the Russian Social Democratic Party was held in a church.

Lenin, Martov, and Plekhanov dominated the meeting, but each came to different conclusions. Lenin, who was tense and pale and seemed to many to be on the verge of a nervous breakdown, rejected all compromises. He insisted that the party should follow the program outlined in *What is to be done*? He called for a powerful central organization of professional revolutionaries acting in the name of the proletariat, and this central organization would receive full powers and act like a dictatorship. Trotsky, who agreed with Lenin during the early stages of the Congress, put forward the ingenious suggestion that the dictatorship of the proletariat would not be the dictatorship of a minority but the dictatorship of the vast majority over itself and he spoke of the necessity of "the leadership's organized distrust of the members." This was grotesque but it reflected the mind and purposes of Lenin, who bitterly attacked any opposition to this thesis. Trotsky's attack on the Jewish Socialist Bund, which had many thousands of members among Jews in Poland, Lithuania, and White Russia, and included many of the most politically conscious workers in Russia, was vehement. They would not accept the dictatorship in this form, and they regarded Trotsky as a renegade. Lenin attacked just as vehemently the Marxists who were known as "Economists" because they regarded higher wages and the improvement of working conditions as essential to any Marxist program. The crux of the debate came over the draft rules of the party. Lenin's draft of Rule I read: "A Party member is one who accepts the Party's program and supports the Party both financially and by personal participation in one of its organizations." Against this, Martov moved an amendment to substitute for the words after "financially": ". . . and who gives the party his regular personal cooperation under the direction of one of the party organizations." The scarcely perceptible difference concealed a profound difference of attitude. It was the difference between working for an absolute dictatorship by a handful of professional revolutionaries and a popular government elected after a successful revolution. Martov's amendment was adopted by a majority, but it was a hollow victory, for the Economists and the Jewish Socialist Bund seceded from the Congress.

Although Trotsky followed Lenin in favor of the hard, centralized organization, he was less happy when Lenin proposed a reorganization of the editorial board of *Iskra*. He wanted a board of three persons: Plekhanov, Martov, and himself. Zasulich, Axelrod, and Potresov were to be dismissed as ineffective and inefficient. This appeared to be an act of unnecessary cruelty, absurdly ill-timed. Lenin insisted; Martov resigned from the editorial board; Trotsky, who had been proposed as a member of the editorial board, felt that Lenin was overstepping the limits of decency; Zasulich felt that she had received a mortal blow. The unhappy Congress finally broke up. Following the secessions, Lenin's group won by a majority of two votes and became known as the *Bolsheviki*, meaning members of the majority, and Martov's group became known as the *Mensheviki*, meaning members of the minority.

Trotsky attended a meeting called by Martov in September to decide what could be done to heal the wounds. But the wounds were past healing. Some temporary bandages were wrapped round them. For a while Mensheviks were permitted to write for *Iskra*, which now appeared under the editorship of Lenin, Plekhanov, and Axelrod. The Mensheviks even captured *Iskra* for a brief period, and Lenin resigned from the editorial board. Trotsky, worn out by an interminable debate which seemed meaningless, finally broke away from both the Bolsheviki and the Mensheviki, and in August 1904 he published in Geneva a pamphlet vigorously attacking Lenin, justly accusing him of stirring up a totally unnecessary quarrel at the moment when it was abundantly necessary that the Social Democratic Party should have a clear program and go over to the offensive, for the Russo-Japanese War had broken out and the opportunities for revolution had never been greater.

The pamphlet, which he called *Our Political Tasks*, has something in common with Karl Marx's *Herr Vogt*. It is too virulent to be credible and too ephemeral to be worth translating into English. Throughout he attacks Lenin as the new Robespierre; he becomes "Maximilien Lenin" and is presented as a caricature of Jacobin intolerance, a man who would send Marx to the guillotine for his moderation. His voice rising shrilly—for the pamphlet reads like an extended speech of denunciation—Trotsky describes him as an abject example of revolutionary incompetence, an adroit statistician and slovenly lawyer, a firebrand without a grain of common sense. Some of these statements came back to haunt him when in due course he fell into the hands of Stalin.

But there were more important things in the pamphlet than sterile attacks. He looked toward a successful revolution which was not managed by a tight and inflexible organization. "A proletariat capable of exercising its dictatorship over society will not tolerate any dictatorship over itself," he wrote. He was thinking out the situation afresh without benefit of Lenin's rules and regulations. He wrote in an article published at the end of 1904 a precise account of how the revolution would come about.

A tremendous amount of revolutionary energy has been accumulated. It should not vanish without a trace, it should not be dissipated in scattered engagements and clashes, with no coherence and no definite plan. All efforts ought to be made to concentrate the bitterness, the anger, the protest, the rage, the hatred of the masses, to give their emotions a common language, a common goal, to unite, to solidify all the particles of the masses, to make them feel and understand that they are not isolated, that simultaneously, with the same slogan on the banner, with the same goal in mind, innumerable particles are rising everywhere. If this understanding is achieved, half of the revolution is done.

We must summon all revolutionary forces to simultaneous action. How can we do it?

First of all we ought to remember that the main scene of revolutionary events is bound to be the city. Nobody is likely to deny this. It is also evident that street demonstrations can turn into a popular revolution only when they are a manifestation of *masses*, i.e. when they embrace in the first place the workers of factories and plants. To make the workers quit their machines and stands; to make them walk out of the factory premises into the street; to lead them to the neighboring plant; to proclaim there a cessation of work; to make new masses walk out into the street; to go thus from factory to factory, from plant to plant, incessantly growing in numbers, sweeping away police barriers, absorbing the new masses they happened to come across, crowding the streets, taking possession of buildings suitable for popular meetings, fortifying those buildings, holding continuous revolutionary meetings with audiences coming and going, bringing order into the movements of the masses, arousing their spirit, explaining to them the aim and the meaning of what is going on; to turn, finally, the entire city into one revolutionary camp, this is, broadly speaking, the plan of action.

The article is called "The Proletariat and the Revolution." The words "dictatorship of the proletariat" are never mentioned: there is no need for it, since the revolution will find its own leaders.

It was a remarkably prophetic article. In the following year, without a party, divorced from Lenin, neither Menshevik nor Bolshevik, he led a revolution which very nearly succeeded.

THE
YEAR
1905

PART THREE

The proletariat of the entire world looks to us with expectation.

NEARLY A REVOLUTION

6

The year 1905 began badly for Russia. On January 2, after a long and desperate siege, Port Arthur, the Russian naval base in the Far East, surrendered to the Japanese army of General Maresuke Nogi, thus demonstrating for the first time that an Oriental army was more than a match for a Western army trained in modern warfare. Not only the Russian army but the Russian fleet were destroyed, for the Japanese captured the heights overlooking the harbor and shelled the fleet until there was not a single ship that was seaworthy. The Russian soldiers fought heroically, the Russian officers were inept, the Russian general in command was weak-willed and perhaps treacherous. After the surrender, 878 Russian officers and 23,481 men marched out of Port Arthur as prisoners of war.

A stunned and despairing people heard the news and asked where the fault lay. Most thought the fault lay with the government, the inefficient and always hesitant autocracy that was out of touch with popular feeling and clung to its feudal prejudices as though wedded to them. It dealt harshly with social unrest but otherwise seemed lacking in any plans or principles.

Its prestige was severely damaged by the surrender and by the end of the year, after more shattering defeats, it had almost no prestige left.

Three weeks after the surrender of Port Arthur there occurred a still more shameful defeat in St. Petersburg. Once again there was a surrender, but of a very different kind—a surrender of moral authority, by shooting at men, women and children marching peacefully across the great square facing the Winter Palace in order to present a petition to the Tsar.

On January 22, "Bloody Sunday," Father George Gapon, an Orthodox priest and former prison chaplain, led the march of about 120,000 people through the streets of St. Petersburg. He had written out a petition which was a model of its kind, forceful and intelligent, in the appropriate style of supplication toward a benevolent and understanding ruler; and if the tone seems to us now obscurely mediaeval, we must remember that in 1905 mediaeval habits of speech were still current in Russia:

> Sire! We, the workers and people of St. Petersburg, of various classes, our wives, our children and aged and helpless parents, are come to Thee, Sire, to seek for truth and protection. We are become beggars, bowing under oppression and burdened by toil beyond our powers, scorned, no longer regarded as human beings, treated as slaves who must suffer their bitter lot in silence. And having suffered, we are driven deeper and deeper into the abyss of poverty, lawlessness, and ignorance. We have been strangled by despotism and arbitrary rule, and we have lost our breath. We have no more strength, Sire . . .

So began the long and earnest petition that Father Gapon hoped to present to the Tsar on behalf of the working classes of St. Petersburg, over which he had acquired an extraordinary dominance. The petition made specific demands: open discussions between the workers and the government, an eight-hour working day, a minimum wage of one ruble a day, more hygienic factories, an income tax, an amnesty for political prisoners, universal suffrage, education and medical care, the separation of church and state, and a constituent assembly. They were not excessive demands but they pointed toward a complete change of direction of the government and an end to absolutism. In their backwardness and misery the workers were demanding some of the commonplaces of life in Western Europe.

It was a bitterly cold day, the roads covered with ice and snow, the wind coming in chilling gusts. The petitioners carried crosses, icons, and religious banners, and there were also banners painted with portraits of the Tsar. They sang the deep-throated hymn "God Save the Tsar," and they marched peacefully with linked arms in good order. There were no speeches, no harangues. Father Gapon, who had some connections with the police as a result of his work in the prisons, had arranged that the police would do nothing to disturb the progress of the procession, but here and there soldiers backed by Cossacks blocked off streets and bridges, thus forcing the marchers to make a detour. By 2 P.M. most of the marchers had reached the square. They hoped to see the Tsar standing at one of the windows of the Winter Palace, but the Tsar had left some days before for Tsarskoye Selo. In his place was the Tsar's crusty fifty-seven-year-old uncle, the Grand Duke Vladimir. Seeing the crowd and determined to "teach them a lesson," he issued to the long line of soldiers drawn up in front of the Winter Palace the order to open fire. With this order he sealed the fate of the Romanov dynasty.

The Grand Duke Vladimir had not panicked: he knew exactly what he was doing. He ordered the soldiers to fire into the crowd, not over their heads. To the end of his days—he died four years later—he felt he had done the right thing at the right time, and showed not the slightest sign of penitence.

As the first volley was fired, there came from the crowd a low humming sound, and this was followed by sharp screams and cries that grew louder when the second volley was fired. After that came the panic, as everyone attempted to escape from the square, flinging themselves from right to left, and some turned back fleetingly to look at the windows of the Winter Palace, hoping against hope that at the last minute the Tsar would appear, to call off the soldiers and receive the petition, as though the shooting had been a mistake, as though the nightmare would clear away. The banners and icons fell on the snow; pools of bright red blood appeared; soon there were only the soldiers, the dead, and the desperately wounded on the square.

A commission of lawyers belonging to the Opposition was established to examine the cause of the shooting and to make an estimate of the numbers of the dead and wounded. They concluded that about one hundred fifty had been killed and two hundred wounded. Others were sure the numbers were vastly greater, so that figures of two thousand dead and four thousand wounded were commonly believed. From the point of view of history the numbers had little significance compared with the simple diagram on the icy square: the line of soldiers, the mass of the crowd, and the sudden scattering. There came the realization that the Tsar could not, or would not, help the people, and that thenceforth there could only be war, open or concealed, between the Tsar and the people. A wave of strikes swept over Russia. The strike was the first weapon; the random killing of policemen, the chief supporters of the autocracy, was the second; and then came sabotage, local insurrections, especially in the subject provinces, the secret collection of weapons, the preparation for a massive act of retaliation. All this happened in a year that saw unparalleled disasters for the autocracy and the Russian people alike.

Father Gapon laid a curse on the Tsardom. Writing like a Hebrew prophet, he invoked God to put an end to autocracy with the aid of the people, and he promised that "bombs and dynamite, terror by individuals and by the people" would bring about the downfall of the dynasty.

Neither Lenin nor Trotsky had any part in "Bloody Sunday." They were both living in Geneva. Wildly excited, imagining that the revolution was about to break out, they both wrote editorials in their revolutionary newspapers. Lenin wrote:

> The prestige of the Tsar's name has been ruined forever. The uprising has begun. Force against force. Street fighting has begun, barricades have been thrown up, rifle fire is crackling, guns are cannonading. Blood flows in rivers and a civil war for freedom is blazing. Moscow and the South, the Caucasus and Poland are ready to join forces with the Petersburg proletariat. The slogan of the workers is: Death or freedom.

Few of the things that Lenin was talking about were actually happening. There were strikes all over the country but there were no uprising. Lenin was surrendering to a revolutionary's dream.

Trotsky, who always attempted to write precisely and even pedantically, wrote eleven days after "Bloody Sunday" a delirious article that sometimes resembles a liturgical chant:

> The Revolution has come. With one bound she has lifted the people up scores of steps. In times of peace we would have had to lift ourselves up these steps with immense labor and fatigue.
>
> The Revolution has come and destroyed the plans of so many politicians who dared to make their little political calculations with no regard to the master, the revolutionary people.
>
> The Revolution has come and destroyed scores of superstitions, and has manifested the power of the program, founded on revolutionary logic, of the development of the masses.
>
> The Revolution has come, and the period of our political infancy is over.

While "Bloody Sunday" in the eyes of a Marxist revolutionary was eminently satisfactory and had a proper explanation in revolutionary theory, there was one aspect of it that was startling and disturbing—the marchers were led by an Orthodox priest. It was necessary to explain the priest away, or at least to reduce him to manageable proportions. Trotsky confronted the difficulty head on. He accepted the fact that "the forms taken by the uprising" could not have been foreseen, that there was something perplexing in a revolutionary priest being placed by history at the head of the working masses, and that "he lent these events the stamp of his personality, his conceptions, his rank." Nevertheless the central figure was the proletariat. "The hero, Gapon, did not create the revolutionary energy of the Petersburg workingmen, he only unloosed it. He found thousands of thinking workingmen and tens of thousands of others in a state of political agitation. He formed a plan that united all those masses—for a period of one day." Trotsky seems to be deliberately avoiding the real issue, which is how did it come about that Father Gapon led the masses without calling upon the assistance of professional revolutionaries? What was the secret of his success? Trotsky found some comfort in the fact that Father Gapon was only "a leader for a day." It was the task of the Social Democrats to lead them for all the future with "clear revolutionary thinking, a decisive plan of action, a flexible revolutionary organization which would be able to give the masses a slogan, to lead them into the field of battle, to launch an attack all along the line and to bring the revolution to a victorious conclusion."

Trotsky, confronted by Gapon, is an almost comic figure. He is full of envy and beside himself with annoyance because what he continually calls the revolution has happened in this way, in a totally improper and unforeseen way, led by an Orthodox priest who had no business leading anything. It enrages him that the revolutionaries failed so completely to take advantage of the situation for the excellent reasons that "our organizations are imperfect, our connections with the masses are insufficient, our technique is primitive." In spite of all this he proclaims that Social Democracy alone has the key to the future. "The proletariat of the entire world," he writes, "looks to us with expectation." It would have been much closer to the truth to say that the proletariat of the entire world knew very little and cared less about the expectations of these small groups of Social Democrat revolutionaries living outside of Russia.

Trotsky struck an ominous note in this article. It was a note oftentimes sounded by Lenin with quite extraordinary force. It said in effect: "All others get out! Only we are permitted to bring the revolution into being! All others must be annihilated!" Trotsky wrote immediately after "Bloody Sunday":

> Our fight for a revolution, our preparatory work for the revolution must also be our merciless fight against liberalism for influence over the masses, for a leading role in the revolution. In this fight, we shall be supported by a great power, the very logic of the revolution.

We should therefore not be surprised to find Trotsky later, in agreement with Lenin, doing his utmost to destroy all other revolutionary parties, even those that were close to him, even those that contributed heavily to bringing the revolution about. Again and again Trotsky would come back to the idea that only a monolithic totalitarian party could effectively rule Russia. This was a belief he shared with the Tsar.

Trotsky was still living in Geneva with Natalie on February 17, 1905, when the Grand Duke Sergey was killed by a bomb thrown by Ivan Kaliayev outside the Kremlin. Kaliayev, one of the most courageous and gentlest of revolutionaries, had seen the Grand Duke driving through the streets a few days earlier with his two young children in the carriage. Just in time—for he saw the children at the last moment—he held back the bomb. The Grand Duke Sergey had been the Governor of Moscow and had just resigned on the curious grounds that he had not dealt sufficiently firmly with the workers and students. In fact he had dealt with them harshly, and his very harshness was leading Moscow to the verge of revolution. He was torn to shreds by the bomb. Kaliayev made no attempt to escape and was hanged, believing to the last that his act was necessary and beneficial. He was a good poet and one of the few political assassins with a conscience.

It was an age of murders and disasters, but this year they followed one upon another more rapidly than at any time since the Napoleonic wars. Father Gapon, who incarnated the revolution for a day, fled from Russia and was hunted by the Russian police: he was found hanged in an abandoned cottage in Finland in April 1906, and it was certain that he had not hanged himself. It was widely believed that he was murdered by the Social Revolutionaries who suspected that he was a police informer, but it is more likely that the police finally caught up with him. The desperation of the government and the police had spawned a multitude of *agents-provocateurs* who successfully muddied the revolutionary stream: a friend might be an enemy, an enemy might be a friend: and this fear of the *agent-provocateur* had the effect of hardening the revolutionaries who became increasingly harsh and intolerant toward one another. This was a new menace, and no one had yet succeeded in finding an antidote to this pervasive poison.

The drum roll of disasters continued through the spring and summer. On May 27–28 the entire Baltic fleet was destroyed in the Straits of Tsushima by a Japanese fleet under Admiral Togo. This was a disaster of even greater magnitude than the fall of Port Arthur. The Baltic fleet had traveled round the Cape of Good Hope with the aim of sweeping the Japanese navy out of the sea. It fell into all the traps the Japanese carefully laid for it. The remnants of the fleet, after being battered by the Japanese, surrendered ignominiously, flying white flags made of bedsheets. Of the numbers of Russian dead there is no accurate accounting. Three cruisers, including the *Aurora*, succeeded in limping away from the battle and finally reached Manila, where they were interned by the American authorities. The *Aurora* returned to Russia and became one of the links between 1905 and 1917.

The Japanese were inflicting terrible defeats on the

Russians in the Far East. They were also fanning the revolutionary flame in Russia, pouring huge amounts of money into the coffers of the revolutionaries. Colonel Akashi Motojiro, the chief of the Japanese secret agents in Europe, gave money to Lenin and Trotsky and to the Polish revolutionary Josef Pilsudski. Indeed, he gave money to every revolutionary organization that asked for it, for he had unlimited funds at his disposal. Letts, Finns, Poles, Armenians, and Georgians benefited from his beneficence. Lenin was deeply involved with the outfitting of the *John Grafton*, a gun-running steamer, which, it was hoped, would land enough guns and ammunitions near St. Petersburg to arm a revolutionary army. Colonel Akashi was involved with the same project. The ship ran aground off the coast of Finland, and although the Japanese colonel believed that the arms reached their destination, it appears that they fell into the hands of the Russian police. Japanese money helped to finance the mutiny in the Black Sea, which came to an end when the *Potemkin* took refuge in a Rumanian port. Revolutions are expensive. Behind all the revolutionary efforts made in 1905 there can be seen the kindly smiling face of the Japanese colonel.

A week after "Bloody Sunday," having secured a forged passport from a friendly student, Trotsky left Geneva with Natalie. According to his own impatient philosophy, he should have rushed to St. Petersburg. Instead he took the train to Munich. His reasoning was characteristic: he told himself that he could not act until he had consulted the man he regarded as the wisest and most learned of revolutionaries. In socialist and Social Democratic circles this huge, fat, jellylike man was known as "Parvus," which means little, insignificant, unimportant.

Sometimes the real makers and shapers of history are little known. They glory in the shadows, speak in whispers, vanish into the crowd, and at exactly the right moment they emerge to utter a prophecy or issue a command, or like Colonel Akashi they spread around the money that fuels a revolution or a mutiny, and soon there comes a time when scarcely anyone remembers that they were present at the creation. They are the gray eminences who are all the more daring because they bear no outward responsibility.

Such a man was Israel Lazarevich Helphand, a Russian Jew born in 1867 at Berezino in White Russia. He was descended from generations of Jewish stevedores who worked in Odessa, and like them was rootless, improvident, strong-willed, engrossed in the mercantile world. His ambition, announced early in life, was to be a revolutionary and to acquire a vast fortune. He succeeded in both aims. He was in his twenties when he changed his first name to Alexander. As Alexander Helphand he was sometimes an acute business man. As Parvus he wrote critiques of socialist and social democratic policy which were among the most brilliant of his time. He was also known as Molotov, meaning the hammer: this pseudonym was later stolen from him by another and more famous revolutionary.

Trotsky had known and corresponded with Parvus for a long time, admiring him above all as a theoretician with a remarkable grasp of practical affairs. Trotsky had dreamed of revolution as something attainable in the future, perhaps the long distant future; Helphand was more impatient, saying: "Why not now?" In later years Trotsky said of him: "In spite of his originality and ingenuity of thought he failed utterly as a leader." This was not fair; he never wanted to be a leader. Instead he wanted to be the hidden leader, the *éminence grise*, the man who thinks out the scenario and permits others to act the roles. Later in the year, in St. Petersburg, he would show that he possessed a phenomenal flair for the kind of hidden leadership that gave him the greatest pleasure.

Trotsky wanted to show him the article he had written on Bloody Sunday. He was especially concerned with the forms of the revolution and how it came about that it was led by a priest. Parvus agreed that Father Gapon was merely incidental. The masses had appeared on the streets and performed a political act effectively "disguised under a priest's cloak." Neither of them could understand that Father Gapon, simply because he was a priest, gave legitimacy to the procession and also granted it a theoretical invulnerability, for it was inconceivable that the soldiers would shoot at the priest. But the inconceivable happened. Neither Trotsky nor Parvus understood the role played by Gapon, who was by no means "incidental."

When Trotsky first heard the news of "Bloody Sunday" with all its promise of rising revolutionary ferment, he did what he nearly always did when he was greatly excited. He turned pale, was unsteady on his feet, and nearly fainted. It forced him, as it forced all the other revolutionaries, to reach out for sudden conclusions, sudden changes of plan. Lenin remained outside of Russia. Trotsky recognized an essential need to return, to learn what was really happening and to fan the flames. The visit with Helphand had prepared him with a theoretical underpinning for the present revolt; what about the practical affairs of the revolution? Natalie decided to go on ahead to search out some convenient hiding places for her husband. She found St. Petersburg seething: the police and the Cossacks were hunting down known revolutionaries: order was being maintained. The Tsar and the government were pretending that nothing had happened on "Bloody Sunday." The war was still going on in the Far East and would continue well into the summer.

In February Trotsky slipped into Kiev bearing a passport made out in the name of a certain Corporal Arbuzov. He was always in danger of arrest, moved from house to house, staying briefly with a lawyer who was terrified out of his wits by the thought of what would happen to him if the police knew that he was harboring a fugitive from justice. After leaving the unhappy lawyer he went to live with a professor of the Kiev Technological Institute, and when this proved too dangerous he moved in with a widow. His most imaginative hiding place was an ophthalmic hospital, where he was plagued by a nurse who periodically dropped harmless medicinal drops in his eyes and vigorously gave him footbaths. When the nurse was out of sight, the eye doctor and Trotsky would commune merrily with one another, pleased with the trick they had played on the nurse.

Trotsky could not have chosen a better place than Kiev for his revolutionary work. Here he met Leonid Krassin, a rich and well-respected engineer, outwardly an outstanding example of the bourgeoisie while being in fact a dedicated revolutionary in charge of all Bolshevik activities in Russia and second only to Lenin in the party. Krassin was unimpressed by the intellectual squabbles of the Congress; he thought in terms of practical affairs—weapons, ammunition, bombs, propaganda; he liked Trotsky. Somewhere in the Caucasus he possessed his own secret printing press where he printed Trotsky's pamphlets and proclamations. For Trotsky the chief surprise was that his revolutionary writings appeared for the first time in good type on fine paper.

With the help of Krassin he made his way to St. Petersburg, finding refuge in the Konstantinovsky Artillery School in the apartment of its chief medical officer, Dr. Alexander Litkens. It was an odd hiding place, for artillery officers were everywhere, a military doorman guarded the apartment and turned a blind eye to the streams of Bolsheviks and Mensheviks who came to visit Trotsky, who used the name of Vikentiev and called himself a landowner. All the time the police were looking out for him. Just as dangerous as the police were the spies and *agents provocateurs* who had infiltrated the party. Trotsky, neither Bolshevik nor Menshevik but in a curious way both Bolshevik and Menshevik, found himself dealing with the activists of both parties in St. Petersburg. And when the police by the skillful use of an *agent provocateur* captured the entire Menshevik organization, he knew he was in extreme danger. To avoid arrest, revolutionaries sometimes met in the woods outside St. Petersburg. Natalie attended one of these meetings in the woods to celebrate May Day. Suddenly mounted Cossacks appeared from nowhere, arrested Natalie and the other revolutionaries, and carried them off to brief jail terms. A few days later Trotsky crossed the border into Finland, which was a Russian possession but considerably safer for revolutionaries than St. Petersburg, which was now honeycombed by the police.

He found an isolated boardinghouse on the shores of a lake, his only companions being the Finnish owner of the boardinghouse, his dying wife, a Swedish writer living with an English actress, and his own thoughts. The writer and the actress absconded without paying their bills, the owner of the boardinghouse ran after them to Helsingfors, and in his absence the wife died. The name of the boardinghouse was *Rauha*, meaning "peace." There was more peace than Trotsky could tolerate. But just at this time there broke out the long-heralded explosion in St. Petersburg, and he left the sepulchral house, the pines, and the lake shrouded in mist, and took the train to the capital. In a few days he was acting as virtual governor of the city, its most untiring journalist and revolutionary leader.

In the middle of October fifty printing shops came out on strike, elected delegates to form a council or *soviet*, and invited others to join them. The response was immediate, and within a few days most of the workmen in the city were on strike. Soon the strike began to extend to the railroads. The city came to a standstill, and the Tsar's ministers found themselves confronted by another government that called itself the Soviet of Workers' Deputies, that issued orders and saw that its orders were obeyed. The Soviet issued orders to the Tsar's ministers: the autocracy must be curbed, the people's will must be heard, the rights of free speech and assembly must be guaranteed, all classes must have the right to vote, and the parliament (the Duma) must have the right to pass judgment on the acts of the administration. All this was hammered out by the deputies without very much assistance from the three revolutionary parties, the Social Revolutionaries, the Bolsheviks and the Mensheviks. Georgy Khrustalov-Nosar, a strikingly handsome twenty-six-year-old lawyer who had won fame for defending the causes of workers, was elected first chairman of the St. Petersburg Soviet of Workers' Deputies. Trotsky, who was the same age, was appointed vice-chairman. History has dealt unfairly with Khrustalov-Nosar, and this is largely the fault of Trotsky, who claimed wrongly that the lawyer was nothing more than a figurehead. The workers' deputies did not think so. They applauded Khrustalov-Nosar's speeches but they applauded Trotsky's speeches louder, because he whipped them up to a state of dramatic excitement. At all costs he was determined to fan the flames. The Russo-Japanese war had come to an end with the Treaty of Portsmouth at the end of August, and the problems of the government were made all the greater by disaffection among the returning soldiers.

Trotsky was in his element: endlessly making speeches, endlessly writing articles. He was helped by Parvus, who arrived in St. Petersburg with a large amount of money which he fed into the revolution. He bought a small liberal newspaper, the *Russkaya Gazeta*, and watched its circulation mount from 30,000 to 100,000, and by early December it reached the half-million mark, largely because Trotsky's inflammatory speeches were displayed on the front page. Trotsky also contributed to *Nachalo* (The Beginning), the Menshevik paper, which also acquired a formidable circulation. The Bolsheviks had a small paper, *Novaya Zhizn* (New Life), which never gained a circulation above 50,000. In his autobiography Trotsky recorded with pleasure a story told to him by Kamenev, one of the editors of *Novaya Zhizn*. Kamenev took a train journey from St. Petersburg and was astounded when he saw long lines of people at the railroad stations shouting for the revolutionary newspapers. "*Nachalo, Nachalo, Nachalo*," they cried. Then there came a few voices crying out for *Novaya Zhizn*, and then it was "*Nachalo, Nachalo, Nachalo*" all over again. "Then I said to myself with a feeling of resentment that they do write better in *Nachalo* than we do," Kamenev commented.

Novaya Zhizn was harsh and dogmatic, written with the Bolshevik iron temper. *Nachalo* and *Russkaya Gazeta* appealed directly to the people. It was characteristic of the Bolsheviks that when they were invited to participate in the Soviet, they replied through Lenin that they could do so only if the Bolshevik Party was given the controlling power. They backed down and were permitted to take part in proportion to their numbers, which were few. Lenin did not arrive in St. Petersburg until November 10.

With Parvus providing the money and his experience of publishing, Trotsky found himself in control of an immensely powerful propaganda machine. While Khrustalov-Nosar attempted to keep to a middle path, hoping to force the Government into a series of confrontations relating to the workers' grievances, especially those connected with individual freedoms and the eight-hour day, Trotsky was working toward open insurrection. He wanted to arm the workers and to transform the strike into a revolution. The workers succeeded in acquiring arms but never enough of them: hundreds of revolvers, thousands of knives, daggers, knuckle-dusters, and wire thongs. In St. Petersburg there was nothing remotely resembling an armed insurrection; the workers knew the strength of the garrison troops, and the Soviet of Workers' Deputies knew its limitations even though Trotsky declared that it possessed unlimited power. The Tsar and his ministers were aware of its power. On October 31, on the advice of his ministers and much against his will, Nicholas II published an imperial manifesto conceding certain constitutional rights to the people. Nearly everything the Soviet demanded was granted, but though the manifesto was signed with Nicholas II's own hand and bore the imperial seal, it was clear that he intended to remain an autocrat, and between autocracy and the constitutional government demanded by the strikers there could be no agreement.

On the day when the imperial manifesto was published, huge crowds formed outside the Technological Institute in St. Petersburg and outside the university. The triumph of the strikers seemed complete. They were congratulating themselves on their victory, when Trotsky advanced on the platform holding up a copy of the manifesto. "Citizens!" he cried, "Today it has been given us and tomorrow it will be taken away and torn into pieces as I am now tearing into pieces this paper-liberty, before your very eyes!"

It was a theatrical gesture wonderfully calculated to disturb the peace. Out of such things are revolutions made. But the imperial manifesto was not simply a piece of paper. Though he hesitated for two days before signing it, and always regretted it, Nicholas II at the moment he placed his signature on the page had allowed the walls of autocracy to be breached. All his attempts to restore the full powers of the autocracy were to fail.

Trotsky continued to be the leading spirit of the Soviet. He seemed to possess some sixth sense by which he knew what the workers would be thinking tomorrow and therefore had the advantage of being able to announce their thoughts today. Anatoly Lunacharsky, a future commissar of education, remembered someone saying in Lenin's presence: "Khrustalov's star is waning and now the strong man in the Soviet is Trotsky." Lenin's face darkened for a moment, and then he said: "Well, Trotsky has earned it by his brilliant and unflagging work."

The imperial manifesto, offered so quickly after the strike, had the effect of dulling the revolutionary fervor of the workers. Soon the strike was called off, while the Soviet continued to exist as a deliberative body serving the interests of the workers. The Government was determined to destroy it. On December 5 Khrustalov-Nosar was arrested.* Trotsky promptly assumed the role of chairman of the Soviet, a position he occupied for only eleven days.

One of Trotsky's last acts as chairman was to deliver his own manifesto to the government. It was called "A Manifesto on the Finances of the Empire" and called upon the people to refuse to pay all dues and taxes

---

*Georgy Khrustalov-Nosar (1879–1919) became a Menshevik in 1907 and shortly afterward abandoned revolutionary work to become a journalist. In 1917 he appeared in St. Petersburg and as a former chairman demanded to be admitted into the Soviet. He headed the short-lived "Khrustalov Republic" during the Civil War until he was captured. The Bolsheviks, who had always hated him, shot him.

demanded by the government, to demand that all savings be withdrawn from the banks, to refuse to the government repayment on foreign loans, and to insist that all salaries be paid in gold or metal coin. Parvus, the *éminence grise* with one waving foot emerging from behind the proscenium arch, was the real author of the manifesto, and he may have guessed that this was the final insult, the final provocation. The government decided on extreme measures. While the executive committee of the Soviet was meeting on the afternoon of December 16 in the building of the Free Economic Association, they heard the heavy footsteps of Cossacks, soldiers, and police in the corridors. A trade-union spokesmen was concluding a speech in favor of resuming the general strike when a police officer entered the room. Trotsky ran to the balcony and then shouted: "Comrades, do not offer any resistance!" and told them to break the locks of their revolvers before they were arrested. Then he darted back to his chair and rebuked the police officer who was interrupting the speaker.

"Please do not interrupt the speaker," Trotsky said in his most commanding tones. "If you want to take the floor, you must give your name and I shall ask the meeting whether it wishes to listen to you."

The officer nodded, for he understood proper procedures. Trotsky asked the members of the Soviet whether they would allow the officer to speak "for the sake of information." The members agreed; the police officer read the warrant; Trotsky proposed that they should now take up the other items on the agenda. When the officer began to protest, Trotsky rebuked him.

"Please do not interfere," he said. "You have had the floor; you have made your statement; we have acknowledged it. Does the meeting wish to have further dealings with the policeman?"

"No."

"Then please leave the hall."

The officer left, to return a few moments later with a platoon of soldiers. It was obvious that they were all about to be arrested.

In a calm voice Trotsky said: "I now declare the meeting of the Executive Committee of the Soviet of Workers' Deputies is closed."

It would not meet again until 1917.

PRISON AND EXILE 7

Trotsky was taken to the Kresty Prison in the Viborg quarter of St. Petersburg. Although Kresty means "Cross," thus suggesting intense suffering and anguish, it was in fact one of the least oppressive of Russian prisons, where a prisoner had nearly all the privileges of a comfortable provincial hotel except that he was not allowed to leave his room when he pleased. There was electric light and central heating. There was a thick wooden door with an ordinary lock, a bed, a chair, a table, a holy icon in one corner and a *parasha* in the other. This was a bucket half-filled with water, which served as a toilet and was removed once a day. Plumbing was still in its infancy in Russia, and there were provincial hotels with equally inadequate toilet facilities.

Above the table the prison rules and regulations were displayed. They were not especially onerous, nor were they numerous. Civility toward the guards was demanded, but on the whole the guards were courteous, and a sensible prisoner behaved courteously toward them. On the other side of the prison rules was a price list of articles in the prison shop. The list was fairly extensive and included cakes, chocolates, and sweets. Eau de cologne could also be bought, and this helped to obscure the stench from the *parasha* during the hot summer. Many of the inmates were middle-class students and teachers with socialistic tendencies and expensive tastes. The prison had an excellent library, and none of the inmates wore prison uniform.

Trotsky is supposed to have said: "The Kresty is paradise. It is the only place where I can ever get any work done." He enjoyed its monastic calm more than its luxuries, worked steadily every day, filled his room with books, ordering some from the prison library and others from neighboring bookshops, and wrote pamphlets that were immediately published and brought him a small income. His principal work was a study of rent, never completed, which he carried about in all his journeys: it was finally lost about 1919 during the Civil War. Another important work written in the Kresty Prison had the title *Sum Totals and Perspectives*, by which he meant the accomplishments and prospects of the revolutionary movement. It was at this point in his life that he discovered French literature, reveling in Flaubert and Maupassant, happiest when he was lying on his prison bed and absorbing page after page of Gallic sensitivity. He said later that it gave him a physical delight to read in French, although he did not yet know the language well. It was like sipping a fine wine or inhaling the smoke of a good cigar. Although he spoke German passably well and was at ease in the technical language of Marx's works, he was more at ease reading French novels. For German novels he had no taste whatsoever.

There survives a photograph of Trotsky taken inside his cell at the Kresty Prison. He sits in front of the cell door with his hands folded on his lap, wearing a high collar, a dark suit, and well-polished shoes, and he looks completely poised and calm, as though he did not have a worry in the world. With his thick, curling, black hair and small pointed beard, he could be taken for a highly intelligent Jewish business man with a palatial town house, three or four secretaries, and a growing family, who collects art in his spare time. He wears his elegance as easily as he wears his intelligence. At this time he was a revolutionary in danger of severe punishment for his part in an uprising, one of the people most hated by the autocracy, which had its own way of breaking the spirits of its adversaries.

It would take more than prison to break Trotsky's spirit. His calm concealed a seething pride and a profound faith in his own revolutionary career. He did not regard himself as a revolutionary only; he was a leader of revolutionaries, the teacher of the art of revolution. While his domination of the Soviets had not quite the historic importance he imagined it to have, it was nevertheless an extraordinary event and he was well satisfied with his accomplishment. He had found the crack in the structure of government; he had widened it and shown how the whole structure could be brought crashing down.

Sum Totals and Perspectives has importance as a theoretical study. The book is lacking in organization and suffers from an ill-concealed megalomania. He undoubtedly exaggerated the importance of the revolution of October 1905, which was not in fact a revolution at all; it was at best a series of strikes in preparation for an uprising which never took place. Trotsky will say: "The influence of the Russian revolution on the proletariat is immense," and again, "The colossal influence of the Russian revolution manifests itself in . . ." He rarely mentioned his own participation as the leader of the Petersburg Soviet but is all the more present because he identified himself with it. He suffers from the terrible necessity of self-aggrandizement which is man's human response to prison bars.

Trotsky's judgment on the 1905 revolution was not, however, the main theme of the book, which was largely concerned with working out a theory of revolution, and especially the next revolution. How will it come about? By what stages? In what order? Who are the enemies, and how will they be liquidated? He offers a blueprint for the coming revolution which is remarkably precise and informative and describes very closely what happened when the Communists took power in 1917. It should be quoted at some length precisely because of its prophetic character:

> The proletariat can achieve power only at a moment of national upheaval, of sweeping national enthusiasm. The proletariat assumes power as a revolutionary representative of the people, as a recognized leader in the fight against absolutism and barbaric feudalism. Having assumed power, however, the proletariat will open a new era, an era of positive legislation, of revolutionary politics, and this is the point where its claim to be the recognized spokesman of the will of the nation may be endangered.

> The first measures of the proletariat—the cleansing of the Augean stables of the old regime and the driving away of their inhabitants—will meet the active support of the entire nation whatever the liberal castrators may tell us of the power of some prejudices among the masses. The work of political cleansing will be accompanied by democratic reorganization of all social and political relations. The workers' government, impelled by direct pressures and demands, will have to intervene decisively in all the relationships and activities of the people.

> The first task will be to dismiss from the army and the administration all those who have stained their hands with the blood of the people; it will have to disband all the regiments that have polluted themselves with crimes against the people. This work will have to be done immediately, long before the establishment of an elected and responsible administration and before the organization of a popular militia. This, however, will be only the beginning. The workers' democracy will soon be confronted with the problems of the length of the working day, the agrarian question and the problem of unemployment. The legislative solution of these problems will show the *class character* of the workers' government. It will tend to weaken the revolutionary ties between the proletariat and the nation; the economic differentiation among the peasants will acquire a political expression. Antagonism between the component parts of the nation will grow in proportion as the policies of the workers' government become more definite, lose their general democratic character and become *class policies*.

> The lack of individualistic bourgeois traditions and

anti-proletarian prejudices among the peasants and the intelligentsia will help the proletariat to assume power. It must not be forgotten, however, that this lack of prejudices is based not on political understanding, but on political barbarism, on social shapelessness, primitiveness, and lack of character. These are all qualities that can hardly guarantee support for an active, consistent proletarian policy . . .

The proletariat will be compelled to carry the class struggle into the villages and thus to destroy the slight community of interests undoubtedly to be found among all the peasants. In its further advance the proletariat will have to find support by setting the poor villagers against the rich, the rural proletariat against the agrarian bourgeoisie. This will alienate the majority of the peasants from the workers' democracy. Relations between village and city will become strained. The peasantry as a whole will become politically indifferent. The peasant minority will actively oppose proletarian rule. This will influence part of the intellectuals and the petty bourgeoisie of the cities.

Thus, the more definite and determined the policy of the proletariat in power becomes, the more narrow and more shaky becomes the ground beneath its feet. All this is extremely probable and even inevitable.

Two features of proletarian politics which will inevitably meet with the opposition of the proletariat's allies are *collectivism* and *internationalism*. The strong adherence of the peasants to private ownership, the primitiveness of their political conceptions, the limitations of the village horizon, its isolation from world-wide political ties and allegiances, are terrible obstacles in the way of revolutionary proletarian rule.

To imagine that Social Democrats will participate in the provisional government, playing a leading role in the period of revolutionary reforms, insisting upon giving them the most radical character and all the time enjoying the aid and support of the organized proletariat—only to step aside when the democratic program is put into operation, to leave the completed edifice at the disposal of the bourgeois parties and thus to open an era of parliamentary politics where the Social Democrats form only a party of opposition—to imagine this would mean to compromise the very nature of the workers' government. It is impossible to imagine anything of the kind, not because it is "against principles," but because it is absolutely *unreal*, it is utopianism of the worst kind, it is the revolutionary utopianism of Philistines . . .

A proletarian government must necessarily take decisive steps to solve the problem of unemployment. Representatives of labor in a revolutionary government cannot meet the demands of unemployed workers with arguments about the bourgeois character of the revolution. Once, however, the government ventures to eliminate unemployment—no matter how—a tremendous gain in the economic power of the proletariat is accomplished. The capitalists whose pressure on the working class was based on the existence of a reserve army of labor will soon realize that they are powerless *economically*. It will be the task of the government to doom them also to *political* oblivion.

Trotsky's argument for the kind of revolution he wanted should be studied closely not only for what it contains but for its deliberate omissions. Implicit in the argument but never mentioned is the rule of an elite revolutionary group commanding the operation. The dictatorship of the proletariat is a fiction for the dictatorship of a group of professional revolutionaries devoted to carrying out an established policy by which all classes are to destroyed or totally regimented. The rich peasants are to be destroyed by the poor peasants, the capitalists will be doomed to political oblivion, the army and the bureaucracy will be purged. Implicit in the argument is a period of civil war, for it is unthinkable that the classes will bow down to the will of a government which rejects parliamentary government in any form. It is a blueprint for absolute tyranny exercised not simply by a minority but by a very small minority.

Trotsky shared Lenin's contempt for the peasantry: they are depicted simply as the servants of the state, the poor peasants being set against the rich peasants, thus neutralizing one another. All power is given to the proletariat in theory; in practice the power remains in the hands of the revolutionary elite. The state becomes a monolithic organism determined to suppress the

legitimate aspirations of more than three-quarters of
the population. All who reject the program are doomed
to political oblivion, which can only mean that they are
exiled or killed.

The author of this merciless tract was well aware that
there would be resistance and opposition. He recognized two periods of danger to the revolutionary movement. The first was immediately after the assumption
of power when the revolutionary government, lacking
legitimacy and having no roots among the people, is
unable to convince the nation that it possesses the
power and authority to act. In Trotsky's words, "this is
the point where its claim to be the recognized spokes-
man of the will of the nation may be endangered." The
second storm signal occurs when the policies of the
revolutionary government are rigidly defined. In Trotsky's words, "the more definite and determined the
policy of the proletariat in power becomes, the more
narrow and more shaky becomes the ground beneath
its feet." From the peasantry, with its deep roots in
tradition and age-long fear of the cities and the urban
proletariat, Trotsky expects to find the greatest resistance. Implicit, too, in the argument is the fact that the
peasants are weak and their resistance can be overcome by the armed power of the proletariat.

Marxist jargon is not pretty, and Trotsky makes no
effort to make it more palatable. The heavily weighted
words are moved like iron chessmen across the board:
checkmate is accomplished in four separate moves. A
classless society is not brought into being; instead
there are three classes: the rulers, the proletariat, and
the peasantry. Nothing at all is said about professional
men: doctors, architects, engineers, chemists, physi-
cists, town planners, professors, nor is anything said
about the fate reserved for poets, writers, sculptors,
painters. Like the peasantry they are presumably to be
made subservient to the ruling elite and the industrial
proletariat. They have very little place in the new
scheme of things.

Trotsky describes the coming of the revolution as
passionlessly as though he were describing a chemical

experiment. He is aware that the test tubes may explode, that the experiment may fail, that he may be arrested and executed before the experiment is completed. He is speaking about the uprooting and destruction of countless people, of violent alterations in government, of the substitution of one absolutism by another, and all the time he speaks like a professor describing the interaction of chemicals. The tone is cold, mechanical, inhuman, for the revolution will be embarked upon without enthusiasm. It is ordained and inevitable by reason of Marxist theory.

Like Marx, Trotsky fails to define "the dictatorship of the proletariat." It is like the pillar of fire by night that marched in front of the Israelites, leading the way to the land of milk and honey; it is mysteriously generated, without form or substance. If he fails to tell us anything about the elements that form the dictatorship, it may be that he is aware of the terrible formula: the dictatorship of the proletariat = the dictatorship of one man.

But while he refuses to define the dictatorship, he describes the advantages that will flow from it:

> The domination of the proletariat means not only democratic equality, free self-government, the shifting of the burden of taxation to the propertied classes, the dissolution of the standing army into a people's militia, the abolition of compulsory payments to the Church, and also recognition of all revolutionary changes made by the peasants (seizures of land). . . . But is it not possible that the peasants will remove the workingmen from their positions and take their place? No, this can never happen. This would be in contradiction to all historical experience. History has convincingly shown that the peasantry is incapable of an independent political role.

Trotsky's simplicities are sometimes breathtaking: he announces his proclamations with such force and conviction that while reading them we almost believe them. The revolutionaries in Russia might have been more successful if they had paid more attention to the peasantry; the Chinese Communist revolution showed that the peasantry was indeed capable of being an independent political force.

After a few months Trotsky was transferred to the Peter and Paul fortress situated on an island in the Neva. This was the most closely guarded prison in Russia and also the most prestigious, reserved for those who presented a direct threat to the monarchy. Here Dostoyevsky, Chernyshevsky, Nechayev, Bakunin, and many other revolutionaries had suffered the awful silence of solitary confinement. Trotsky was among the very few who was perfectly happy in the fortress, reveling in the silence which, as he said, allowed him to think. He was permitted books and writing paper, and continued to write at great length. Parvus, who was arrested in April, almost went mad in the Peter and Paul fortress. The lack of physical and mental exercise, the darkness of his cell, and the knowledge that he was absolutely in the hands of an implacable enemy, shattered his spirits and left him without resources. Parvus recovered slowly, threw himself into preparation for his trial, and learned to his sorrow that he would not be put on trial at all. He was given an administrative sentence of three years' exile in Siberia, and having concealed a large sum of money on his person he was able to escape from his place of exile without any great difficulty.

The trial of the fifty-one members of the Soviet opened in St. Petersburg on October 2, 1906. Originally there were fifty-two members but one had already been shot "by administrative order." The members of the Soviet were accused of armed insurrection against the state. Some four hundred witnesses were called, and of these about two hundred actually testified during the trial. Trotsky's father and mother came up from Yanovka to attend the trial, the father quiet and dry eyed, the mother falling sometimes into uncontrollable fits of weeping, and sometimes she would look up proudly to catch the eye of her son, who looked as though he was quietly enjoying himself and quite certain that he was the most important of the defendants.

The court was a little afraid of him, for it was well

aware of his oratorical gifts. As anyone might have guessed, he offered no defence: he attacked. In his powerful, rasping voice he proclaimed that the workers had good cause for insurrection. They were armed—with justice. They had not prepared an uprising; instead, they had prepared *for* an uprising, which was something else. He went on:

> What is an uprising? Not a palace revolution, not a military conspiracy, but the uprising of the working masses. The president of this court addressed the following question to one of the witnesses: did he regard a political strike as an uprising? I forget what the witness replied, but I believe and affirm that a political strike, contrary to the doubts of the president, is indeed an uprising. This is not a paradox! Yet it may seem to be a paradox from the point of view of the indictment. I repeat: my concept of the uprising—and I shall presently demonstrate this—has nothing in common but its name with the conception as understood by the police and the prosecution. I say that a political general strike is an uprising!
>
> What exactly is a political general strike? It has only one thing in common with an economic strike: in both cases the workers suspend work. In everything else they are absolutely dissimilar. The economic strike has its own fixed and narrow goal, that of putting pressure on an employer by placing him temporarily outside the competitive field. It interrupts work in a factory in order to achieve changes within the limits of the factory. The nature of a political strike is very different. It exerts no pressure on individual employers; it does not as a rule present any specific economic claims; its demands are directed over the heads of the employers and consumers who are cruelly affected at the state power itself. How does the political power affect the state power? By paralyzing it!

By going over to the offensive Trotsky was deliberately assuming a far greater share of the guilt than the other defendants. He admitted that the general strike in October created anarchy, but it was precisely as a result of this anarchy that there came the imperial manifesto of October 31. And it was not only the workers who created anarchy: the Tsarist government went about deliberately creating a state of confusion:

> The autocracy, basing its strength on bayonets, natural-
> ly tried to introduce confusion, chaos and disintegration
> into the colossal process of fusing together the popular
> forces whose center was the Soviet of Workers' Deputies.
> On the other hand, the Soviet, resting on the confidence,
> discipline, activity and unanimity of the working masses,
> could not fail to understand the terrible threat to popular
> freedom, civil rights and inviolability of the person repre-
> sented by the army and the harsh instruments of power
> held in the same blood-stained hands that wielded them
> up to October 31. Between these two organs of power
> begins a titanic struggle for influence over the army—the
> second stage of the developing popular uprising.

Trotsky was not in the least bashful when he insisted
that the workers were *preparing for* the uprising which
could only be carried out with the help of armed force,
and more particularly with the help of the disaffected
armed forces. Inevitably, if the workers and disaffected
soldiers united against the regular army, there would
be civil war. The question of civil war was adroitly
avoided. To the question: Did the Soviet understand
that the regular army under the orders of the autocracy
was prepared to strike hard at the workers? Trotsky
answered: "Yes, the Soviet thought so; it had no doubts
on this score; it was aware—firmly aware—that the
fatal hour would strike sooner or later."

The crime was armed insurrection. The pedagogue
addressed the president of the court and explained
patiently that general strike = insurrection, and armed
insurrection is only possible when some of the soldiers
have come out on the side of the workers. He was
splitting hairs and confusing the issue, which was a
very simple one. At what point can a general strike,
which obviously threatens the state power, be suppressed by the massive use of military force? At what
point dare the revolutionaries engage the military? In
Moscow, there was a different story. There the Bolsheviks came out in open insurrection on December 10,
1905, and from the second or third day the revolutionary

war became nothing more than a mopping up campaign with the Bolsheviks in full flight or in hiding. The St. Petersburg Soviet of Workers' Deputies never officially planned an armed rebellion: unofficially it was proposed many times. The prosecution was dealing with facts. Trotsky brilliantly overrode the facts and addressed the court as a teacher instructing them on the precise meaning of the words "uprising," "armed rebellion," and "strike." In his closing statement he went on to ask the government to define the meaning of "government":

> I ask you: What are we the accused to understand by the term "government"? Does any such thing exist in our country? The government has long since broken with the people, and sustains and supports itself solely upon the Black Hundreds and upon its military and police forces. What we have is not a popular government. It is an instrument for mass murder. I cannot describe in any other way a government machine that is tearing to pieces the living body of our country. And if I am told that the pogroms, the murders, the burnings, the rapes—if I am told that everything that happened in Tver, Rostov, Kursk, Siedletz—if you tell me that Kishinev, Odessa, Byalystok are the form of government of the Russian Empire—then I will agree with the prosecution that in October and November we were arming ourselves directly and immediately against the form of government of the Russian Empire.

In spite of the batteries of lawyers and the hundreds of witnesses and the revelation that the Soviet had acquired arms, although these arms were very few, the prosecution put on a bad case. The first parliament created by the imperial manifesto of October 31 met on May 10, 1906, and was dissolved by the prime minister, Peter Stolypin, less than three months later on the order of the Tsar. In its brief course this parliament, known as the First Duma, began to examine the actions of the police critically. Count Urusov showed that the police and the government immediately after the proclamation of October 31 had organized bands of armed vigilantes, called the Black Hundreds, whose sole purpose was to bring about pogroms of the Jews all over Russia, apparently in the belief that this would satisfy the people and turn their minds away from social purposes. Documents were found showing that reports on the activities of the Black Hundreds were frequently submitted to the Tsar, who at no time showed the least disapproval. A certain Lopukhin, a recently dismissed police official, wrote to one of the defense lawyers, offering what appeared to be proof that a pogrom in St. Petersburg was averted by the action of the Soviet of Workers' Deputies. It appeared that leaflets printed on behalf of the Black Hundreds to justify the killing of Jews had been produced on the police printing press, and that in general the police were far more subversive of public order than the Soviet. A certain General Ivanov, one of the chiefs of the gendarmerie in charge of investigating the deputies, a man whose fat, ungainly body became the delight of the caricaturists, admitted in court that he received very little help from the police. "I went to their headquarters, and they stole my briefcase and all its documents," he said. "I should have known better, because they always do that." There was laughter in court, but it was not amusing. The police were outside the law.

The sentences were handed down on November 15. All the members of the Soviet were found innocent except for fifteen, who were sentenced to exile in Siberia for life and the deprivation of all civil rights. Trotsky was one of the fifteen.

Trotsky went into exile in high spirits. In the sole of one boot he carried a passport with a false name, and there were gold coins packed solidly inside his high heels. He intended to escape and did so at the first opportunity about forty days after leaving St. Petersburg at a place called Berezov, in Ostyak territory, not far from the Arctic Circle, where Prince Alexander Menchikov, boon companion of Peter the Great, was once exiled. He slipped away at night, hidden in the frozen hay piled on a light deer-sleigh driven by a drunken tribesman. When they were some distance from Berezov he got out of the hay and sat with the driver, who remained drunk throughout most of the long journey. It scarcely mattered, for a drunken tribesman retains his sense of direction. They drove south across a vast snowy wasteland and forests of white fir trees in the silence of winter. It was like a landscape in a dream. The three deer driving the sleigh could run for forty-eight hours without taking food, although their food lay plentiful under the snow. At long intervals the sleigh would stop, and the deer would dig holes in the snow with their hooves, and eat the soft moss underneath. The snow was so deep that sometimes the deer would be almost up to their ears before they reached the moss. Sometimes they came upon Ostyak settlements, which offered no danger. There were no roads, no telegraphs, and if the Ostyaks suspected that he was a political prisoner running away from his place of exile, they had no desire to inform the police. The sleigh glided smoothly and silently like a boat on a crystal-clear lake. Here and there they came upon animal tracks: the trail of a fox, the footprints of weasels and ermine, and the delicate, pointed tracks of partridges. Sometimes they saw the huge footprints of clumsy elk.

The journey went so well that Trotsky sometimes stirred himself to a sense of excitement by wondering whether the Ostyaks would attempt to murder him in the belief that he was a rich merchant. Somehow he had procured a revolver and was relatively safe. Fear entered the paradise of snow, and then vanished, while he contemplated great white fir trees whose branches had withered away in the forest fires of summer, and now they looked like rows of great candles. These orderly rows produced a profound impression on him, on the mathematical temper of his mind. If only the world could be rebuilt in mathematical order! If only everything could be reduced to mathematical simplicity! It is astonishing how often he evokes the satisfaction of watching things on parade: soldiers, books on shelves, Russian fences, rows of trees. $1 + 1 + 1 + 1 + \ldots$ gave him an immense pleasure.

In the silence of the plains of snow, there was no

sense of space, or time, or distance traveled. Nikivor, the driver, said that only the Archangel Michael had measured the distances here. Once, according to the old legend, an ancient crone had attempted to measure them with her crutch, but she gave up in despair.

The Ostyaks, too, had almost given up in despair. They were a society in full decay, disease ridden, without schools, without medical care, continually drunk, the women as drunk as the men: Russian civilization had brought them nothing except alcohol and some particularly vicious Russian swearwords which they incorporated into their speech. The children were pretty, the men and women savagely ugly. Like so many other things about the Ostyaks, this too was inexplicable.

At no other time did Trotsky describe landscapes so well. It was a landscape that seemed to come out of ancient Russian fairy tales, full of beauty and horror.

Forest, forest, endless forest. . . . Here again there is an immense area ravaged by fire, though not so recently, and you can see the young shoots growing on the old charred trunks.

"What causes these fires?" I ask Nikivor. "Did people light bonfires?"

"Who would have bonfires in this country?" he replies scornfully. "In summer not a living soul comes here. All the traveling is done along the river. No, the fires are caused by a cloud, the cloud comes and sets the forest alight. Or else one tree rubs against another in the hot dry wind and it strikes sparks because the trees are so dry. The wind starts a fire, the wind puts it out. The resin and bark burn away, the needles burn, the trunk remains standing. In a few years the burned-out trees will fall, rotted away."

There are so many trunks around us, all looking as though they might fall at any minute. Some are held up only by the thin branches of other trees. One had fallen across the trail but the top was caught in another so that we could barely pass, by stooping. Then came another stretch of great trees, and soon we came to a path leading down to the river.

"These pathways are useful for catching ducks in the spring," Nikivor observes. "They fly downwards, you know. Just before sunset the hunters stretch a net across the path between the trees, right up to the top. The birds cannot see the net because of the darkness. Then the hunters pull a string, the net falls and covers them. You can bag fifty ducks in this way. Then you bite them."

"What do you mean—bite them?"

"Well, you have to kill them or they'd fly away. So you get your teeth into their necks and bite them—it's the quickest way. There are streams of blood flowing out of your mouth. Of course, you can smash their heads with sticks, but biting is better."

Traveling in this way, they covered nearly three hundred miles in a week. Toward the end Trotsky's account trails off, and we are left in some uncertainty how he continued the journey, which is not surprising since he wrote it shortly after he escaped from Russia, it was not advisable to reveal escape routes, and it was necessary to conceal the names of the people who befriended him on the way. At Rudniki he took a train on a narrow-gauge railroad to Perm. Then to St. Petersburg. Soon he was standing in the School of Artillery in the house of his friend Dr. Litkens, his sentence of exile for life over in two months.

But in another sense it was not over: he was to remain in exile for many years. He left St. Petersburg by boarding a train at the Finland station—the secret police entered the carriage, looked him over, and walked on—and settled down in a small village near Helsingfors, where he met Lenin and Martov, who were preparing a party congress to be held in London. Here, in Finland, they were briefly reconciled, and Trotsky wrote his poetic account of his journey across the snows, which became popular in socialist circles all over Europe.

For him, as for Lenin, the years of exile were scarcely endurable. Unlike Lenin, Trotsky showed no interest in being the head of a party: he was Bolshevik and Menshevik, fluid, wanting his freedom. He settled at last in Vienna—"the old imperial, hierarchic, vain and futile Vienna," as he called it—and he probably settled there because of all European cities it was the one that most resembled Odessa. It was a place where people were kind to him and could tolerate him, where there was a feverish intellectual life, and where the Social Democratic Party had deep roots, though he affected to despise the Austrian party members and said that all the time he was in Vienna he was looking across the border toward the more powerful socialist minds of Germany. It was the Vienna of Rilke, Trakl, Wittgenstein, Freud, Adler, Musil, and the young Hitler. The giants were emerging, or had already emerged.

He lived in three rooms in the working-class suburb of Hütteldorf with Natalie and the two sons she had given him, Lyova born in 1906 and Sergey born in 1908. He was an indulgent father, enjoyed playing with his sons and taking them on walks, but enjoyed writing and studying more. Natalie did the housework and attempted to make ends meet with the meager money he earned as a correspondent or as the editor of the paper *Pravda*, which came out at irregular intervals.

In September 1911, Peter Stolypin, the reactionary prime minister of Russia, was shot to death by a Jew, Mordka Bogrov, in the Kiev Opera House in the presence of the Tsar. Bogrov was in the pay of the police, and the assassination, which was never fully explained, provided the police with an excuse for a massive pogrom in Kiev. For Friedrich Adler's magazine *Der Kampf*, Trotsky wrote an article on terrorism:

Whether a terrorist attempt, even a "successful one," throws the ruling class into confusion depends on the concrete political circumstances. In any case the confusion can only be short-lived; the capitalist state does not base itself on government ministers and cannot be eliminated with them. The classes it serves will always find new people; the mechanism remains intact and continues to function.

But the disarray introduced into the ranks of the working masses themselves by a terrorist attempt is much deeper. If it is enough to arm oneself with a pistol in order to achieve one's goal, why the efforts of a class struggle? If a thimbleful of gunpowder and a little ball of lead is enough to shoot the enemy through the neck, what need is there for a class organization? If it makes sense to terrify highly placed personages with the roar of explosions, where is the need for a party? Why meetings, mass agitations, and elections if one can so easily take aim at the ministerial bench from the gallery of parliament?

In our eyes individual terror is inadmissible precisely because it *belittles the role of the masses in their own consciousness*, reconciles them to their own powerlessness, and turns their eyes and hopes toward a great avenger and liberator who some day will come and accomplish his mission.

The anarchist prophets of "the propaganda of the deed" can argue to their hearts' content about the elevating and stimulating influence of terrorist acts on the masses. Theoretical considerations and political experience prove otherwise. The more "effective" the terrorist acts, the greater their impact, the more the attention of the masses is focused on them—the more they reduce the interest of the masses in self-organization and self-education.

There is nothing surprising in this argument; both the Mensheviks and the Bolsheviks had outlawed individual acts of terrorism. What is interesting is the vigor and subtlety of the argument. But there were not many such articles during this period when he seemed to be floundering in a Sargasso Sea, without power, without influence, hating Vienna or pretending to hate it, living on loans and selling things in the pawnshops, and without a career. His career in fact consisted of waiting impatiently for the next revolution.

He was a man of extremes, an organizer of revolts and desperate escapes, a conspirator and agitator, an orator and writer. He could do all these things superbly, but Vienna was not the place where he could practice them to his own advantage. He was not a good speaker in German; he was a worse speaker in French; he was terrible when he spoke English. He joined the Austrian Social Democratic Party and became a member in good standing, but he was not regarded as one of its major orators or as one of its major figures.

He suffered from the disease of exiles, quarreled with those who helped him, and was sometimes cruel to

those he loved. Interested in psychiatry, he studied the
works of Freud and Alfred Adler, who befriended him.
Sometimes Natalie and the children would spend the
summers in the Adler country house near Innsbruck.
Adler's wife was Russian by birth, and Adler's daughter Alexandra remembers Natalie's gay laughter, and
her sadness when it was time to return to the misery of
Hutteldorf. Adler's son Kurt remembers how as a boy he
used to play football in the park with young Lyova. A
policeman came along and told the boys it was absolutely verboten to play football. Suddenly Trotsky was
in the park, haranguing the policeman so authoritatively that thereafter the children played in the park as
often as they pleased.

In 1912 Trotsky's financial situation improved when
Kievan Thought, one of the most prestigious newspapers in southern Russia, invited him to become a
foreign correspondent covering the Balkan War. He was
an excellent correspondent, learned a great deal about
the conduct of wars, and fought magnificent battles in
Belgrade and Sofia "with those youngsters barely dry
behind the ears, who wield their censor's scissors
indiscriminately even on theoretical articles where
there is nothing at all about the war."

One of the chief fruits of Trotsky's travels in the
Balkans was his friendship with a Bulgarian doctor
called Christian Rakovsky. Born in September 1873, he
was six years older than Trotsky. He belonged to the
landed gentry; at the age of fifteen he became a
revolutionary and at nineteen he was arrested in Switzerland for physically assaulting an *agent-provocateur*.
He studied medicine in Paris and philosophy in Germany. He was on the *Potemkin* in the Black Sea in 1905
when it mutinied and was the agitator chiefly responsible for the mutiny. He was one of those men who leave
little trace in history books but change the course of
history. Trotsky loved him. With his fine Roman head,
his French manners, his Bulgarian warmth, his precise
German intelligence, he was the companion Trotsky
had always desired.

For Trotsky the Balkan wars provided an opportunity

for studying the nature of war. The battles were fought in mountainous countries, where ambushes and surprise attacks followed the pattern of medieval wars. The Serbs, Greeks, Montenegrins, and Bulgarians were in revolt against the Turks; and all Russian sympathies were on the side of the enemies of the Ottoman empire. Trotsky wrote for *Kievan Thought* an article on the Bulgarian atrocities against the Turks, which created a furor for a week. He disliked the Turks but saw no reason why atrocities committed against them should not be reported.

He returned to Vienna not knowing what was to become of him, still poor and improvident, writing occasional articles and making occasional speeches. His one great accomplishment—the 1905 Soviet—was far behind him. In his own mind he intended to be an actor performing in the center of the stage, but he remained in the wings. For a few more years he would be compelled to continue the career of a revolutionary waiting for a revolution.

WANDERINGS ON THE PERIPHERY OF WAR

PART FOUR

Imagine you are in Tver under the vigilance of the police and you are about to be deported to Tokyo, a place where you have not the slightest intention of going. That is approximately my situation . . .

THE VILLAGE OF ZIMMERWALD 8

On a cloudless summer day the old order perished. A few minutes before eleven o'clock in the morning of June 28, 1914, a young Serbian nationalist, Gavrilo Princip, fired two shots at an automobile slowly backing out of a street it had entered by mistake. The Archduke Franz Ferdinand, the heir to the Austro-Hungarian throne, and his wife were killed. In an extraordinarily short space of time the great powers Britain, France, Russia, Germany and Austria called up the reserves and prepared for war, and they went about it automatically, blindly, without counting the cost, all making mistakes—the same mistakes. On August 1, Germany declared war on Russia, and there was no turning back.

In all the countries at war the socialists and the Social Democrats voted for war credits. In Trotsky's eyes this was the greatest mistake of all, for it meant in his eyes the repudiation of socialist principles, socialist programs and socialist ideals by the very men who had been elected to parliament in order to bring socialism about. The forces of the left, which had grown powerfully during the previous ten years, had surrendered to the forces of nationalism. Only a very few socialists and Social Democrats spoke against the war, their voices drowned in the storm of euphoria that spread over all these nations now that the war had actually broken out. For Trotsky there was only one comfort—wars end in revolutions.

On August 3, at three o'clock in the afternoon, deeply depressed because he had just heard of the assassination of the French socialist Jean Jaurès in Paris, Trotsky walked into the office of the head of the Austrian political police in the company of his friend Friedrich Adler. The policeman said it was quite possible that all Russians living in Vienna would be arrested the following morning.

"Then your advice is to leave?"

"The sooner the better."

"Good. I will leave with my family for Switzerland tomorrow."

"Hm . . . I would prefer that you do it today."

At 6:10 p.m. Trotsky and his family, having abandoned nearly all their possessions, were on the train bound for Zurich.

Exile in Zurich gave him an opportunity to write a book called *War and the International*, in which he attacked the sleepwalking leaders who blundered into the war. He also attacked the socialists who did nothing to obstruct the military organization. He raged against the German Social Democrats whom he had sometimes admired in the past. When the Social Democratic newspaper *Vorwärts* urged the German workers to "hold out until the decisive victory is ours," he commented that it was "a case of an ulcer of slavish sentiments bursting open and foul pus crawling over the pages of the workingman's press." What he feared most of all was that the war would not only exhaust society's productive resources but would also exhaust the moral forces of the proletariat. He foresaw a long war. Writing in October 1914, he hoped it might be possible against all odds and against all the evidence for the proletariat to bring about an end to the war. The Social Democrats should inscribe on their banner:

"Immediate cessation of the War." The warring governments must be shown that they were not struggling for
national self-preservation but embarking on a campaign of mutual national annihilation, and the only
proper program was to institute the United States of
Europe—without monarchies, without standing armies,
without ruling feudal castes, without secret diplomacy.
He did not explain how this could be done, but insisted
that it would be done because the future lay with
revolutionary Marxism. "The epoch into which we are
entering will be *our* epoch," he wrote. "Marxism is not
defeated. On the contrary, the roar of the cannon in
every quarter of Europe heralds the theoretical victory
of Marxism." Having finished the book, he left for Paris
to become the French correspondent for *Kievan
Thought*.

In the summer of 1915 the Italian socialist deputy
Ordino Morgari went to Paris to meet Emile Vandervelde, the Belgian socialist who had been elected
president of the International. Morgari wanted Vandervelde to convene a meeting of the International on
neutral soil to protest against the war, to summon the
working classes to down tools and prevent the war from
continuing. Morgari's hopes were quickly dashed. Vandervelde replied that he had no intention of convening
a meeting of the executive committee as long as a
single German stood on Belgian soil. Morgari thought
this was an insufficient answer, and protested. What
harm could it do? Was it possible that Vandervelde
could on his own responsibility prevent the International from doing its duty? An idea occurred to him. Was it
possible that the International was a hostage of the
Entente? "Yes, we are hostages," Vandervelde replied.
"Will you are least permit the neutral countries to hold
a conference?" Morgari asked, but Vandervelde rejected any conference whatsoever under the auspices of
the International.

Morgari was not satisfied with these replies and
sought out many other socialists in Paris. He met
Martov and Trotsky in a café on one of the Grands
Boulevards and outlined his plan for a conference to be

held in Switzerland without Vandervelde's approval and outside the authority of the International, indeed against the International. Morgari knew what he was doing, and it made sense. Trotsky, who describes his meeting with Morgari in his autobiography, pretends that it was completely ineffectual and that they merely chattered about pacifism and the need to restore international connections until Morgari, warming to the subject that really interested him, enlarged on the subject of false passports that would have to be obtained for the delegates to enable them to enter Switzerland. Trotsky has a good deal of fun at Morgari's expense, describing how the Italian deputy's voice dropped to a tragic whisper when he mentioned the false passports and how someone else, terrified by the turn in the conversation, hurriedly called a waiter, paid for the coffee they had been drinking, and hurried out. "That was the end of the meeting," Trotsky wrote. "As we walked back with Martov, we laughed a lot, gaily, but not without a certain anger."

Trotsky's description of the meeting with Morgari is not entirely trustworthy. No doubt Morgari was full of his own importance and no doubt his voice dropped to a conspiratorial whisper, but there was nothing foolish in his desire to hold a conference somewhere, somehow, against the war. Nor was it foolish to discuss false passports. In France in 1915 anyone talking about false passports in a café was well-advised to lower his voice.

Trotsky himself was the chief beneficiary of this meeting in a café. The conference that Morgari wanted so much was held in the village of Zimmerwald high up in the mountains near Berne. The conference is historically associated with Trotsky, who wrote the document which came to be known as the Zimmerwald Manifesto. Attached to this document, like footnotes, were two very short addenda, one signed by Lenin, Radek, and Zinoviev, and the other by Trotsky.

The conference was held during September 5–8. All the delegates met in Berne and were driven to Zimmerwald in four stagecoaches. Robert Grimm, a prominent Swiss socialist, who was later to be of considerable assistance to Lenin at the time when he was about to cross Germany in a sealed train, made all the arrangements and acted as host to the thirty-eight delegates. Grimm and Trotsky appear to have hand-picked the delegates, and some of them were obviously included for no other reason than to add to the numbers. Yet for a formal conference they were very few, and Trotsky has described how, as the coaches climbed up the winding mountain roads, the delegates laughed about the fact that half a century after the founding of the First International, it was still possible to seat all the Internationalists in four coaches.

The truth was that they represented no one but themselves; they were not delegated and were therefore not delegates. Nor were they united in their purpose, for they quarreled vehemently. Lenin objected to the presence of Martov. Angelica Balabanoff was refused voting rights. Two "delegates" came from Germany, two from France, two from Italy, three from Russia, three from Poland, two from Switzerland, one each from Rumania, Bulgaria, Sweden, Norway, and Holland. The "delegate" from Holland was Henrietta Roland-Holst and the "delegate" from Rumania was Trotsky's friend Christian Rakovsky. Surprisingly Austria was not represented. Though they claimed to represent eleven countries, the "delegates" came mostly from France, Italy, and Switzerland, where they lived in exile or enjoyed official positions in the socialist party. The German delegation, headed by Georg Ledebour and Adolf Hoffman, both deputies of the Reichstag, brought greetings from Karl Liebknecht, who had been imprisoned for his opposition to the war.

Lenin was the "spoiler." More than any of the others he embroiled himself in bitter controversies, while attempting to dominate the conference and bend it to his will. He wanted them to agree upon a manifesto with teeth in it; and in his own draft manifesto he urged all socialist members of parliament to resign and to lead the workers out on the streets until the governments were toppled, and afterward there must come into existence a new International to coordinate the worldwide revolution. Such an International would be invested with full powers and would, at least in theory, act as a sovereign body.

Most of the people who came to Zimmerwald knew Lenin in person or by reputation, and they were a little afraid of him, for he was the master of the trenchant and damning word. They were not prepared to sign their names to a document calling for immediate uprisings. Trotsky, who played the role of the conciliator, moving quickly and lightly over the no man's land separating the extreme left from the moderate left, succeeded in keeping the peace. In comparison with Lenin he appeared modest; he knew the habits of the Western world and maintained a studied politeness. In fact, he was as hungry for revolution as Lenin and thinking along the same lines—a sudden paralyzing blow at the heart of the government, the workers on the streets, the iron "dictatorship of the proletariat." He served as the conciliator, appeared to be in the middle, but was secretly with Lenin, with Lenin's policies rather than with the man. There was a stubborn rivalry between them, but their aims were the same.

Angelica Balabanoff, an exceedingly perceptive woman, was puzzled by Trotsky's role at the conference. She had heard him out-Lenining Lenin in the violence of his ideas, yet he appeared to be at home among the moderates. She therefore asked Lenin for an explanation. "Why does he hold apart from your group?" she asked. Lenin answered quickly in a voice colored by irritation: "Don't you know? It's ambition, ambition, ambition!"

This was not the whole truth. Lenin, Zinoviev, and Radek were all violently ambitious and were all the more ambitious because their fortunes had sunk so low. Yet there was a difference in the qualities of their ambitions. Lenin's ambitions were absolute: he saw himself as the embodiment of the dictatorship of the proletariat, and he regarded Zinoviev and Radek as his servants jumping at his commands, as obedient to him as their inferior intellects would permit. Trotsky saw himself as no man's servant and was aware that his intellect was at least the equal of Lenin's. Also, he knew the arts of conciliation, which Lenin had never learned.

So now in the tiny village in the mountains Trotsky sat among the "delegates," calming them, seeking a consensus, making himself invaluable on all sides, so that it was generally agreed that he should write the final declaration and submit it to the conference after Lenin's draft manifesto was rejected. Trotsky's Zimmerwald Manifesto deserves to be quoted at some length because it is a document of historical importance and because it involves a deliberate act of deception brilliantly carried out to advance his cause. In all, three drafts of the manifesto were produced and then submitted to a seven-man commission. The three drafts consisted of Lenin's draft, a draft by the moderate socialists, and Trotsky's intermediary draft attempting to bridge the gap. Here are the introductory paragraphs of Trotsky's version which was accepted when it was realized that no perfect consensus could be reached and that the tenuous unity achieved during the conference was likely to be broken if there was any further wrangling:

Workers of Europe!
The war has lasted more than a year. Millions of bodies lie on the battlefields, millions of men have been crippled for life. *Europe has become a gigantic slaughterhouse of men.* All civilization, created by the labor of many generations, is doomed to destruction. The most savage barbarism is now celebrating its triumph over everything that had previously been regarded as the pride of mankind.

Whatever may be the truth about the immediate responsibility for the outbreak of the war, one thing is certain. The war that has brought about this chaos is the result of imperialism, of the endeavors of the capitalist classes of all nations to satisfy their greed for profit by exploiting human labor and the natural treasures of the entire earth.

Economically backward or politically weak nations are threatened with subjugation by the Great Powers, which are attempting by blood and iron to change the map of the world according to their interests as exploiters. Entire peoples and countries like Belgium, Poland, the Balkan states, and Armenia, are threatened with the fate of being torn asunder, annexed in whole or in part as booty in the game of compensations.

As the war continues, the real driving forces are revealed in all their baseness. The veil that has concealed the meaning of the world catastrophe from the understanding of the peoples is falling away shred by shred. The capitalists of all countries, who are coining the gold of war profits out of the bloodshed of the people, proclaim that the war is being fought for the defense of the fatherland, for democracy, and for the liberation of oppressed nations. *They lie!* . . .

Workers!

Exploited, disenfranchised, scorned, they called you brothers and comrades at the outbreak of the war when you were being led to the slaughter, to death. And now when militarism has crippled, lacerated, degraded and destroyed you, the rulers demand that you surrender your interests, your aims, your ideals—in a word, *slave-like submission to the civil peace.* You are forbidden to express your views, your feelings, your pain; you are not permitted to set forth your demands and to fight for them. The press is muzzled, political rights and liberties are trodden upon—this is the way *military dictatorship* rules with an iron hand . . .

The struggle is the struggle for freedom, for the reconciliation of peoples, for *socialism.* We must assume the task of fighting for peace—for a peace without annexations or war indemnities . . .

Never in the history of the world has there been a more urgent, a more noble, a more sublime task, and its fulfillment must be our common aim. No sacrifice is too great, no burden too heavy to achieve this goal: peace among the peoples.

Working men and working women! Mothers and fathers! Widows and orphans! Wounded and crippled! We call to all those who are suffering from the war or in consequence of the war, we cry out over all frontiers, and over the smoke-filled battlefields, the devastated cities and villages:

Workers of all countries, unite!

This document was signed by nineteen "delegates"

including Lenin, Robert Grimm, Georg Ledebour, Adolf Hoffmann, and Henrietta Roland-Holst, the only woman among the signatories. For some reason Trotsky did not sign. Lenin, having signed, characteristically added a disclaimer like a codicil to a will. "The manifesto," he wrote, "contains no clear pronouncement about the methods to be used to fight the war." The method to be used was revolution, but since it was impolitic to mention the word in a document intended to have a wide circulation, Lenin added carefully, so that no one should have any illusions about his preferred method: "We shall continue, as we have done all along, to advocate in the socialist press and at meetings of the International, a clear-cut Marxist position in regard to the tasks with which the proletariat is confronted in an age of imperialism."

Having explained indirectly that the Zimmerwald Manifesto left very much to be desired and had avoided the main issue, Lenin then gave it his stamp of approval, saying: "We vote for the manifesto because we regard it as a call to struggle, and in this struggle we are anxious to march side by side with the other sections of the International."

This was not quite the end of the matter. Trotsky and Henrietta Roland-Holst had introduced an amendment condemning the socialists who had voted for the war appropriations. Georg Ledebour had protested vigorously, saying he would not sign the manifesto if the amendment was included. Finally it was agreed that the manifesto "contains all that is implied" in the amendment, which could therefore be abandoned with a clear conscience. In a final paragraph Trotsky explained the circumstances which brought about the rejection of the amendment.

These two notes, one by Lenin and the other by Trotsky, were sometimes added to the Zimmerwald Manifesto, but were usually omitted. They were purely personal statements without any force or any authority except that which came from their names. At this time they were very little known. Both of these notes had one thing in common: they were deceptive, for they encouraged the reader to believe that the "delegates" were in agreement. In his autobiography Trotsky wrote that there were distressing disagreements on many occasions during the conference, and for the most part they were between Lenin and the majority.

Most of the conference was held in the open air, in the garden of the Zimmerwald Hotel. When there were disagreements, Lenin had the pleasant habit of absenting himself from the conference table and playing with the dogs of the hotelkeeper, while he left to others the task of hammering out a formula which would embrace both sides of the argument. Here Trotsky describes what happened when Lenin saw the dogs playing on a patch of sand in the garden on a bright summery day:

> Vladimir Ilyich suddenly got up and left the table. Half-kneeling, he started laughing and tickling first one dog, then the other, under their ears, along their bellies, lightly, delicately (to use Gorky's expression). There was spontaneity in Lenin's gesture. One is tempted to say that he behaved like a little urchin, so carefree, so boyish was his laughter. He glanced at our commission as if he wanted to invite the comrades to take part in this lovely diversion. It seemed to me that people looked with some astonishment: everyone was still preoccupied by the serious debate. Lenin went on stroking the animals, but in a less ebullient manner. He then returned to the table and refused to sign the proposed text of the manifesto. The discussion began anew with fresh violence.

There was, as Trotsky recognized, much method in this madness. The dogs provided a useful stage prop, an excuse for his delaying tactics, an interlude of recreation before he returned to the attack. Lenin was determined that his knifelike will should prevail, but in fact it did not prevail. In spite all his maneuvers he was forced to agree to the Zimmerwald Manifesto after being permitted to write his own minority report, which said in effect that he agreed without enthusiasm and with guarded approval. In one of his speeches at the conference Trotsky summed up the situation of Lenin in one sentence when he declared: *"Der linke Flügel der Partei ist disorientiert.* [The left wing of the Party is disoriented.]" This was one way of saying that it had gone mad, that it was out of touch with reality, and that it had lost its effectiveness.

Trotsky, however, shared many of Lenin's hopes and beliefs. He foresaw that the war would end in revolution and that the task of the revolutionaries was to prepare the ground for the coming revolution. Any means were permissible to turn the war into revolution, for it was more important that capitalism should be destroyed than that any of those abstractions, "Germany," "France," "Russia," "England," should be victorious. The enemy was the ruling class in every nation. The argument plainly depended upon simultaneous revolutions in all the fighting nations: if Russia had a revolution, and Germany did not, what then? Lenin seemed to believe that a revolution in Russia would be followed twenty-four hours later by a revolution in Germany, and then almost automatically the revolutionary fire would blaze in France and England. It was almost an article of faith that one revolution would give birth to another, and so ad infinitum. They had forgotten that revolution is a luxury which only a very weak country can afford and that nations like France and England possess an essential resilience which permits them to ride out a revolutionary tide. In France, too, there were men still living who remembered the horrors perpetrated by the Commune and the even greater horrors perpetrated by the reactionaries who slaughtered the Communards. The revolution, on which they debated at such length at Zimmerwald, looked deceptively simple. "The struggle is the struggle for freedom, for the reconciliation of peoples, for socialism," said the Zimmerwald Manifesto. But the kind of revolution Lenin envisaged had very little to do with any form of freedom except the freedom to obey. Ever since 1903 Lenin had believed that the revolution would be directed by a revolutionary elite of hardened and determined men. Trotsky, less dogmatic, and more of a humanist, possessing a more subtle attitude toward people, felt that the hard-core revolutionary elite might not be sufficient to sustain the revolution. Trotsky looked warily toward all the accidents that might arise; Lenin was contemptuous of accidents and willed them away.

After Zimmerwald, Lenin and Trotsky did not meet again until they both reached St. Petersburg in 1917. Trotsky returned to Paris, carrying copies of the manifesto in his luggage. When passing through customs at the frontier, he took care to place some Russian monarchist propaganda on top of the manifestoes; and seeing that Trotsky was a loyal citizen of the Tsar, the customs officer smiled and waved him into France.

In Paris, Trotsky continued to work on *Nashe Slovo* and to send articles to *Kievan Thought*, continually hounded by the police, continually visiting the censorship office. The Zimmerwald Manifesto was censored, which is not surprising, since it called for an immediate armistice and a peace without annexations or war indemnities. The French government was in no mood for such frivolities. But censoring the manifesto was like censoring a religious tract: the more it was censored, the more widely it became known. *Nashe Slovo* itself was under attack. The Russian ambassador to France complained that it was undermining the war effort, and in the Russian embassy articles from the newspaper were translated into French and sent by messenger to the Ministry of War with appropriate comments by the ambassador himself. The newspaper was receiving attention in high places; so was Trotsky. Jean Longuet, a deputy in the French parliament who happened also to be the grandson of Karl Marx, discussed the case of the newspaper and its chief editor with Aristide Briand, premier and foreign minister of France, an orator in the same class as Trotsky. Briand was a man with a clearcut mind and profoundly intelligent. Longuet thought he was presenting a convincing case when he was suddenly interrupted. "Do you know that the *Nashe Slovo* was found on the persons of the Russian soldiers who murdered their colonel in Marseilles?" Briand asked, and at this point Longuet retired from the contest. He did not know; nor did Trotsky, who made inquiries and learned that a certain Colonel Krause had been stoned to death in Marseilles by his own soldiers who were later found to be in possession of copies of *Nashe Slovo*. Trotsky became convinced that these copies were planted on the soldiers by an agent of the Russian government sent to France from England. The Krause affair sealed the fate of the newspaper. Not only must the newspaper be closed, but Trotsky himself must be banished from France. He could go anywhere he liked. This was satisfying at first but he soon discovered that no country wanted him. England and Italy refused to give him a visa; Switzerland, which he regarded as a last resort, proved to be adamantly opposed to granting him a visa under any terms. Holland and Scandinavia, where he might be welcomed, could only be reached through England. He was not permitted to remain in France and was continually under surveillance. Incensed by the order of banishment, Trotsky wrote off a letter to Jules Guesde, one of the founding fathers of French Marxism, whom Briand had invited into his cabinet as a minister without portfolio in an attempt to placate the left wing. Trotsky had forgotten or did not know that Guesde was no longer a minister in the National Cabinet and at this precise moment in October 1916 possessed no office at all. It was a very long letter covering seven closely printed pages when Trotsky later printed it, and it is unlikely that Guesde took the trouble to read all of it.

Written in fury, the letter reads like a speech. We hear the rolling thunder, and almost we can see Trotsky on the rostrum, his right arm jerking menacingly as it always did when he was excited, his voice rising to the shrill scream of a knife grinder and falling again only to rise again, drumbeat and piercing whistles, tearing of silk, sound of marching feet. There is scarcely another piece of his prose that so effectively suggests the quality of his speeches. Here is part of the long letter:

To the Minister of State, Monsieur Jules Guesde:
Before quitting the soil of France under the escort of a police officer, who personifies the liberties over whose

defence you stand guard in the National Cabinet, I deem it my duty to express to you a few thoughts which, while they are most likely not to be any use to you, will at least be of use against you. In expelling me from France, your colleague, the Minister for War, did not think fit to indicate his reasons for suppressing the Russian newspaper *Nashe Slovo*. I was one of its editors and for two years I suffered all the torments of the censorship operating under the aegis of the same Minister of War.

Nevertheless I shall not conceal from you the fact that for me there are no mysteries about my expulsion. You felt the need to adopt repressive measures against an international socialist, one of those who refuses to be the defender or the slave of the imperialist war.

* * * * *

You believed, you hoped, that the proletariat of France, bled white in this senseless and hopeless war by the crime of the ruling classes, would continue to tolerate quietly, to the very end, this shameful pact between official socialism and the worst enemies of the proletariat. You were mistaken. An opposition has come forward. In spite of martial law and the frenzy of nationalism which, whether it is royalist, radical or socialist, always preserves its capitalist substance—the revolutionary opposition is gaining ground every day.

* * * * *

Perhaps you will console yourself with the thought that we are few in numbers? Yet we are greater in number than the police of all ranks believe. In their professional myopia they fail to see the spirit of revolt rising from every hearth of suffering and spreading throughout France, throughout all Europe, in the suburbs where the workman live, in the countryside, in the shops, and in the trenches.

* * * * *

Jules Guesde, get out of your military automobile, leave the cage where the capitalist state has imprisoned you. Look around you! Perhaps fate for the last time will have pity on your wretched old age and permit you to hear the muted rumble of approaching events. We expect them, we summon them, we prepare for them! The fate of France would be too terrible if the Calvary of its working class did not bring about a great revenge, where there will be no room for you, Jules Guesde, and for yours.

Expelled by you, I leave France with a profound faith in our triumph. Over and above your head, I send fraternal greetings to the French proletariat, which is awaking to its great destiny!

Without you and against you: Long live socialist France.

Having composed a masterpiece of savage invective against an old man who had never harmed him and who no longer possessed any power, Trotsky waited to see exactly what the French government was going to do with him.

9 A FROLIC THROUGH SPAIN

One day toward the end of October 1916 two plainclothes policemen knocked politely on the door of Trotsky's small apartment on the Rue Oudry, a short street running off the Boulevard St. Marcel, and Natalie let them in. They announced that they had some business with her husband, they would wait for his return, and meanwhile they hoped she would not be inconvenienced by their presence. There was no telephone; no messengers could be sent to warn Trotsky; and Natalie quietly surrendered to the inevitable. When Trotsky came home, he was immediately placed under arrest but in the gentlest and quietest way possible. They explained that he would be under arrest only for a little while—the time it took to get him to the Spanish frontier. They hoped they were not unduly disturbing him, and when Natalie asked them questions they kept doffing their hats with an exquisite and infuriating politeness. *Excusez, madame!*

When Trotsky had time to ponder his arrest, it occurred to him that everything seemed to happen like a farce in a tenth-rate stage show. One of the plainclothes men was short and elderly with a broad potato nose such as you find in Russia, the other was a heavyset, middle-aged man, completely bald and dark-skinned—"as black as pitch," Trotsky said with some exaggeration, for the *Sûreté Générale* was not in the habit of employing Negroes to make important arrests. They were equally polite, equally firm. When they said, "Please make it easy for us," they meant, "Don't make any trouble for us or you will regret it!" Trotsky was given a little time to arrange his affairs and to say farewell to a few friends, while the policemen politely removed themselves from the apartment, standing guard outside the door. When at last Trotsky entered the car, one of the policemen carefully arranged the rug like a well-trained chauffeur.

In the train taking them to the Spanish frontier they sat together in a third-class compartment. It appeared that the elderly policeman was something of a geographer: he knew the names of places in Russia and recited them. In this way Tomsk, Irkutsk, Kazan, Novgorod, and Nizhni Novgorod were evoked in the express train to remind Trotsky of a land that seemed infinitely far away. The tall, dark-skinned man regarded himself as a philosopher, and between bites on a pork sausage he announced: "The Latin people are marking time; the others are leaving them behind. What is happening in literature? Decadence all along the line! In philosophy, the same! Nothing has happened since the time of Pascal and Descartes. The Latin race is marking time." Trotsky waited expectantly for more revelations, but there was a long pause and at last the philosopher said gloomily: "Some time back you had Tolstoy, but Ibsen is more comprehensible to our people." Then he was silent again.

Then it was the turn of the elderly man who began to talk at length about the Trans-Siberian railway, which offered some measure of hope to the world and by implication denied the pessimistic conclusions of his younger colleague. "Yes, we lack initiative," he said. "Everyone wants to be a government official. It's sad, but you can't deny it."

The dark man interrupted with a dissertation on the

art of following suspects through the streets of Paris.

"It isn't efficient any more," he said. "The Metro has killed it. People who are being shadowed should be ordered never to use the Metro. This is the only way in which shadowing can be perfected."

The elderly man commented: "We often follow a man, and sometimes we haven't the faintest idea why we are doing it."

"You see," said the dark man, "we policemen have to be skeptics. You people have ideas, but we have to protect the established order. Take the Great Revolution. What a movement of ideas! The Encyclopedists, Jean Jacques Rousseau, Voltaire! And fourteen years after the Revolution the people were more miserable than ever. Read Taine. . . . We policemen are conservatives by the very nature of things. Skepticism is the only philosophy that accords with our profession. After all, no one chooses his own path. Free will does not exist. Everything is determined by the course of events." A moment later, raising his wine bottle to his mouth, taking a long drink, and corking the bottle, he was ready with more revelations. He said: "Renan was of the opinion that all new ideas come too early, and that's a fact!" He had just said this when he caught sight of Trotsky's hand on the handle of the door. Was it possible that Trotsky would open the door and jump into the darkness? Cautiously Trotsky placed his hand in his pocket. After a long night journey without sleep, they were coming into the railway station at Hendaye, whence it was only a short distance to Irún on the Spanish side of the border.

The two policemen behaved impeccably, respectfully, with the proper detachment. *"C'est fait avec discré-tion, n'est-ce pas?"* the dark one said, taking leave of his prisoner on Spanish soil. He hoped the prisoner would also show discretion. "You may take the tramway from Irún to San Sebastián. It would be best if you assumed the appearance of a tourist, thus avoiding the suspicions of the Spanish police, who are extremely distrustful. And from this moment I don't know you, do I?" Then the policemen turned their backs on him and walked back to France, where they telephoned their superiors to announce that their mission was accomplished. Some time later a telegram was dispatched from the Prefecture of Police in Paris to the police authorities in Madrid: "Leon Trotsky, a dangerous anarchist, crossed the frontier at Irún. Intends to settle down in Madrid."

Trotsky's account of his subsequent wanderings survives by a curious chance only in Spanish. In a book called *Mis Peripecias en España* (My Vicissitudes in Spain), published in 1929 in Madrid in a translation by Andrés Nin, one of the founders of the Spanish Communist Party, we have the text of Trotsky's diary based on a small edition published in Russia in 1926. All copies of the Russian edition appear to have perished. Some extracts from the diary are printed in Trotsky's autobiography, but one has to read the full diary to get the flavor of his two months of wandering through Spain, one comic incident following after another, one absurdity following hard on the heels of the last.

Although he was under police surveillance during the entire period, and was arrested briefly, Trotsky enjoyed himself. He knew no one in Spain, did not speak Spanish, had almost no money, and was completely bewildered by Spanish society, which was even more feudal than Tsarist Russia, but he resolved to extract the utmost amusement from his situation. He had spent all his days immersed in revolutionary activities. Now for the first time since his school days he was in a situation where revolutionary activity of any kind was impossible. He was free of all his burdens.

He spent only a day or two in San Sebastián, where his hotel bedroom was adorned with a picture, *La Muerte del Pecador* (The Death of a Sinner), showing a two-headed devil snatching the sinner from the hands of a weeping angel. Contemplation of the picture led him to some acute reflections on the fate of the human soul, and then by natural progression to the subject of military uniforms in Spain. "The military uniforms are complicated," he wrote. "It would appear that they are the product of mature reflection. They do not give the impression of being serious."

In fact nothing in Spain gave "the impression of being serious," except its art. He went to Madrid, wandered round the streets, happily fell in with a few Frenchmen who were able to inform him about the curious failings in the Spanish character, watched the ceremonial arrival of Marcos Avellaneda, the new ambassador from Argentina, at the Royal Palace to the music of a military band—Trotsky enjoyed the band—and spent most of his time in the Prado examining the paintings of Rembrandt, Ribera, and Goya. After seeing the paintings he wrote in his diary some weighty observations on the new forms of art that would appear after the war, for it was inconceivable that this most terrible of wars would not change the nature of man's perceptions. He appears to have made these observations on November 7, 1916, in his small room in the Hotel de Paris in Madrid. Exactly a year later he was leading the insurrection in Petrograd.

Madrid amused him, saddened him, and sometimes delighted him. He especially enjoyed the brilliance of the city at night in the glare of electricity and gaslight. Paris had been dark at night, in fear of enemy airplanes. Madrid gloried in its illuminations, its Paris fashions, its gaiety, thus vividly demonstrating the advantages of peace over war.

Early in the afternoon of November 9, when Trotsky was in his hotel room, a maidservant knocked on the door and asked him to come out in the corridor. In this way he found himself under arrest, for the two gentlemen waiting outside were policemen, unpleasant looking and obviously up to mischief. They told him he would be detained.

"For how long?" he asked.

"For an hour or two," they answered. "We need certain information about you."

They took him to the police station. They did not keep him for an hour or two. For seven hours he sat on a leather divan, from two o'clock to nine o'clock in the evening, waiting to be examined. He remembered that he sat on the divan without once changing his position during those seven hours. At last he was led upstairs to an office where he was cross-examined by a small group of Olympian figures commanded by a tiny, bald-headed man who made up for his stature by a tremendous sense of his own importance. How did you come to Spain? Deported by the French authorities. Why? Pacifism. Were you at Zimmerwald? Yes. What did you do there? I wrote the Manifesto. Did you take part in the discussions? Yes, of course. What are your ideas? Trotsky told them, though they could have understood little, for the information was conveyed through an incompetent interpreter. It appeared that they regarded him as an anarchist. One of the policemen sighed: "If you only knew the amount of money we spend prosecuting our anarchists." *Our* anarchists! Trotsky pointed out that whatever else he was, he was not one of *their* anarchists. "You mustn't hold me responsible for the Spanish anarchists—and the Russian police." They had obviously received a dossier from the Russian secret police; just as obviously they were having some difficulty deciphering it. The Russian secret police knew Trotsky well and they were under no illusions about his beliefs and they would never have described him as an anarchist. This description seems to have come from a careless police agent in France.

Finally the little police chief announced that the Spanish government could not tolerate the presence of the accused on Spanish soil, that he must be thrown out of the country immediately, and that meanwhile his movements would be subject to "certain restrictions."

"Is it permissible to know the reason?" Trotsky asked politely.

"Your ideas are far too advanced for Spain," he was told, and soon he learned what was meant by "certain restrictions." At midnight he was taken to prison in a cab.

Prisons were old friends; he was accustomed to them and knew how to deal with them. If he was not afraid of them, it was because he found them admirable places for quiet study and contemplation. The Model Prison was shaped like a star, with five galleries radiating from the center, and each of the galleries was four stories high. There was the peculiar silence of a prison at night, "impregnated with heavy vapors and nightmares." He was marched up iron stairways and locked in a large, dimly lit cell with a bed, a chair, a crucifix, and barred windows, and there was a small aperture in the windows which permitted fresh air to come in. Fully clothed, he lay down on the bed and contemplated the various intricate lines of force that had brought him in winter to a jail cell in Madrid; and thinking about these things, he laughed himself to sleep.

Prison is always an invigorating experience provided the stay is short. Trotsky remained in the Model Prison for three days. He learned that strict equality among the prisoners did not exist, that there were three classes of cells, A, B, and C, and with each class there was a different set of privileges. In A the prisoner had the privilege of paying the government one and a half pesetas a day for his accommodation with the right to two hour-long walks during the day. In B the prisoner paid 75 centimes for his accommodation and was permitted to walk about only for half an hour. In C, the cells being about the size of a cupboard, he was permitted very little walking and paid nothing. Trotsky's cell belonged to A class and was paid for by the government: an admirable arrangement.

During his walk the following day Trotsky encountered the self-styled "King of Thieves," a man who had practiced his trade all over Europe and was now contemplating a visit to Canada, where he hoped to practice his trade even more profitably. He asked Trotsky's advice. "Canada?" Trotsky replied. "Well, you know there are many farmers there and a young bourgeoisie with a deep sense of property, like the Swiss." It was not a very helpful answer, and the King of Thieves was somewhat irritated, as he had a perfect right to be.

Sometime later Trotsky was told that the Spanish government had decided to expel him and wanted to know which country he would like to be expelled to. This was not a game he enjoyed playing, nor did he enjoy being fingerprinted and measured anthropometrically. He resisted fingerprinting with vigor until it became clear that they were absolutely determined; then, with studied nonchalance, he gazed out of the window while they rolled his blackened fingers and thumbs on a piece of paper. For anthropometric measurements it was necessary for him to remove his boots. He resisted again, and claimed later that he drove the anthropometrists into a state of total confusion. When all this was over, he encountered the prison chaplain in the corridor. The chaplain murmured: *"Paciencia, paciencia."* For once Trotsky found himself in full agreement with a priest.

One of his few visitors in prison was Anguiano, the secretary general of the Spanish Socialist Party, who had just been released from a two-week prison sentence for saying something improper about a saint. Anguiano was in close contact with the leaders of the French and Italian Socialist parties and was bombarding them with appeals to help Trotsky obtain a visa for France and Italy. This was a serious matter, for Trotsky was afraid of being deported to Russia. The French and Italian Socialists did what they could, but no visas were granted. Quite suddenly, on the morning of his third day in prison, he was informed that he would be sent to Cádiz, a city in southwestern Spain, where he would be permitted to cool his heels while the Spanish government in its own good time decided what to do with him. He was asked whether he would like to pay the fare, and answered that he saw no reason to pay for a journey he did not want to take to a city he had not the least desire to visit. The long-suffering Spanish police bowed to Trotsky's unanswerable logic, and the Spanish Crown paid the fare of the prisoner and his police escort.

What puzzled him was why he was being sent to Cádiz, of all places. What was there about Cádiz which made them think this was a suitable habitation for him? He could see no logic in it except that it was far from Madrid, but there were many other places in Spain even further from Madrid. It occurred to him that from the moment he took flight from Berezov near the Arctic Circle he had been traveling southwest in more or less a straight line to the ultimate edge of Europe and the Atlantic Ocean.

Cádiz, which the Romans called *Jocosae Gades*, was no joke. Once it was one of the richest cities in the world; now it was fading tranquilly away among the dusty palm trees and overornate Christmas-cake buildings. Trotsky, wandering in the bright sunshine in the middle of winter, dogged by his police guards, restlessly attempting to get out of Spain and pursue his career as a revolutionary, thought the place unreal, improbable, and farcical. He spent six weeks there in a state of bemusement. The Spanish authorities offered to put him on a ship going to Cuba.

"You will go to Havana," he was told.

"Havana?"

"Yes, Havana."

"I won't go voluntarily."

"Then we may have to take you on board and put you under the hatches."

The secretary of the German consul acted as interpreter, and it was clear that the secretary thought him unreasonable.

"You should come to terms with reality (*sich mit den Realitäten abzufinden*)," he was told.

A ship for Havana was leaving the next day. For Trotsky, Havana was simply Spain writ smaller, a place where he was liable to be arrested and reduced to inconsequence. He marched to the telegraph office and sent urgent telegrams to socialist friends in Madrid, the minister of the interior, the head of the secret police, prime minister Alvaro Romanones, liberal newspapers, republican deputies, and everyone else who could conceivably help him to avoid being put on the ship early the next morning. "I mobilized every argument that could be compressed within the limits of a telegram," Trotsky wrote with some satisfaction. "Imagine," he wrote to the Italian deputy Serrati, one of the recipients of the deluge of letters he wrote after his visit to the telegraph office. "Imagine you are in Tver under the vigilance of the police and you are about to be deported to Tokyo, a place where you have not the slightest intention of going. This is approximately my situation in Cádiz on the eve of my expulsion to Havana." Having sent the telegrams, he returned to the prefecture and loudly demanded that, rather than be placed on the ship going to Cuba, they should permit him to remain in prison while awaiting a ship to New York, and he insisted that this information be immediately telegraphed to the authorities in Madrid at his expense. They sent the telegram, allowed him to remain free, and hoped that arrangements for putting him on the ship for New York would not be too long delayed.

In theory he was in the custody of his guards; in fact he could do very much as he pleased. When he wanted them, they were at his service. When he went to bookshops, they helped him to buy books. He acquired in this way a map of the Atlantic Ocean, dated 1846, an English-French and a Spanish-German dictionary. One of the policemen pointed to a book in Spanish on the will and suggested that he should buy that too. It was probably an oblique compliment. The police were his leisurely custodians; they vanished when they had other things to do. In Paris, during his last months in France, they had followed him everywhere. If he went to a cinema, they kept watch outside. If he suddenly turned into a Metro, he would hear them coming down the steps after him. If he jumped into a taxi, they would pursue him in another taxi. Trotsky enjoyed outwitting them, but it was nerve-wracking to be constantly pursued. In Cádiz it was nerve-wracking not to be pursued. They seemed to be inviting him to escape, perhaps hoping that he would go on one of the ships in the harbor and vanish from sight.

Cádiz was almost paradise; the sun shone and cooling winds came from the sea; the greatest war in history did not exist, for there was no news about it in the newspapers. Trotsky took refuge in the municipal library, where no voices from outside were allowed to penetrate and where the clock had stopped. He also visited the museum where there was a dubious Van Dyck, a dubious Rubens, and an authentic Murillo. In Cádiz authentic Murillos abounded, for the artist had lived there and while painting *St. Catherine* for the Church of Santa Caterina, he accidentally fell from the scaffolding and died.

Trotsky was perfectly happy wandering through the crowded streets that "smelled of wine, grease, garlic and human poverty." Chance encounters brought him some entertaining stories. He was amused by one of his guards who marveled at the number of telegrams Trotsky was capable of sending, an accomplishment that would have been quite impossible without the aid of Señor Marconi, the great Spanish inventor. "What a head Marconi must have," the guard said. "He is not a foreigner, he is one of ours, a Spaniard." Trotsky tried to disabuse him. It was no use. The guard was absolutely convinced that Marconi was a Spaniard. "I am sure he is a Spaniard," the man said with total conviction. Once he was invited by a sacristan to visit the catacombs, and refused the offer on the grounds that he was enjoying the fresh air, the palm trees, the sunlight, and the sea, and would find none of these down below. One day he watched a peculiarly unpleasant brawl taking place in the old harbor, and it occurred to him that a gigantic screw jack will eventually be needed to raise the culture of the masses. He was like a princely traveler who is a little put out by the coarse behavior of the natives.

Meanwhile in his studious fashion he frequented the municipal library, where the only sound came from the bookworms eating through the eighteenth-century folios. He took copious notes which he later incorporated in his diary. Three historical works particularly interested him: Bourgoing's *Description of Modern Spain*, Adam's *History of Spain since Its Discovery by the Phoenicians to the Death of Charles III*, and de Merlhiac's *Concerning the Freedom of the Seas and of Commerce*, all published between 1807 and 1818. They were all

French, but Adam's *History* was originally written in English. It was a vast, four-volume compendium of the available knowledge of Spain, and he found in it a good deal of quite useful information about royal arrogance, revolutions and counterrevolutions, murders, the auto-da-fé, conspiracies, and invasions. As he read leisurely about the long distant past he sometimes made caustic notes on the Spanish character and particularly the character of the politicians:

A historian of the Spanish revolution tells us about politicians who will brand the popular movement as madness and criminality five minutes before victory is achieved, and then they will cheer the victors. "These accommodating gentlemen," says the historian, "appeared in all the revolutions one after another and out-shouted all the rest." The Spaniards call these people Pancistas, a word derived from Panza. From this same word comes the name of our old friend Sancho Panza.

Panza means "belly" in Spanish: Trotsky enjoyed these pleasant discoveries. He found the Spaniards amusing but not particularly interesting. In the intervals of compiling notes and reading from enormous musty folios, he continued to bask in the sunlight. Natalie, writing from Paris, complained that she was living through one of the worst winters on record—"nothing but cold, rain, snow, mist and mud."

Gradually the little pieces of the jigsaw puzzle were being put together. The Spanish government finally bowed to his desire to go to America. Letters and telegrams in his favor were being sent to Madrid in a steady stream. As the author of the Zimmerwald Manifesto he was not unknown; there were many helping hands; Natalie was working on his behalf from Paris and he continued to send urgent telegrams to Madrid, until they were weary of him. A ship was leaving Barcelona for New York toward the end of the month. The Spanish authorities were happy to let him go. He was put on the train to Madrid with the customary guards, and in Madrid he was allowed once more to visit the museums and art galleries. In this way he was able to study Zurbarán's saintly monks and Goya's portrait of Manuel de Godoy, Duke of Alcudia and Prince of the Peace, who acquired Queen Maria Luisa as his mistress. Trotsky thought he could see in Godoy's foolish face exactly the same expression he had seen in the face of Prince Potemkin, who acquired the Empress Catherine the Great as his mistress. In the Prado he found Goya's painting of King Fernando VII and thought it "execrable, unworthy of the artist's brush." This was a very odd verdict considering that critics unanimously regard it as one of Goya's most admirable creations mingling affection with brutal satire.

Then he was on the train again to Barcelona and freedom. As usual, the police were heavy-handed. They would let him go but first they must make his life miserable. Taken to police headquarters, he was detained for three hours. Incensed by the untoward behavior of the police, he sent off another telegram to the prime minister of Spain: "On my arrival in Barcelona I wasted three hours at the Jefatura de Policia without being permitted to eat or wash." He expected an apology but received none. Natalie and his two sons had arrived in Barcelona, and there was a happy reunion. The boys were delighted by the sea and the abundant fruit. Trotsky entered into his notebook some cursory remarks on the Catalan character; he regarded them as "the privileged smugglers of Spain," enterprising and hard-headed. He admired their industry and he developed an affection for Barcelona which he did not possess for Cádiz. Barcelona was real, Cádiz was comic opera.

Too late he learned that the Italian socialists were completing their arrangements for him to return to Switzerland through Italy. If he had been able to remain in Spain a day or two longer, he might have been able to make his headquarters in Zurich. He blamed Alexander Izvolsky, the Russian ambassador to France, for the delay, and there is no doubt that

Izvolsky was keeping an eye on him and doing everything possible to keep Trotsky out of Europe.

So it happened that on December 28 the S.S. *Monserrat*, with a cargo of refugees from warring Europe, and with Trotsky and his family on board, set out for New York. The weather was magnificent until they sailed into the Atlantic. On the last day of the year they passed Gibraltar, where someone observed that there were no less than sixty-five British warships guarding the straits.

There was a doctor on board; he examined the passengers one by one, and there was tragedy when he discovered that one of the passengers was suffering from trachoma and would not be permitted to land in the United States. Most of the passengers were seasick. Only Trotsky's sons were enjoying themselves. They encountered one of the ship's firemen and reported breathlessly to their father that the man was a republican.

"How do you know?" Trotsky asked. "How did you understand what he was saying?"

"No difficulty. He said: 'Alfonso' and then pretended to be holding a revolver and went *paf, paf, paf.*"

"Yes, he must certainly be a republican," Trotsky commented.

The boys were so pleased with their newfound republican that they gave him some dried grapes and other dainties. Trotsky met the twenty-year-old republican and was happy to know he was not the only revolutionary traveling on the ship.

There were storms in the Atlantic. The S.S. *Monserrat* took on water and limped along. The third-class passengers, ill fed and full of anxiety about what would happen to them in New York, lay listless on the deck. Trotsky spoke to few people; the passenger-list showed scarcely anyone worth talking to. He rested, slept, read, paced the deck, gazed at the huge waves that threatened to drown the small Spanish tub, and pondered what the year 1917 would bring.

10 DICTATOR OF AMERICA?

After a stormy seventeen-day journey across the Atlantic, the S.S. *Monserrat* dropped anchor in New York harbor at three o'clock in the morning of January 13, 1917. Nearly all the passengers were shaken out of their sleep by the deafening roar of the anchor chains. Soon people of half a dozen nationalities, all refugees from Europe, were leaving their cabins and making their way to the deck for their first view of the New World and of its largest, wealthiest, and most audaciously designed city. What they saw on that cold, dark Sunday morning was not very much. It was raining hard, there was a driving wind, and it was bitterly cold. Huge skyscrapers loomed in front of them. Trotsky, standing on deck, was not at first impressed by the skyscrapers and he called New York "a wet mountain of buildings."

A curious incident happened when they were being examined by the medical doctors sent on board the ship to discover whether any of the passengers were suffering from communicable diseases. When Natalie stepped up to the doctor's table in the second-class lounge, she was wearing a veil. There was nothing surprising in this—many women wore veils—but Trot-

sky was shocked beyond measure by the unceremoni-
ous way in which the doctor lifted the veil and then
made a motion with his fingers to lift up her downcast
eyelids. Trotsky thought the doctor wanted to see
whether she was suffering from trachoma, but it is more
likely that he simply wanted to see what she looked
like and to make an estimate of her general health. For
Natalie, it was evidently an affront. Trotsky was proud
of her behavior. In some diary notes written many years
later he wrote: "N. did not protest, said nothing, did not
step back; she was just surprised. She glanced at the
doctor questioningly and blushed a little. But the
coarse Yankee immediately dropped his hands and
stepped back apologetically; there was such an irre-
sistible dignity of womanhood in her face, in her
glance, in her whole figure." He was very proud of her
when a few minutes later they stepped down the
gangplank to the New York pier.

Thereafter the word "trachoma" is mentioned fairly
often in Trotsky's writings and speeches. He liked the
sound of it, and the image of those bluish-gray jellylike
eyes could be applied to his enemies who were unsee-
ing and appalling to look upon. "America was working
for Europe at war," he commented in his autobiography. "She needs cheap labor, but it must be labor
without trachoma, without anarchism and other diseases of the sort." Quite suddenly on board a ship in New
York harbor the word "trachoma" entered his vocabulary, to be used with quite extraordinary effect whenever he was in a mood for denunciation.

Trotsky's fame and popularity had preceded him, and
he was warmly welcomed by the leaders of the small
groups of Left-wing Socialists in New York. They helped
him to find a small apartment on 164th Street, the
Bronx, at a rent of eighteen dollars a month, which he
could well afford, for he was soon writing articles for
socialist newspapers and being paid for them and he
was also making two or three speeches a day, for which
he received twenty or thirty dollars. Most of the time he
remained in New York, but he made at least one trip to
Philadelphia.

The Bronx apartment was well furnished and provided with common American conveniences. They included electric light, gas cooking-range, bath, telephone, automatic service elevator, and a chute for the garbage. The telephone particularly entranced him, for he had never previously possessed a private telephone. His two sons were fascinated by the modern conveniences, and they too succumbed to the lure of the telephone. New York, the city of skyscrapers and labor-saving machines, profoundly impressed Trotsky who wrote later that it was "the fullest expression of the modern age and no other city in the world could compare to it." But this enthusiastic tribute was balanced by a severe condemnation of "capitalist automatism" and "the moral philosophy of the dollar." The capitalists were in charge; they stole from the people; they were busily employed in converting the people into blindly obedient automatons.

Trotsky encountered few capitalists while he was in the United States. He met one capitalist shortly after his arrival in America. This was the Negro janitor of the apartment house in the Bronx who absconded with the tenants' rent money after Natalie had given him three months' rent in advance. This was upsetting, and Trotsky was in despair until he learned the janitor had acted very selectively: he robbed only those tenants who had already received a receipt from the landlord. Natalie had not yet been given a receipt. The thief wrapped up her money carefully and concealed it in a crate full of crockery which was being stored in the basement. Natalie eventually got her money back, and Trotsky wrote rather sententiously that the incident helped him to understand "the black problem" in the United States. He thought the janitor was "a delicate fellow indeed," adding that he always regarded him gratefully and sympathetically.

It was all very odd, of course—the thieving janitor converted overnight into a hero, "the moral philosophy of the dollar" held in abeyance for the time it took for the thief to slip away. Black America was represented by a man so astute that he was able to steal from the rich without harming the poor. Almost the janitor was a revolutionary.

There was no lack of incidents helping him to understand the problem of the United States. Nikolay Bukharin, a friend and close associate of Lenin, had recently been deported to the United States from Scandinavia as "an undesirable alien." He was a theorist and propagandist, a dedicated Bolshevik, a man who belonged to one of the lower ranks of the aristocracy, possessing considerable keenness of mind and gentleness of spirit. In argument he was rarely trenchant; he had no reputation at all as a public speaker; his harsh theories were at odds with his kindness and geniality. He was then twenty-nine years old. On the first or second day after Trotsky's arrival, Bukharin took him by the arm and said: "There is something you absolutely must see—the New York Public Library. It's open until late in the evening—think of that!" Without further ado, Trotsky was taken to inspect the library which was the only library known to the revolutionaries which did not close at five o'clock.

Madame Alexandra Kollontay was another Bolshevik who was living in New York. She was an apostle of "free love," and at forty-five she was still beautiful. Trotsky half despised Bukharin for his slow brain and he had no feeling at all for the seductive Kollontay, who was soon writing to Lenin in Switzerland, informing him of the arrival of Trotsky in New York, his vast popularity, and the revolutionary theories he advanced so casually and so easily. "What a swine he is!" Lenin wrote back, reflecting Kollontay's own distaste for the upstart who was capable of making a speech on any subject whatever and holding his audience spellbound.

Trotsky's capacity to hold men spellbound was observed in Brooklyn the day after he landed from the boat. On the evening of January 14, Ludwig Lore, a leading Left-wing Socialist, held a meeting in his house to discuss the coming revolution in America. He was a heavyset man with a thick black mustache and wavy black hair, who looked a little like a head waiter but possessed a keen and enquiring mind. About twenty people were invited. Among those who have been identified were Trotsky, Bukharin, Madame Kollontay, Grigory Chudnovsky and a revolutionary known as V. Volodarsky, whose real name was Goldstein. These represented the Russian exiles. Sen Katayama represented Japan and S. J. Rutgers represented Holland. Ludwig Lore, Louis Boudin, Louis Fraina, and John D. Williams of Boston represented the United States. The meeting had been arranged some days earlier, and the coming of Trotsky was totally unexpected. He was invited to talk about revolutionary trends in Europe and to discuss the strategy by which the Left-wing Socialists in America would rise to power.

Trotsky dominated the meeting, which lasted well into the night. Bukharin, following Lenin, wanted the Left-wing Socialists to break away entirely from the Socialist Party; he would have nothing to do with them and attacked them mercilessly. Trotsky presented a more moderate strategy. The Left-wing Socialists would remain within the Socialist Party but they would have a newspaper of their own. The question was put to the vote, Trotsky won, and it was agreed to form a committee to examine how they would proceed to bring a newspaper into existence. At the second meeting of the group about a week later it was decided to produce not a newspaper but a political magazine to appear every two months. There was no longer a feeling of urgency; the revolution in the United States was still far away.

Although these conferences in Ludwig Lore's sitting room seemed fairly innocuous because they represented political forces that had not yet fully emerged in the United States and would never take deep root there, they were not unimportant. The continuing quarrel between the Left-wing Socialists and the Right-wing Socialists was being fought out in Brooklyn. The Left-wing Socialists were opposed to gradualness; they thought calmly about immediate action, bloody uprisings, the total destruction of the capitalist system. The Right-wing Socialists spoke of "socialism in our time" and respect for the human person. Ironically it was the gentle charming Bukharin with his aristocratic good manners and his rather childish enthusiasm for every new idea who represented the extreme Left and Trotsky, the tough-minded spellbinder, who represented the moderates. In his book *The Roots of American Communism*, Theodore Draper wrote: "Twenty-four hours after Trotsky's arrival, he and Bukharin were able to carry on their European feud in terms of an American movement almost wholly foreign to both of them. In fact, their American dispute was virtually a continuation of their European disagreement."

Although their disagreements ran deep, they were able to work together. Bukharin was the editor of *Novy Mir* (New World), which had its editorial offices in a dingy building on St. Mark's Place in New York. Trotsky was invited to join the editorial board, which included Volodarsky and Chudnovsky. *Novy Mir* had a small circulation and appeared to be wholly ineffective, but its influence was out of all proportion to its circulation. Hard, abstract thinking about revolution, of a peculiarly Russian kind, was encouraged; and the dogmas of nineteenth-century revolutionary writers like Belinsky, who thought all the works of Shakespeare were not worth a pair of boots, and of Chernyshevsky, who wrote a famous novel about a revolutionary leader who was like a prophecy of Lenin, were discussed as though they were eternal truths. But these theoretical essays and the revolutionary ideas behind them percolated down into the American socialist movement at a time when the movement needed perhaps some stiffening. The trouble was that the Russian theories were so abstruse, so absolute, and so devoid of common humanity that they often confused rather than helped the American Socialists. Trotsky congratulated himself that "the ideas of *Novy Mir* found their way into the wider circles of American workers." So they did, but the workers found them too often indigestible.

Ludwig Lore fell under Trotsky's spell. He wanted his new friend to address all the small revolutionary organizations in New York and to write in as many newspapers as possible. He became Trotsky's manager and interpreter. There were many Socialist parties, most of their membership coming from East European immigrants who still spoke their native language, knew very little about America, and dreamed of a revolution in a country where they were still strangers. The Russians, Ukrainians, and Letts had their own Socialist parties. The Lithuanians had two parties, one in Manhattan, the other in Brooklyn. There was a small Bolshevik group and a group of Social Revolutionaries. The Socialist Propaganda League of America was the only group with any native English-speaking Americans in it, and it was pathetically small. Trotsky addressed all these groups, hurried from one meeting to another, worked, wrote articles and editorials for *Novy Mir* and the *Jewish Daily Forward*, and seemed to be everywhere at once. He negotiated with the German and Finnish communities and sometimes seemed to act as though the revolution in America had already begun and he was cheering them on the barricades.

Ludwig Lore and Sen Katayama came to the same conclusion: in Trotsky they saw the long-sought-for leader of the American revolution, the man who could rouse the masses into action and topple the capitalists from their thrones. They were quite serious about this. Sen Katayama spoke of the coming reorganization of the Left, which would then place itself under the direction of Trotsky, and Ludwig Lore thought that within a year Trotsky would have ignited the whole Socialist movement in America under his authority. Ludwig Lore was far from being a foolish man, yet he warmed himself with visions of Trotsky as the Socialist dictator of America.

Trotsky's popularity in New York is difficult to understand until we remember that most of his listeners were Jews and he came to them almost as a Messianic figure. He spoke of a world of equality, fraternity, and liberty acquired through the application of Marxist principles. The harsh and throbbing voice spoke of a world where there were no masters, no slaves, no poverty, no heavy labor. One blow delivered at the right time and the right place would destroy capitalist society to its foun-

dations; the millennium would come; the perfect society was almost within reach. He would show later that it
was perfectly possible to destroy a capitalist society by
stabbing at its heart, but the perfect society was still
infinitely far away.

Bukharin, who was normally kindly and amiable,
was deeply disturbed. The affairs of *Novy Mir* were not
taking place as he desired. Increasingly Trotsky assumed the position of editor in chief. His air of conscious superiority was immensely irritating and frus-
trating. He was more brilliant than anyone else, worked
harder than anyone else, saw more clearly than anyone
else, and all this was to his credit. But there were those
who found him to be gratuitously insulting, vain, opinionated, and liable to be carried away by his own
rhetoric. He was always the cat who walked alone, and
he walked surefootedly. Bukharin felt that Trotsky was
walking over him. He resented Trotsky's dominance,
and said so, only to be reminded that there was work to
be done and Trotsky was doing it. Many years later,
when Trotsky was fighting for his political life, Bukharin remembered the many veiled insults he had received and took his revenge.

Meanwhile, Bukharin continued to present an amiable appearance to the world and insisted that there
were no fundamental differences between them. Trotsky belonged to no political party and called himself an
independent Marxist. Bukharin hoped to win him over
to the Bolsheviks.

On February 17, 1917, there was held in New York a
conference which was intended to bring about a united
front among all the Socialist parties in America. It was
called "The International Conference of Socialist Organizations and Groups" but the high-sounding title was
a misnomer. The International Conference was attended by delegates from among the Russian, Ukrainian,
Lettish, and Lithuanian Socialist parties, and there
were only two or three Americans. Once more Trotsky
was the star speaker. Once more there was an attempt
to hammer out a program for a Socialist revolution in
America by a handful of East European immigrants

who spoke no English, had rarely traveled outside the New York area, and were totally ignorant about the real conditions in America. But if they knew little about America, they were deeply and intimately aware that Russia was in a state of convulsion, for there were signs during that long winter that Russia was at breaking point with widespread misery among the people and a general disintegration of the government. The revolution had already begun, but the leaders had not yet appeared. All the signs pointed to a violent revolution in Russia before the coming of the spring.

Trotsky triumphed easily at the conference. He urged the American Socialist parties to accept the manifesto he wrote at the conclusion of the Zimmerwald conference: the war must be brought to an end without annexations or reparations and the Socialists must take power—not the Socialists who voted for war but those who were resolutely opposed to the warmongers, to capitalists, to the privileged aristocracy, to the existing forms of government. On this basis "the embryo of the Third International" would come into being. He painted a future society which, having passed through the fires of revolution, would be clear and untainted as crystal. This future society was much closer than people believed. Bukharin violently disagreed, for he was neither as hopeful as Trotsky nor did he feel that the Third International would come about in the manner described by Trotsky.

America was drifting into the war. President Wilson had severed diplomatic relations with Germany, and America was already on a war footing. Trotsky believed, or pretended to believe, that America's entry into the war could not be long postponed because it would bring untold advantages to the capitalists. He was a man with a considerable conspiratorial bent and he saw the war as a gigantic capitalist conspiracy. The capitalists controlled the factories, which processed all the products made by men. It was not a new idea but he expressed it brilliantly in an article that was printed in Yiddish in the *Jewish Daily Forward* on January 30, 1917:

All the European countries involved in the war have been transformed into immense factories processing material for the front. So much bread, so much pork, so much human flesh. Only the pig does not surrender its individuality so readily, does not meekly accept military discipline and is not given to self-sacrifice. Leave all that to man. Assure a man that he is the elect of nature, that his highest ideals demand that he sacrifice himself for the capitalist God, which calls itself the Fatherland, and he is in your pocket. They dress him up and put him in a stinking trench, and the elect of nature, this king of the universe, is soon covered with lice and filth. And when his time comes, he is taken from this hole and put in a more permanent one, only now he is dead.

By waging fierce struggles, men in ancient times succeeded in establishing laws that protected them from arbitrary rule and capricious government. But these hard-won rights are anathema to the Factory that supplies human and other flesh to the war, the slaughter-house of freedoms. A democracy like France, for example, says to her soldiers: "You are being called upon to defend democracy and your glorious legacy. To accomplish this most effectively, we shall have to curtail your freedom, your individual rights, your democracy." The first step in this direction comes with the institution of censorship. Officially, the purpose of censorship is to prevent the enemy from gaining easy access to useful information. In fact, from the very beginning censorship has been a weapon in the hands of the ruling class to destroy dissent.

Trotsky goes on to describe his own warfare against the French censors, who were at least as bad and incompetent as the censors he confronted when he was a correspondent in the Balkan wars. Censorship was a game played by blind men, and he offered lovingly remembered examples of their blindness. Since he had to visit the censors' office every day in Paris, this was a subject on which he could speak with authority, but it was not, as he said, the first step in the direction of suppressing human rights, since at a time of war all rights except those reserved by the high command and the government are simultaneously suppressed. Trotsky, knowing most about censorship, gave it prime importance. It was a rhetorical game, and he played successfully all the rhetorical games he knew.

In Paris there had been almost no speechmaking; in Spain there was none at all; in New York he was sometimes making four or five speeches a day. He found his voice. The Social Democrats in Brooklyn and Manhattan, mostly Jewish refugees from Russia and Lithuania, were providing him with a weapon of inestimable importance simply by listening to his speeches. He played on them, as in a few months he would play on the bewildered and half-starving people of St. Petersburg.

Among many of his listeners there was a widely held belief that Trotsky was pro-German. The belief was well founded. It was not that he wanted a German victory so much as that he wanted a state of affairs that would give birth to revolution, and he believed that a German victory would ensure a revolution. How he came to this conclusion is unclear. He appeared to believe that the moment the war ended the workers would turn on the factory owners and the soldiers would turn on their officers. This was no doubt a satisfactory belief, but there was not a shred of evidence for it.

Dr. Ziv, whom he had known long ago when they were both young revolutionaries in Nikolayev, happened to be in New York. He attended one of Trotsky's speeches delivered at Cooper Union, and was surprised by the small attendance and the ease with which he found a seat in the front row. Such things happened rarely. Usually, according to Dr. Ziv, four or five other speakers came on the podium, uttered their speeches and went quietly, and then Trotsky came forward to a storm of applause.

In America the popularity of a speaker is measured by the length of time he is prevented from beginning his speech. His popularity is expressed by more or less frenzied applause, whistles, thumping of the feet and other noisy and effective means. This is called "cheering."
No one could tell how long the cheering would have

lasted if Trotsky, who had not yet acquired a taste for American ways, had not brought it to an end very quickly by an abrupt gesture of impatience and when he saw that his signs of impatience were ignored, he began his speech at the height of the applause. Suddenly the audience grew quiet.

It is difficult for me to give an opinion about the speech of a man whom I regard as an opponent. But I have to say that Trotsky's speech made a very strong impression on me from the artistic point of view. While listening to him I experienced a real and absolute ecstatic pleasure even though I categorically rejected all the ideas on which he based his speech. He was the model of the perfect orator.

According to Dr. Ziv, who had excellent reasons for studying the speaker very closely and listened to many of his speeches, Trotsky was not a natural orator. On the contrary, every word had been carefully prepared; the exact weight to be given to his words had been calculated in advance; he gave the impression of a man who would avoid demagoguery at all costs, though he remained a cultivated demagogue. He addressed himself to the cultured persons in the audience. At some point in the speech he would describe the horrors of war, and he did this so dramatically that he had the audience on the edge of their seats.

He told them that every evening in Paris the lights went out and the city was plunged into darkness, and this was not because the Parisians feared the coming of the Zeppelins but because France was in a state of abject economic decline. Coal supplies were running out, to such an extent that you would see women with sacks on their backs gathering the small pieces of coal fallen in the streets, and then they would go home to their freezing children and cook a little food for them. While the French people starved, the corrupt and decadent government permitted every kind of atrocity against the Germans, and they did this with the sanction and agreement of their allies. Black colonial soldiers were sent into battle and they would return with sacks filled with the ears of German soldiers. This story particularly impressed the audience, which groaned with horror. Dr. Ziv observed that Trotsky did not attack the politicians who made the war possible. Instead, he attacked the socialists who entered the bourgeois governments of national defense, men like Emile Vandervelde, Albert Thomas, and Jules Guesde, who were characterized as traitors. And having inveighed against the traitors and described the horrors of war, he would point to the peaceful and beautiful world which would come into existence once the socialists were in power everywhere. From the horrors of war he ascended to the realm of abstractions, and he did this so easily that Dr. Ziv wondered how any logical person could accept his arguments, which were always obscure but never more obscure than when he called upon the allies to lay down their arms and surrender to Germany, the most efficient of nations, and therefore the one most likely after the inevitable revolutionary war to embrace the logic and efficiency of socialism.

About a month after Trotsky's arrival there was a meeting between him and Dr. Ziv, who asked about what had happened to all the others who had met in Shvigovsky's nursery garden and been arrested. "And what about Parvus?" Dr. Ziv asked. "Making his twelfth million," Trotsky replied, shrugging his shoulders. They played chess. Dr. Ziv won the first game, Trotsky demanded a second and won, and that was the end of their chess. Dr. Ziv concluded that Trotsky hated losing so much that he would not dare to play a third game. Outwardly they were on good terms, and whenever they met Trotsky would put his arms round his friend's shoulders and say to the small group that followed him around: "This is my old friend, Grigory Ziv, who only needs to spend a couple of months in France to become a good socialist."

Trotsky's visit to New York was an unalloyed triumph. He accomplished exactly what he wanted, he acquired a following, he improved his oratory, he raised audiences to a fever-pitch of excitement, he earned some money. Above all, he saw in himself the makings of a revolutionary leader. He was determined to reach Russia as quickly as possible. When he applied to the Russian consulate-general, he asked to be repatriated as "a passenger of note," not as one of a herd of political refugees. The consul-general, who knew a great deal about Trotsky's inflammatory speeches, answered that he would be treated according to the rules, and that "eggs do not teach the hen." Trotsky snapped back: "Mr. Consul, evidently you have not yet grasped the fact that the time has come for the eggs to teach the hen."

This exchange, and others, did nothing to endear Trotsky to the consular authorities, who telegraphed the Ministry of Foreign Affairs in St. Petersburg to warn them that Trotsky was on his way. The Russian consul informed the British consul in New York, who in turn informed the Foreign Office in London. Since Trotsky was sailing on the Norwegian ship *Christianiafjord* which would put in at Halifax and one of the English ports, it was necessary for him to have a transit visa. He was given a questionnaire to fill up at the British Consulate General and was told that everything was in order. All this took a good deal of time; there was much running to and fro; and in the midst of it all his younger son, who had just recovered from a bout of diphtheria, decided to wander out into the street and solve a problem that had been plaguing him for some time. He lived on 164th Street and he wanted to discover whether there was a 1st Street. He therefore wandered south until some friendly policemen found him and took him to the station house, where he remembered his father's telephone number. When he was found, he was calmly playing checkers with a policeman.

On March 26, 1917, a farewell party was given for Trotsky at the Harlem River Casino at 127th Street and Second Avenue. About eight hundred guests, mostly Russian and German socialists, attended. His speech, or rather speeches—for he spoke first in Russian and then repeated exactly what he had said previously in German—were all the more fiery because he was aware of the drama of the occasion. He analyzed the causes of the war, then the course of the war, the February Revolution in Russia, and the Provisional

Government of Prince Lvov, which took power after the abdication of the Tsar. He denounced Prince Lvov and all his ministers, and prophesied their downfall. Emma Goldman, the American anarchist leader, knew both Russian and German and endured the whole speech twice, each time marveling at his lucidity and brilliance, at the same time disagreeing with everything he said. It was not an uncommon attitude. Trotsky was an artist, a performer, an orator in the style of Robespierre, who was never more convincing than when he uttered a palpable untruth or prophesied something that could not happen and therefore did not happen. Among those who listened to Trotsky's speeches was a certain Inspector Tunney of the New York police department. The inspector was also a part-time agent of the military intelligence department of the United States Army.

The police department had excellent reasons for being at the Harlem River Casino. They were seriously considering whether to arrest him. His speeches were becoming increasingly subversive and inflammatory. To his own followers he urged defiance of the law, the destruction of the existing social system, and the overthrow of the government. Almost his last words in New York were an order to his followers "to keep on organizing until you are able to overthrow the damned rotten capitalistic government of this country."

Either on this day or a few days earlier Trotsky had his last meeting with Frank Harris, novelist, editor, and *bon vivant*. Trotsky said his ship would be touching at Halifax, Nova Scotia.

"Good God!" Harris replied. "You surely won't trust yourself to an English port?"

"Why not?" Trotsky asked. "The English are our allies!"

The English, however, did not regard themselves as Trotsky's allies.

Harris again warned him of the danger of traveling to an English port. Trotsky shrugged his shoulders.

"However much they dislike me personally," he said, "they can do nothing!"

Trotsky's self-assurance, his belief that he could not

possibly be arrested by the English, was laughable. At
the British Consulate General in New York they had
told him that his papers were in good order. Why
should he disbelieve them?

At the Harlem River Casino a small sum of money
amounting to $128 was raised to help him pay the
expenses of his journey. Characteristically he divided
it up among the seven other political refugees who
were making their way to Russia. With just enough
money to reach Russia, he took his family on board the
Christianiafjord light-heartedly, carrying the bunch of
flowers presented to him at the dockside. His wife, and
his two sons, aged nine and eleven, were excited by the
prospect of sailing to Russia. The ship sailed on March
27. A week later, on April 3, it dropped anchor in
Halifax. British naval authorities and the local police
came on board to examine the passengers' documents.
American, Dutch, and Norwegian passengers were allowed to proceed; the Russian passengers with two
exceptions were ordered off the ship. Trotsky, after a
grueling cross-examination, refused to leave of his own
free will and had to be carried bodily down the gangplank. Orders to arrest him had come from the British
Foreign Office and were transmitted by the Admiralty
radio.

Trotsky protested vehemently, saying that he had
been arrested illegally, a statement that was illogical,
since they had a perfect right to arrest anyone they
regarded as dangerous to the Allied cause, whether or
not he had been given a transit visa. Trotsky stood by
the law: he was a Russian citizen, he had committed no
crime, he possessed valid documents. Colonel Morris,
who interrogated him, answered: "You are dangerous
to the present Russian government. You are dangerous
to the Allies in general."

He was removed to a prison camp in Amherst, Nova
Scotia, while Natalie and the boys were held in the
house of a police agent and later in a hotel. Trotsky was
treated as though he was a prisoner of war with only
those privileges permitted to prisoners of war, that is to
say, he had no privileges. In Spain he was allowed to
bombard government officials with letters and tele-

grams; in Canada he was not permitted to write to anyone, and when his children went out into the street they were closely followed to see that they never went near the post office or a postbox. He was in serious danger of spending the rest of the war in the camp at Amherst in the company of eight hundred German prisoners of war, the majority of them being German sailors. The camp was in fact an old, dilapidated iron foundry with three tiers of bunks arranged around the walls. It was heavily guarded, unpleasantly crowded, and completely cheerless. There was only one satisfaction: he spoke German and could therefore converse with the German sailors and teach them the doctrines of revolution.

One interesting document of this time survives: the two-page form, headed "Prisoners of War," in which Trotsky describes his own vital statistics, an officer briefly describes the circumstances of his capture, and his left and right thumbprints are recorded for posterity. Thus we learn that Trotsky, Leon Bronstein, was captured on April 3, 1917, that he was five feet eight-and-a-half inches tall, weighed 170 pounds, and had black hair and black eyes. To the question "State whether with the Colours or in the Reserve," he answered, "Political exile, have not escaped military service." He was born in Gromokley in the province of Kherson in Russia. To the question "Home address," he answered, "Wife, taken off Halifax, N.S., from same ship." He signed the document, "Russian Citizen, Leon Trotsky."

In this document his eyes are described as being black. These words were written by Colonel Morris, who examined him several times. Curiously, many people wrote about his black eyes. They were in fact bright blue.

While in the prison camp Trotsky learned from American newspapers that Lenin had returned to St. Petersburg and was addressing meetings of workers. He was also attacking the Provisional Government. The German prisoners of war were soon being offered lectures on the significance of the February Revolution in Russia and the importance of Lenin. Trotsky also gave lectures on the significance of the Zimmerwald Manifesto which he wrote. Some of the prisoners were impressed by the antimilitarist arguments of the manifesto.

Trotsky's fate depended entirely on the actions of officials of the Russian and British Foreign Offices. They were busy men, and they could be pardoned if they overlooked the files relating to Trotsky. The foreign minister of Russia was Paul Miliukov, and he appears to have thought that nothing would be gained by urging the British to release Trotsky, who was rumored to have received subsidies from the German government. It was known that he had made pro-German speeches in New York. The obvious inference was that he was in German pay. News of his arrest had reached St. Petersburg, and on April 16, Lenin or one of his close assistants wrote in *Pravda*: "Can one even for a moment believe the trustworthiness of the statement that Trotsky, the chairman of the Soviet of Workers' Delegates in St. Petersburg in 1905—a revolutionary who has sacrificed many years to a disinterested service to revolution—that this man has anything to do with a scheme subsidized by the Germans? This is a patent, unheard-of, and malicious slander of a revolutionary." Lenin, too, was being attacked for receiving German money. Miliukov did nothing for several days. He was very busy, the plight of Trotsky was not of the utmost importance, the Russians were still at war with Germany, and it was quite obvious that Trotsky would be a thorn in the side of the Provisional Government. It was Alexander Kerensky, the minister of justice, who said it was intolerable that Trotsky should be interned, argued for his immediate liberation, and insisted that Miliukov request the Foreign Office in London to free this redoubtable revolutionary.

On April 29, twenty-six days after his arrest, Trotsky was told in Amherst that he was a free man. A Danish freighter was in the harbor, ready to take him to Sweden. In this way, with a burning hatred of the English, Trotsky set out for Russia in an agony of impatience. Eighteen days later he arrived in St. Petersburg, hoping against hope that he had not arrived too late to take charge of the revolution.

TRIUMPH AND TRAGEDY

PART FIVE

You want to take the road of destruction. Be careful. Out of this chaos, like a phoenix out of the ashes, there will come a dictator . . . You are recommending childish prescriptions—arrest, kill, destroy! What are you—socialists or the police of the old regime?

THE CRASH THROUGH THE DOOR

11

On March 15, 1917, Vladimir Ilyich Ulyanov, better known as Lenin, spent the morning working quietly in the library set up in a deconsecrated Dominican Church in a tree-lined corner of Zurich. When he had finished his morning's work, he arranged his books neatly on the table and walked home to the single room on the Spiegelgasse he shared with his wife, Nadezhda Krupskaya. The Spiegelgasse was one of those narrow, medieval streets, once inhabited by mirror makers, now full of cheap lodging houses. At the top of the street there was a sausage factory that spread a foul stench over the surrounding area. As he walked up the steep, cobblestoned street, his iron-studded mountain boots struck sparks off the cobble-stones.

The room at No. 14 Spiegelgasse was dark and miserable, with only a few sticks of furniture, and the windows were tightly shut to keep out the fumes of the sausage factory. Krupskaya had suffered from bronchial pneumonia during the winter; she was still ill, and moved slowly; she was making a little money from proofreading, which gave her headaches. The family was very poor, and Lenin had been wondering for some time whether he would have to take a full-time job. They shared a light lunch, Lenin did the washing up, and he was struggling into his old, worn overcoat, about to return to the library, when there came a violent knocking on the door.

A moment later a young Polish revolutionary, Mieczyslav Bronski, burst into the room, shouting: "There's a revolution in Russia! Haven't you heard?"

Lenin was dumbfounded: he had not heard it, had not expected it. He turned to Krupskaya with an expression that implied total disbelief. Where had Bronski learned it? From the newspapers. There was nothing to be done except to hurry down to the newspaper stand on Bellevue Platz, which looks over the Lake of Zurich. Here the newspapers were exhibited free. Headlines announced the Russian Revolution, but Lenin still could not believe it. "Probably the Germans are lying," he grumbled. They were not lying. The Revolution had broken out in earnest. The small group of excited Russian political exiles hovering over the newspaper stand were shivering in the cold wind coming from the lake.

From this moment there began Lenin's determination to return to Russia at all costs and to wage his own war against the revolutionaries. But how to return? He thought of being smuggled across France to England, and then taking ship to St. Petersburg. There were many ruses, many plans, many negotiations. In twenty-five days, a remarkably short space of time, the daring plan of bringing Lenin to Russia by way of a sealed train through Germany and Sweden was worked out in all its details. The instigator of the plan was the sinister Dr. Alexander Helphand, whom Lenin had once known well and now cordially disliked. The first eight numbers of Lenin's *Iskra* were printed on Helphand's private printing press hidden away in his house in Schwabing in the outskirts of Munich. The printing press was provided with a self-destruct mechanism in the event of a police raid. Lenin's admiration for Helphand had cooled considerably; he distrusted a man who combined a passionate desire for wealth and an equally passionate desire to be a revolutionary.

Nevertheless it was Helphand who through his connections with the German General Staff and the German Social Democratic Party was able to set in motion the plan to bring Lenin through Germany in a sealed train. The Kaiser himself had taken part in the discussions; General Ludendorff gave it his approval; the German Foreign Office was deeply implicated. Lenin knew about these negotiations in a general way, but not in detail. "I will negotiate with the devil, if necessary," he said, "so long as I can get back to Russia."

185
THE
CRASH
THROUGH
THE
DOOR

On April 8, 1917, some thirty Russian political exiles with their wives and two children set out on a sealed train through Germany. Among them were Lenin, Zinoviev, Radek, and Sokolnikov, who all played major roles in the Revolution. Trotsky, writing his *History of the Russian Revolution*, speaks of a "sealed train," putting the words in quotation marks, as though he did not regard it as sufficiently sealed. In fact the train consisted of a single engine and a single carriage with second- and third-class compartments, and it was effectively sealed by the simple method of locking all the doors of the compartments occupied by the Russians and only the door opposite the compartment occupied by two German officers remained unlocked. The carriage was given extraterritorial rights: no German might enter it, no Russian was permitted to set foot on German soil. The two German officers on the train were present simply as observers and representatives of the government; they told the engine driver where to go and reported to Berlin whenever they arrived at a railroad station.

It was an uneventful journey, inordinately slow and for Lenin exquisitely boring, for he wanted nothing so much as to reach Petersburg in the shortest possible time. The Revolution had already taken place: his problem now was to subvert it, to make it change its direction and its character. Unfolding before him was something he had never previously dared to hope for: the transformation of the Provisional Government of Russia into "the dictatorship of the proletariat" represented by himself and his chosen ministers.

Although Lenin insisted that everyone on the train

must pay the proper fare, and although the exiles had almost no communication with the Germans, and although they were traveling "extraterritorially," there was not the least doubt that they were traveling through enemy country at the enemy's invitation and concurrence. They were therefore liable to be arrested for treason when they reached Russian soil. The German government had offered large sums of money to the Bolshevik Party in order to foster the Revolution, and this too was accepted either during a mysterious twenty-hour wait in Berlin or later in Sweden. To accept money from an enemy was treasonable; to foster revolution in wartime was also treasonable. The closer they came to Russia the more apprehensive Lenin became about the possibility of being arrested. It was perfectly possible that he would be arrested by the military after crossing the frontier, that he would be tried by a drumhead court-martial and summarily executed.

But when he crossed the frontier from Sweden into Finland, which was then a part of Russia, the frontier guards waved him into the country over the protests of some British officers who were assisting the guards. The British were watching out for Lenin; they knew he was on the sealed train; they followed his movements through Sweden and were well aware of the danger he represented. Yet they could do nothing to prevent him entering Russia. He had thought of himself as a revolutionary who would not live to see the revolution, as an old man living out his last days in Switzerland in terrible isolation and poverty, and this was true, but there was something else that was true. By the purest accident he had arrived in Russia just at the time when people where realizing that the Revolution was lacking in direction and purpose. The people were looking for a savior, for someone who had the power and authority to lead them out of the war. He was already a legend, and he was accordingly treated as legendary figures are treated—with curious ceremonies, fanfare, banners, searchlights.

When Lenin stepped off the train at the Finland Station, which was decorated with red banners, there

187

THE
CRASH
THROUGH
THE
DOOR

was no court-martial, no march to the execution ground. Instead he was greeted with the singing of *The Marseillaise* and was then led by a young officer to inspect an honor guard of Baltic sailors standing rigidly at attention. Then he was taken to the reception room formerly reserved for the Tsar, where a delegation from the Petrograd Soviet led by Nikolay Chkheidze welcomed him in the name of the Soviet. Chkheidze, who was terrified by Lenin, said bravely that he hoped Lenin would help to calm the stormy waters of political life in the capital and thus help to close the ranks of the entire democracy. Lenin detested Chkheidze, who was a Menshevik—he hated Mensheviks more than he hated capitalists—and he ostentatiously paid not the slightest attention to the welcoming speeches. Instead he looked gravely at the ceiling or toyed with the immense bouquet of red flowers given to him when he stepped off the train. When the welcoming speeches were over, he announced in his harsh, gravelly voice that the predatory imperialist war was the beginning of a civil war all over Europe and that the Russian Revolution of February 1917 would be followed by a greater revolution that would not stop until it had brought about the worldwide socialist revolution. Capitalism was about to fall; the bourgeois governments were about to fall; the war was about to end, for the people would soon turn their weapons against their capitalist enemies. It would all happen very soon, tomorrow or the next day, and nothing could prevent it. He spoke to them as a prophet. He was still speaking when a crowd of workmen and soldiers burst through the glass door of the imperial reception room, lifted Lenin on their shoulders, and carried him out into the square outside the Finland Station. Lenin was unaccustomed to being carried on people's shoulders. He kept saying: "Be careful, comrades!" He made another speech in the square and still another when he was lifted onto the turret of an armored car. Searchlights were criss-crossing the square. Two or three thousand people had gathered; red banners with gold letters were waving in the wind; there was deep snow on the ground, and a biting wind. Slowly, between speeches, a procession of armored cars made its way in the direction of the Kshesinskaya Palace, which had been the home of the *prima ballerina assoluta* Kshesinskaya before the Bolsheviks confiscated it.

From the moment when Lenin heard about the outbreak of the Russian Revolution to the moment when he returned to Petersburg in triumph there had passed a month and a day.

Trotsky's arrival in Petrograd, formerly St. Petersburg, was more modest. Although he wrote in his autobiography that he received a tremendous welcome and was greeted with speeches by Uritzky and Fyodorov, and was lifted triumphantly on men's shoulders, it is abundantly clear that he was not being received with the same fanfare as Lenin. In spite of his former fame as the leader of the 1905 Soviet, he was comparatively little known, commanded no party, had few followers, and had no propaganda organization working for him. He had come at a period when the excitement was dying down. The snow had melted, the ice had thawed, the long winter was over, and Petrograd was licking its wounds.

Following the February Revolution, Russia was being ruled by a Provisional Government and also by the Soviet of Workers' and Peasants' Deputies which had elected an Executive Committee (the "Ex-Com"). In effect there were two governments locked in continual conflict, and no one had worked out any modus operandi by which these governments could operate successfully. There was even a third government dominated by General Polovtsoff, commanding the military forces in Petrograd, and his staff. General Polovtsoff was theoretically subservient to the minister of war but in fact often issued orders under his own authority, and his growing power threatened both the Soviet and the Provisional Government. He commanded a large and capable intelligence staff which infiltrated all the existing political parties and he kept a sharp eye on Lenin and Trotsky.

189

THE
CRASH
THROUGH
THE
DOOR

On the day following his arrival in Petrograd, Trotsky attended a meeting of the Ex-Com. Nikolay Sukhanov, the great historian of the Russian Revolution, a man of courage and intelligence who somehow succeeded in being present at all the dramatic moments of that dramatic year, was on the platform when Trotsky entered the room, to be greeted rather drily by Chkheidze, the president of the Soviet, and warmly by many of the deputies. From the floor came a demand that he should address the Soviet, and he did so, at first nervously, because he had had little time to study the situation, and then, gaining strength from the warmth of his listeners, he embarked with all the appropriate oratorical flourishes on the coming world revolution which would come about as a result of the revolution in Petrograd; and though not a Bolshevik, he spoke in the authentic Bolshevik tone. Sukhanov remembered that his arms flailed wildly and his cuff kept continually shooting out of his sleeve so that it was in danger of flying across the room, and he would pull it back. Trotsky also attacked the Soviet for having come to a working agreement with the Provisional Government—an agreement that was never fulfilled—but he attacked cautiously, uncertain whether he had caught the mood of the audience and visibly confused by some hecklers. "From the onset he did not expect any sympathy," Sukhanov wrote. He was in a defiant mood; it paid off; the Bolsheviks observed that he was speaking as if he were one of their own. But a few days later, on May 10, during a conference with Lenin he refused to take a seat on the editorial board of *Pravda*, saying that he did not regard himself as a Bolshevik and it was necessary for them to debolshevize themselves, by which he meant that it was necessary for them to moderate their harsh policies if they were to achieve their goals. He already knew that Lenin's harshness was an end in itself.

At the beginning of June there was held the first All-Russian Congress of Soviets. 822 delegates with voting rights attended; the Bolsheviks numbered 105 and were therefore outnumbered by eight to one. The largest number of delegates were Social Revolutionaries, and then came the Mensheviks. Trotsky was among the ten delegates of a splinter party that called itself the "United Social Democrats."

During a speech by Tsereteli, the brilliant Georgian who had been appointed minister of posts and telegraph, Lenin, in two words, announced his program. Tsereteli had just said: "At the present moment there is no political party that would say: 'Give the power into our hands, go away, we will take your place.' There is no such party in Russia." Lenin shouted from his seat: "There is!" Then he mounted the rostrum and declared: "The citizen minister of posts and telegraphs has just stated there is no political party prepared to take the entire power upon itself. I say there is! No party can refuse this! We are prepared at any moment to take over the entire power."

These words were a direct threat to the state power and also to the power of the Soviet, and when Lenin went on to proclaim that it was the duty of the Soviet to wrest power from the Provisional Government, it was not difficult to follow his reasoning: the Soviet destroys the Provisional Government, the Bolsheviks then destroy the Soviet in the midst of the confusion.

Kerensky in measured words warned his audience that the road that Lenin recommended could only end in the loss of the Russian people's hard-won liberties and the dismemberment of the country.

"You want to take the road of destruction," he said. "Be careful! Out of this chaos, like a phoenix out of the ashes, there will come a dictator—and it will not be me! . . . You are recommending childish prescriptions—arrest, kill, destroy! What are you—socialists or the police of the old regime?"

It was certain the Bolsheviks were planning an insurrection. They were still a minority party, with only 105 voting delegates at the Congress out of a total of 822 delegates. They had no mandate from the people. If they succeeded, it would be by force and terror, by a sudden blow at the heart of the government, by a series of conspiratorial acts that would take the city by surprise.

191
THE
CRASH
THROUGH
THE
DOOR

Trotsky was in agreement with the Bolsheviks on the necessity of insurrection. He formed himself into a one-man revolutionary party and continually delivered speeches to groups of workers and soldiers in Petrograd. From early morning to late at night he was racing through the city, well dressed, almost dapper, wearing a goatee that curled up a little, his blue eyes lit with revolutionary fire and his thick curly black hair waving in the wind. In the Cirque Moderne on the other side of the Neva he addressed crowds of many thousands, but in his speeches he did not call for insurrection. The cry was: "All power to the Soviet." He played on the people like a musician playing on an instrument, and sometimes he fell into a trance state when it seemed to him that he and the people were one, that there was no barrier between them, and he had only to command and they would do what he commanded. He wrote:

I usually spoke in the evening at the Cirque Moderne, sometimes quite late at night. My audience was composed of workers, soldiers, hard-working mothers, street urchins, the oppressed underdogs of the capital. Every square inch was filled, every human body compressed to its limit. Young boys sat on their father's shoulders; infants were at their mothers' breasts. No one smoked. The balconies threatened to fall under the excessive weight of human bodies. I made my way to the platform through a narrow human trench, sometimes I was borne overhead. The air, intense with breathing and waiting, fairly exploded with shouts and the passionate yells of the Cirque Moderne. Above and around me was a press of elbows, chests and heads. I spoke from out of a warm cavern of human bodies; whenever I stretched out my hands I would touch someone, and a grateful movement in response would give me to understand that I was not to worry about it, not to break off my speech, but keep going. No speaker, no matter how exhausted, could resist the electric tension of that impassioned human throng . . .

Such was the Cirque Moderne. It had its own contours,

fiery, tender and frenzied. The infants were peacefully sucking the breasts from which approving or threatening shouts were coming. The whole crowd was like that, like infants clinging with their dry lips to the nipples of the revolution. But this infant matured quickly.

Trotsky did not explain how breasts could approve and threaten, or why the babies' lips were dry when they sucked at the nipples of the revolution. But there was no doubt that in his own mind he was the breast and the milk, the source of revolutionary nourishment. He was riding higher than anyone in Petrograd. His friend Anatoly Lunacharsky, who was also racing around the city making speeches, believed that "under the influence of his tremendous activity and blinding success certain people close to Trotsky were even inclined to see him as the real leader of the Russian revolution," and Moses Uritzky, another prominent revolutionary later to be killed by an assassin, said: "Now that the great revolution has come one feels that however intelligent Lenin may be, he begins to fade beside the genius of Trotsky."

Lenin made speeches only on important occasions. Trotsky made speeches at all times and on all occasions, whenever he felt there was a need for them.

These speeches were like the steady flame that keeps the kettle simmering. They contributed in a measurable degree to the revolutionary excitement of the time, but they did not appreciably help people to decide between the various parties, nor did they help people to decide on the future course of the revolution. Trotsky hinted at an uprising; he did not declare openly for an uprising. He excited them, exasperated them, fanned their enthusiasm for change, upbraided them for not having made any changes, and vividly described what would happen once the Soviet had acquired full power, which it was bound to do since the Provisional Government was obviously in a state of decay. His speeches acted like drugs, leaving them dazed and almost delirious.

But the Provisional Government was not yet in decay, it commanded the support of the army, the police, the bureaucracy, most of the middle class, and many of the workers who saw no advantage in a direct confrontation between the Soviet and the Provisional Government. The Bolsheviks were in a minority. The Social Revolutionaries, about to split into a left and right wing, had a vast following among the workers and peasants, the liberal Cadets or Constitutional Democrats represented the professional classes, and the Mensheviks were the communists "with human faces," and they too had a large following among the workers. But only the Bolsheviks under the direction of Lenin had developed a precise, brutal, and absolutely uncompromising plan of action that did not depend upon events but existed as it were beyond and in spite of events. It was fueled by a kind of Messianic belief that a socialist government in Russia would lead inevitably to socialist governments all over the world. Lenin's hope was that the Soviet and the Provisional Government would suffer a paralyzing shock, and the Bolsheviks would then step in to assume absolute power, whereupon he would proclaim immediate peace with Germany and the beginning of the world revolution. Lenin therefore could look upon the day to day happenings in Petrograd with the detachment of a man looking at them from afar. For him the events in Petrograd were only important in as far as a seizure of power would be the prelude to world revolution. The Bolsheviks were playing for much higher stakes than any other party.

The largest hope of the Bolsheviks was that the Provisional Government would deliver a paralyzing blow upon itself, like a scorpion stinging itself to death. The government might simply fall, leaving a vacuum. At all costs it was necessary to test the government, to calculate its strengths and weaknesses, to maintain the pressure by continual street demonstrations. To the surprise and alarm of the Bolsheviks the government was strong enough to order a massive offensive against the Germans and Austrians. Just before the offensive, the Soviet, pitting itself against the government, ordered a show of strength of its own. Huge processions of workers with banners wound through the streets of

193
THE
CRASH
THROUGH
THE
DOOR

Petrograd and out into Mars Field, where the chief delegates to the All-Russian Congress stood on the reviewing stand. They observed that most of the banners bore the Bolshevik slogans: *Down with the ten capitalist ministers! All power to the Soviets! Bread, Peace and Freedom!* This came as a shock, for it showed that the Bolsheviks were rapidly increasing in power and influence and were far better organized than most of the delegates had suspected. The Bolshevik *coup de théâtre* amounted to a victory over the Soviet, a visible claim to leadership of the Revolution, but it was not a claim that the delegates were willing to concede.

Although Bolshevik and Social Revolutionary agitators had been actively encouraging rebellion and desertion in the Russian army, the army was also far better organized than the delegates had suspected. What came to be known as the Kerensky offensive opened on June 29, 1917, under cover of a barrage from thirteen hundred guns, with thirty-one Russian divisions advancing along a wide front. The Russian generalship was superb; the Germans and Austrians retreated. Kerensky was able to report to the Provisional Government from the front: "Today is the great triumph of the revolution. The Russian revolutionary army has assumed the offensive." So it had, and for two weeks the Russians advanced, only to be halted by a massive German counteroffensive on July 16. Then the Russian armies reeled back, and thereafter there was no effective Russian army in the field. There was nothing except its own inertia to prevent the German army from advancing on Petrograd and Moscow. There was also, in the eyes of the Bolsheviks, nothing to prevent a seizure of power by bringing the workers out on the streets and advancing on the government buildings.

On July 17 the Bolsheviks attempted a *coup* which was more serious than a *coup de théâtre* and not quite a *coup d'état*. They brought the workers out on the streets together with about six thousand sailors from the naval base at Kronstadt, a Bolshevik enclave. The sailors took possession of the Peter and Paul Fortress, where the Russian Tsars were buried close to the

195

THE
CRASH
THROUGH
THE
DOOR

dungeons where political prisoners were imprisoned. The sailors thronged the street outside the small Kshe-sinskaya Palace. Here, from a balcony overlooking the street, Lenin addressed them with a curiously perfunctory speech, demanding that they should demonstrate "firmness, steadfastness and vigilance." He was suffering from a heavy cold, could not think clearly, and knew that at this particular moment he was incapable of leading an insurrection. But the demonstrators were still thronging the streets, an angry crowd descended on the Tauride Palace, where the Central Executive Committee of the Soviet had its offices, and Victor Chernov, the minister of agriculture in the Provisional Government, was seized by some people who recognized him and threw him into an automobile obviously with sinister intentions. People were shouting confusedly. Chernov's followers were going to use machine guns to rescue him, and it is likely that there would be a bloody battle in front of the palace. Trotsky rushed out of the palace, thrust his way through the crowd, leaped on the front of the automobile, made a quick gesture demanding silence, and gave a short ringing speech on proper behavior during a time of revolution, ending with the words: "Those in favor of violence to Chernov raise their hands!" The conjuring trick was performed so expertly that no one dared to raise a hand, and Trotsky turned politely to the minister, saying: "Citizen Chernov, you are free!" Then with Chernov at his side he walked back to the palace.

There were other brave and equally risky conjuring tricks performed that day. Fyodor Dan, a brilliant Menshevik leader, confronted the 176th Infantry Regiment marching in full battle order on the Tauride Palace. He harangued them without knowing whether they had come to arrest the Central Executive Committee or to join the Soviet. As a member of the Soviet, he ordered them to protect the palace by mounting guard over it, so that the demonstrators, now armed, would be kept at bay. This they did, somewhat to their own surprise. The demonstrators were still roaring through the streets, there were bloody skirmishes, street battles, arguments that spilled over into murders and ugly fistfights, but on the morning of the second day the streets were quiet again and the Kronstadt sailors returned to their island fortress, abandoning the Peter and Paul Fortress to the government. No leader had emerged with the power to challenge the government; no revolutionary party had the trust of the workers; on all sides there had been displays of futility and impotence. Lenin fled the scene, hiding first in a haystack in the small village of Razliv and then making his way to Finland. Just before going into hiding Lenin had met Trotsky and said: "Now they will shoot us down one by one! This is the right time for them!" The danger to Lenin and Trotsky was all the greater because the government had taken possession of some documents that showed more or less conclusively that they had received large sums of money from the German government. Trotsky was in character when he refused to go into hiding. He was placed on trial not by the government but by the Mensheviks and Social Revolutionaries in the Soviet. He was found guilty and thrown into the Kresty Prison, which he regarded less as a prison than as a place where he could conduct his affairs in reasonable comfort. A deputation of Kronstadt sailors visited him in his cell to seek his advice about whether they should defend the Winter Palace, the seat of the government, or take it by assault. He told them to wait.

August was a time for the healing of wounds, for taking stock, for preparing for the next leap into the unknown. It was a time when energy was wasted on unreal problems, when the Soviet and the Provisional Government danced around each other, provoked each other, and showed conspicuously that they were both irrelevant and incapable of governing in a way that would have been approved by a majority of the people. Kerensky made the mistake of appointing General Lavr Kornilov to be commander in chief of the Russian Army. Kornilov, a Siberian Cossack with Kalmuck features, made the mistake of believing that he was the destined "man on the white horse," the savior of Russia. He proposed to arrest Kerensky and the Provisional Gov-

ernment, to dissolve the Soviets in Moscow and Petrograd, and to rule with dictatorial powers. Kerensky
successfully tricked him into making avowals he had
not intended to make; and the army Kornilov hoped to
lead to Petrograd melted under the pressure of agitators sent into its midst. The long-drawn quarrel between Kerensky and Kornilov exhausted much of the
remaining strength of the government. What the Bolsheviks had hoped for—that the government should
sting itself to death like a scorpion—was now happening. Kerensky arrested Kornilov, appointed himself
commander in chief, ruled with the help of an inner
cabinet comprising himself, two moderate socialists,
and two liberal army officers, and realized too late that
a tide was rising which would soon drown the government and all its institutions.

On September 25, 1917, Lenin from his hiding place in
Finland issued his famous call for armed insurrection.
It was not obeyed. Much more work had to be done
before the revolutionaries would be able to seize power. Alliances had to be made, there were inevitable
compromises among the parties to be prepared, a
whole system of operations had to be worked out, and
luck, too, must be constrained to play its part. The
Bolsheviks, after what appeared to be irretrievable
defeat following the July Days, were now again in the
ascendant. Trotsky, released from prison after being
condemned by the Soviet, returned to the Soviet to work
among those who had persecuted him, those Social
Revolutionaries and Mensheviks whom he now regarded with scorn and bitter contempt. The seat of the
Central Executive Committee was now the Smolny
Institute, a former school for young ladies of gentle
birth, with gardens looking over the Neva and with a
convent surmounted by a beautiful smoke-blue cupola.
In these unlikely surroundings all the revolutionary
parties met, conferred, battled against one another,
and decided by vote whether they were for insurrection
or against it. At the end of September on the demand of
the Bolsheviks nearly a thousand delegates voted for a
new presidium. Amid increasing tension the votes were

197
THE
CRASH
THROUGH
THE
DOOR

counted. There were 519 votes for the Bolsheviks, 414 for the old presidium, with 67 abstaining. Trotsky was elected chairman of the presidium, regaining the position he last occupied in 1905. The presidium consisted of 13 Bolsheviks, 6 Social Revolutionaries, and 3 Mensheviks. As a result of this vote Trotsky took charge of the revolution.

The Bolsheviks were now in command of the Soviet at a time that could scarcely be more propitious for them. Economic chaos was mounting. The German fleet was ravaging the Gulf of Finland, and the German army appeared to be moving toward Petrograd. Kerensky was attempting to remove pro-Bolshevik troops from the capital, and Trotsky was doing his best to ensure that they would remain. Kerensky was attempting to strangle the Soviet, and Trotsky was attempting to isolate Kerensky. The inevitable effect of this dance of death would be a civil war while the Germans advanced: the bloodiest of wars. Lenin blindly trusted in a European revolution to save the situation, while Kerensky blindly trusted in the good sense of the Russians to come together at this most dangerous moment in the life of the nation. At the beginning of the year Russia had thrown off the despotism of the Tsar. Was it possible—was it to be believed—that before the end of the year, after only a few months of political freedom, the Russians would be forced to endure the despotism of Lenin, who had never concealed his intention to make peace with Germany, to force the people into a mold he had already designed, and to rule by decree and by force?

Zinoviev, who had accompanied Lenin into exile, and Kamenev, who was Trotsky's brother-in-law and a man who weightily considered the solutions of problems, independently came to the conclusion that an uprising at the present time was doomed to failure because there was not the slightest hope of a European revolution. They were terrified that Russia would become the battleground of Germans, Right-wing Russians, and Left-wing Russians, with the Germans sweeping everything before them. Having come to this conclusion, and having informed Lenin that the time was not yet ripe for insurrection, Zinoviev and Kamenev felt the full brunt of Bolshevik displeasure. When Lenin slipped into Petrograd in disguise on the night of October 23—he shaved off his beard and mustache, wore a wig, and for added protection covered three-quarters of his face with a bandage—he was outraged when he heard that Zinoviev and Kamenev were against an immediate insurrection. So was Trotsky, who headed the Military Revolutionary Committee. This committee already acted as a de facto government. It was wholly under Trotsky's control, issued orders that were obeyed by most of the regiments stationed in the capital, most of the factory workers, and all the Kronstadt sailors. It acquired arms by the simple process of sending a worker with an order for arms signed by Trotsky to an arsenal. It requisitioned automobiles, houses, and stocks of paper. When the government ordered that the printing works where a Bolshevik newspaper was being printed should be closed down and its doors sealed, Trotsky sent his well-armed Red Guards to break the seals and to start the presses rolling. And when the government ordered the Telephone Office to cut off the telephones to and from the Smolny Institute, Trotsky sent a detachment of troops to mount guard on the telephone operators and to ensure that the calls went through. The Military Revolutionary Committee ordered the printers to stop printing pro-government pamphlets and posters, and the printers obeyed the order. Kerensky ordered the cruiser *Aurora*, now anchored in the Neva, to put to sea. The sailers sent a deputation to Trotsky to ask what they should do and were told to stand by and await further orders. The Peter and Paul Fortress, at his orders, surrendered its supply of weapons to the Red Guards. The insurrection had already begun, the city had already been occupied, the Red Guards were already on the march without the government being made aware of what was happening. The Military Revolutionary Committee had acted brilliantly, secretly and purposefully. It had found the answer to the problem: How do you create an insurrec-

199

THE
CRASH
THROUGH
THE
DOOR

tion so silently that scarcely anyone of importance knows that it is taking place? It was an interesting problem, for the success of the insurrection depended precisely on its secrecy.

On the night of November 6, Trotsky was alone in his room on the third floor of the Smolny Institute, exhausted by a long and sleepless week. Power streamed from his hands, for he alone was responsible for the hundreds of orders issued by the Military Revolutionary Committee. He had appointed the members of the committee; on his own authority he had signed the sheets of paper that provided him with weapons of all kinds, and was in absolute command. During the night his Red Guards were making their rounds, quietly seizing the railroad stations, the state bank, the post office, the telegraph office, and all the other offices from which the Provisional Government derived its strength. In the morning the citizens woke up and saw nothing amiss. The trams were running, the shops were open, schoolchildren were going to school, and scarcely anyone realized that this day would pass into history. It was a bitterly cold day with low scudding clouds in the sky, the rain falling at intervals and the wind whistling along the Nevsky Prospect.

At ten o'clock in the morning Trotsky announced that the Provisional Government had fallen. The statement was a little premature. The Provisional Government would exist for another sixteen hours. Quietly, during the day, the grip tightened. An ultimatum was sent to the ministers sitting in the Winter Palace. They rejected it. During the afternoon Lenin, who had been hiding in the working-class district of Vyborg, arrived at the Smolny, still wearing his wig and the bandage over his face, looking more like a conspirator than anyone else in the building. Kerensky had slipped out of Petrograd by car, hoping to reach his troops in the outskirts of the city and as commander in chief lead them back to capture the city now ruled by Trotsky. The Red Guards were surrounding the Winter Palace, moving cautiously, exchanging rare shots with the handful of troops who were guarding it. The great revolutionary battle,

201
THE
CRASH
THROUGH
THE
DOOR

the storming of the Winter Palace, never took place. Instead the Red Guards and the sailors spent the whole afternoon and evening moving into position, and it was not until one o'clock in the morning that they began to infiltrate into the enormous palace. At 2:10 A.M. Vladimir Antonov-Ovseyenko burst into the Malachite Room and announced to the ministers of the Provisional Government who were sitting very soberly around a malachite table lit by a single shaded lamp that they were all under arrest. A former officer in the Tsarist army, Antonov-Ovseyenko did not in the least resemble a revolutionary. He wore a wide-brimmed hat pushed back over his head, and his red hair hung to his shoulders. Chalk white with weariness, for he had not slept for thirty-six hours, he announced very quietly that they had been arrested by the order of the Military Revolutionary Committee and would be taken to the Peter and Paul Fortress. They seemed relieved.

While waiting for the news to come from the Winter Palace, Lenin and Trotsky rested on the floor of one of the committee rooms at the Smolny. When the news came at last, Lenin gave an odd little smile and said: *"Es schwindelt."* ("My head is spinning.") As he said this he made a little circling movement with his hand around his head.

Trotsky and Lenin had won the gamble. By ruses and conspiracies, in secrecy and silence, they had brought the Provisional Government to its knees. They had achieved the power they had always wanted. They proclaimed a government with Lenin at the head and Trotsky as commissar for foreign affairs. They were men without illusions, ruthless and unscrupulous, determined to bring about a new form of society which was only the old society writ large and far more oppressive. It was the wrong revolution at the wrong time, in the wrong place, with the wrong leaders. During the next three years, as the result of their assumption of power, Russia would suffer all the horrors of civil war, famine, and invasion, and afterward there would come the burdening bureaucracy and the thousands of prison camps. The Bolsheviks would proscribe all other political parties, paying special attention to the Mensheviks. They built up a force of secret police so powerful that it was able to reach out into the families of everyone in the country, killing without mercy and often for no reason at all. They opened the way for Stalin, who ruled Russia for nearly thirty years as though he detested everyone in it. They ruled by decree and suffered no one to argue with them; they were a law unto themselves.

It had been easy to destroy the Provisional Government; it was not so easy to destroy the Germans who occupied large areas of Russia and threatened Moscow and Petrograd. Soon Trotsky would be faced with more serious problems than the capture of a dozen ministers sitting round a table.

THE FORTRESS OF BREST - LITOVSK 12

Sometimes in the midst of a war there are long pauses when the order comes down from the high command that no guns must be fired, and during these pauses mysterious people can be seen moving across the battle lines for purposes that are rarely explained. They identify themselves by secret signs, wear disguises, whisper in such low tones that their words are scarcely audible, and vanish as quietly as they came. Their names are rarely known and seldom appear in the history books. They are the secret agents whose task is to find out exactly what is happening in the rear of the enemy lines, and they are prepared to pay huge sums for this information. Sometimes they are double agents and they profit from both sides.

Throughout the war the Germans had been sending their agents to Russia. A surprisingly large number of German officers had been taught to speak Russian faultlessly. The German high command knew from day to day what was happening in the Russian court, and then in Prince Lvov's cabinet, and then in Kerensky's cabinet, and when the Bolsheviks took power there were still German agents in the capital and in all the large towns. The German intelligence system was accurate and efficient, and it was funneled in the winter of 1917 into the German-occupied fortress of Brest-Litovsk, which served as headquarters for Major-General Max Hoffman, the brilliant chief of staff of the Commander in chief in the East, Prince Leopold of Bavaria. The prince was a nonentity; the general was the driving force. The town of Brest-Litovsk had been set on fire by the retreating Russians in July 1916, and now from his office high up in the fortress the general looked down on a ruined city covered with a merciful blanket of snow.

The general, at forty-eight, was a heavyset man with a round moon-face, who resembled in the softness of his appearance a middle-aged ecclesiastic. In fact, he was all steel, and ranked with Hindenburg and Ludendorff among the greatest generals Germany had produced. He read and spoke Russian perfectly, he was knowledgeable in Russian ways, he was familiar with the great mass of reports sent to him by his agents, and he believed he understood what was happening in Russia. When Lenin sent to Brest-Litovsk a deputation to sue for peace, there was a general belief in Germany that General Hoffman would deal with it briskly and permit no nonsense. He had vast sums of money at his disposal and he possessed vast resources in men and matériel. What he called "the unholy mob of Bolsheviks" would be confronted with German intelligence and German steel.

But when the delegation representing the Soviet government arrived in Brest-Litovsk, he found himself at a disadvantage. In the first place the delegation was much larger than he had expected, and its leaders were not the kind of people he was accustomed to talking to. At the head of the delegation was Adolf Yoffe, a Jew, a typical revolutionary intellectual, with a long history of clandestine activity behind him. He had a pleasant soft voice and dark burning eyes and was heavily bearded. Lev Kamenev, also Jewish and also bearded, possessing a mind that moved cautiously and uncompromisingly, but with more guile than Yoffe, represented what may be called the Leninist faction, for he was very close to Lenin and understood the workings of his mind. The three others in the delegation were Lev Karakhan, an Armenian who acted as secretary-general of the delegation, astute and wily, possessing a gift for speech-making with a heavy Armenian accent; Grigory Sokolnikov, a close friend of Trotsky with a clean-cut mind and a commanding presence; and Anastasia Bitsenko, a member of the Social Revolutionary Party, who had spent seventeen years as a prisoner in Siberia for having assassinated a former minister of war, General Sakharov. She was a tall, thin, intense woman, gray-haired, intelligent, and silent. She had evidently been included in the delegation for decorative purposes, and General Hoffman was inordinately startled by her appearance at Brest-Litovsk.

He was even more startled by the presence of representatives of the common people, who, like Anastasia Bitsenko, took no part in the discussions and were introduced in order to provide symbolic character, just as a stage director will give half a dozen nondescript people walk-on parts to represent the total population of Moscow. There was a soldier, Nikolay Byelakov, an "old codger," sullen, gruff, concealing his uneasiness with a constant air of defiance; Fyodor Olich, a tall young sailor who took pride in the neatness of his uniform; a young workman called Obukhov, dark faced, curly haired, insolently enjoying every moment of his sudden elevation to prominence; and finally there was the old peasant, Roman Stashkov, who was completely bewildered by the turn of events. Yoffe and Kamenev had seen him trudging through the snowy streets when they were driving toward the Warsaw station, they had stopped the automobile, hauled the old peasant onto it, and told him he was an official delegate under instructions "to go to Brest-Litovsk to make peace with the Germans."

In this happy-go-lucky manner the Soviet delegates obtained some colorful window dressing, but their intentions were deadly serious. They also brought with them nine naval and military officers headed by Admiral Vasily Altvater to advise them on matters concerning the armed forces. Yoffe's instructions were to secure from the Germans a six months armistice, the promise that no German troops were to be transferred from the Eastern Front to the Western Front, and the evacuation of German soldiers and sailors from some islands in the Gulf of Riga. His aim was to produce a détente and a status quo. He was hoping that in the space of six months the entire German population would be engulfed in a revolution.

General Hoffman took careful note of the elements of symbolism, charade, and sheer absurdity in the Soviet delegation, but discounted neither the intelligence of Yoffe nor the determination of Lenin and Trotsky acting behind the scenes. He was also well aware that Lenin and Trotsky were not yet solidly in power and might be overthrown, that the Bolshevik delegation was not so much concerned with signing an armistice as with exerting pressure by means of propaganda, and that the prospects of coming to any workable agreement with them were very remote. If the negotiations broke down, he proposed that the German army would march into St. Petersburg and occupy the city.

Trotsky knew exactly what he wanted to accomplish: "To arouse the masses of Germany, of Austro-Hungary, as well as that of the Entente—this is what we hoped to achieve by entering into peace negotiations." Unlike the Germans, who simply stood and waited at Brest-Litovsk, prepared to advance or go forward, thinking only in military terms, Trotsky was thinking in fluid terms, hoping for the disintegration of the German front, seeking temporary alliances with the United States, France, and England, using all kinds of feints and ambushes to mislead the enemy, the many enemies, for he regarded the British, French, and American governments as being just as guilty as the Germans. It was usually Trotsky's fate to lock horns with intellectual inferiors. It soon became apparent that neither General Hoffman nor the German foreign minister, Richard von Kühlmann, were in any way his inferior. And indeed at the first meeting of the delegations, Adolf

Yoffe, who spoke for Trotsky, seemed to be overwhelmed by the weight of German intelligence confronting him. He was like a man who had entered a bull ring armed with a rusty sword and found himself face to face with bulls with lowered heads, red eyed, and with horns sharpened to a razor edge. The Germans did not parade their power—it was something they possessed naturally.

Yet, as the conference continued, it became more and more evident that the power of the Germans was no longer absolute. They dictated their terms, insisted on their conditions, won arguments, and even at a later stage marched across southern Russia and carved out for themselves a small empire, but this power, however brutal and efficient it appeared to be, lacked any enduring quality. It resembled an oak tree hollowed out by ants that falls at the first kick. And Trotsky, too, continually feinting and bluffing, without an army to enforce his claims, engaged in maneuvers designed to put Hoffman and Kühlmann off balance, was equally powerless. The treaty of Brest-Litovsk, which ended with Russia's submission to Germany's most extreme demands, was an object lesson on the insignificance of treaties. The Germans by gaining a small empire gained nothing, and the Russians by losing it gained nothing either.

The first meetings were holding operations. They were deliberately drawn out because the Russians were still hoping for the social-democratic revolution that would sweep through Germany and Austria, leapfrog over Switzerland, take root in France, and spread into England. Alternatively, the Western Powers might penetrate into Germany, and General Hoffman's army on the Eastern Front might be compelled to fall back. Neither of these two things happened, and the Central Committee of the Communist Party—the new name replaced the old Social Democratic Party (Bolsheviks)—found it almost impossibly difficult to make any decisions. Lenin wanted peace at all costs. Yoffe, Radek, Dzerzhinsky, Uritzky, Kollontay, and others wanted revolutionary war but were not clear how such a war could be conducted. Others, like Stalin, waited on the sidelines and did not commit themselves. Trotsky was the pragmatist. He wanted an armistice on the best terms available, and if possible he would talk the Germans to a standstill. But whatever they wanted or said they wanted, the members of the Central Committee found themselves in a quandary, for none of these suggested solutions offered much hope. Trotsky finally concluded that the best solution was "Neither Peace nor War." It was brilliant; it was new; it was memorable; and it seemed if not examined too closely to provide a novel intellectual solution, or at least a way out of the morass. The Germans were not in the least impressed with it and dismissed it out of hand.

The Bolsheviks had won the Revolution, and were in danger of losing Russia to the Germans.

Lenin viewed the loss of vast areas of Russia with a certain equanimity. Once, when Trotsky asked him what they would do if the Germans continued their invasion and marched on Moscow, he replied:

> We shall withdraw further East, to the Urals, all the time declaring our readiness to conclude peace. The Kuznetz Basin is rich in coal. We shall set up an Uralo-Kuznetz Republic based on the regional industry and the Kuznetz coal and supported by the proletariat of the Urals and by as many workers as we can move with us from Moscow and Petrograd. We shall hold out. If need be we shall retreat even deeper, beyond the Urals. We may reach Kamchatka, but we shall hold out. The international situation will be changing a dozen times; from the redoubt of our Uralo-Kuznetz Republic we shall spread out again and we shall return to Moscow and Petersburg. But if now we senselessly involve ourselves in a revolutionary war, if we let the elite of our working class and our party perish, then, of course, we shall return nowhere.

There is not the slightest doubt that Lenin, driven into a corner, was showing a quite extraordinary interest in the Uralo-Kuznetz Republic. There were members of the Central Committee who were not quite sure where the Uralo-Kuznetz Republic was or whether it existed, or whether Lenin was joking. Trotsky, out of loyalty and friendship, professed to believe that the nonexistent Republic was a device to demonstrate his conviction that all was not lost. Lenin, he suggested, was pointing to the immensity of Russia as a reason for hope and a warning against the strategy of despair. "Fortunately we were never reduced to the Uralo-Kuznetz Republic," Trotsky commented. "Nevertheless one can assert that the Uralo-Kuznetz Republic, which never materialized, saved the Union of Russian Soviet Federal Socialist Republics."

Quite obviously it did nothing of the kind. The imaginary republic was born of despair. Trotsky was inclined to praise Lenin at all times and to pardon his most dangerous errors. He wrote that Lenin approached the Treaty of Brest-Litovsk with inexhaustible revolutionary energy, when in fact he was as confused as everyone else.

Since the discussions were going badly, Yoffe was summoned back to Petersburg for consultations. He, too, was bewildered, for it appeared that no armistice was possible under any terms acceptable to the Russians and there was nothing they could do to prevent the Germans from advancing wherever they pleased. An armistice merely provided them with an excuse for making whatever territorial demands occurred to them.

Trotsky decided, at Lenin's urging, to take over the negotiations. A brilliant debater, he was prepared to engage Hoffman and Kühlmann in a prolonged debate on matters of revolutionary principle, territorial acquisitions, self-determination, and expropriations. By the sheer power of his logic he would demonstrate the need for the Germans to retreat to their own frontiers. But once he arrived at Brest-Litovsk, logic deserted him. Kühlmann greeted him with the remark that it was better to deal with the principal than the emissary. Trotsky thought it was an attempt at flattery, and bristled. He wrote later that the incident had the same effect on him as stepping on something unclean, and he was so shocked that he involuntarily started back. Kühlmann's remark was ordinary, accurate, and commendable, for it is always better to deal with the principal than the emissary. Thereafter they dueled, and took joy in their dueling, but Kühlmann was at least as good a duelist as Trotsky. He had an army behind him. Trotsky, on his way to Brest-Litovsk, had seen the Russian trenches facing the German positions, and there were no soldiers in them.

Trotsky detested Brest-Litovsk, the burned-out city under the snow. He enjoyed his brisk morning walks, but hated seeing the notices which read: "Any Russian found in this place will be shot." The notice did not apply to Russian commissars, but there was nothing to say that they were specifically excluded. Invited to lunch by Prince Leopold of Bavaria, he curtly refused; and when he discovered that lesser members of his delegation were on good terms with their German counterparts, he ordered an end to fraternization. The Germans had placed automobiles at the disposal of the Russians; these too were rejected. When Count Czernin suggested that the library Trotsky had abandoned in Vienna at the beginning of the war could be sent to Moscow, Trotsky thanked him politely, but he bristled when the Count a few moments later asked him to intervene in the case of two prisoners in Russian hands. Count Czernin was the Austrian foreign minister; he lacked Hoffman's brutal intelligence and Kühlmann's grace of mind, but he was far more human than either of them. There was even something commonplace about him, which must have been refreshing to the observers who saw Hoffman, Kühlmann, and Trotsky exhibiting their intellectual skills—scoring points, adding them up, and each pronouncing himself the victor.

When Trotsky arrived at Brest-Litovsk he was disconcerted to discover that the Germans had granted the Ukrainian *Rada* a seat at the conference table. Some young students who claimed to be duly appointed representatives of the Ukrainian government were given the privileges of emissaries and allowed to speak at length about the iniquities of the Russian Communist Party. Trotsky treated the Ukrainians with supreme contempt by pretending that they did not exist, while Count Czernin, looking to the Ukraine for wheat to feed the starving Austrians who were on the verge of revolution, treated them with favorable attention. Alexander Sevruk and Mykola Liubinsky, the two most outspoken of the Ukrainian delegates, deserve a place in history, for they fought Trotsky's fire with a savage and unrelenting fire of their own and they were fearless in their denunciation of Lenin's cruelty.

On January 18, 1918, Trotsky left Brest-Litovsk to confer with Lenin. He was on his way to Petersburg when Lenin dispersed the Constituent Assembly, the first democratically elected parliament in Russia, where the Bolsheviks were in the minority. At Lenin's orders a guard entered the Tauride Palace, where the Assembly was meeting, and told the delegates to go away "because the guards are getting tired." Fearing harassment, the delegates had brought candles and food and were preparing to spend the night debating. They left the Tauride Palace and were never permitted to return.

Trotsky exulted in the simple logic of the operation, which was so swift, so brief. "There was no skirmish at all," he wrote, "only a simple and pathetic demonstration of the rearguard of 'democracy,' bowing itself off the stage, armed with its candles and sandwiches."*

Lenin cut the throat of democracy by sending a single guard into a palace. The guard represented the power of the terror which was now in full bloom. All that the Russians had fought for over so long a period was now snatched from them. Henceforth Russia would be ruled by a dictatorship, with Lenin and Trotsky as the duumvirs, until in due course a single dictator emerged.

But if it was a simple matter to disperse the Constituent Assembly, it was a much more difficult matter to get rid of the Germans, who obstinately remained on Russian soil and showed no desire to leave. They, too, possessed a vast appetite for the wheatfields of the

*The Socialist Revolutionaries polled 16,500,000 votes; the Bolsheviks 9,023,963; other anti-Bolshevik parties 10,650,000. About 27 million voted against the Bolsheviks, and a third of that number voted for them.

Ukraine. When Trotsky returned to Brest-Litovsk he had the satisfaction of learning that Soviet forces were advancing into the Ukraine, the *Rada* had collapsed almost at the same moment when the Germans signed a separate treaty with it, and there seemed to be some hope that Germany would not advance into Russia. Presented with the German demands, Trotsky saw that his hopes were misplaced. The fall of the *Rada* meant very little to the Germans, who could always produce another one to take its place. Trotsky made a thundering speech rejecting all the German terms, refused to sign an armistice, and returned to Petrograd with the satisfaction that he had upheld revolutionary honor by placing the Germans in a predicament—"No War and No Peace." Like Lenin, he was still placing his trust in the expected revolutionary uprising in Germany which would inevitably destroy the German military cast and bring about the demoralization of the German army. It did not happen. The German high command gave the order to advance, and Hoffman had the satisfaction of seeing the German army scooping up vast areas of Russia without firing a shot. "It is the most comic war I have ever experienced," he wrote. "It is waged almost exclusively in trains and cars. One puts on the train a handful of infantry men with machine guns and one gun, and one rushes to the next railroad station. One seizes the station, arrests the Bolsheviks, entrains another detachment and travels farther."

Such an act was not entirely unexpected, but both Lenin and Trotsky professed to be taken by surprise. Trotsky sounded out the British, the French, and the Americans to learn whether they could offer any aid, and realized that if it came it would come too late, and there existed no machinery to bring it about. Lenin held to his view that "peace at all costs," so long as the Soviet government survived, was the only logical course. Trotsky, while sympathizing with the views of those who wanted to continue the war and not in the least convinced by Lenin's arguments, nevertheless sided with Lenin on the grounds that Lenin, having now taken command of the Revolution, must be permitted to make the ultimate decisions. "I am not sure that he is right, but I do not want to do anything that would interfere with the party's unity," he declared. "On the contrary, I shall help as much as I can. But I cannot stay in office and bear personal responsibility for the conduct of foreign affairs." This was as close as he came to an admission of failure. Lenin also made an admission of failure, for he offered to resign, and there were many who wanted to see him go. The question was debated in the Tauride Palace, so lately occupied by the elected deputies from all the Russian provinces, but the debate was without meaning, because the Germans had issued their last ultimatum and commanded the Soviet delegates to appear at Brest-Litovsk or face the consequences of a full-scale invasion of Russia rather than the partial invasion which had now become inevitable. On the afternoon of March 3, 1918, Yoffe signed the armistice in the presence of Prince Leopold of Bavaria, General Hoffman, and the plenipotentiaries of the Austro-Hungarian Empire, Bulgaria, and Turkey, which claimed large areas of the Caucasus now under the control of its armies.

The treaty of Brest-Litovsk showed the failure of Soviet diplomacy. Trotsky, by his speeches, only encouraged the Germans to act more harshly than they had originally intended. He deliberately exasperated them; they in turn decided to crush him. He proved to be an incompetent diplomat.

One of Lenin's favorite sayings during this time was one that reflected his fear of a full-scale German invasion. He said: "The German beast springs quickly." Now it sprang. With no opposition the German army poured across the Ukraine, occupied the Crimea and advanced toward the Caucasus, reaching the Don River a thousand miles to the east of Brest-Litovsk. The ignominy of the Russian surrender did much to stiffen opposition to Lenin's regime. The Germans advanced into Estonia and Finland, threatening Petrograd. Lenin ordered the seat of government to be moved to Moscow.

For fear that the people of Petrograd would rise in protest, all the arrangements for the transfer of the government were conducted in secret.

In the Kremlin, Lenin and Trotsky occupied adjoining apartments in the Kavalersky Building opposite the Potyeshny Palace, known as the "Pleasure Palace." There was very little pleasure to be found. By the surrender at Brest-Litovsk, Russia lost a third of her population, a third of her agricultural land, more than half of her factories, and nine-tenths of her coal mines. Only a year had elapsed since the abdication of Nicholas II.

In March 1918, shortly after his arrival in Moscow, Trotsky was appointed commissar of war, a post he would continue to hold until January 1925. The task he confronted was the most difficult he had ever faced. He would have to arouse a half-starving and demoralized people into actively supporting a revolutionary war on a battlefield that extended from the gates of Warsaw to Vladivostok. He had to organize supplies, appoint generals, train recruits, plan battles. The infant republic fought battles against sixteen armies, and survived. Indeed, it thrived on the very impossibility of success, taking nourishment from every failure, never more successful than when its soldiers were hopelessly outnumbered. Trotsky, who had never studied military affairs except when he was a war-correspondent in the Balkans, showed himself to be an extraordinarily gifted military commander. He had commanded the forces that brought about the revolution in Petrograd; he now commanded all the armies that regained the lost territory of Russia. When it was all over, ambition had been burned out of him, and he was only a husk of himself.

THE ARMORED TRAIN 13

On August 7, 1918, Trotsky left Moscow on a special train bound for Kazan. The mission was urgent, for it was known that the Red Army in Kazan was in grave danger from the artillery of the Czechoslovaks and the Whites under Admiral Kolchak. The special train was hastily put together, all available guns, ammunition, and medical supplies were packed into the railroad cars, and in addition there were two hundred hand-picked Red Army troops who, if necessary, could be thrown into battle. Communication had broken down, and when Trotsky left Moscow he did not know that Kazan had already fallen and the remnants of the Red Army had been thrown back on Svyazhsk, a small town on the right bank of the Volga originally built by Ivan the Terrible as a fortress and staging post for his own successful conquest of Kazan when it was ruled by a Tatar Khan.

Everything now depended on defending Svyazhsk, for if it fell the Czechoslovaks and the Whites would have no difficulty making their way to Nizhni Novgorod by boat and from there following the railway across the southern plains to Moscow. Svyazhsk had one advan-

215

tage. It was nearly an island, for the Svyaga River curled round the town before falling into the Volga. If there were sufficient guns, if there was a capable commander, and if the people were in good heart, Svyazhsk could be made impregnable. But the Red Army had lost most of its guns to the enemy and was demoralized. There was a good commander, Vatsekis, a Latvian and former colonel of the imperial general staff. He could do little, unless there were reinforcements. The train journeyed slowly, for the railway workers were not yet on the side of the revolution. Trotsky impatiently scanned maps, read French novels, listened to radio bulletins from all over Europe and sometimes stopped the train to get on the direct telephone line to the Kremlin. Surprisingly, most of the telegraph wires were still up, and he was able to reach Moscow. He was not able to reach Svyazhsk. Moscow said it had received only scanty news from Svyazhsk but believed it was still holding out.

Trotsky's special train drove into the little railroad station and stopped. He addressed some soldiers gathered in the station yard, summoned Vatsekis to a conference, handed out guns, ammunition and medical supplies, announced that he was staying there until Kazan was conquered, and that the carriages would be his command post. As for the train, it was ordered back to Moscow to bring more men, more guns, more supplies to the small town. The carriages, standing in the wretched station yard, became the symbol of resistance against an unyielding and dangerous enemy.

The train had arrived only just in time, for the people in Svyazhsk had almost given up hope. The young journalist Larissa Reissner, daughter of a German landowner and a Polish mother—she was twenty-three years old and would die of typhus before she was thirty—happened to be in Svyazhsk during those rainy August days. She described how everyone hoped the rain would continue, for the enemy airplanes rarely flew when the weather was bad, but as soon as there was a clearing in the clouds they came and dropped bombs on the nearly defenseless town. The enemy knew that Trotsky's train was there, and the airmen aimed for it. They all missed. Meanwhile Trotsky was summoning, as though by magic, more defenders, more guns, more supplies. Svyazhsk, a barely discernible dot on the map, was being regarded by Moscow as the key to the defense against all the armies converging from the East. Everything needed for the coming offensive was obtained. Soon there were newspapers, boots and overcoats; even letters came; and the food was a little better. Trotsky acquired a new and highly skilled staff of soldiers and sailors uncompromisingly dedicated to the conquest of Kazan. In the early days of the Civil War their names would be spoken with bated breath: Rosengoltz, Smirnov, Mikhailov, Mezhlauk, Kobozov, another Smirnov, Raskolnikov, and in the thirties nearly all of them were shot by Stalin because they were Trotsky's associates. In Svyazhsk they were saving the revolution.

There were bloody skirmishes, sudden assaults, feints, ambuscades. Kazan stood on a high bluff overlooking the river and could only be taken by assault. Trotsky hoped to take the city with the help of a number of small torpedo boats floated down through the rivers and canals from the Baltic Sea. The aim was to destroy the fleet attached to the Czechoslovak army in Kazan, then to engage them in battle, and then to take the city by storm. To destroy the fleet and the shore batteries, Raskolnikov, the former commander of the Kronstadt sailors, decided to send a flotilla of torpedo boats silently, with no lights, on a dark night, against Kazan with the intention of creating the greatest amount of destruction. The ruse worked perfectly. Trotsky insisted on accompanying Raskolnikov on the commander's flagship, the *Prochny*, meaning the "Endurable," which sailed close to the city, set fire to barges loaded with munitions and food supplies, shelled the city, and nearly came to disaster when its steering gear was damaged, and for a brief while it was drifting helplessly alongside an enemy barge under the muzzles of White Guard artillery. The steering gear was quickly repaired, and all the ships returned safely to Svyazhsk.

For a fantastic moment Trotsky had been in hideous danger, and this danger took the form of burning barges and exploding ammunition on a river that seemed to have caught fire.

Trotsky was exhilarated by the adventure, and with Raskolnikov planned a still more formidable raid against Kazan in the future. Meanwhile he toughened up the spirits of the soldiers and sailors under his command. To deserters he was totally merciless; they were shot after a drumhead court-martial. Twenty-seven soldiers, all members of the Communist Party, and several of them old militants who had served the party from the beginning of the century, were sent to the firing squad "as an example to others." In his autobiography Trotsky assures the reader that he passed death sentences only on "two officers and a few privates." Larissa Reissner pointed out that the executions were dictated by a fact that had very little to do with their desertions. Within the army, members of the Communist Party were becoming increasingly unpopular because they usually chose or received the "cushy jobs." They were regarded as people exempt from the law; they deserted at will; they were known to be cowards. Trotsky was determined to put an end to their privileged position. The execution of "two officers and a few privates" was therefore a rather excessive rebuke to Communist Party members in the army to remind them that in the fighting line they were no better or no worse than non-party members.

The memory of the executed Communists followed Trotsky throughout the rest of his life. Those who detested him found confirmation in the image of the cold, proud, and bloody-minded leader with a thirst for theatricality; and when Trotsky in due course quarreled violently with Stalin, who was infinitely more bloody minded, these executions were remembered against him. Stalin, who bitterly contested Trotsky's leading role in the Civil War, would ask slyly how he defended Svyazhsk and answered: "By killing Communists."

The truth was that Trotsky's army was in desperate straits, in danger of collapsing from within. Revolution-

ary discipline could be maintained only with the utmost difficulty in spite of the fact that every officer was
being advised and watched closely by a political commissar, whose duty was to affirm the absolute rights of
the revolution over all other rights. The miserable
conditions in Svyazhsk accounted for the chaos and
disorder, but they did not, in Trotsky's view, offer
anyone a license to run away. He made this clear in an
order issue on August 14, 1918:

> I learn that the detachment of partisans from Petrograd
> has deserted its positions.
> I have ordered Commissar Rosengoltz to investigate the
> facts of the matter.
> The soldiers of the Red Army of Workers and Peasants
> are neither cowards nor scum. They want to fight for the
> liberty and happiness of the toiling people. If they retreat
> or fight badly, it is the fault of their commanders and
> commissars.
> I give this warning: if a unit retreats, the first to be shot
> will be the commissar, the second will be the commanding
> officer.
> Courageous soldiers will be rewarded according to their
> merits and will be given commissions.
> Cowards, profiteers and traitors will not escape bullets.
> I answer for this pledge before the whole Red Army.

The need for ruthlessness was imposed upon him by
the White Guards and Czechoslovaks fighting against
him. They were well equipped, brave, ruthless, and
cunning. On August 28, Boris Savinkov, a brilliant
novelist, former terrorist, and audacious soldier, took
part in an extended encircling movement to take
Svyazhsk from behind, thus cutting the line to Moscow
and forcing the defenders to fight on two fronts. The ma-
neuver was brilliantly executed. The Whites swooped
down on a railroad station at a place called Shikhrana,
killed everyone in the station, blew up a munition train,
cut the line, and then advanced on Svyazhsk, moving
along the railroad. An armored train, mounted with
naval guns, happened to be in Svyazhsk, and was sent
against them. The armored train was called "Free

Russia." The commander of the train panicked, abandoned the train, fled back to Svyazhsk "in order to report," and soon the Whites were within a mile of Trotsky's headquarters. Trotsky ordered every available man into the battle against the advancing Whites—his own guards, radio operators, cooks, orderlies, and clerks, and everyone he could get hold of in Svyazhsk itself. It was a rabble army of about four hundred men against no one knew how many Whites. They fought through the night, and by the morning the Whites were withdrawing the way they came. While the battle was going on, Trotsky remained in his train, virtually alone, studying a map by the light of candles, giving orders over a field telephone. With a little more luck Savinkov might have captured Svyazhsk and made Trotsky prisoner. The Kazan newspapers reported variously that Trotsky had been killed, taken prisoner, had been flown out just in time, and that his dog was captured as a trophy. This puzzled Trotsky, who had never in his life kept a dog. The curious legend of the dog he left behind him was repeated by the Whites many times during the Civil War.

On September 1, 1918, there came a coded telegram from Moscow, telling him that an attempt had been made on Lenin's life, that the extent of his wounds was still unknown, and that he must return at once. He immediately left for the capital, and during his absence the army of Svyazhsk took Kazan by assault.

By the time Trotsky reached Moscow, Lenin was already out of danger and convalescing in a villa at Gorki outside Moscow. Trotsky went to visit him and was rewarded with the "love look" that sometimes appeared in Lenin's eyes when he listened to Trotsky's stories about the front. Once, as Trotsky remembered the words, Lenin said: "The game is won. If we have succeeded in establishing order in the army, it means we can establish it everywhere else. And the revolution—with order—will be unconquerable." They were, and still regarded themselves as being, the two leaders of the revolution.

Soon Trotsky was once more traveling to the front, to

the many fronts, in his armored train, which became more essential, more complex, and more demanding, so that in time Trotsky himself became, as it were, the personification of the train and acquired characteristics which belonged more to the train than to the man. In his black leather uniform, he generated energy and drove himself relentlessly. His style became more staccato, the rhythms of his life were fused into the rhythms of the train. When he made speeches, he spoke from the roof of the train, heroic against the background of dramatic skies. Had not Karl Marx said that "revolution is the locomotive of history"? He was the man astride the iron horse, the hero cultivating his own legend, the former antimilitarist turned into a Napoleonic figure.

Trotsky described the train as "a flying apparatus of administration," but this was to describe it by its lowest denominator. It was advertisement, threat, drumhead court-martial, punishment and reward, arriving when least expected. The converted Pullman, which had belonged to the Tsarist minister of railways, was equipped with all the luxuries that Trotsky's inventive mind could contrive. In the armored train there was a library, a bath, a printing press, a radio station, an electric power station, a restaurant, a clubhouse for the guards and special service men, two automobiles, a secretariat, storerooms for guns, medical supplies, and clothing for the soldiers, and Trotsky's own office with the maps hanging on the wall and the nailed-down typewriters and comfortable armchairs. In time the armored train would expand; there would be more storerooms, more offices. Altogether about one hundred twenty men were employed on the train. Above all, the armored train was a singular reminder of one man's personal power.

This, of course, was one of the problems. Trotsky gloried in the train, with which he identified himself, and there were many who were envious and believed that he was taking too much glory to himself. The train gave him unlimited mobility, he was continually in touch with the Kremlin by telephone and radio, he was himself one of the major sources of authority and power; nevertheless he was cut off from the main source of power by his very mobility, by the fact that he was communicating by messages and not face to face. He was sometimes totally unaware and always indifferent to the plots that were being mounted against him even in those early days by Stalin, who spent more time in the Kremlin and had the ear of Lenin. Trotsky had chosen as his representative in the Kremlin a twenty-seven-year-old former army doctor Ephraim Sklyansky, a man of great resourcefulness but no match for Stalin. Trotsky called Sklyansky "the Carnot of the Revolution." This was not quite true. Sklyansky was the faithful messenger boy, the pleader in the high court of Lenin, the man who could be relied upon to carry out Trotsky's instructions to the letter. Trotsky's chief agent in the Kremlin was Lenin himself, whose theoretical knowledge of civil war was being improved daily by the reading of Trotsky's often voluminous reports. Yet the trust between them was not quite absolute. Lenin would listen to sly jokes told about Trotsky, enjoy them, and laugh a little uneasily.

Of Lenin's general admiration for Trotsky there could not be the slightest doubt. It was proved, as Trotsky later pointed out in his autobiography, by a remarkable document given to him by Lenin during the course of a meeting of the Politburo. Lenin wrote his statement in red ink on his official stationery low down on the page, thus leaving space for Trotsky to write whatever order he pleased above it:

R.S.F.S.R.*
Chairman of the Soviet
of People's Commissaries,
Moscow, the Kremlin.
July, 1919

COMRADES:
Knowing the strict character of Comrade Trotsky's orders, I am so convinced, so absolutely convinced, of the

---

* R.S.F.S.R. stands for Russian Soviet Federated Socialist Republic, the name originally given to the country by Lenin. On December 30, 1922, the name was changed to the Union of Soviet Socialist Republics.

correctness, expediency, and necessity for the success of
the cause of the order given by Comrade Trotsky that I
unreservedly indorse this order.

V. ULYANOV / LENIN

Like the armored train, this document was a superb
and legendary gift, and Trotsky was well aware of its
implications, although he probably erred when he
suggested in his autobiography that it implied a direct
rebuke of Stalin, who was continually intriguing
against him in military affairs. In effect, Trotsky was
receiving an accolade, for the order only reinforced
powers he already possessed.

Curiously, no history of the train was ever written. At
various times Trotsky thought of writing it, just as he
thought of writing a history of the Red Army from its
beginnings to the end of the Civil War. But many of the
essential documents vanished into the Archives of the
War Ministry, and though he made copies of most of his
own messages to the Kremlin dictated on the train,
there were not enough of them to provide a full-scale
study. These carbon copies, in purple on flimsy paper,
survive today in the Houghton Library at Harvard
University. And perhaps he did not write the history of
the train or the Red Army for a reason that may be
perplexing but is nevertheless worth pondering. As war
minister he saved Russia during the Civil War. His
triumph was complete. He had every reason to believe
that without him Russia would have been in ruins and
what was left of the country would be under the heels of
the invaders, British, Czech, French, and Japanese
together with the White armies. Although he possessed
a towering pride, he also possessed a certain modesty
and reserve. If he wrote about the Civil War, and still
more if he wrote about the train, he would necessarily
have to present himself in some fashion as the hero of
the story, and from this he recoiled. He was proud of his
great conquests and almost indifferent to public ac-
claim.

Although the engine and the machine-gun cars were
armored, the train was in fact very vulnerable. A spiked
rail, a log, a charge of dynamite could have derailed it.

It was shelled, bombed from the air, machine-gunned and peppered with rifle bullets, but only once was it derailed, and this happened when it was traveling at about twenty miles an hour near a station. As a result of a faulty switch, part of the train was thrown onto an embankment, Trotsky's carriage was tip-tilted, and although the door was crumpled and he was unable to open it, he had no difficulty getting out through the window. It was very dark. He was afraid of an ambush and expected to hear bullets, but there was only silence broken by a few pitiful cries, like the whimpering of a child, coming through the darkness. A man came down the line, swinging a lantern. To Trotsky's relief it was the commander of the train, there was no ambush, and what appeared to be a child's voice belonged to one of the guards who had been pinned down by part of the machinery. He was rescued without difficulty, suffering from nothing more than a few bruises. The restaurant car was smashed to splinters, and altogether eight cars were destroyed. No one had suffered any serious injuries.

Such things gave him a sense of inviolability. He could have been killed a thousand times during those journeys which, according to a rough guess by one of the men in the train, covered a distance of over 200,000 kilometers. From the train's newspaper *V Puti*, meaning "On the Road," it would be possible to reconstruct the various journeys. There were date lines from Chelyabinsk, Samara, Vyatka, Petrograd, Balashov, Smolensk, Rostov-on-Don, Novocherkask, Zhitomir, and many more. Sometimes Trotsky felt that he had spent all his life on the train, that there would be no end to it, and that life consisted of an armored train and an armored automobile that would take him far into the country only to bring him back to the train. In the automobile he was in even greater danger than on the train, for the Civil War was a war of movement, of quick advances and quick retreats, and sometimes they were very close to enemy lines and on a few occasions they were inside enemy-occupied territory. On the steppes they always ran the risk of meeting a Cossack patrol. Then, too, there was the risk of the automobile breaking down far from anywhere. Once, when they were fording a river, the automobile got stuck in midstream. Trotsky raged, cursed his Estonian driver, and threatened all kinds of punishments until the driver answered: "I beg to state that the engineers never foresaw that we should have to sail on water." Trotsky was placated by the man's irony and remained in good humor for the rest of the journey.

Alfred Rosmer, a friend of Trotsky's from his Paris days, accompanied him on one of his journeys in 1920. Rosmer marveled at the number of books in Trotsky's carriage, dictionaries, encyclopedias, technical works of all kinds. There was a French section with novels bound in yellow paper. He was surprised to discover a copy of Stéphane Mallarmé's *Verse and Prose Works*. From this traveling workshop Trotsky poured out a spate of orders, pamphlets, and posters; he edited the newspaper; he wrote one of his major works, *Terrorism and Communism*, dictating to two secretaries and then endlessly revising the manuscript. He told Rosmer that he acquired the best information from the London and Berlin radios and the worst information from the Paris radio.

Terrorism and Communism is part history, part exhortation, part defense of his past actions, and part springboard for some of his own wilder theories on the subject of revolution and the dictatorship of the proletariat. One of his favorite subjects was the militarization of labor, that is, the total dictatorship over the proletariat, the permanent militarized labor force. "The foundations of the militarization of labor," he wrote, "are those forms of State compulsion without which the replacement of capitalist economy by the Socialist economy will for ever remain an empty sound." All labor must be under military discipline; it was totally absurd to expect the dictatorship to survive without compulsion and the most extreme form of discipline; and those who proclaimed that forced labor was always unproductive were deadly wrong for the good reason that "freely-hired labor" was no better than convict labor, since the hirer was nothing more than the prison governor. The argument is tortuous; the words "discipline," "authority," "compulsion" follow one another pell-mell on the page. He is inventing the militarized authoritarian state, and we are invited to imagine factories where every worker has a man in a black leather jacket behind him, pointing a gun at him. Out of the pounding rhythms of the locomotive there came the most terrible and audacious of all his inventions.

Much of the book takes the form of a concentrated attack on the Marxist theoretician Karl Kautsky, who wanted communism with a human face, without compulsion. Trotsky answers that there can be no communism without compulsion, even extreme compulsion, and he never stops to inquire how many bureaucrats, policemen, and *agents provocateurs* are necessary to enforce the iron laws of the state. "Most men," he announces categorically, "try to avoid labor." Therefore they must be forced to labor, according to the Marxist maxim: "He who does not work, neither shall he eat." "The very principle of compulsory service is for the Communist quite unquestionable," he says, as though it were a matter that had never been questioned.

Because he was living on a railroad train, Trotsky attached extraordinary importance to locomotives in the building of a new society after the Civil War. He offered a four-stage scheme, based on the use of militarized labor, for the rehabilitation of the ravaged country "unless we want to melt the town into agriculture and transform all of Russia into a peasant state." The four stages were:

1. Transportation must be supported, even at the minimum level. Bread must be secured for the towns, fuel and raw materials for industry, fodder for the cattle.
2. Machines must be built in the interests of transport and the storage of raw material and fuel. *The most essential machine is the locomotive.*
3. Machines must be built in the interests of the production of articles of prime necessity.

4. The production of articles of personal or secondary significance on the widest possible scale.

The scheme, as Trotsky outlined it, showed only that he was incompetent to deal with the vast problems of industrial recovery.

About the same time that he was writing *Terrorism and Communism* on the train, there occurred to him another of those brilliant ideas that from time to time enlivened the monotony of his endless journeys. It was nothing less than the invasion of India, a direct thrust into the Indian subcontinent from a huge military base in the Urals. The Red Army would conquer India and set in motion a huge Asiatic revolution to offset the reverses that were being suffered in Europe and Russia—the Soviet republic of Hungary had been destroyed, Riga and Vilna had been lost, much of the Ukraine was in enemy hands, Petrograd was under attack, and Odessa looked as though it might fall. Soon Kiev would fall to the army of General Denikin, and the White armies would be racing toward Moscow. At this juncture, during the worst time of the Civil War, Trotsky wrote an enormously long meandering letter to the Central Committee of the Communist Party, urging that the refugees from the Ukraine should be sent to the Urals to help build a gigantic military base and that a cavalry corps of thirty to forty thousand men should be sent through Afghanistan into the plains of India. "The road to Paris and London," he announced, "lies via the towns of Afghanistan, the Punjab and Bengal." He wrote:

There is no doubt at all that our Red Army constitutes an incomparably more powerful force in the Asian terrain of world politics than in the European terrain. Here there opens up before us an undoubted possibility not merely of a lengthy wait to see how events develop in Europe, but of conducting activity in the Asian field. The road to India may prove at the given moment to be more readily passable and shorter for us than the road to Soviet Hungary. The sort of army which at the moment can be of no great significance in the European scales can upset the unstable balance of Asian relationships of colonial dependence, give a direct push to an uprising on the part of the oppressed masses and assure the triumph of such a rising in Asia.

So he went on for page after page, celebrating imaginary future triumphs while the area of Russia controlled by the Communist Party gradually diminished to a square about eight hundred miles wide and eight hundred miles broad with Moscow in the center. The Red Army in the Ukraine had been decimated and General Yudenich, armed by the British and supported by the long-range guns of the British Navy, was advancing on Petrograd. Obviously, Trotsky had not even troubled to look at a map of Afghanistan. His judgment foundered on the vision of revolutionary Asia rising to compensate for all the revolutionary failures in the West. The letter written on August 5, 1919, at the worst hours of the Civil War, suggested that if it was necessary to write off the Russian Revolution, he was prepared to start all over again in Asia.

Meanwhile the fighting continued, and in the small rump of Russia that remained the armored train traveled, stopped, issued orders, and went on again through a landscape of desolation. In the middle of October 1919, the train steamed into the Nicholas Station in Petrograd, and Trotsky stepped out and took command of the defense of the city. Zinoviev, nominally in charge, had lost his nerve. Trotsky found him lying on a sofa, complaining about the difficulties of his task. There was nothing to be done except disregard Zinoviev's existence and rally the people of Petrograd with threats, speeches, orders, and a *levée en masse*. Trotsky threw his train crew into the organization of the defense, and he made it clear that he would fight in every street, in every house. The advance forces of Yudenich could see the gold cupola of St. Isaac's Cathedral gleaming in the faint October sun. The Red Army defending the city was being thrown back, but a new army was being formed within the city. It consisted of clerks, laborers, women, boys, everyone who could hold a rifle. Women were digging trenches along the Neva: machine guns were set up at street crossings; barricades were being raised. Trotsky was determined that when the Whites burst into the gigantic city, they would find a labyrinth of stone, every house a stronghold. Every window, every attic, every cellar would be a source of danger. Some streets would be barricaded with barbed wire, a street nearby would be left undefended, but there would be a hidden machine-gun post waiting for the first soldiers of Yudenich's army. The order of the day, of every day, was: "Hold Petrograd at all costs." One day, when inspecting a division headquarters at Alexandrovka, he saw a column of troops in full retreat. There was only one thing to be done. He mounted a horse, charged them, ordered them back into line, made them turn to face the enemy, and rode with them for a mile until he heard "the sickly-sweet nauseating whistle of the bullets," and at last returned to headquarters in a truck.

The house-to-house defense of Petrograd was never tested, although British tanks appeared in the suburbs and Yudenich's army seemed poised to enter the city. By throwing all his reserves at the invaders, Trotsky threw them back. The tide turned. Yudenich's army fled. With the knowledge that they had saved Petrograd, the Bolsheviks took heart. Soon Denikin's army in the Ukraine was rolled back, Kiev was relieved, the armies in the south began to yield, and by the spring of 1920 the Civil War was over, and there remained only a mopping-up campaign.

For his services in the defense of Petrograd, Trotsky was awarded the Order of the Red Banner. Petrograd, too, was awarded the order. To Trotsky's chagrin there was a third recipient of the order—Stalin, who had played only a minor role in the defense of the city. The fact that he was granted the order demonstrated neither his courage nor his military ability but the power he had generated within the Politburo. Trotsky observed with some satisfaction that when the orders were presented in a ceremony held in the Bolshoy Theater, Stalin quite properly failed to appear.

The Civil War came slowly to its end, but suddenly a new war appeared. The Poles invaded the Ukraine and captured Kiev. In the eyes of the Russians the cat had bitten the tiger and must be suitably punished. Lenin was adamant; he believed or half-believed that the arrival of the Red Army on Polish soil would bring about a Soviet Poland. Trotsky, too, was convinced that the Polish bourgeoisie had ordered the invasion and would inevitably go down to defeat in a workers' revolution. Mikhail Tukhachevsky, a twenty-seven-year-old officer, was given overall command of the Red armies which reached the outskirts of Warsaw in August 1920, only to be hurled back by a sudden powerful counteroffensive made all the easier by a grave defect in the grouping of the Red troops, who were so sure of themselves that they permitted a wide break in their lines. Through this break Marshal Pilsudski poured his troops, bringing about a rout of the Red armies. The Poles captured 70,000 prisoners, 200 guns, and 1,000 machine guns. It was a decisive defeat, and little more was heard during meetings of the Politburo about Soviet Poland.

Trotsky, as minister of war, was as responsible for the defeat as anyone. In later years he wrote that he had objected to the war from the beginning, which was not true, and had assented to it "in order to go along with Lenin," which was perhaps only partially true. The truth was that he had hoped like all the Politburo to enter Red Warsaw in triumph, and soon it would be the turn of Red Berlin, and Red Paris. Warsaw was the key to Europe: not Afghanistan. When the invasion failed, he made the best of it and was one of those who suggested that at the peace conference Poland should be given generous boundaries.

The wars were over, or nearly over. In the spring of 1920 Trotsky took his first holiday since the beginning of the Revolution. He took over the palatial country house of a rich Muscovite about twenty-five miles out of Moscow, installing himself in two large rooms on the second floor. The frost had damaged the plumbing, the grand staircase was too rickety to be used, and the second floor was therefore reached by a ladder. The

country house possessed a large collection of paintings, including Canalettos, and these were now taste-
fully arranged in the enormous drawing room on the
ground floor which had been turned into a public
museum. The large windows of the rooms on the upper
floor looked out on vast tree-covered plains with some
low hills on the horizon. It was very quiet there: an
ideal place for a man to recuperate, to be visited by his
doctors—for his health was giving him cause for
anxiety—to do some leisurely hunting and some unhur-
ried writing. In particular he was working on the
manifesto of the Communist International which would
meet in the summer; inevitably it would become a
small book or a thick pamphlet. Meanwhile, he received occasional visitors and discovered what many
active men have discovered before him: solitude and
leisure sometimes act like poisons. He went out for
walks and found himself just as restless as before.
Hunting quietened him, perhaps because it involved a
certain amount of ingenuity and had a deliberate
purpose. He enjoyed hunting because it blanked out his
mind to other things. "The attraction of hunting," he
wrote, "is that it acts on the mind like a poultice on a
sore."

Trotsky on the second floor of the palatial country
house was acting in character. He had rarely lived long
in any one place; he was the permanent refugee, never
putting down roots, always wandering, happiest when
he was in his armored train and every morning saw the
dawn from a new place. The house in the country was
only a tent, soon to be abandoned. The Canalettos and
the grand staircase which no one was allowed to
descend for fear that the entire structure would collapse were forgotten. After two months Trotsky returned
to Moscow.

In the autumn of the year the war flared up again in
the south. General Peter Wrangel, who had escaped to
Constantinople, assumed command of the remnants of
Denikin's White Army scattered in the region north of
the Black Sea. There were about 130,000 men in his
army, well-equipped by the French who were determined, unlike the British and the Americans, to make

one last attempt to wrest Russia from its Communist rulers. Wrangel set up his headquarters in the Crimea. He was a brilliant general commanding troops who had lost their morale, yet he fought on, contesting every inch of ground, sometimes inflicting heavy losses on the Red Army, which was determined to drive him into the sea.

On the morning of October 27, Trotsky set out in the armored train for the south to inspect the defenses, to discuss problems with the field commanders, and to see the front for himself. That same day he drew up a proclamation, which was printed in *V Puti*, enumerating many of the campaigns in which the train had taken part and ending with the words "Let this campaign be the last." The train spent two days in Kharkov, the headquarters of the southern command, where General Mikhail Frunze, later to succeed Trotsky as commissar for war, was in command, and where Trotsky had the opportunity to see his friend Christian Rakovsky, who was now president of the Ukraine. So they talked all day and through the night, and the train moved south again, and at Alexandrovsk a huge automobile was unloaded and Trotsky drove across endless snow-covered fields for a rendezvous with a Red commander and his staff officer. Night had fallen; it was very cold; there were no signposts on the roads. He had a rather stormy meeting with the commander in a small, cluttered house, a map spread on the table, the only light provided by a candle. The young commander was a Petrograd worker; the staff officer was a professional. They argued, and finally Trotsky made his decision, and the argument was over. Trotsky returned to his train and headed for Moscow. The train, which was heavily loaded, and therefore driven by two engines, headed north at moderate speed. Just when it steamed into Moscow, there came news that Wrangel's forces had been decisively defeated and the survivors were being carried away from the Crimea on French warships.

It was November 14, 1920. The last campaign of the Civil War was over.

THE NIGHTMARE OF KRONSTADT 14

For the Russian people the winter of 1920–21 brought the peace of exhaustion. In Petrograd and Moscow and all the war-torn areas of the south and east the people were close to starvation and emotionally drained. It was a hard, savage winter; telegraph lines were down; food trains from Siberia and the North Caucasus were stalled and sometimes abandoned in snowdrifts; there was massive unemployment due to lack of fuel; and the people who had trusted the Soviet government for so long found themselves at last questioning its competence to rule and demanding explanations for its dictatorial acts. In the trade unions especially there was a growing feeling that Lenin and Trotsky had outlived their usefulness. The government called itself "the dictatorship of the proletariat" but was singularly lacking in its understanding of the workingmen.

The working class was growing restless and rebellious, and it would grow more restless and more rebellious as the terrible winter continued. On January 22, 1921, the meager bread rations for Petrograd, Moscow, and other large cities were cut by a third. On

February 6, *Pravda* announced that the country was confronted with a grim fuel crisis. Six days later nearly all the large industries of Petrograd, including the famous Putilov metal works, closed down for lack of fuel. The bread lines grew longer, and the death rate soared. Even in *Pravda* there were long articles by men who spoke openly of the widening gap between the government and the workers, between the dictatorship of the proletariat and the proletariat itself. The country was being ruled by an incompetent bureaucracy and a Tcheka which was coming more and more to resemble the murderous *oprichniki*, the black-coated palace guard of Ivan the Terrible. Communism had lost its human face.

Lenin and Trotsky regarded themselves as superb artisans of revolution, and at the time of the revolution and under war communism they were able to control and command the state machinery. Now, at a time of precarious peace, they could feel the state machinery slipping out of their hands and they consequently acted with an increasing impatience and intolerance. Neither of them had the slightest experience or understanding of economic forces: they gave orders and were surprised when their orders were disobeyed not because the Russians were unwilling but because economic forces prevented them; nor did their study of Marxist theory suggest any response to the question: What happens when the proletariat is sick to death of the dictatorship which acts in its name?

By the spring of 1921 it was becoming obvious that extreme measures would have to be taken. Trotsky recognized two alternatives: the total mobilization of labor with the entire labor force under strict disciplined regimentation or a relaxation of state controls leading to a certain amount of private industry. It was generally believed that Trotsky preferred the first to the second, his absolutist mind demanding an absolutist solution, for he had envisioned the working force as an army under military discipline working for the state. In fact, even before Lenin, he proposed most of the stratagems included later under the generic name of the New

Economic Policy. But these were propositions only, and he was not himself in a position to impose these ideas on the government. Similarly with the trade unions which he wanted to dissolve on the grounds that the workers needed no special protection from the state. Many of the workers saw in the trade unions their only protection against the all-devouring state, but only on condition that they were in control of the trade unions: the danger was that the government would appoint the trade-union officials, who would simply issue orders from above.

The popular image of Trotsky at this time was of a man who arrived easily at harsh, rigorous, and inhuman solutions, while Lenin, the "little father," proposed the more kindly and human solutions. In fact, Lenin was harsh and rigorous at all times; Trotsky was far more human, far more sensitive to the needs of others, and he possessed a much wider knowledge of world affairs and therefore knew how the outside world judged the Communist government and sometimes acted accordingly. They formed the duumvirate, and lesser mortals lay in their shadow.

One of these lesser mortals was Grigory Zinoviev, whose official posts included being chairman of the executive committee of the Petrograd Soviet. He had all the powers of the governor of the city. Confronted by unrest and near-rebellion, he acted exactly as a medieval governor might have acted. The workers, who were locked out because there was no fuel for their machines, were joined by workmen from the Trubetskoy factory, the Baltiisky mills, the Galernaya dockyards, and many more. They attempted to hold demonstrations in the streets. Zinoviev gave orders that they should be dispersed by the military, especially by the armed *kursanty*, the cadets in the military school. The workers were unarmed; many were shot; others were arrested by the Tcheka. Zinoviev reported to Lenin and Trotsky in Moscow that the unrest in Petrograd was caused by White conspirators. He declared martial law on February 24, 1921, called for more troops, placed a curfew on the city, forbade all meetings "whether in the open or in enclosed places," and proclaimed that anyone who disobeyed these orders would be dealt with with the severity appropriate in time of war, by which he meant they would be shot.

Among the interested observers of the street demonstrations and the subsequent shootings were some delegates from the naval fortress of Kronstadt, an island guarding the approaches to Petrograd. They were in sympathy with the Petrograd workers and they hoped they could prevail upon the government to put an end to rule by decree and to moderate its policies. Their reports on the situation in Petrograd were accepted by the sailors of Kronstadt, whom Trotsky and others had described as "the finest flower of the Revolution." On March 1 the Kronstadt Soviet held a mass meeting on the island attended by about sixteen thousand sailors, Red Army men, and workmen. An invited guest was Mikhail Kalinin, who had the title of President of the All-Russian Soviet Executive Committee, which meant that he was the President of the Soviet Union. As President, he was greeted with full military honors, military bands, and banners.

The mass meeting was asked to examine a resolution drawn up by sailors of the warship *Petropavlovsk*. There was overwhelming agreement with the resolution, although Kalinin, of necessity, argued against it. What the sailors wanted and were prepared to go to almost any lengths to obtain was a society where there was freedom of choice within the framework of communism. They did not yet know that this was impossible. They thought they were demanding a few elementary changes in the methods of communist rule, and they were to learn that these changes involved a complete change of direction of the communist state, for which neither Lenin nor Trotsky were prepared.

The resolution adopted at Kronstadt has survived, and reads as follows:

Resolution of the General Meeting
of the Crews of the First and Second Squadrons
of the Baltic Fleet March 1, 1921

Having heard the Report of the Representatives sent by the General Meeting of Ship Crews to Petrograd to investigate the situation there, Resolved:

1. In view of the fact that the present Soviets do not express the will of the workers and the peasants, immediately to hold new elections by secret ballot, the pre-election campaign to have full freedom of agitation among the workers and peasants.

2. To establish freedom of speech and press for workers and peasants, for Anarchists and Left Socialist parties.

3. To secure freedom of assembly for labor unions and peasant organizations.

4. To call a non-partisan conference of the workers, Red Army soldiers and sailors of Petrograd, Kronstadt, and Petrograd province, no later than March 10, 1921.

5. To liberate all the political prisoners of the Socialist parties, as well as all workers, peasants, soldiers and sailors imprisoned in connection with the labor and peasant movements.

6. To elect a commission to review the cases of those held in prisons and labor camps.

7. To abolish all the political sections because no party should be given special privileges in the propagation of its ideas or receive the financial support of the government for such purposes. Instead there should be established educational and cultural commissions, locally elected and financed by the government.

8. To abolish immediately the armed guards who suppress the traffic in foodstuffs.

9. To equalize the rations of all workers, with the exception of those employed in trade detrimental to health.

10. To abolish Communist detachments in all branches of the Army, as well as Communist guards kept on duty in mills and factories. If such guards or military detachments are deemed necessary, they are to be appointed from the ranks, and in the factories only with the agreement of the workers.

11. To give the peasants complete liberty of action with regard to their land and also the right to keep cattle which they must look after themselves without employing hired labor.

12. To demand that the Army in all its branches and our

      comrades the *kursanty* shall concur in our resolution.
13. To demand that the press shall give extensive publicity to our resolutions.
14. To create a mobile Control Commission.
15. To permit workmen to take part in small scale labor provided they do not employ hired labor.

Such was the charter proposed by the Kronstadt sailors and passed by an overwhelming majority of the men in the fortress and on the ships.

Four days later the Petrograd Soviet met in the Tauride Palace under the chairmanship of Zinoviev. A heavy guard of *kursanty* and Tchekist soldiers with fixed bayonets surrounded the chairman, who believed he was in danger of being assassinated. He denounced the Kronstadt sailors in a shrill voice and accused them of betraying the Republic. For the first time a public audience heard the name of General Kozlovsky who, according to Zinoviev, had organized the conspiracy. The former Tsarist General Kozlovsky was acting as an adviser on artillery at Kronstadt and had been appointed by Trotsky. He was not leading anything. He simply obeyed the orders of the Provisional Revolutionary Committee which the sailors had established.

Lenin and Trotsky, receiving their information from Zinoviev, thundered against the Kronstadt sailors, describing them as mutineers engaged in a conspiracy led by a Tsarist general and Social Revolutionary traitors. Moscow broadcast denunciations of the uprising, although in fact there had been no uprising, and *Pravda* bitterly attacked the mutineers who were being financed by the French secret service. It is unlikely that either Lenin or Trotsky believed that the French secret service had anything to do with it. Defiant sailors were demanding more freedom, and the government had not the slightest intention of giving it to them. They must therefore be shown to be in the pay of a foreign power; they were reptiles, and must be stamped out. Trotsky appears to have thought at first that the sailors could be argued out of their position or that a compromise could be reached, but Lenin was adamant. At all costs the movement must be crushed.

Trotsky arrived in Petrograd by special train on the night of March 4–5, 1921. He immediately went into conference with Zinoviev, ordered the disarming and imprisonment of the disaffected soldiers of the Petrograd garrison, approved Zinoviev's plan for arresting the families of the sailors who had homes in Petrograd, and issued an ultimatum:

> The Workers' and Peasants' Government has decreed that Kronstadt and the rebellious ships must immediately submit to the authority of the Soviet Republic.
>
> I command all who have raised their hands against the Socialist fatherland to lay down their arms at once. The obdurate are to be disarmed and turned over to the Soviet authorities. The arrested commissars and other representatives of the Government are to be liberated at once. Only those surrendering unconditionally may count on the mercy of the Soviet Republic.
>
> Simultaneously with this warning I am issuing orders for the suppression of the mutiny and the subjection of the mutineers by armed force. Responsibility for the harm that may be suffered by the peaceful population will fall entirely on the heads of the counter-revolutionary mutineers.
>
> This warning is final.
>
> Trotsky
> Chairman of the
> Revolutionary Military Council
> of the Republic
> Kamenev*
> Commander-in-Chief

The sailors refused to submit. They announced on their radio and in their newspaper, the *Kronstadt Izvestia*, that they would fight only in self-defense and would not attack. They had arrested the Bolshevik commissars in Kronstadt, but had committed no other

---

* Sergey Sergeyevich Kamenev was made commander in chief of the armed forces of the Soviet Republic in July 1919. He was a former colonel commanding the 30th Poltava Regiment at the time of the October Revolution. He owed his appointment to Trotsky, who drew most of his army commanders from the ranks of former Tsarist officers. In September 1918, after the battle of Kazan, he succeeded Vatsekis in command of the Eastern front. He is not to be confused with Lev Borisovich Kamenev, who was one of the major figures in the Central Committee and Trotsky's brother-in-law.

crimes against the state. They hoped to hold off the attackers until the ice melted, when they would be doubly secure. The fortress was well provided with heavy artillery, but the heaviest guns pointed west, for the purpose of the fortress was to blast out of the sea all enemy ships advancing on Petrograd. They had four dreadnoughts armed with twelve 12-inch guns, two cruisers armed with 10-inch guns, and three more cruisers armed with 6-inch guns. There were no ice-breakers and all the warships were caught in the ice. Provisions and fuel were running low, but there was enough ammunition to last a long siege. There were other fortresses nearby, but these were on land and their guns could be turned on Kronstadt, for they remained loyal to the government. The sailors rejected Trotsky's ultimatum and waited for the first blow.

The first direct attack came on the night of March 8 during a violent snowstorm. Most of the attackers were beaten back, and the few who arrived under the walls of Kronstadt surrendered to the machine gunners who appeared unexpectedly in the mist and snow. The naval shells, provided with short fuses, made huge lakes in the ice, and hundreds of the attackers were drowned. Political commissars reported that morale was low and many soldiers were wondering aloud why they should be fighting against their brothers. These reports were seen by Trotsky, who called up more student cadets and ordered the disbandment of regiments with low morale. The *Kronstadt Izvestia* celebrated the arrival of Trotsky in Petrograd in an editorial entitled "Let the Whole World Know":

> Field-Marshal Trotsky, standing up to his knees in the blood of the workers, has fired the first shot against revolutionary Kronstadt, which rose up against the government of the Communists to restore the real power of the Soviets.

Although many thousands of pages were later written about the causes of the Kronstadt uprising, there can be little doubt that the *Kronstadt Izvestia* was perfectly accurate when it said that the aim of the sailors was "to restore the real power of the Soviets," by which they meant the Soviets' or councils of soldiers', sailors', workers', and peasants' deputies. The Soviets had no voice. All decisions were made at the top. No discussions were permitted. Zinoviev, an incompetent administrator, should have been removed long before, but there existed no channel by which the people could express their contempt for him and their distrust of his policies. In theory the Soviets were powerful instruments of government. In fact Zinoviev ruled like a dictator, obedient only to the dictators who ruled from Moscow. It was a situation made for rebellion, and the Kronstadt sailors, who were traditionally the first to revolt, took courage from their traditions. Lenin and Trotsky, accustomed to solving problems with extreme brutality or by annihilating the problem makers, had no difficulty convincing themselves that this was pure and simple mutiny to be punished by death. The Kronstadt sailors must be wiped out. Their legitimate grievances must be characterized as treacherous demands, and once they had been suitably punished they must be thrown into the trash can of history.

Two more attacks on Kronstadt took place, on the 10th and 12th of March, and were repulsed with great losses to the attackers. Trotsky had ordered the reduction of the rebel fortress "at all costs," and on March 16 there came the all-out attack with Tukhachevsky's soldiers advancing across the ice in overwhelming numbers. They were robed in white sheets; so were many of the defenders. By dawn on March 17 the attackers succeeded in reaching the outer defenses of Kronstadt, cutting through the barbed wire and establishing a foothold on the island. Fighting continued through the day, and by the early morning of the 18th the town and the warships were in the hands of Tukhachevsky's forces and the Tchekists who had accompanied them. Fierce hand-to-hand fighting continued for several hours. Captured sailors were put up against a wall and shot or roped together and led off across the ice to prisons in Petrograd. The Tchekists showed no mercy, unlike the sailors who had spared all their Communist prisoners. Some of the sailors, including their leader, Stepan Petrichenko, escaped to Finland, but the greater number were either killed in battle or by firing squads. The government of Finland sent a note to the Soviet government demanding that it pick up the thousands of bodies lying on the ice which would inevitably be swept onto the Finnish shores when the thaw came.

Alexander Berkman, the American anarchist who happened to be in Petrograd at this time, wrote two unhappy entries in his diary:

> March 17. Kronstadt has fallen today. Thousands of sailors and workers lie dead in its streets. Summary execution of prisoners and hostages continues.
>
> March 28. The victors are celebrating the anniversary of the Commune of 1871. Trotsky and Zinoviev denounce Thiers and Galliffet for the slaughter of the Paris rebels.

Something had gone terribly wrong, and Trotsky, even more than Lenin, was responsible. In his autobiography Trotsky scarcely mentions the Kronstadt rebellion and says nothing at all about his own involvement with it; it was something that happened in passing, and far away, or so he would lead us to believe. But in fact he was at the heart of it, giving orders, urging the use of the utmost force to reduce the fortress and the utmost terror to prevent anything like it happening again. Lenin and Trotsky made a special journey to Petrograd a few days later and were photographed with a large group of soldiers who had taken part in the suppression of the uprising.

Kronstadt was a symbol of the government's inadequacy to deal with a changing situation. Because it was a dictatorship, it was cut off from the people, did not know what the people were thinking and feeling, and was indifferent to their suffering. The thousands of bodies lying on the ice, attackers and defenders alike, testified to the government's malice, stupidity, and absurdity.

In his posthumously published life of Stalin, Trotsky

devotes a single sentence to the rebellion: "Suffice it to say that what the Soviet government did reluctantly at Kronstadt was a tragic necessity; naturally the revolutionary government could not have 'presented' the fortress that protected Petrograd to the insurgent sailors only because a few dubious Anarchists and Social Revolutionaries were sponsoring a handful of reactionary peasants and soldiers in rebellion." This kind of argument was unworthy of Trotsky and had the disadvantage that it was a direct lie. The Kronstadt sailors were not "a handful of reactionary peasants and soldiers in rebellion" and they were not sponsored by "dubious Anarchists and Social Revolutionaries" any more than they were sponsored by General Kozlovsky. The ghosts of the dead sailors were not so easily laid.

Years passed, the Kronstadt rebellion was gradually forgotten, and Trotsky maintained his silence. It was not until 1938 that he felt the need to assert his complete innocence at a time when it was beginning to be believed that the seeds of Stalin's total inhumanity and ruthlessness were to be found in the early years of the Revolution, that in fact Lenin and Trotsky had conceived the monstrous regime of Stalin, not intentionally, but as it were accidentally, having laid down the inhuman and merciless rules which Stalin would later use to his own advantage. Trotsky replied in two essays published in January and June 1938. The first was a more or less theoretical defense of the suppression, based on the supposition that the Kronstadt sailors were counterrevolutionaries, anarchists, Social Revolutionaries, and White officers determined to bring down the government. The second article was a more personal statement designed to rebut the accusation of Anton Ciliga in his book *In the Country of the Big Lie* that more than ten thousand seamen had been shot at Trotsky's orders. Trotsky replied:

The truth of the matter is that *I did not participate in the least in the suppression of the Kronstadt rebellion, nor in the repressions following the suppression.* In my eyes this very fact is of no political significance. I was a member of the government. I considered the quelling of the rebellion necessary and therefore bear responsibility for the suppression . . .

The decision to suppress the rebellion by military force, *if the fortress could not be induced to surrender, first by peace negotiations, then through an ultimatum*—this general decision was adopted with my direct participation. But after the decision was taken, I continued to remain in Moscow and took no part, direct or indirect, in the military operations. Concerning the subsequent repressions, they were completely the work of the Tcheka . . .

I slipped aside completely and demonstratively from this affair. Concerning the repressions, as far as I remember, Dzerzhinsky had personal charge of them and Dzerzhinsky could not tolerate anyone's interference with his functions (and properly so).

The italics were supplied by Trotsky to emphasize his innocence, his distance from the affair. He would give the impression that he was in Moscow throughout the rebellion and that he played no role whatsoever, but accepted full responsibility because he was minister of war while at the same time rejecting all responsibility as an individual. The argument was unconvincing and proved nothing except his versatility in argument. The Kronstadt sailors continued to be shot in batches in the Petrograd prisons three months after the end of the uprising.

During this harsh winter there were other massacres equally horrible and less well known. While Trotsky was on an inspection tour in the Urals, the Red Army invaded Georgia, which had declared its independence on May 26, 1918. Georgia was a sovereign state ruled by a Menshevik government, with its own ambassador in Moscow. The attack, organized by Stalin with the approval of the Politburo and therefore with the approval of Lenin, came as a bolt from the blue. Trotsky was not consulted. He heard about it while he was in Ekaterinburg on February 21, 1921, and immediately sent off an urgent telegram to Sklyansky asking when the operation began and by whose orders. He learned that there had been a Bolshevik uprising which the Mensheviks had brutally suppressed, and the Red Army had therefore entered the country to safeguard it from Menshevik tyranny. The uprising was imaginary; there was no suppression; Georgia was at peace. When the Red Army crossed the frontiers, the Georgians resisted but were overwhelmed after hard fighting. Then the Tchekists took over, there were mass arrests and executions, all political parties except the Communist Party were banned, and Stalin together with his lieutenant Ordjonikidze became the undisputed rulers of the conquered territory. In vain Lenin called upon Ordjonikidze "to behave with special respect toward the sovereign organs of Georgia and to show special attentiveness and caution in dealing with the Georgian population." The terror continued, and Georgia which had enjoyed its independence for so short a time became a satrapy. The invasion showed, if it showed nothing else, the immense power of Stalin to do as he pleased. Once again Trotsky proclaimed his innocence, insisting that he had known nothing about the invasion until it was a *fait accompli*, forgetting that he as much as any man had helped to create the conditions under which a sudden and murderous invasion could be brought about with the greatest of ease. The government was lawless; it attacked Poland, because it thought wrongly that Poland was weak; it attacked the Kronstadt sailors and massacred them without listening to their legitimate grievances; it attacked Georgia and massacred the Georgians although it had signed a treaty of friendship with the legitimate government. Stalin intended to go on and invade Persia for no better reason than that Persia was on the border of Russia. In the eyes of Stalin and of Trotsky legitimacy meant nothing. In the name of the dictatorship of the proletariat any country could be attacked with impunity.

When Stalin established his own government in Georgia, he placed his own creatures in positions of command. He had no use for the small group of Georgian Bolsheviks who had remained in Georgia under Menshevik rule. They had their own leaders, their own traditions, their own way of looking at life. Stalin threw them into prison, executed some and made life intolerable for the rest. News of the repression of Georgian Bolsheviks reached Lenin during the last clouded months of his life, before his brain failed and he was removed from the scene. Almost his last political act was to denounce the oppressors of the Georgian Bolsheviks and to attempt to form a bloc with Trotsky against Stalin and Ordjonikidze, but by then it was too late.

Mistakes were being made all along the line. The government appeared to be incompetent to govern except by decrees enforced by means of the secret police, mass arrests, executions, long terms of imprisonment, and slave labor. The dream of a truly communist society was receding fast. Among the leaders Lenin alone felt a profound disgust for the way things were going, and now at last, when it was almost too late, he introduced a measure called the New Economic Policy which permitted trade to flow again by legalizing private traders and by restoring small-scale capitalism. He went about it cautiously. All through the spring and early summer the subject was debated in the Politburo; objections were raised and overridden; there were endless speeches. Finally, in August, the decree permitting private trading especially by the peasants was promulgated. "Every peasant must now know and remember that the more land he plants the greater will be the surplus of grain which remains in his complete possession," says the decree. In this way the peasants were encouraged to become capitalists, to sell their grain and produce at the current market prices. They would pay a graduated tax, and no longer would the armed Tchekists be able to descend on their farms and confiscate whatever they wanted. Small traders flourished, the economic lifeblood began to flow, people were given an incentive to work, and suddenly it was as though a huge weight had been lifted from the Russian people. "What is the danger," said Lenin, "considering that we retain full control of the factories, the transportation system, and foreign trade?" The knowledge that the whole country would benefit by free

Police photograph of Trotsky in his early twenties. *(Wide World)*

Trotsky (*second from left*) with a group of exiles during a pause on their way to Siberia.

General Ivanov addressing the court at Trotsky's trial in 1906.

Trotsky in his cell while awaiting trial.   (Pathfinder Press)

Lenin addressing a meeting on Sverdlov Square, May 1920,
with Trotsky beside him.
(Three Lions)

Trotsky outside the armored train of the Chairman of the
Revolutionary Military Council   *(Three Lions)*

Sergey Sedov, Trotsky's younger son.

Trotsky addressing mass meeting at Copenhagen in 1932.

Trotsky and his son Lyova at Royan in August 1933.

(Isaac Don Levine)

trading, even in a restricted form, came lamentably late. Trotsky preferred a continuation of war communism with labor armies under strict discipline and a continuation of requisitions. He delighted in seeing people lined up in orderly rows performing the tasks he had given to them. Fortunately he was outvoted, and the New Economic Policy came into being at Lenin's insistence as the only possible policy that would bring the country out of economic stagnation.

Almost overnight there came a feeling of liberation among a long-suffering people. Hope sprang in the air and danced before their eyes, for it seemed that many other oppressive laws were about to vanish. The New Economic Policy, known as NEP, represented a state of mind of quite extraordinary ebullience which found its expression in the music, the arts, and the writing of the period. It was even possible to hope that open criticism of the government would be permitted, and there was serious talk that an opposition newspaper might be encouraged. Above all, men hoped that the Tcheka, which had long outlived its usefulness, would be disbanded, that the all-powerful bureaucracy would be tamed, and that people would no longer live in fear.

For a little while it looked as though the worst was over.

15 THE LONG DEATH OF LENIN

In character Lenin and Trotsky were poles apart. It could be seen in their appearance, their way of walking, their way of issuing commands and making speeches, in their handwriting and their way of asking questions. They were men who wanted to dominate and were absolutely ruthless in their pursuit of domination, without scruples, without remorse. At whatever cost in human life they worked to overthrow the existing social system, and they dreamed of world revolution with themselves as its chief artificers. They knew exactly what they wanted, and they had thought deeply and brilliantly on how to obtain it. On most essential matters they were in total agreement. Nevertheless, their characters were so different and they were so abrasive in different ways that it is something of a miracle that they were able to work in harmony for so long.

In appearance Lenin was short, stocky, compact. He had a remarkably fine head, powerful features, a look of considerable distinction. There exists a photograph taken of him when he was in hiding in 1917, wearing a wig and without his beard and mustache. It was a remarkably youthful face, handsome and compelling. He could be taken for a ship's captain or a highly skilled mechanic, a man of great experience in the practical affairs of the world. With the beard he looked more the scholar, somewhat remote and impractical. He had a habit of cocking his head a little sideways when asking questions and this gave him an oddly sardonic appearance; in fact he cocked his head to one side because one eye had been damaged in a bicycling accident. He had great patience, asked short questions and listened intently to lengthy replies, hoping that somewhere in the reply there would be the answer to his question. Nearly always courteous, he could be witheringly brutal in summing up people's characters; and he prided himself on his judgment of character, and was often wrong. His handwriting, always quick, nervous and fluid, seemed at odds with the hard outlines of his ideas.

Trotsky, on the other hand, was tall, supple, accommodating, possessing an almost feminine grace of manner. Unlike Lenin, who was intensely practical even when he was dealing with totally impractical ideas, Trotsky lived a highly charged imaginative life and was much more instinctive in his actions than Lenin. He had the type of mentality that permits the act to be followed by the thought. He acted, and found the explanations and justifications later. Throughout most of his life he was an actor playing a role, dramatizing himself both for the public and himself. He dressed well, took pains with his appearance, and acquired many of the techniques of the actor. In addition, he possessed a wonderfully resonant voice which ranged from melting sweetness to raucous screeching, and he was at all times fully in control of it. He cut his beard and mustache according to his roles: trimmed at Brest-Litovsk, heavy and ragged during the Civil War, trimmed most carefully when he was in exile. He designed his own uniforms and during the Civil War appeared in at least six different uniforms, the most flamboyant being worn during the early stages of the war. Like Lenin he lived chastely; unlike Lenin he had an eye for beautiful women and enjoyed their company and could be very chivalrous. Lenin was surrounded by female secretaries, while Trotsky's secretaries were nearly always male. Trotsky's handwriting was unusually clear, upright and methodical, its machine-like precision learned during the years he was writing revolutionary tracts for a hectograph machine. Neither Lenin nor Trotsky had much feeling for painting or sculpture and they were both bored by ballet and opera. Lenin's taste was for nineteenth-century Russian authors, particularly Pushkin, Chernyshevsky, Tolstoy, and Turgenev. Trotsky reveled in French novels, particularly Flaubert, and read widely, if not always approvingly, in modern Russian literature.

It was not only that Lenin and Trotsky were poles apart, but they appeared to belong to different species, different races. They came to revolution by different roads and with different motives, Lenin's driving force arising out of passionate indignation over the execution of his older brother, hanged for an attempted assassination of Alexander III, while Trotsky found his driving force in an almost messianic belief that all the world's injustices could be put right by revolutionaries. Trotsky was a European, feeling at home in the West, and Lenin felt at home only in Russia. Trotsky was fastidious, intensely self-conscious, seeing himself in his mind's mirror, and Lenin was without any trace of self-consciousness and he was so little fastidious that he would wear the same crumpled suit for years, day after day, without having it washed or pressed. He was indifferent to all creature comforts, and was perfectly content to live in small cluttered rooms. Trotsky enjoyed large, spacious, undecorated rooms with the books in orderly rows. He prized neatness. Lenin was happy with a disorderly desk, papers piled on papers. When he wanted a particular paper, he usually knew where it was, although he had to struggle through a mountain of other papers to find it.

One day Lenin asked Trotsky what gave him the greatest pleasure when he was making his great journeys on his armored train during the Civil War. Trotsky thought for a while and said: "The neat fences." Lenin roared with laughter, and whenever Trotsky returned from one of the distant battlefronts, Lenin would say: "Did you see any fences?" For Trotsky a neat fence of freshly cut pine boards was a thing of beauty: it imposed order on a disorderly world. Lenin was surprised that so small an amount of neatness could give Trotsky such immense pleasure.

Perhaps it was because they were so different and therefore complemented one another that they were able to exist together as a duumvirate with so little friction. There were disagreements between them; brief quarrels sometimes flared up, but they were the quarrels of friends certain to be cleared up without bitterness, for they needed each other. Each had his separate sphere of influence, but the spheres overlapped. Stalin claimed later that Lenin and Trotsky were continually at loggerheads, but the surviving documents show them so often in agreement on matters of principle that it is as though a single mind was working. On most subjects they each knew what the other was thinking, and they came to the same conclusions by the same logical processes. What they had in common was their sharp, brutal, revolutionary intelligence. All their conscious lives they had been revolutionaries and they knew how revolutions work.

If Lenin had been at loggerheads with Trotsky, he would not have permitted him so much power and would have found reasons to recall him, to clip his claws. In his autobiography Trotsky describes their frequent meetings which were gay with laughter or somber with those heavy decisions which would soon become the laws of the land. They were pleased with each other, admired each other, and spoke to each other on a level of intimacy, like brothers. On military matters Lenin deferred to Trotsky, to the outrage of Stalin, who also regarded himself as a military authority. Trotsky was evidently speaking the truth in his autobiography when he described the vast powers that had been given to him:

> During the war I had practically unlimited power. The revolutionary tribunal held its sessions in my train, the

fronts were subordinate to me, and the bases auxiliary to the fronts—and at times nearly the entire territory belonging to the republic, not occupied by the Whites, consisted of bases and fortified regions.

Although Stalin, Zinoviev, Kamenev and others attempted at various times to place a limit on Trotsky's military powers, they always failed. In Lenin's eyes he was the one indispensable person in the cabinet. If Stalin, Zinoviev, or Kamenev died, the Soviet state would continue on the course set for it without any perceptible change and without a shudder; if Bukharin died, since he was the theorist of the party and theory had long ago been transformed into action, it would be the same; but if Trotsky died before the Civil War was over, the Red Army would immediately suffer from the absence of his coordinating power, his absolutely ruthless determination, his imaginative grasp and understanding of all the factors, both tangible and intangible, that bring about victories. The only possible alternative as minister of war would be Lenin himself, and he had neither the knowledge nor the energy to command the Red Army.

And what if Lenin died?

This thought, uppermost in the mind of Stalin, had become almost unthinkable to the vast majority of the Russian people. In a few years he had established himself as the ultimate authority, the father figure, the stern and forgiving icon whose image hung in almost every house and room in Russia. In the popular imagination he was somehow divorced from the bloody excesses of the revolution, though he had assented to them and encouraged them. Lenin had replaced the Tsar. But when a Tsar dies, the succession is assured, the government does not fall, there is no more than a brief interregnum until the new Tsar ascends the throne. Lenin had made no plans for the succession. Once, long ago, Trotsky was offered the post of Lenin's deputy. He refused it, either out of pride or because he thought the presence of a Jew in the highest place in the government would be resented by the Russian people or again out of a sense of humility. Lenin actually proposed at a meeting of the Central Committee that Trotsky be appointed chairman of the Soviet of People's Commissaries, the Soviet equivalent to prime minister, and Trotsky leaped to his feet, protesting. "Why not?" Lenin asked. "You were head of the Petrograd Soviet when it seized the power." Trotsky moved to reject the proposal, without debating it. He had not the slightest intention of assuming that particular burden. All this happened in the early months of the revolution when Trotsky was thinking of retiring from the government altogether and devoting himself to writing. With his great record of achievement, with his status as a living legend, he was the logical choice as Lenin's successor.

Lenin began to die in December 1921, having ruled Russia for a little more than four years.

He began to complain of headaches, vertigo, weakness, sleeplessness—sleeplessness was the worst. When he rose from his chair, he would sometimes have to grip the table to prevent himself from falling down. His skin was sallow, his face seemed drained of blood, his hands trembled, and during the following months people who knew him observed that he seemed to shrink, even his face and his huge Socratic forehead seemed to become much smaller. He continued to work, but with intense difficulty. He was only fifty-one and looked like an old man.

He was so ill that he went to live on his estate in the village of Gorki, not far from Moscow, being driven there in a superb Rolls-Royce provided with caterpillar treads to take him over the snow. His brain was clear, he could still write lucidly, and he continued to send directives to the party leaders. "I am ill and stupid," he wrote, but the statement was only half true. He was not in the least stupid, but his body was very weak, he suffered from terrible stomach upsets, he could not sleep, and his brain kept racing as he pondered all the problems of the young Soviet state. But by the end of March 1922 he was well enough to attend the Eleventh Communist Party Congress and to deliver a speech attacking the bureaucracy, their inefficiency and lack of direction. "The machine tears itself out of our hands," he said, "as though there is a man who drives it, but the machine does not go in the direction where it is driven." He was speaking not only about the bureaucracy but about the entire state apparatus which he had created. Trotsky, who also spoke at the Congress, said very much the same thing more reasonably, without Lenin's passionate indignation. Six days later Lenin spoke very briefly and then declared the Congress closed. He never spoke in public again. At this Congress, where Stalin did not speak, Kamenev, Lenin, Rykov, Stalin, Tomsky, Trotsky, and Zinoviev were elected to the enlarged Politburo, and Stalin became General Secretary, a position that would permit him to gather vast powers in his hands.

Seven weeks later Lenin had his first stroke. It left him paralyzed on the right side, he could no longer speak or walk, and even when he made signs it was impossible to understand what he was trying to communicate. A few days earlier, while fishing in a channel of the Moskva River, Trotsky slipped and tore the ligaments of his foot. Of the duumvirate one was mortally ill, the other was immobilized. Trotsky remained in bed and heard about Lenin's stroke from Bukharin. "The doctors," said Bukharin, "are absolutely at a loss."

This was not quite true. The doctors knew what had happened and were hopeful that he would recover the power of speech and the use of the right side of his body, and in fact with their treatment he did recover. By July he was walking and talking. In October he returned to the Kremlin and presided over meetings of the Politburo. He tired easily, but looked better than he had looked for some time.

On the morning of December 13, 1922, Lenin had his second stroke. There was vomiting, nausea, pain, weakness, yet he remained completely coherent. The doctors insisted that he should leave the Kremlin immediately and return to Gorki, but somehow he succeeded in doing everything he intended to do that day.

One of the things he intended to do was to ensure that a certain Nikolay Rozhkov, a former Menshevik and author of a well-known history of Russia, should be prevented from living in Moscow, where he wanted to work in the libraries. Lenin, obsessed with a continuing hatred for the Mensheviks, and alarmed because the Politburo had permitted him to return to Moscow, wrote an angry letter to the Politburo, once more denouncing the professor, who was in fact quite harmless. "This Rozhkov is the enemy!" Lenin thundered, and it was his custom to denounce Rozhkov to everyone who entered his office, painting him in the blackest colors, so that it was a wonder the man escaped arrest and execution. When Lenin thundered, things usually happened. This time he thundered, and nothing at all happened.

Shortly after noon he received Stalin, who remained with him for about two hours. We do not know what was said: it was probably about the trade monopoly, the troubles in Georgia, where Stalin had acted with extraordinary high-handedness, and the forthcoming plenary session of the Central Committee. Stalin wanted to open free-trade ports in Petrograd and Novorossisk on the Black Sea, and Lenin was absolutely determined to have nothing to do with capitalist enterprises of this kind. What is certain is that Lenin argued vigorously with Stalin and that they took up opposing positions, and it appears likely that Lenin bitterly upbraided Stalin. The dying Lenin confronted the implacable Stalin, who had already embarked on the course that would bring him to supreme power. Stalin observed that Lenin was sick and would not last very much longer. The time had come for Stalin to set in motion the vast bureaucracy he controlled in order to offset any decisions by Lenin to remove him or to reduce his power. It was a crucial meeting, a parting of the ways. And beyond the fact that they had now at last found themselves on a collision course, and that all this was revealed to them in the two-hour meeting, we cannot be sure exactly what happened.

Early in the afternoon, after Stalin had gone, Lenin dictated an urgent letter to Trotsky imploring him to bring up the question of the monopoly at the plenum and "to defend our common view of the unconditional necessity of preserving and enforcing this monopoly." The letter clearly implied that Lenin would be unable to speak and had chosen Trotsky as the champion of his ideas against Stalin.

This second stroke, actually two strokes in quick succession, was not in itself very destructive. It caused Lenin great discomfort but did not impair his brain. The doctors feared however that it was the preliminary tremor before the earthquake; they expected a third, more massive stroke that would either kill him or paralyze him so completely that he would be reduced to the state of a vegetable. They wanted him to retire to Gorki, but the weather was too bad, the roads were blocked with snow, they discussed taking him there by air sleigh, that is, a sleigh powered by an airplane engine with a propellor, and then decided it would be safer altogether if he remained in the Kremlin. If he had gone to Gorki, it is unlikely that he would have been able to compose and organize the remarkable series of letters, directives and memoranda dictated during the following ten weeks before his brain failed; nor would it have been possible for him to place in a safe hiding place those letters that had to be concealed. Stalin had his spies and agents everywhere, even in Lenin's secretariat, and was now more than ever determined to move into the vacuum caused by the slow withering away of Lenin's authority.

The most famous of these letters, addressed to the Congress of the Communist Party, has been described as his last will and testament. It is neither will nor testament; he leaves no property, but names six heirs and comments on all of them. He comes to no final decision but leaves the Communist Party to make its own choice. He clearly prefers Trotsky but not to the extent that he will say outright that Trotsky is worthy of the succession; and he emphasizes that Stalin is the least worthy and must be removed from office. It is abundantly clear that Lenin had not wrestled with the problem of the succession; he had thought about it,

pondered some of its implications, and arrived at no
certain conclusions. During the morning of December
23 Lenin, allowed by his doctors to dictate for four
minutes a day, summoned one of his secretary typists,
Maria Volodicheva, and dictated the first paragraphs of
what would become a lengthy letter to the Congress in
which he proposed, following Trotsky, that the decisions of the State Planning Commission should acquire
legislative force and that fifty to a hundred members of
the working class should be recruited to the Central
Committee. On the following day he dictated for a
considerably longer period and for the first time expressed his fear of a major split in the party. He said:

> Comrade Stalin, having become General Secretary, has
> unlimited authority concentrated in his hands, and I am
> not sure whether he will always be capable of using that
> authority with sufficient caution. Comrade Trotsky, on the
> other hand, as his struggle against the Central Committee
> on the question of the People's Commissariat for Commu-
> nications has already proved, is distinguished not only by
> outstanding ability. He is personally perhaps the most
> capable man in the present Central Committee, but he has
> displayed excessive self-assurance and shown an exces-
> sive preoccupation with the purely administrative side of
> the work.
>
> These two qualities of the two outstanding leaders of the
> present Central Committee can inadvertently lead to a
> split, and if our party does not take steps to avoid this, the
> split may come unexpectedly.
>
> I shall not give any further appraisals of the personal
> qualities of other members of the Central Committee. I
> shall just recall that the October episode with Zinoviev and
> Kamenev was, of course, no accident, but neither can the
> blame for it be laid upon them personally, any more than
> non-Bolshevism can upon Trotsky.
>
> Speaking of the young Central Committee members, I
> wish to say a few words about Bukharin and Pyatakov.
> They are, in my opinion, the most outstanding figures
> (among the youngest ones), and the following must be born
> in mind about them: Bukharin is not only a most valuable
> and major theorist of the party, but his theoretical views
> can be classified as fully Marxist only with great reserve,

for there is something scholastic about him (he has never made a study of dialectics and, I think, never fully understood it).

On the following day he added two brief paragraphs concerning Bukharin and Pyatakov:

> As for Pyatakov, he is unquestionably a man of exceptional will-power and ability, but shows too much zeal for administrating and the administrative side of the work to be relied upon in a serious political matter.
> Both of these remarks, of course, are made only for the present, on the assumption that both these outstanding and devoted party workers fail to find an occasion to enhance their knowledge and amend their one-sidedness.

Lenin remarked about both Trotsky and Pyatakov that they showed too much zeal for the administrative side of their work. What he meant by this is not entirely clear, since he approved of good administrators and often spoke of the terrible lack of them in Russia. Clearly administrative ability was not enough: the new leaders must possess a deep knowledge of Marxist dialectics and, implicit in his argument, a larger knowledge of historical and social forces. They lacked the large view. It was as though he was saying: "They all need more training and experience. Bukharin is lost in his theories. Trotsky and Pyatakov are enmeshed in administrative affairs. Stalin is too cruel, while Kamenev and Zinoviev are too weak." He was not only arriving at unsatisfactory conclusions but by insisting far more on their faults than on their virtues he was putting himself in a position where it was impossible to make a choice. One quality that was rated highly by Lenin was assurance. Could it be said that Trotsky with his "excessive self-assurance" was of lesser merit than Pyatakov with his "exceptional will-power"? The ambiguities of judgment were clouding the issue.

Ten days after dictating his summary of six men's characters and their suitability for the succession, Lenin dictated to another secretary, Lydia Fotieva, an indictment of Stalin intended to remove him from the list. He said:

> Stalin is too rough, and this defect, although quite tolerable in our midst and in dealings among us Communists, becomes intolerable in a General Secretary. That is why I suggest that the comrades think about a way of removing Stalin from that post and appointing another man in his stead who in all other respects differs from Comrade Stalin in having only one advantage, namely, that of being more tolerant, more loyal, more polite, and more considerate to the comrades, less capricious, etc. This circumstance may appear to be a negligible detail. But I think that from the standpoint of creating safeguards against a split and from the standpoint of what I wrote above about the relationship between Stalin and Trotsky it is not a detail, or it is a detail that can assume vital importance.

Lenin himself was not especially noted for those bourgeois virtues which he found so lacking in Stalin: tolerance, loyalty, politeness, consideration, lack of caprice. He had institutionalized many kinds of treachery and should not have been so surprised when he learned that Stalin was ruthlessly reaching out for power. But his words were prophetic: the relationship between Stalin and Trotsky was not a detail. On the contrary, this totally unnecessary personal quarrel was to bring about such convulsions in Russia that there was scarcely anyone in the country except the police who did not suffer from it.

Lenin's indictment of Stalin was final. He regarded Stalin as an intolerable menace to the party. Stalin derived some comfort from the opening words. "In these times," he declared, "it was necessary to be rough." But even Lenin, who regarded the killing of the royal family, the aristocracy, the landlords, the bourgeoisie, the Mensheviks, the Social Revolutionaries, and all the other parties in Russia with detachment, could never have guessed how rough Stalin could be.

Nevertheless he knew how savagely brutal Stalin could be to Lenin's wife, Nadezhda Krupskaya, for on

December 22 Stalin had telephoned her and cursed her
with extraordinary violence for permitting Lenin to
study party documents at a time when he was under his
doctor's orders to rest, an order reinforced by a decision
of the Central Committee. He threatened to have her
put on trial before the party disciplinary committee.
What provoked this outburst was a message dictated
by Lenin to his wife on the previous day addressed to
Trotsky and urging a display of unity and an unrelenting attack against those who were fighting the trade
monopoly. Krupskaya added a brief note: "V.I. also
requests you to telephone your reply." The message
was sent by hand to Trotsky, who was in bed and
suffering from lumbago. Trotsky answered that he was
in total agreement with Lenin and would continue the
fight. Stalin heard about the incident: the messenger
may have opened the letter and copied it, or Stalin may
have tapped Trotsky's telephone, or someone in Lenin's
entourage may have overheard him when he was
dictating to his wife. It is certain that Stalin heard
about it, and it is equally certain that Lenin heard
about Stalin's denunciation of Krupskaya over the
telephone either on the same day or a few days later.
Stalin had counted on Lenin's early death or at least on
Lenin's silence, and it appeared that Lenin was quickly
recovering and fighting back from a position of
strength.

For two more months Lenin occupied himself with his
work: documents were read to him, he dictated articles,
he considered, dismissed, and considered again a vast
reorganization of the party. "We are forced to consider
a radical change in our entire view of socialism," he
said, but never made clear exactly what direction he
wanted to pursue. His health fluctuated. There were
days when he was completely lucid, other days when
he had neither the will nor the energy to speak. On
March 5, 1923, he dictated two important letters. The
letter to Trotsky urged and demanded that he should
take up the Georgian question against Stalin. The letter
to Stalin demanded a formal apology for his tirade
against Krupskaya; unless the apology was forthcom-

ing Lenin proposed to break off all relations with Stalin. The letter to Trotsky was signed "with best comradely greetings," the letter to Stalin was signed "respectfully yours," the coldest and most formal of greetings.

With these two letters the dramatic quarrel between Lenin and Stalin came to an end. Four days later Lenin suffered his third stroke and took no further part in the affairs of Russia. On May 12 he was carried out of the Kremlin on a stretcher and for the rest of his life, except for a visit to the Kremlin in October for a last look at his office and his books, he remained in Gorki.

When Lenin's biographers describe the last months of his life, they usually assume the tone of solemnity appropriate to the slow death of a great prince. They generally forget that while there is great sadness and also fear concerning the succession of power, there is an element of relief. He was so dominating a figure that the little men grew weary in his shadow. His reign which was so brief and so momentous would soon be over and they would be free to walk in the sunlight.

In Russia there was now no final authority; there was a vacuum not yet clearly defined as a vacuum. Stalin, Kamenev, and Zinoviev ruled and did not rule. As always when a dictator is dying, there was outward calm and inner confusion, the government marking time or moving forward by its accumulated momentum. The weather vanes begin to spin even when there is no wind. This is the time when the principle of indeterminacy becomes an almost physical fact of life, when a very small event can set a country spinning in an entirely new direction. Trotsky was well aware that history is a series of accidents. One of those small accidents happened when a tiny blood vessel burst in Lenin's skull. Another happened in October 1923 when Trotsky went duck hunting and while walking to a waiting canoe suddenly found himself wading through icy-cold water and immediately began to suffer from chills. The duck hunt was abandoned and he returned to Moscow, where he was put to bed, suffering from influenza and those violent changes of temperature that had plagued him at intervals throughout his life. In the middle of January 1924, when he was recovering but still weak, his doctors insisted that he should go to the south to avoid the rigors of a Moscow winter. It was decided to send him to Sukhum-Kaleh on the eastern shore of the Black Sea, where it was always summer. The train had reached Tiflis, the capital of Georgia, when one of his secretaries came to him with a decoded telegram from Stalin, saying that Lenin was dead. Trotsky was suffering from a high temperature. He read the telegram and then handed it to his wife, but she had guessed already. A few minutes later he was able to reach Stalin on the direct wire and was told that the funeral would take place the next day, that it would be impossible for Trotsky to return in time, and it was better that he should continue his treatment. Stalin, who was in charge of the funeral arrangements, knew very well that the funeral would not take place the next day, and in fact it took place six days later. Trotsky was being deliberately excluded from the ceremonies.

Even if Trotsky had attended the ceremonies, it would have made little difference. He could not have appeared publicly in Moscow, where the streets were covered with snow and sleet and an icy wind was blowing. While still in the railroad station at Tiflis he wrote a eulogy of Lenin "the unique, the only one." The eulogy reads like an incantation on the theme "Lenin is no more, Lenin has gone from us." The eulogy covers two pages and appears to have been written in a fever at white heat:

> Lenin is no more. Like gigantic rocks crashing into the sea, the words fall on our consciousness. Beyond belief, beyond thinking . . . How shall we go forward, how shall we find the road, shall we not lose our way? For Lenin, comrades, is no more . . . May the sting of the needle which we shall feel in our hearts every time we remember that Lenin is no more be for each of us an admonition, a warning, a summons . . . In grief, sorrow, and affliction we bind our ranks and hearts together, uniting for the new battles ahead.
>
> Comrades, brothers, Lenin is no more.
> Farewell, Ilyich! Farewell, our leader!

The train went on to Sukhum-Kaleh, where the mimosa was in full bloom, the palm trees waved in the sea breezes, the camellias glowed among their glossy leaves, and the sun shone strong on their faces. On January 27, 1924, he heard the great salvo of artillery which announced that at this precise moment the funeral was taking place outside the Kremlin wall.

He was in a stupor, his will paralyzed, and he could not even bring himself to write a letter of sympathy to Krupskaya, whom he deeply loved, admired, and respected. He was shaken a few days later when he received from her a letter of sympathy:

Dear Lev Davidovich,

I write to tell you that about a month before his death, as he was looking through your book, Vladimir Ilyich stopped at the place where you sum up Marx and Lenin, and asked me to read it over again to him: he listened very attentively, and then looked it over again himself. And here is another thing I want to tell you. The attitude of V.I. toward you at the time when you came to us in London from Siberia has not changed until his death. I wish you, Lev Davidovich, strength and health, and I embrace you warmly.

N. Krupskaya

In the spring Trotsky left Sukhum-Kaleh and returned to Moscow. He still conducted the affairs of the Ministry of War and attended the meetings of the Politburo; he continued to write books and articles; his health improved and he was ruddy-faced. But ambition was burned out of him. He watched Lenin's successors performing a ritual dance, a few steps forward, a few backward, a bow, a flourish, and sometimes the dancers were brilliantly illuminated and at other times they vanished into the shadows. He had no overmastering desire to join them in the dance. It was as though he were standing on another planet, watching them from afar.

THE
DESCENT
INTO
HELL
PART SIX

They are carrying away my father, Lev Davidovich
Trotsky! My father, who gave no victory—

THREE BOOKS 16

I n 1924, the year of Lenin's death, Trotsky published three books. They were *Literature and Revolution, Problems of Everyday Life,* and *Lenin: Notes for a Biographer.* Although *Literature and Revolution* has become famous, perhaps because the title promises so much, none of these books shows him exerting his full strength and they may be classed among his minor writings. They were written when he had many other things on his mind, when he was simultaneously fighting for power while abandoning all hope of power, and when he was living under the shadow of Lenin's illness. He wrote these books for many reasons, and not the least of these reasons was to deaden the pain of an ambiguous situation. The second-in-command of the Revolution, the close friend and companion in arms of Lenin, was now virtually powerless.

Literature and Revolution, which was first published in July 1924 with a dedication to Christian Rakovsky, was an attempt to lay the basis for a philosophy of revolutionary art. It fails partly because Trotsky had few of the makings of a philosopher, partly because he knew comparatively little about the many writers and poets of his time and was out of sympathy with most of them, and partly because the book assumes the form of a polemic against all those who have not spoken worthily of the revolution. The polemic is also a lament over the literature that never came to birth. He therefore presents an aggrieved face to the world and reminds us that in the future great philosophers and artists will arise to make amends for the present unsatisfactory state of affairs. Indeed, at the very end of the book he announces that "there is no revolutionary art as yet." But this is a matter of small consequence, for under the aegis of the Communist Party there will ultimately come into being a Communist man who "will develop all the vital elements of contemporary art to the highest degree." This is a satisfying conclusion, but even more satisfying conclusions are promised. "Man will become immeasurably stronger, wiser and subtler," he wrote. "His body will become more harmonized, his movements more rhythmic, his voice more musical. The forms of life will become dynamically dramatic. The average human type will rise to the heights of an Aristotle, a Goethe, or a Marx. And above this ridge new peaks will arise."

But this was mythology, not literary criticism and not philosophy. In his more sober moments he would not see "the average human type" in quite so exalted a position.

The number of writers and poets whom Trotsky thoroughly detested was far greater than the number he approved of. In fact he approved of exactly one poet, the rest being consigned to various mansions of oblivion. The good poet was Demian Bedny, whose crude revolutionary jingles are now forgotten. "Demian Bedny did not and will not create a school," Trotsky declared. "He himself was created by the school, called the Russian Communist Party, for the needs of a great epoch that will not come again."

Although Russia had rarely known so many poets of the first magnitude as those who were coming to maturity at the time of the Russian Revolution, Trotsky would have none of it. Anna Akhmatova was dismissed with contempt. He wrote that her poems concerned "herself, an unknown person in a derby or in spurs, and inevitably God." This was clever but less than helpful. Of Vladimir Mayakovsky he wrote that he would describe a love affair as if he were describing the migration of nations. This, too, was clever, but others before Trotsky had observed that Mayakovsky was incapable of writing without introducing the sound of thundering hooves. Trotsky praises Mayakovsky's great early poem called *A Cloud in Trousers*, written before the Revolution, and wonders why his poems written after the Revolution are so mechanical, so frenzied, and so shapeless. He is particularly affronted by what he calls "Mayakovsky's intimacy with the Revolution," by which he means Mayakovsky's rather immodest way of presenting himself in his poems as standing beside Lenin and leading him on to victory. "He fills the squares, the streets and fields of the Revolution with his personality," Trotsky complains. "The poet is too much in evidence." The complaint is justified, but Mayakovsky himself could answer that it was precisely because he filled the squares, the streets and fields of the Revolution, that he wrote his glorious and sometimes shoddy poetry.

Trotsky was hard to please. He disliked Symbolist poetry, had an aversion to the Moscow Art Theater, loathed Andrey Biely, Vasily Rozanov, Marina Tsvetaeva, Boris Pasternak, Boris Pilniak, Vsevolod Ivanov, Sergey Essenin, and thirty others. At the beginning of the book he puts in a good word for a wonderful short-story writer called Nikolay Tikhonov but takes it away at the end of the book after learning that Tikhonov has written a story about a grocery store. The greatest poet of the time was Alexander Blok; Trotsky would be well content if the entire body of his works vanished provided that his poem *The Twelve* survived. Like a schoolmaster chastising modern Russian literature, Trotsky gives failing marks to everyone except the execrable Demian Bedny, whose jingles are now unreadable. One poet is castigated for his diffidence, another because he belongs to a worn-out tradition, a third because he has not understood what the Revolution is all about. Boris Pilniak is "nothing but a romantic." Andrey Biely is "nothing but a corpse." All belong to "the manure heap of history."

What puzzles Trotsky is the inadequacy of modern Russian literature when confronted with the central event of Russian history—the Revolution. Some element of paranoia is involved, for was he not the center of the central event? He rages too loudly to be completely convincing, and his hatred of so many great writers does not preclude a certain envy. He continually asks himself: "Why did they fail to write superbly about a superb epoch?" and he answers that the fault lay with the bourgeoisie and their lack of understanding of the cataclysmic importance of the Revolution. He does not ask whether something went wrong with the Revolution.

What he wanted was "socialist realism," although this combination of words had not yet come into existence. "The Revolution is strong to the extent it is realistic, rational, strategic and mathematical," he wrote. What he meant by this was the Revolution had clearly defined outlines, a sharp and linear logic, a deliberate precision. In fact, it had none of these, but it pleased Trotsky to imagine that it did. He demanded of writers and poets that they too should be "realistic, rational, strategic and mathematical." Their failing was that they rejected mathematics and were devoted to the imagination alone. Trotsky understandably opposed this view of affairs and asked rhetorically: "Can it be that the Revolution, the same one which is now before us, the first since the earth began, needs the seasoning of romantic outbursts, as a cat ragout needs hare sauce?" He never minimized the importance of the Revolution—the first since the earth began.

From time to time in *Literature and Revolution* Trotsky, putting aside his larger and more dangerous claims, turns his attention to other subjects besides literature and revolution. Perturbed by the absence of any viable revolutionary art or any that he approved of, Trotsky finds himself contemplating the art of the

Middle Ages and the Renaissance. For the first and last time in his life, he bestows his approval on Christianity:

The Christian myth unified the monumental art of the Middle Ages and gave significance not only to the temples and the mysteries, but to all human relationships. The union of the religious point of view of life with an active participation of it made possible a great art in those times. If one were to remove religious faith, not the vague, mystic buzzing that goes on in the souls of our modern intelligentsia, but the real religion, with God and a heavenly law and a Church hierarchy, then life is left barren without any place in it for the supreme confrontations of hero and destiny, of sin and expiation.

This is not a passage which would have found favor in the eyes of Lenin, who regarded religion with contempt and loathing. Trotsky recognized that a great art had emerged out of "the real religion, with God and a heavenly law and a Church hierarchy," and this gave meaning to "the supreme confrontations of hero and destiny, of sin and expiation." Without religion "life is left barren." Yet he was in no mood to embrace Christianity to find meaning in his life. Having celebrated Christianity, he quickly turns savagely against it, remarking that it "reflected the contradictions of life and solved them fictitiously." Then comes the *coup de grace*: "Mediaeval society overcame the growing contradictions by transferring the promissory note to the Son of God; the ruling classes signed this note, the Church hierarchy acted as endorser, and the oppressed masses prepared to discount it in the other world." This was clever, but it cannot be reconciled with his previous statement. He seemed to hope that out of the bloody struggle for communism there would emerge a myth at least as potent as Christianity, perhaps in the person of the all-knowing Lenin who died at the height of his power and fame of a sickness that left him half paralyzed and close to madness. He did not know then that his own role, so legendary that it cried out for myth making, would be canceled in the history books; whole pages would be torn out; he would be reduced to a cypher who took no part in the Revolution, or if he did it was only to betray it.

In *Literature and Revolution* Trotsky performed the revolutionary service of demanding that the Revolution should have some meaning in terms of culture, religious feeling, the sense of man's tragic destiny on earth and the knowledge of man's insufficiency to deal with the problems presented by his own existence. He was not concerned with morality but with the laws governing human society; and if he did not go very far, he went further than the Communist theoreticians who were too lazy to think and accepted as self-evident fact that the laws governing human society had been sufficiently studied by Marx and there was no need for further study. Trotsky was trying to break through the deadening rhetoric of dogma without much success, but it was to his credit that he was the only Bolshevik leader to make the effort.

Problems of Life showed Trotsky in an unfamiliar role, that of a moralist earnestly seeking to resolve some of the moral problems raised by the Revolution. Significantly very little was said about the major problems. He had nothing to say about the arbitrary use of power, the mass executions, the torture chambers for extracting confessions, the labor camps, the harshness of a regime which seemed to regard the people as potentially hostile elements who must be disciplined into total obedience. He had nothing to say about the lack of a free press, or about the government's insistence that there could be no freedom of assembly under Communist rule, or about rule by decree. It never seemed to have occurred to him that all these things were morally wrong and that the Revolution was therefore doomed to exist in a moral vacuum, and that the crimes of the dictatorship would be endlessly repeated until the day came when the government was overthrown.

While he refused to discuss major problems, he enjoyed his quiet and somewhat casual discussion of minor problems—marriage, the Church, the purpose of life, the proper attitude toward death, the uses of polite language, of icons, of ceremonies, of bureaucracy. He did not always resolve the problems but sometimes hinted at a solution. In his eyes the Revolution had been won and it was now time for the people to think seriously about the demands of culture and of economic reconstruction. The future was full of promise; there were no longer any impediments to the growth and strengthening of human personality; under the dictatorship of the proletariat life was beginning again free from capitalist exploitation. He assumes the aspect of an elderly uncle who assumes some responsibility for the changed circumstances of the people and is therefore in a position to offer them advice.

Well aware that the Communist Party is unable to move people as deeply as the Church, he urges it to make use of rituals and ceremonies. The party must be more colorful, it must enter more deeply into people's lives. The death of a comrade must be treated with an almost religious respect, with the appropriate music and the firing of blank shots over the grave. But he is not too hopeful that the party will be able to answer the irrational need of the people for rituals and ceremonies:

> The workers' State already has its festivals, processions, reviews and parades, symbolic spectacles—the new theatrical ceremonies of State. It is true that in the main they are too closely allied to the old forms, which they imitate and perpetuate. But on the whole, the revolutionary symbolism of the workers' State is novel, distinct and forceful—the red flag, the red star, worker, peasant, comrade, International. But within the closed cages of family life the new has not penetrated, or at least has done so but little, while individual life is closely bound up with the family. This explains why in the matter of icons, christenings, Church funerals, etc., the balance is in favor of custom. The revolutionary members of the family have nothing to offer in their place.

This was true and needed to be said, but Trotsky was incapable of pursuing the matter to the extent that he would admit that anything had gone wrong. "Marriage easily dispenses with ceremonial," he wrote, thus dismissing out of hand the universal desire of men and women to celebrate their marriages. The icon in the corner of the room was equally expendable. It amused him that tough Communist workmen retained the icons on the grounds that they did not want to disturb their womenfolk by removing them, or simply because it was "habitual" and the rooms looked bare without them. He had a curious idea that the cinema would take over the role of the Church, but on this subject he speaks hesitantly, as though he did not quite believe it. On his own confession he rarely attended the cinema and took little pleasure in it.

He was appalled by the ignorance of the Russian soldiers. At all costs they must be taught to read and write. The ignorance of young workers was equally deplorable and he made the sensible suggestion that they should be provided with technical handbooks "well-printed, well-stitched, of a handy size and inexpensive." But what appalled him most of all was the prevalence of foul language, the innumerable excruciating terms of abuse and the incredible number of swearwords. The upper classes in prerevolutionary Russia had their own vocabulary which sprang, he thought, from "the slave-owners' pride, unshakable power," while the very poor swore out of bitterness, hopelessness, and despair, in the knowledge that there was no escape for their miseries. But why after the Revolution were they still cursing?

He could not guess the reason: he could only point to the phenomenon which could not be explained by his theory of revolution. In a chapter called "The Struggle for Cultured Speech" he wrote:

> The Revolution is, in the first place, an awakening of human personality in the masses, which were supposed to possess no personality. In spite of occasional cruelty and the sanguinary relentlessness of its methods, the Revolution is before and above all the awakening of humanity, its onward march, and is marked by a growing respect for the

personal dignity of every individual, with an ever-increasing concern for those who are weak.

A revolution does not deserve its name if, with all its might and all the means at its disposal the woman—twofold and threefold enslaved as she has been in the past—fails to advance on the road of individual and social progress. A revolution does not deserve its name, if it does not take the greatest care possible of the children—the future race for whose benefit the revolution has been made. And how could one create day by day, if only by little bits, a new life based on mutual consideration, on self-respect, on the real equality of women, looked upon as fellow-workers, on the efficient care of the children—in an atmosphere poisoned by the rolling, roaring, and resounding swearing of masters and slaves, that swearing that spares no one and stops at nothing? The struggle against "bad language" is a condition of intellectual culture, just as the fight against filth and vermin is a condition of physical culture.

Almost unconsciously, for it slipped out of him, he had provided an answer. The revolution which had intended to introduce an egalitarian society had failed; the "masters" were the bureaucrats of the Communist Party, the remaining Russians were their "slaves." The promised new life based on self-respect, mutual consideration, and the equality of women had not emerged and was far from the point where it was possible for it to emerge. The bureaucracy and the Tcheka held the people in an iron grip. The people were terrified of their government and would soon become more terrified, as Stalin increased his power over a murderous bureaucracy.

In *Problems of Everyday Life* Trotsky is already aware that "something has gone wrong." Life has become problematical. In his pedantic fashion he seeks to discover why this has happened. In attempting to solve the problem he resembles a doctor who is confronted with a prostitute in the last stages of syphilis and pronounces that she has a bad complexion and will soon be cured if she takes proper exercise. On the whole it is a kindly book; there are no shafts of savage wit; he is trying to be helpful.

He was also trying to be helpful when he wrote during the months after Lenin's death a book which he called *Lenin: Notes for a Biographer*, the title suggesting that he was merely writing a source book for future biographers. A more accurate title might be *Lenin and I*, for it is largely a recital of their meetings and discussions written with charm and with an acute understanding of Lenin's personality except when he composes a running commentary on Gorky's celebrated essay on Lenin, amusing himself as he congratulates Gorky for his perception in one passage and lambasting him in the next for being insensible to Lenin's real character. In his summing up of Lenin, Gorky described him as "a man of extraordinary will power but in all other respects a typical Russian intellectual." Trotsky roars with rage and can hardly control himself in his excitement. A typical Russian intellectual, indeed! What on earth is Gorky talking about? Doesn't he know that Lenin was a giant of revolutionary thought? Doesn't he know that Lenin transcended all that was petty and narrow in the world of the *muzhik* by the soaring flight of his thought and his most powerful will? Trotsky shouts too loudly to be completely convincing. "Lenin's genius," he proclaims, "consisted, first of all, in transcending all confines." This was to grant Lenin virtues that were meaningless. Gorky wrote that Lenin sometimes "had to hold down his soul by its wings." Once again Trotsky roared his contempt. He explained quite unnecessarily that Gorky was comparing Lenin with the sufferers from a fasionable *malaise*, the sick conscience, the split personality, the man who was a prey to interior conflicts because he had to restrain his love of man, his love of culture. In this way, of course, Gorky had only shown his total and devastating ignorance, for Lenin in Trotsky's eyes was "all of a piece, of very high quality, of complex structure, but with all its components held perfectly together and constituting one solid entity." The same might be said of a lump of coal.

It is fair to say that Trotsky's running argument with Gorky is the least distinguished chapter in a book with many distinguished chapters. Trotsky's aim was to produce a credible Lenin through anecdotes and stories; he told them well and created the atmosphere in which a Lenin could live and breathe; and the final image that emerges is very similar to the image depicted by Gorky, though with one essential difference: Trotsky always sees Lenin in a position of commanding authority, while Gorky sees him in his moments of leisure, reminiscing, justifying himself, and sometimes saying things to give Gorky pleasure.

Trotsky's book is important among other reasons because it shows how casually Lenin embraced the philosophy of total violence, the absolute destruction of his enemies, and by implication it shows how Trotsky shared his enthusiasm for violence. There were many occasions when Trotsky presented himself as urbane, kindly, cultured, generous to his enemies, and incapable of inflicting pain. In fact, Trotsky rejoiced in revolutionary violence. The terror pleased him. He described it as "a remarkable instrument of revolutionary justice," and regretted that the Tcheka sometimes made mistakes by being overzealous. Lenin, as the leader of the Revolution, pronounced very early that he would exterminate everyone who opposed him and carried out his threat without mercy or humanity. A list of names would be shown to him; he would approve, and pass on to more important things. In this way he left to his followers a legacy of murderous repression that long outlived him.

Historically, the decision to kill was taken on the morning of the first day of the Revolution. Kamenev brought up at a meeting in the Smolny the question of whether to repeal the law imposing the death penalty on soldiers who deserted. It had been repealed following the February Revolution, and was reinstituted by Kerensky when he became minister of war. Now, at the moment of victory, Kamenev thought it was right and proper to abandon the death sentence. Trotsky, who was present at the meeting, raised no objection to the abolition of capital punishment. When Lenin learned about Kamenev's proposal he lashed himself into a fury, and shouted: "Nonsense! How can one make a revolution without firing squads? Do you think you can deal with your enemies by laying down your arms? What other means of repression do we have? Imprisonment? No one attaches any importance to this during a civil war when each side hopes to win."

Kamenev explained patiently that he was speaking only about deserters, just as Kerensky had introduced the law only to punish deserters. Lenin angrily insisted that anyone who approved of the abolition of the death penalty was an ignoramus who failed to realize the enormous difficulties that would soon confront the revolution. "An inadmissible weakness, a pacifist illusion!" he said. The proposal had already been agreed upon; a decree had been issued; Lenin in his abrupt way suddenly proposed that the decree should be rescinded. There was a bitter argument, with the majority against Lenin. It was generally agreed that to rescind the decree immediately after issuing it would be unwise. Lenin, who cared nothing about majority opinion, bided his time. After the decree was issued, Lenin paid not the slightest attention to it.

"Lenin," wrote Trotsky, "stressed the inevitability of terror at every suitable opportunity." Lenin, too, had studied terror, written learnedly about it, understood its most labyrinthine mazes. He would talk about it at great length, and many times a day. It was obviously a subject that fascinated him, and he liked to watch the reactions of his listeners to see whether they were as stern and merciless as he was. And if like Kamenev or Bukharin they showed that they were not entirely at ease with terror, he would rebuke them: "Here are those, excuse the word, 'revolutionaries' who imagine we shall achieve our revolution in a nice way, with kindness? What have they learned? What do they understand by dictatorship? What sort of dictatorship will it be if they themselves are ninnies?"

All these statements were merely variations on an original text: "What other means of repression do we have?" In fact, there were many other means, but Lenin deliberately sought out the most extreme means, the most culpable means, the means that led to the horrors of a thousand prison camps. The responsibility was his, and it was shared with Trotsky.

In the autumn of 1924 Trotsky published two volumes of his writings and speeches during the first year of the revolution. The general title of these volumes was a very simple one: *1917*. A lengthy preface entitled "Lessons of October" was an attempt to summarize the exact course taken by the revolution and to discover why it succeeded and why other revolutionary attempts had failed. In the previous year the German Communist Party had made a bid for power, and failed miserably; the outlook for revolution was demonstrably less in 1924 than it had been in the previous years. Why? And also why had there been no careful studies of the October Revolution to examine how it all came about? There had been in fact a conspiracy of silence; there had been too many controversies, too many brutal arguments, while the Revolution was taking place. Outwardly, it appeared to have been planned and carried out with extraordinary precision. In fact, it was built out of compromises, tactical errors, indecision, and it succeeded by the purest accident. Trotsky does not of course accept the fact that the accidental played a large part in it, but he goes to some pains to show that there were many tactical errors and many of the leaders were indecisive. He suggests that the party owes to itself a scrupulous examination of the errors made at the time of the Revolution, for unless it learns these lessons, it may, when confronted with a crisis, go down to defeat.

It is possible that when Trotsky wrote this introductory essay which amounts to only about sixty pages, he was writing in a state of pedagogical innocence. He appears to have been genuinely surprised by the uproar it caused. After the death of Lenin a triumvirate, consisting of Stalin, Zinoviev, and Kamenev, had been created, ostensibly to deal with the day-to-day affairs of the republic until more permanent appointments could be made. Each of them had reasons for preferring not to examine what happened during the Revolution—Zinoviev and Kamenev because they held back and insisted that the uprising was ill timed, and Stalin because he had taken almost no part in it, although he claimed later to have been the chief instigator acting through a mysterious "Center" which was independent of the Military Revolutionary Committee of the Petrograd Soviet. In the introductory essay, Trotsky uses the word "we" when he evidently means "I." To the triumvirate, one of the most offensive passages in the essay was a brief account of the insurrection in which they are not mentioned:

From the moment when we, as the Petrograd Soviet, invalidated Kerensky's order transferring two-thirds of the garrison to the front, we had actually entered a state of armed insurrection. Lenin, who was not in Petrograd, could not appraise the full significance of that fact. So far as I remember, there is not a mention of it in all his letters during this period. Yet, the outcome of the insurrection of November 7 was at least three-quarters settled, if not more, the moment we opposed the transfer of the Petrograd garrison; created the Military Revolutionary Committee; appointed our own Commissars in all army divisions and institutions, and thereby completely isolated not only the General Staff of the Petrograd zone, but also the Government. As a matter of fact, we had here an armed insurrection—an armed though bloodless insurrection of the Petrograd regiments against the Provisional Government—under the leadership of the Military Revolutionary Committee and under the slogan of preparing the defence of the Second Soviet Congress, which would decide the ultimate fate of the state power.

Lenin's counsel to begin the insurrection in Moscow, where, on his assumption, we would gain a bloodless victory, flowed precisely from the fact that in his underground refuge he had no opportunity to estimate the radical turns not only in the mood but also in the organizational ties that took place among the military rank and file as well as the army hierarchy after the "peaceful" insurrection of the garrison of the capital.

Without perhaps intending to do so, Trotsky was claiming that "we" had won by successfully subverting the garrison, by disregarding Lenin's advice, by creating the Military Revolutionary Committee, and by appointing to key positions people who would carry out its orders. All this was true. "We" dominated the revolution. "We" created the situation, and "we" took full advantage of it at exactly the right time. Where Lenin would talk of the power of the revolutionary proletariat, and how the proletariat had taken power in Petrograd, Trotsky more accurately spoke of the members of the Military Revolutionary Committee whom he had handpicked. He was under no illusions about how the revolution was brought about, for he brought it about.

No one reading the official present-day accounts of the Russian revolution and Trotsky's account in "Lessons of October" and later in his *History of the Russian Revolution* could imagine that they were describing the same revolution. Today Stalin's imaginary "Center" is still regarded in the Soviet Union as the engine of the revolution, and its directing force. It can hardly be expected that anyone could believe it in the face of the evidence, but if it is not believed, it is regarded as an acceptable fiction.

About the time of the publication of *1917* Trotsky fell ill again with the mysterious fever which may have been related to the fevers he suffered at intervals throughout his life or to the pneumonia or perhaps influenza which took hold of him in the autumn of the previous year after duck shooting at Kaloshino. "Lessons of October" was attacked in *Pravda*. He was too ill or too disdainful to reply. The vultures were gathering around him. As the attacks on him grew more violent, so his silence became almost deafening. He had become the adversary. It was not a role he could play with joy. He was still commissar of war, he still had many admirers and sympathizers, he still possessed the status of a living legend, and he was still young and capable, if only he was not fever ridden, to strike back. But at this moment he had not the least intention of striking back. It was not pride only: he felt a deep sense of responsibility toward the revolution and wanted at all costs to avoid a brutal collision with men whom he still regarded with some respect, though they had none for him. One of their chief weapons was a letter he had written to Chkheidze in April 1913, which was intercepted by the police and remained in the police archives until discovered after the October Revolution. Trotsky had been editing a paper called *Pravda* in Vienna. Suddenly he learned that the Bolsheviks had appropriated the same title for their paper in Petersburg. Lenin, in the full knowledge that Trotsky was editing a paper of the same name, simply purloined the title. In rage Trotsky wrote a letter vigorously attacking Lenin, describing him as "a professional exploiter of every kind of backwardness in the Russian working-class movement." He wrote: "The entire edifice of Leninism at the present time is built on lies and falsification and bears within itself the poisonous elements of its own decay." The vultures seized upon the long-forgotten letter as evidence of Trotsky's hatred of Lenin, and Stalin in particular rejoiced in this damning evidence of Trotsky's guilt. Zinoviev joined in the hue and cry. He declared that the commissar of war should be deprived of his rank and title, and reduced to the status of the manager of a leather shop.

Early in 1925, while the official denunciations were continuing, Trotsky dictated a short work called *Where Is Britain Going?* in which he prophesies a communist revolution in the British Isles. The work is the fruit of many errors and delusions. Knowing so little, he was compelled to cover up his ignorance with prophecies. Contradictions abound. Britain, doomed to extinction at the hands of colonial America, was nevertheless preparing herself for her historic communist role. He announces that she will inevitably be the first truly Marxist state in Western Europe. He gives no reasons. It is an act of faith. Were not Cromwell's Roundheads comparable with the Red Army? He says as though it was a matter of recorded fact that the Fabian Socialists were the tools of the Conservative Party. As in a vision he sees the dictatorship of the proletariat being proclaimed in the Houses of Parliament, and in the same vision he sees Britain sinking below the seas under the weight of American guns.

When Trotsky failed to understand anything, he resorted to sarcasm. Here he rails against Ramsay MacDonald, J. H. Thomas, and Philip Snowden, the leaders of the British Labour Party:

British pigeon-fanciers, by means of artificial selection, achieve special varieties with a continually shortening beak. But there comes a moment when the beak of a new stock is so short that the poor creature is unequal to breaking the egg shell and the young pigeon perishes, a sacrifice to compulsory restraint from revolutionary activities, and a stop is put to the further progress of varieties of short bills. If our memory is not at fault, MacDonald can read about this in Darwin. Having entered upon MacDonald's favourite course of analogies with the organic world, one can say that the political art of the British bourgeois consists of shortening the revolutionary beak of the proletariat, and so not allowing him to pierce the shell of the capitalist state.

The metaphor is too complex; he handles it badly; the argument becomes grotesque. "We do not intend to prophesy what will be the tempo of the revolutionary process," he writes, and then immediately changes his mind: "but in any case it will be measured in terms of years, or at the most in terms of five years, not at all by decades." He wrote that Britain would be resurrected by the newborn Communist Party, successors of the Chartists, and social reform would come about "on a new and immeasurably broader historic basis."

Where Is Britain Going? is sorry stuff written without enthusiasm or insight. It moves ponderously and betrays the hand of a man who is tired. In the spring of 1926 he went to Berlin to seek a cure for his recurrent fevers. The doctors kept him in a private clinic for weeks, unable to decide what was wrong, until it finally occurred to them that the fault lay with his tonsils. They removed his tonsils, but his fevers continued. Afterward he enjoyed traveling through Berlin as a private citizen, the city so little changed in spite of wars and bungled uprisings by the left and right. He attended a wine festival and briefly took refuge in the Soviet Embassy when it was learned on dubious evidence that there would be an attempt to assassinate him. Returning to Russia, he seemed jauntier than ever.

In January 1925, he had been relieved of his duties as commissar of war and given three minor posts dealing in different ways with industry and production. He was chairman of the Concessions Committee which administered foreign concessions, chairman of the Board of Electrotechnical Development, and chairman of the Industrial-Technological Commission. These were not sinecures; he worked hard, read innumerable technical and scientific books, visited power stations along the Dnieper, inspected laboratories, invited German and American experts to advise on production and costs, drew up tables and graphs showing comparative indices of Soviet and world economy, and thought of himself as half-administrator and half-student, remembering the days when he attended the University of Odessa and seriously contemplated a life devoted to physics and mathematics.

While industrial power fascinated him, the battle for political power continued unrelentingly. In character, in method, in habits of mind, Stalin and Trotsky were poles apart. Stalin brooded on all the injuries he received and exacted vegeance for the least of them; he regarded himself, and had regarded himself ever since Lenin's death, as the rightful inheritor of power. The triumvirate had broken up: Zinoviev and Kamenev now sided with Trotsky, and Stalin knew he must act decisively. On October 25, 1926, during a meeting of the Politburo, Trotsky accused Stalin of being "a candidate for the post of gravedigger of the revolution." Stalin turned pale, rose from the table, controlled himself with immense difficulty, and then rushed out of the room, slamming the door behind him. Some time later Yuri Pyatakov burst into Trotsky's apartment and exclaimed to Natalie and to a few others who were standing there: "Why, why did he say that? Stalin will never forgive him! No, he will avenge himself on him and his children and grandchildren unto the third and fourth generation!" Pyatakov was overwrought: he was like a man who had suddenly seen the vision of the abyss.

The incident made him violently ill, and there was no cure for this illness. In every human sense Trotsky's statement was true, but at the precise moment when he glared at Stalin and called him "the gravedigger of the revolution," Trotsky doomed the small body of his associates who called themselves "the Opposition" and signed his own death warrant.

The campaign to reduce Trotsky to insignificance proceeded apace. In a long series of speeches delivered by Stalin to the chief party members in the winter of 1926, Trotsky was described as the bellwether who has led all the other Oppositionists astray, he was a man who has simply not understood what the Revolution was all about, took no part in it, quarreled violently with Lenin throughout his career, always despised the party as an aristocrat despises the rabble, and was engaged even now in practices designed to destroy the party. Trotsky has become a destructive force which must be rooted out of the Soviet Union if communism is to succeed. In Stalin's view Trotsky was never a Bolshevik; his theory of the permanent revolution was totally irrelevant; his understanding of the revolutionary movements in China and Britain was totally defective; and perhaps worse than any of these things he was himself merely "a series of theatrical gestures," a substance without form and void, and therefore of no interest to the party. A whole book of Stalin's speeches, *On the Opposition*, was later published. The book in its present revised and somewhat bowdlerized version has over nine hundred pages.

Trotsky was now on the defensive and beginning to regret his temporary alliance with Zinoviev and Kamenev. He had once called Stalin "the most eminent mediocrity," and he was now learning that it was possible for a man to be a mediocrity and absolutely ruthless. Stalin had the army, the secret police, the police, the *agents provocateurs*, and the hooligans who would break up with shouts and catcalls any meetings addressed by Trotsky. Street demonstrations in favor of Trotsky were put down with the greatest of ease. Trotsky was reduced to holding secret meetings at night with a dozen or two dozen workmen, as he had done in the days when he was a young revolutionary in Nikolayev; and on the following day there would be a report on Stalin's desk with a detailed account of where he had been and what he had said. The Oppositionists used a secret printing press to print handbills: this too was known to Stalin, who had provided the press through one of his secret agents.

On the eve of the tenth anniversary of the Russian Revolution, the bureau in charge of historical records sent Trotsky a printed questionnaire concerning his participation in the events of October 1917. Trotsky answered with a long letter. Once more, as in "Lessons of October," he went over the familiar ground. The sixty-page letter detailed step by step his services to the Revolution, and went further, for he included in it information that was not asked of him, in particular the full texts of the letters Lenin had written to him, urging that the two of them, Lenin and Trotsky, should form a bloc against Stalin. This letter was the last sustained composition written by Trotsky in the Kremlin.

One day when Stalin was already assuming control of the state power, there was a meeting of Old Bolsheviks in a villa in Zubalova, a suburb of Moscow. It was a summer evening; the Old Bolsheviks were convivial, and there was much drinking. Suddenly Stalin turned to Dzerzhinsky and Kamenev, who were sitting beside him, and said: "To choose a victim, to carefully prepare the blow, to pitilessly avenge oneself—and then to go to bed, what could be sweeter in life?"

The blow had already been prepared. At the Fifteenth Party Congress held a little later in the year, Trotsky and all his followers were summarily expelled from the party and handed over to the secret police.

A LETTER FROM YOFFE 17

T he noose was tightening. There was deep snow in the streets, the days were short and the nights bitterly cold. In the Kremlin, like a man hunched up over a chessboard, Stalin was drawing up those strange diagrams, charts, and lists of names which always accompanied the execution of his plans. All power was already in his hands; it remained only to move cautiously, to permit the victims to tie their own ropes round their necks and to spring the trap.

On November 7, 1927, the tenth anniversary of the Revolution, Trotsky told his wife that they must leave their Kremlin apartment immediately and hide out for a few days in the apartment of his friend Beloborodov, who had left Moscow for a few days to study the strength of the Oppositionist movement in the Urals. In theory Beloborodov was the commissar for home affairs; in fact he had very little power. In history he occupies a small niche, for he was chairman of the local executive committee at Ekaterinburg when he received a telegram from Sverdlov ordering the execution of Nicholas II and all the other members of the imperial family. He carried out the order and telegraphed to Moscow: "Inform Sverdlov entire family shared fate of head. Officially family will be destroyed during evacuation."

In Beloborodov's apartment, surrounded by huge crates of books and documents, Trotsky spent his last few weeks in Moscow. For a few days scarcely anyone knew where he was. Then came young students who stood outside the house to keep guard over him, and then came the secret police, the informers, and the *agents provocateurs*.

On November 14, a week later, Stalin convened an extraordinary meeting of the Central Committee and the Control Commission. At this meeting Trotsky and Zinoviev were expelled from the party, while Kamenev and Rakovsky were expelled from the Central Committee and others were expelled from the Control Commission. The grounds for the expulsion of Trotsky and Zinoviev were that they had taken part in counterrevolutionary demonstrations which amounted to insurrection. Their real crime was that they opposed the absolute dictatorship of Stalin. Many of those who voted for the expulsions were later expelled and still later executed. With the expulsions went the order for their immediate eviction from their Kremlin apartments.

While all this was going on, Adolf Yoffe, who was Trotsky's deputy in the Concessions Committee and had been a close friend of Trotsky for seventeen years, and was now suffering from tuberculosis and an incurable disease of the nerves, sat up in bed in his Kremlin apartment and began to compose with great difficulty a long farewell letter to Trotsky:

Dear Lev Davidovich,

All my life I have thought that a man of politics ought to know how to leave the scene at the right time, as an actor leaves the stage, and it is better to go too soon than too late.

More than thirty years ago I embraced the philosophy that human life has meaning only to the extent that, and as long as, it is lived in the service of something infinite. For us humanity is infinite. The rest is finite, and to work for the rest is therefore meaningless. Even if humanity too must have a purpose beyond itself, this purpose will appear in so remote a future that for us humanity may be considered as an absolute infinite. It is in this and in this alone that I have always seen the meaning of life. And now taking a glance backward over my life, of which twenty-seven years were spent in the ranks of our party, it seems to me that I have the right to say that *all* my conscious life I have been faithful to this philosophy. I have lived according to this meaning of life: work and struggle for the good of humanity. I think I have the right to say that not a day of my life has been meaningless.

But now, it seems, comes the time when my life loses its meaning, and in consequence I feel obliged to bring it to an end, to abandon it.

For several years now the present heads of our party, in accordance with their general policy of not giving work to Communists of the Opposition, have given me neither political nor soviet work whose scope and character would permit me to be useful to the maximum of my capabilities. During the past year, as you know, the Politburo has completely cut me off, as an Oppositionist, from any political work.

My health has kept getting worse. About September the twentieth, for reasons unknown to me, the Medical Commission of the Central Committee summoned me to an examination by specialists who informed me categorically that the state of my health was much worse than I supposed and that I must not stay another useless day in Moscow nor remain another hour without treatment, but go abroad immediately and enter an appropriate sanatorium.

To my direct question, "What chances have I got to get well abroad, and can I take care of myself in Russia without giving up my work?" the physicians and assistants, the practicing doctor of the Central Committee, Comrade Abrossov, another Communist physician, and the director of the Kremlin hospital, all answered simply that the Russian sanitoria could help me in no way, that I must rely upon treatment in the West. They added that if I followed their instructions, they had no doubt that I would be able to work for a prolonged period.

For about two months the Medical Commission of the Central Committee (in spite of having on its own initiative ordered the consultation) took no steps either toward my stay abroad or toward my treatment here. On the contrary, the Kremlin pharmacy, which had always delivered medicines to me according to the prescriptions, was forbidden to do so. I was, in fact, deprived of the help of free medicines, which I had always enjoyed. I was obliged to buy medicines, which were indispensable to me, in the pharmacies of the city. It appears that this took place at the time when the group in power began to visit on the comrades of the Opposition its policy of "Hit the Opposition in the belly."

As long as I was well enough to work I paid little attention to all this, but as I kept getting worse my wife approached the Medical Commission of the Central Committee and personally Dr. Semashko, who has always, publicly, gone to extremes to realize his formula, "Save the old guard." The matter was nevertheless constantly postponed, and all my wife was able to obtain was an extract from the decision of the council of physicians. In this extract my chronic maladies are enumerated, and it is set down that the council insists on my being sent abroad "to a sanatorium of the type of Professor Friedlander's" for a period that may extend to one year.

Meanwhile, nine days ago I took to my bed because of the severity and intensification of all my chronic ailments (as always happens in such circumstances), and especially the most terrible, my inveterate polyneuritis, which has again become severe, forcing me to endure an absolutely intolerable pain and preventing me from walking. For nine days I have received no treatment, and the question of my trip abroad has not been taken up. Not one of the physicians of the Central Committee has come to see me. Professor Davidenko and Dr. Levine, being called to my bedside, prescribed a few trifles which obviously could do me no good, and then admitted that "nothing could be done," and that a trip abroad was urgent and indispensable. Dr. Levine told my wife that the affair was dragging because the Medical Commission evidently thought that my wife wanted to go with me, and "that makes it too expensive." My wife answered that in spite of the state I was in, she definitely would not insist that she or anyone else accompanied me. Whereupon Dr. Levine assured us that, under these conditions, the matter would soon be settled. Dr. Levine told me again today that the doctors could do nothing, that the only thing for me to do was to go abroad immediately. Then in the evening the physician of the Central Committee, Comrade Potyemkin, notified my wife that the Medical Commission of the Central Committee had decided not to send me abroad, believing that a short stay would be futile, and that the Central Committee would not give for my cure more than one thousand dollars and they regarded this as the maximum.

While I was abroad recently I received an offer guaranteeing me twenty thousand dollars in royalties for my memoirs, but considering that they would have to be censored by the Politburo and knowing how the history of the party and of the revolution is falsified in our country, I did not consider it possible to lend a hand to such a falsification. The entire censorship of the Politburo would consist of not allowing a true evaluation of the personages and their actions, either on one side or the other—either of the authentic leaders of the revolution or of those who at present find themselves invested with this dignity. In consequence I see no way of getting treatment without accepting money from the Central Committee, and for all my twenty-seven years of revolutionary work, this committee thinks it can value my life and my health at a sum not exceeding one thousand dollars.

Therefore I believe the time has come for me to put an end to my life. I know the general opinion of the party is opposed to suicide, but I feel that none of those who understand my situation will condemn me for it. If I were in good health I would have found strength and energy to struggle against the situation created in the party. But in my present state I cannot endure a situation in which the party silently tolerates *your exclusion from the ranks*, even though I am absolutely certain that sooner or later a crisis will come which will oblige the party to cast off those who have led it to such disgrace. In this sense my death is a *protest* against those who have led the party to a situation such that it cannot act in any way in the face of this disgrace.

If I may be permitted to compare something big with something little, I will say that the immensely important historical event, your exclusion and that of Zinoviev, an exclusion that must inevitably open a period of Thermidor in our revolution, and the fact that I am reduced, after twenty-seven years of revolutionary work at responsible posts in the party, to a situation where I have nothing left but to put a bullet through my head—these two facts illustrate one and the same thing—the present regime in our party. And perhaps the two events, the little and the big one together, will jar the party awake and halt it on the road leading to Thermidor.

Dear Lev Davidovich, we are bound together by ten years of work in common and, I hope, of personal friendship, and that gives me the right to tell you, at the moment of farewell, what seems to me to be a weakness in you.

I have never doubted the correctness of the way you have shown us, and you know that for more than twenty years, ever since the "Permanent Revolution," I have been with you. But I have always thought you lacked the inflexibility, the intransigence of Lenin, his resolution to remain at the task alone, if need be, in the road he had marked out, sure of a future majority, of a future recognition by all of the rightness of that road. You have always been right politically, beginning with 1905, and I have often told you that with my own ears I have heard Lenin admit that in 1905 it was not he, but you, who was right. In the face of death one does not lie, and I repeat this to you now.

But you have often renounced your right position in favor of an agreement, a compromise, whose value you overestimated. That was wrong. I repeat: politically you have always been in the right, and *now more than ever you are in the right*. Some day the party will understand this, and history will be compelled to recognize it.

Moreover, do not be afraid today if certain people desert you, and especially if the many do not come to you as quickly as we all wish. You are in the right, but the certainty of the victory of your truth lies precisely in a rigorous intransigence, in a most severe rigidity, in the repudiation of every compromise, exactly as that was always the secret of the victories of Ilyich.

I have often wanted to tell you this, and have only brought myself to it now, at the moment of saying good-by.

I wish you energy and courage equal to those you have always shown, and a swift victory. I embrace you. Good-by.

Your,
A. Yoffe

P.S. I wrote my letter during the night between the fifteenth and sixteenth, and today, the sixteenth, Maria Mikhailovna went to the Medical Commission to insist that they send me abroad, if only for one or two months. They told her that in the opinion of the specialists a short stay abroad was absolutely useless. They told her that the Medical Commission had decided to transfer me immediately to the Kremlin hospital. Thus they refuse me even a short trip for the sake of my health, even though all the doctors agree that a cure in Russia is of no use and will do me no good.

Good-by, dear Lev Davidovich. Be strong. You will need to be, and energetic, too. And bear me no grudge.

A.

Yoffe's testament, for it was nothing less, deserves to be quoted in full not only because it is a poignant human document but because it throws light on the intolerable situation of the Old Bolsheviks trapped within the murderous machine they had helped to create. In his sickness and pain he whines a little; it is not a noble or heroic letter, but it is formidably honest. He was not an unintelligent man, and he was well aware that the real reason he was not being permitted to go abroad was that he might succumb to the temptation to write his autobiography or in other ways use his freedom to attack the triumvirate. He detested Stalin, and Stalin in his cold, revengeful way had already consigned him to oblivion. He knew that if he was taken to the Kremlin hospital he would die "under treatment." He seems to have hoped that his wife and son would suffer no ill-effects by his suicide, and if he did, he was profoundly wrong—they were arrested and sent into exile. He hoped, too, that his death in some mysterious way would strengthen the adversaries of the triumvirate, but he must have known that it was already too late and that Trotsky himself was lacking precisely in those qualities that were needed to destroy the inhuman machinery that called itself the government of the Soviet Union. He wrote with a mind made luminous by despair. "The certainty of the victory of your truth lies precisely in a rigorous intransigence, in a most severe rigidity, in the repudiation of every compromise, exactly as that was always the secret of the victories of Ilyich." But it was not Lenin so much as Stalin who showed a rigorous intransigence, a most severe rigidity, and the repudiation of every compromise.

There are ambiguities in this letter, which was almost a salute to the victor. When Yoffe pointed out that his twenty-seven years of revolutionary work were valued by the Central Committee "at a sum not exceeding one thousand dollars," he was making a sardonic joke. He already knew that in their eyes he was worth zero dollars. He foresaw the coming of Thermidor, the period when the revolutionary leaders go hog-wild killing each other, forgetting that there had been many Thermidors ordered by Lenin and that Thermidor was the name of the game of revolution, that it was unavoidable, and that he was himself simply by occupying many responsible positions in the government guilty of crime by association. Yoffe was not an innocent man; he shared the common guilt; and when he hinted at his own innocence he was hinting at something beyond belief. He offered himself as a sacrifice, but his single sacrifice, at a time when millions were being sacrificed, was meaningless.

And it is precisely at this point that his letter acquires a human dimension: at various times in the course of the letter he asks himself whether there is any meaning in his life and in his death. Like Bukharin many years later, he finds no ascertainable meaning. He repeats his belief that in some far distant future his work will be justified because he will have conferred benefits upon the human race. He was probably too intelligent to believe that the far distant future would remember him; like all men he was caught up in the endless maze of self-justification. But now, with the revolver lying beside the telephone on the bedside table, in mortal pain and agony, he concluded that in dying he might be able to instill a little more courage in Trotsky, and this was the meaning and justification of his life. When he learned that the doctors were insisting on taking him to the Kremlin hospital, and no doubt would be coming in a day or two, he decided that he possessed freedom of action for only a few more hours. Trotsky called on the telephone to ask the state of his health. Yoffe answered

evasively and asked Trotsky to come and see him,
presumably for a last farewell and so that he could
place the suicide note, now in a sealed envelope, in
Trotsky's hands. Trotsky was busy and said he would
come later. He had apparently forgotten all about his
friend when two hours later the telephone rang and an
anonymous voice said: "Adolf Abramovich has shot
himself. There is an envelope for you on his bedside
table." Trotsky hurried to Yoffe's apartment. The secret
police, which had been busy monitoring all the telephone conversations of the Opposition, had already
taken possession of the envelope. G.P.U. officers were
already searching through Yoffe's papers. Trotsky
asked them for the envelope addressed to him and was
told that no such letter existed. For a little while longer
Trotsky remained in the apartment, gazing down at the
man whose bloody head lay on a bloodstained pillow.
He observed that Yoffe's expression had not changed;
his face was "calm and infinitely tender," and there
was no sign of suffering. Soon he slipped away.

Yoffe and Trotsky had known each other for more
than twenty years. Yoffe was active in the 1905 revolution; he had been with Trotsky and Parvus when they
were hammering out their theory of the permanent
revolution; he was in Austria when Trotsky was editing
Pravda, and he was one of those who elected to act as
couriers and carry copies of the newspaper into Russia.
He was arrested and sentenced to a long term of exile
in Siberia. Released at the time of the February Revolution, he made his way to Petrograd and became a
member of the two organizations responsible for the
October Revolution—the "October Central Committee"
of the Bolshevik Party and the Military Revolutionary
Committee of the Petrograd Soviet. Trained as a physician, he had no military knowledge, but he had a keen
brain and an uncanny knack for knowing the limits of
the possible. Lenin had complete faith in him and made
him the leader of the first delegation of the peace
negotiations with the Germans at Brest-Litovsk. He was
the Soviet ambassador to Germany in the stormy days
of 1919 and signed the peace treaty with the Poles after

the disastrous 1920 war. He represented the Soviet Union at the Genoa Conference in 1923 and was sent to China to win Dr. Sun Yat-sen to the Soviet cause; in this he was very largely successful. Later he became the Soviet ambassador to Japan. He had made history and been a part of history, and he had employed all his intellectual agility, daring and physical courage in the service of the Bolshevik cause in spite of the fact that he suffered from a hereditary nervous disease and was in great pain unless he took pain-killing drugs.

The government decreed that the funeral should take place on November 19, a working day. The coffin containing the body of Yoffe lay in state in the building of the Commissariat of Foreign Affairs on Lubyanka Square. A crowd of about ten thousand milled about in the street, blocking all traffic, so that Trotsky had some difficulty reaching the coffin in time for the funeral procession to the Novodevichy Cemetery. Trotsky was accompanied by Radek and Muralov, and among those who marched in the procession were Stalin's wife, Nadezhda Allilueva, and Rakovsky, who was Trotsky's closest friend. It was a cold, blustery winter day with whirling snow gusts. The procession sang revolutionary songs including a song composed in honor of Trotsky: "Long live Trotsky—the leader of the Red Army." But when they reached the cemetery gates, the mourners were told by an officer in command of a small detachment of troops that only twenty people would be permitted to accompany the coffin to the grave. The crowd forced its way in, defying the authorities.

It was the custom to make many speeches at the graves of departed Bolshevik leaders, and at least eight speeches were made. Chicherin made the formal speech on behalf of the Central Committee. Trotsky, Zinoviev, Kamenev and Rakovsky made speeches. Rakovsky, close to tears, took the red flag covering the coffin in his hands and declared: "Like you we shall follow the red flag to the end, and we make this oath to you now on your tomb." Trotsky's speech was surprisingly calm; he appealed for the restoration of party unity, did not mention Stalin by name, and made what amounted to a set speech. "The life of Yoffe, not his suicide, should be the model for those he has left behind. The struggle goes on! Everyone must remain at his post!" The only vehement speech was made by Zinoviev, who spoke of the crimes of Stalin, his accumulation of personal power, his betrayal of the rights of party members, and his deliberate misrepresentation of the party's wishes and purposes. Then it was all over and the people made their way to the cemetery gates, while the snow fell and a chilling wind made them draw the flaps of their fur caps over their ears.

An American journalist, Louis Fischer, wrote that after the funeral ceremonies he came upon Trotsky with some of his supporters hiding in a brick shed, pacing up and down like a caged animal, in deadly fear. It is much more likely that Trotsky was simply sheltering from the wind and the snow, and that he was pacing to keep up his circulation, and that he was not afraid. He was waiting for arrangements to be made to escort him out of the cemetery to his waiting car. And when at last Trotsky left the cemetery and passed close to the military detachment at the gate, one of his followers ran up to the soldiers and shouted: "Red Army comrades! Give a cheer for the leader of the Red Army, Comrade Trotsky!" The soldiers stared straight ahead, as though they had not heard. There was dead silence. Trotsky stood some distance away, silent, staring at the ground. Ten years had passed since the October Revolution which he had brought into being, but none dared to raise a cheer for him. Then, followed by Zinoviev and Kamenev, he entered his car.

The procession to the cemetery was the last public gesture of the Opposition. There would be many more gestures, all of them in private, in prison cells, in remote places of exile, and in the small tiled room in the basement of the Lubyanka Prison, where one by one nearly all the Opposition leaders and their followers were shot in the back of the head. Stalin received a full report of the speeches made at the grave. In his own time and at his own pace he would punish the speechmakers.

Stalin liked to tell a story from one of Krylov's fables about a hermit and a bear who grew very fond of each other. One day, while the hermit was sleeping, a fly settled on his nose. The bear was solicitous and gently waved the fly away. But the fly kept coming back and continued to settle on the hermit's nose. The bear asked himself what should be done, concluding that he must kill the fly so that the hermit could sleep peacefully. He picked up a huge stone and when the fly next settled on the hermit's face, he brought the stone down with immense force on the fly, crushing it to death. He also crushed the hermit's skull.

"The Opposition," Stalin liked to say, "is just like that bear." But it was really Stalin who was like the bear. In order to crush the Opposition, Stalin set about crushing Russia, and in order to rid himself of Trotsky he had the idea of banishing him to some far away place where he would be quite harmless, where the secret police would keep their eyes on him, where all his correspondence would be opened, and where he could be expected to die of misery and despair.

THE ARREST OF A WARLORD 18

Trotsky was not the kind of man ever to submit, ever to surrender. His pride and also his intelligence forbade it; and in addition to his personal pride as a man there was the more exalted kind of pride by which he saw himself as a historical figure. He was deeply aware of his place in history. He would not under any condition permit his image to be tarnished.

Stalin, confronted by an adversary he detested with an obsessive hatred, was determined to tarnish the image, to reduce him to zero. He controlled the huge propaganda machine, the bureaucracy, and the secret police. It was therefore not difficult for him to arrange matters in such a way that Trotsky should be made to look ridiculous. The masses must know that all his sins had been uncovered, that he was in total disgrace, that he had confessed his crimes and had willingly accepted his punishment. Unfortunately Trotsky was quite incapable of confessing his crimes or willingly accepting punishment. It was therefore necessary to proceed cautiously, and with all the more caution because there were likely to be demonstrations in his favor at the railroad station. There were perhaps a hundred thou-

sand people in Moscow who were on the side of
Trotsky. In time they could be picked up one by one:
tortured, exiled, killed. But this was not the time for
mass arrests and monstrous punishments. Stalin was
determined to proceed cautiously. First, Trotsky must
be made to suffer the utmost indignity. Secondly, the
demonstrations at the railroad stations must be reduced to a minimum.

While the scenario for Trotsky's deportation was
being worked out with great care, Trotsky himself
maintained the pose of a man superbly indifferent to
his fate. He rejected deportation; he would go only
under force. Nevertheless he supervised the packing of
his books, linen, furniture, clothes, manuscripts and
records with the efficiency of a general disposing his
army in proper order. What chiefly disturbed him was
that Natalie had a severe cold and her health was
being jeopardized by all the excitement, the visitors
bringing flowers and gifts, the constant ringing of the
telephone, the apartment transformed into a maze of
boxes and packages, all of them listed and numbered.
Trotsky summoned Dr. Fyodor Gautier, who had also
been Lenin's doctor, and after examining Natalie, the
doctor said: "She cannot go now. She is too ill. You
must postpone the deportation."

Obviously, the deportation could not be postponed at
a doctor's orders. Stalin had left the entire matter to the
G.P.U., and their will would prevail. Departure had
been set for 10 P.M. In the evening the family sat round
the table, waiting to be carried off by the secret police.
Young Victor Serge, the most faithful and intelligent of
his followers, describes Trotsky as looking terribly ill,
but oddly serene and even majestic with his halo of
hair already turning white. Serge feared the worst: he
thought Trotsky would be placed on the train and then
vanish—there would be "a most regrettable accident."
But the order given by Stalin to the G.P.U. did not
include a sentence of death. This would come many
years later.

Trotsky and his family waited around the table in an
unaccustomed silence. The telephone did not ring. No

one came to visit them. They brooded silently. At ten
o'clock, the hour when the train was supposed to leave
Yaroslav railroad station, there came a call from the
G.P.U. "The departure had been postponed," said the
anonymous voice. "For how long?" Trotsky asked. "For
two days. You leave the day after tomorrow."

About thirty minutes later they learned the reason.
There had been a demonstration at the railroad station
such as had not been seen since the time of the
Revolution. Thousands of people had converged on the
station, shouting "Long live Trotsky!" They had taken
possession of the platform and the train, they stood on
the rails to prevent the train from leaving, and they
mounted a large portrait of Trotsky on the roof of the car
they believed reserved for Trotsky. They defied the
G.P.U. officers who were milling around the station,
and when the rumor started that Trotsky had already
been smuggled onto the train, they went through it
carriage by carriage. There was some fighting. People
were arrested and beaten up. There was continual
uproar for about an hour and a half. Finally someone
announced that the train would not leave until January
19, and about the same time Trotsky was told it would
leave on January 18. It left on January 17.

Once more Trotsky's apartment was filled with well-
wishers. Rakovsky was there, and so was Maria Ivan-
ova Yoffe together with a crowd of young people who
had raced to the apartment from the station. Breathlessly they described what had happened, as though it
was a triumph. They were sure Trotsky would be
allowed to remain in Moscow; they believed the government could not face another demonstration like the
one they had just seen. Long after midnight the jubilant
visitors left and Trotsky went to bed. He did not awake
from a deep sleep until eleven o'clock the next morning.

The G.P.U. came just as Trotsky was finishing a late
breakfast. Some were in uniform, others in civilian
clothes. They were deployed around the apartment like
a small army, one guarding the door, another the
telephone, others following the movements of each
member of Trotsky's family, while two or three kept

their eyes fixed on Trotsky. He was informed that he was under arrest in accordance with Article 58 of the penal code—the article dealt with the punishment for acts of treason and counterrevolutionary activities—and he would immediately be conveyed under escort to Alma-Ata. The telephone was ringing constantly, but no one answered it.

Although Trotsky and every member of his family were being closely watched, they all succeeded in slipping away into the bedroom and locking the door. Trotsky was still wearing pajamas. He refused to dress, and he refused to leave the apartment except under duress. The locked door posed a problem to the G.P.U., who telephoned to headquarters to find out the proper course of action for removing one of the founding fathers of the Soviet Union from his bedroom. Trotsky took advantage of the delay by quietly reciting into his dictaphone the last message he would ever give from Moscow to his followers. Headquarters gave its instructions: the door must be broken down and Trotsky physically removed from the premises. The upper part of the door was frosted glass; a hammer smashed the glass, and an arm groped through the shattered glass to turn the lock. The first man into the room was a certain Kishkin, who had been an officer on the armored train. He was hysterical. He shouted: "Shoot me, Comrade Trotsky, shoot me!"

"You're talking nonsense, Kishkin," Trotsky said. "No one is going to shoot you! Do what you have to do!"

Many years later it was remembered of Kishkin that he had once said "shoot me" to Trotsky, thus establishing the fact that he was secretly one of Trotsky's followers. He was shot.

Trotsky was wearing bedroom slippers. Because there was thick snow on the ground and it was twenty degrees below zero, the G.P.U. officers pulled off his slippers, made him put on his snow boots, wrapped him in his fur coat, and clamped a fur cap on his head, and when he folded his arms, refusing to leave the apartment, they lifted him bodily and carried him down the stairs to the waiting car, while Natalie, their two sons,

Yoffe's widow, and the young wife of Beloborodov, the former minister of the interior and a close family friend, came running after them. As he ran down the stairs, Lyova Sedov, Trotsky's eldest son, pulled all the doorbells, shouting at the top of his voice: "They are carrying Comrade Trotsky away!"

In spite of the fact that on the previous night thousands of people had been demonstrating at the railroad station, none of the Oppositionists had kept watch on Trotsky's apartment and hardly anyone saw them being carried away.

Why Yoffe's widow and Beloborodov's wife were allowed to accompany them is something of a mystery. Apparently they hurled themselves into the car, and in the excitement and confusion the G.P.U. officers scarcely noticed them. There were at least nine, perhaps ten, people in the car which was driven at breakneck speed to the Yaroslav station. Once Sergey, the younger son, attempted to leap out of the car because they were passing the place where Lyova's wife was working and he wanted to warn her, but the G.P.U. officers held him by the arms and prevented him. When at last they reached the Yaroslav station, they found it had been transformed into an armed camp. Cavalry surrounded the square; soldiers with stacked rifles were everywhere; machine guns and armored cars were stationed at the approaches. The station itself was deserted except for the white-aproned porters, conductors, and railroad officials who went about their affairs as though nothing was happening.

Suddenly the car came to a halt outside the main entrance of the railroad station. Trotsky was still resisting. He would go on the train only if they carried him onto it. Six men were carrying him, while G.P.U. men in uniform with drawn revolvers marched in front. Trotsky, loosely wrapped in a fur coat, his face blue with cold, his arms dangling, still wearing his pajamas and having lost his snow boots, was being carried through the station as though he were a piece of luggage or a carcass of beef. Natalie followed him, weeping, her hair disheveled, her small face pinched with fear and misery. She was leaning heavily on the arms of a G.P.U. officer. Neither Trotsky nor his wife were recognizable: they resembled strange, small caricatures of themselves. An American correspondent who happened to see them being brought into the station thought at first that they were heavily made-up actors taking part in a charade.

Suddenly Lyova, the older son, racing blindly through the railroad station as though he had been shot out of a cannon, began shouting at the top of his voice: "Comrade workers, look what is happening! They are carrying away my father, Lev Davidovich Trotsky! My father, who gave us victory—" He thought he was addressing workmen, but most of the men in the railroad station were secret service men. Lyova was twenty-two years old, brave to foolhardiness; he had elected to accompany his parents on their journey. He was the herald of a great prince, running before him, shouting: "Soviet comrades, look at the prisoner! He is Trotsky, Lev Davidovich, my father! Why don't you do something? Can't you see it is Trotsky, Trotsky, Trotsky?"

Lyova became hysterical, his voice rising to a shrill scream that echoed against the vaulted roof of the station. He tripped and fell, and then got up and screamed: "Comrades, look! It is Trotsky! They are taking him away!"

Sergey was so outraged by the spectacle of his father being carried away like a carcass of beef that he did something that was extremely dangerous—he attacked one of the G.P.U. officers with his fists, and suddenly Lyova was by his side, and they were all struggling. Yoffe's widow and the young wife of Beloborodov were running behind Trotsky, tears pouring down their faces. Sergey and Lyova were subdued, and then let free. Trotsky and Natalie were pushed onto the train, where Lyova joined them. On the platform two women and a young man remained to bid farewell to two men and a middle-aged woman who were going into exile without any possessions at all, without a book or a handkerchief and with only the few rubles that Lyova was carrying in his pocket.

Trotsky had been told that his books, his archives, and his clothes would follow him on another train, but he had no assurance that this would happen. He knew only that he was being sent to some far distant and desolate place on the edge of Russia, in the company of G.P.U. men and soldiers of the Red Army, and perhaps he was being sent nowhere at all but only to his death.

Everything had been arranged by Stalin in such a way that Trotsky would be made to suffer the utmost indignity. Almost immediately there began in the Soviet Union the long process by which a man is reduced to a nonperson. One by one his friends were rounded up, deported, killed, or won over to the ruling power after making abject confessions of their crimes, for it was already a crime to have known Trotsky. It served Stalin's purpose that Trotsky the man should vanish out of sight but Trotsky the enemy should remain; he was the bogeyman to be conjured up whenever there was need to bring forth an arch-enemy, an arch-conspirator, an arch-oppressor. Trotsky was permitted to go on living but only on condition that he remained invisible. Meanwhile Stalin continued to weave fantasies about the man he had reduced to zero. Quite suddenly Trotsky's name was removed from history, his books were removed from the shelves, his theories were perverted or borrowed outright and given new names. If he was mentioned at all, he was made to look ridiculous: a monster of pride, a traitor to Lenin, a perverter of Marxism for his own purposes, ready to offer the Soviet Union to the highest capitalist or fascist bidder. It was not true, but against this drumroll of accusations Trotsky possessed no effective voice. In all the remaining years of his life he would be one man waging war against the most powerful propaganda machine in the world.

At the moment when Trotsky was thrown on the train in the Yaroslav station, his historical role came to an end. There remained twelve years for him to write his memoirs and innumerable articles, to protest, to hammer out and perfect a theory of revolution, and to attempt to build up out of his own ideas a powerful revolutionary force that would sweep all the other revolutionary forces away. In this he failed, as he failed in so many things. Yet the blue-faced man in the fur coat, the pajamas, and the stockinged feet had changed the course of history more than any man of his time, and he knew it, and this was his consolation.

"They are carrying away my father, Lev Davidovich Trotsky! My father, who gave us victory—"

THE FATHER OF APPLES 19

Every day they traveled eastward, and they observed that the farther they were from Moscow the more considerate were the guards and the more they seemed to be at peace with themselves. They left Moscow without books, wearing only the clothes they stood in, without even a toothbrush or toothpowder or a cake of soap. This proved to be an advantage, for now they were reduced to their essential beings, stripped of all defenses, naked to their enemies; and they drew strength from their nakedness. Trotsky was at his best in times of disaster; he was very tender with Natalie, comforting her and pretending to a gaiety he did not feel. They were alone in their compartment, lying down at full length on the seats, facing one another, holding hands. The door was half-open, but the guard who stood outside was not visible and his voice was rarely heard.

At first the train traveled slowly, for the region around Moscow was deep under snow. Natalie had a fever and seemed exhausted, shivering, saying little. Lyova was in an adjoining compartment. He was not a prisoner, he could stretch his legs on the station platforms, and he could buy small necessities. His presence was comforting, but the G.P.U. guards were watching him closely, and it was obvious that his presence on the train was known in Moscow. Trotsky was disturbed because there was no guarantee that he would see his books and archives again; he had been told that they would be sent on another train, reaching Frunze, in Kazakhstan, twelve days later. But there was not the slightest proof that this would happen, and for all he knew his books and papers were filed away in the archives of the G.P.U.

At Samara they were given a change of underwear, soap, toothbrush, and tooth powder. Here, too, they received meals from the station restaurant but were not allowed to move along the platform. The Communist Party had officially denied that Trotsky was being deported to the east, and it was therefore necessary that he should not be seen during the journey. There were altogether about twenty guards on the train, and at each station a report on Trotsky's actions and behavior was telegraphed to Moscow. The reports were necessarily brief, for he did nothing except comfort Natalie, read the newspapers bought at the railroad stations, think, and sleep. He slept very little and often thought about death. Once he murmured: "I didn't want to die in a bed in the Kremlin." The guards had informed him that he was being deported to Alma-Ata in Kazakhstan, but he did not entirely believe them. It was possible and even likely that he would be sent to some even more remote and distant place.

At Frunze they found their luggage, climbed into an autobus, and set out over the snow-covered wastes toward the mountain passes that led down to Alma-Ata, a town of earthquakes and floods, icebound in winter, surrounded by fields of red poppies in the spring, malaria-ridden during the hot summer. Alma-Ata means "Father of Apples" in the Turkic language, and there were many apple orchards. The journey over the snowfields and the mountains was a nightmare; they were caught in a blizzard; the temperature dropped below zero; and though they found refuge for the night in a small hut used as a mail station, the stove was not lit and they nearly froze to death. Lyova slept on a bench, Trotsky and Natalie on a table. "It is very different from our apartment in the Kremlin," Natalie commented, looking at the small, low-ceilinged hut, the cold stove, the sheepskins piled on the table, the small windows thickly encrusted with frost. Early the next morning they set off again over snow as smooth as glass and somehow they made their way over the pass to arrive at Alma-Ata long after midnight, being set down in a bleak mid-nineteenth-century hotel where two small rooms were reserved for them, and on either side of them were rooms reserved for their guards and the local G.P.U. officials. Their improbable address: Hotel Jetysa, Gogol Street, Alma-Ata, Kazakhstan.

From the beginning of their exile they knew they were being watched closely. They pretended they had full freedom to act as they pleased, to talk to whomever they pleased, to write to friends and acquaintances all over Russia, and to continue the struggle against Stalin from this small town near the frontier of China. They forgot that all their letters were opened and that merely to write to someone was to incriminate him, and if a visitor came to see them, the G.P.U. were immediately on his trail. Thus it happened that one of Trotsky's old-time secretaries, the tall, handsome, fair-haired Sermuks, made the journey to Alma-Ata and actually had the audacity to rent a room in the Hotel Jetysa. He managed to have one brief conversation with Trotsky, and then the G.P.U. spirited him away. He died in prison. Another friend and protégé of Trotsky made his way to Alma-Ata, set up as a carter, carried on secret conversations with Trotsky in the public baths, and he too vanished. From April to October 1928, Trotsky wrote eight hundred letters and sent about five hundred telegrams to his political followers, and it seems never to have penetrated his mind that he was acting incautiously and that every one of his correspondents would be interrogated and punished by the G.P.U. After October he received no more correspondence, for the G.P.U. had decided that they had all the information they needed. His letters, to which he attached extreme importance, hoping to revive the Opposition by an ever-widening campaign of letter writing, were in fact instruments of death.

Trotsky had the illusion that he was still politically powerful, still a force to be reckoned with. In the small house he rented near the G.P.U. building, he worked at tables piled high with manuscripts and newspapers, while Lyova served as his secretary, and a charming young woman, who reported daily to the G.P.U., worked as his typist. In the summer he took a house in the country set in a flowering apple orchard under the shadow of the white mountains. The house was very close to other houses rented to G.P.U. officials, and the peasant owner regularly informed on him to the G.P.U. Sometimes Trotsky went fishing in the mountain streams; sometimes he went off alone with a gun and shot quail, pigeon, and pheasants; and there were days when he worked in the orchard, helping the peasant to gather the huge, red Alma-Ata apples. Between bouts of malaria, he worked as though he was still a high official of the state; all the time the G.P.U. was watching him.

Outwardly calm, Trotsky was the prey to inner anxieties. He may have known or guessed that Stalin was seeking a way to get rid of him. Voroshilov was supposed to have said: "If he dies in Alma-Ata, we won't hear about it for a long while."

On December 16, 1928, Trotsky received an ultimatum from a certain Volynsky, a high official of the G.P.U. sent especially from Moscow. The ultimatum was verbal, not in writing. Volynsky said:

> The work of your political sympathizers throughout the country has lately assumed a definitely counterrevolutionary character; the conditions in which you are placed in Alma-Ata give you full opportunity to direct this work. Therefore the collegium of the G.P.U. has decided to demand from you a categorical promise to discontinue your activity, or else the collegium will be obliged to change your conditions of existence to the extent of com-

pletely isolating you from political life. In this connection the question of changing your place of residence will arise.

Trotsky regarded this demand of a verbal promise as intolerable and unacceptable. If the promise was demanded in writing, he would reply in writing; at least there would be a record, and all his past experience warned him that if he gave a verbal promise or a verbal rejection, it would eventually be distorted, changed beyond recognition. "Change of residence," "completely isolating you from political life"—these words had a hollow, graveyard sound. They meant a violent alteration in his life, and not for the better. Perhaps he would be murdered; perhaps he would be imprisoned somewhere within the Arctic Circle; he was being threatened as never before.

He decided that he had only one recourse: to write to the Central Committee. Probably only Stalin and the senior members of the G.P.U. would see the letter; the letter was therefore directed at Stalin, whose name was not mentioned (though he used the word "Stalinist") and took the form of a stinging rebuke. This letter, written the same day as the meeting with Volynsky, was at once a plea, a warning, an attack, a recital of wrongs committed and of hopes deferred, a statement of principles, and it included a total rejection of the ultimatum. In his anger, he said some things that were hopelessly wrong-headed and silly, as when he declared that "the world bourgeoisie and international Menshevism have both blessed this war; the judges have long ago awarded 'historical rightness' to Stalin." He accused the regime of being "blind, cowardly, and utterly inept." It was "unbalanced, false, contradictory, and unworthy of confidence." "Creatively, it is impotent." He accused the regime of living off the remnants of the ideas of the Opposition. He said:

> The greatest historical strength of the Opposition, despite its momentary weakness, lies in the fact that it keeps its fingers on the pulse of the world historical processes, that it clearly perceives the dynamics of class forces, that it

foresees the future and prepares for it consciously. To renounce political activity would be to renounce the preparation for the coming day.

At this point it becomes clear that he is himself the Opposition, the one with his finger on the pulse of world historical processes, the one who foresees the future. He alone knew; all others were ignorant. Stalin, reading the letter, could measure the depths of Trotsky's despair from this paranoid claim to all-seeing wisdom. Never before had Trotsky claimed so clearly that the destiny of the world depended on his own destiny, that he was "the preparer for the coming day."

When they are deeply moved and especially when they are in a state of anguish, men often shape their thoughts into the form of a liturgical chant. So in this long letter to the Central Committee, Trotsky gives way to a chant which is a repudiation of the renunciation demanded of him:

> To demand that I renounce my political activity is to demand that I abjure the struggle for the interests of the international proletariat, a struggle I have been waging for thirty-two years, during my whole conscious life . . .
>
> To renounce my political activity would mean to give up the struggle against the blindness of the present leadership . . .
>
> To renounce my political activity would mean to give up the struggle against the stifling regime that reflects the growing pressure of the enemy classes on the proletarian vanguard . . .
>
> To renounce my political activity would mean to acquiesce to the economic policy of opportunism that is undermining and shaking the foundations of the dictatorship of the proletariat . . .
>
> To renounce my political activity would mean to submit passively to the blunting and the direct falsification of our most important weapon, the method of Marxism . . .

This repudiation in the form of a prolonged chant remains curiously unconvincing, perhaps because the repetitions do not reinforce one another and there is no particular order of ideas. Self-justification is a difficult art; it was one he had never mastered. He was a man who could stand on his feet and make a two-hour-long speech without, it seemed, taking breath. Soon enough we come to realize that this letter to the Central Committee was a speech in his own defense that needed a public audience to be effective.

After the liturgical chant came the lamentations and the litany of the dead. So many people had been killed by Stalin that Trotsky scarcely knew where to begin. His daughter Nina, by his first wife, was expelled from the party and denied the opportunity to work. She died of tuberculosis in a Moscow hospital not long after he was exiled to Alma-Ata. He received a letter from her, written shortly before her death, seventy-three days after she wrote it. Obviously the letter had been held up by the G.P.U., for what purposes he was never able to fathom. He believed that Stalin had hastened her death.

Then there was Georgy Butov, a young engineer who had been placed in charge of the secretariat of the Revolutionary Military Council during the Civil War. He was small and frail and very pale; his private life was unhappy; all his energies were concentrated on the work of the secretariat. He was arrested and ordered to provide the G.P.U. with incriminating evidence against Trotsky. He refused. He knew he would perish. Thrown into prison, he went on a hunger strike that lasted fifty days and died in September 1928. Trotsky spoke only of these two deaths, symbolic of all the other deaths visited upon the Opposition. He concluded the letter on a note of defiance: "To each his own! You wish to continue with policies inspired by class forces hostile to the proletariat. We know our duty. We will do it to the end."

There was some method in Trotsky's madness. The letter was full of derision and undisguised hatred, calculated to exasperate Stalin and to provoke him into action. At all costs it was necessary to break out of the circle, even at the risk of death. He calculated that Stalin would not kill him, because he was one of the founding fathers of the Soviet Union, because he was so widely known, and because he needed Trotskyism as a whipping dog. Little did he know what Stalin dared do.

About the same time that Trotsky was writing the letter, Natalie also wrote a letter complaining about the misery of living in exile:

> Since the end of October we have received no letters from home. We get no answers to our telegrams. In short, the postal blockade. Naturally it will not stop there. We await something else. At present we are all sick with malaria. It is Lyova who is sickest: he is running a continual temperature of 39 degrees [103–4 Fahrenheit].
>
> Severe cold. The cold in our rooms is torturing. Houses here are not built for cold weather. The price of wood is incredible.
>
> Natalia Ivanovna

Although letters no longer arrived, the newspapers still came to Alma-Ata. *Pravda* was full of talk about the struggle against the Right. Trotsky believed that the pendulum would soon swing to the struggle against the Left. He was not disappointed.

Volynsky, the emissary of the G.P.U., remained in Alma-Ata, watching. It was obvious that Trotsky's fate was being decided in Moscow. It was equally obvious that Stalin was weighing many alternatives as he attempted to decide the exact measure of punishment to be accorded to Trotsky. At a meeting of the Politburo, Stalin announced that the fit punishment was expulsion from the Soviet Union. According to rumor Rykov, Bukharin, and Tomsky vehemently objected, and Bukharin sobbed and screamed, protesting against the decision. It may be true, and if so the information is most likely to have come from Bukharin. But the majority sided with Stalin and the order for deportation was drawn up in the appropriate bureaucratic manner, with every word weighed carefully. Trotsky was no longer *tovarishch*, "comrade"; he became *grazhdanin*, "citizen." This, too, was part of the punishment.

The order read as follows:

Considered: The case of citizen Trotsky, Lev Davidovich, under article 58/10 of the Criminal Code, on a charge of counter-revolutionary activity expressing itself in the organization of an illegal anti-Soviet party, whose activity has lately been directed toward provoking anti-Soviet actions and preparations for an armed struggle against the Soviet power.

Resolved: Citizen Trotsky, Lev Davidovich, to be deported from the territory of the U.S.S.R.

On January 20, 1929, there was a commotion in the street outside Trotsky's house. Armed guards posted themselves at the entrance and the exits. Volynsky entered with the writ of deportation which was dated January 18 and had been transmitted by telegraph. Asked to sign a slip of paper acknowledging that he had been informed of the Politburo's decision, Trotsky wrote: "The decision of the G.P.U., criminal in substance and illegal in form, has been announced to me, January 20, 1929. Trotsky." He knew very well that it was not the decision of the G.P.U.

The armed guards watched closely, while Trotsky asked the inevitable questions. If he was being deported, where was he being deported to? What country would accept him? Once Volynsky turned to Trotsky's son and said: "Where are they taking you?" as though the secrets of the Politburo had somehow been confided to him. The writ was an order for Trotsky's expulsion but said nothing about the wife and son. They were told that somewhere in European Russia they would be met by an officer of the G.P.U. who would tell them what country they would be sent to. Evidently Stalin had not yet made the final arrangements for the deportation, and perhaps in the end it would prove to be impossible to deport him. If this happened, it would make little difference to Stalin, who had a large number of alternative punishments in reserve.

Trotsky was given exactly one day to pack his belongings, books, manuscripts, and archives, and to prepare for the journey. At dawn on January 22 an autobus arrived outside the house to take them on the first stage of their journey. Everything was loaded into the bus and at once they set out over snow-covered plains and through icy mountain passes. At the summit of the pass over the Khungai Ala Tau mountain they encountered a blizzard. The powerful tractor waiting to tow them across the pass stuck in the snowdrifts and almost vanished under the snow, together with the seven automobiles it was towing. It was one of the worst winters on record, and Trotsky commented ruefully that he had arrived in Alma-Ata in a snowstorm and was leaving in a snowstorm; it was as though Stalin had inflicted this punishment on him. But he was one who escaped the full fury of the storm. Seven men and some horses were frozen to death on the pass that day.

Somehow the tractor was lifted out of the snow, but it made little progress. Sleighs were brought up. Archives, manuscripts, and books were piled on the sleighs, and in seven hours they traveled about twenty miles. Here and there as they made their way to the lowlands they saw the shafts of sleighs sticking out of the snow. The Turkestan railway, the famous Turk-Sib, was then being constructed, and the snowy wastes were littered with what could still be seen of the construction material. The workmen and their horses had taken refuge from the snowstorm in the winter camps of the Kirghiz.

At Frunze a train was waiting for them to take them to European Russia. Now there were two G.P.U. officers accompanying them: Volynsky and an even more senior officer called Bulanov, who was continually in contact with Moscow on the direct wire. It was Bulanov who at last informed Trotsky that he would be exiled to Constantinople, and though Trotsky objected vehemently there was absolutely nothing he could do about it. He thought his vehement refusal carried some weight and wrote in his autobiography that Moscow foresaw everything except his refusal to leave voluntarily.

The long, wandering train journey across Russia screamed his impotence. He was not allowed to talk to Moscow: the talking was done by Bulanov. He could not escape from the train, for there was a large escort of soldiers on board. He could not, as in the days when he commanded his own armored train, tell it where to go. Moscow was choreographing the enterprise, listening to a stream of reports, ordering the train to turn into a siding or to proceed at full speed at its pleasure.

Trotsky demanded that he should be allowed to see his younger son, Sergey, and his daughter-in-law, Anya, the wife of Lyova. This message was conveyed to Stalin, who saw no reason not to humor the man who was his declared enemy. At Ryazhsk, an industrial town two hundred miles southeast of Moscow, Sergey and Anya became passengers on the train. Instead of three there were now five members of the Trotsky family under close guard, on a slow train to nowhere, in the depth of winter. The train avoided large towns and finally came to rest on a siding near a small abandoned station somewhere in the snow-covered forests of Kursk. It was a place, wrote Trotsky, "which has sunk into a stupor between two stretches of thin woods." There they remained for twelve interminable days, while Stalin deliberated with the Politburo in his leisurely fashion. Food and newspapers were brought every day from a railway station up the line; most of the food was canned and soon there was a small mountain of empty cans outside the train. The newspapers reported the purge of the Oppositionists in Georgia, for Stalin was at last falling upon his own people. The temperature dropped to 53 degrees below zero. Suspended in time, surrounded by snow, Trotsky waited out his last days on Russian soil rereading Kluchevsky's *History of Russia* and the works of Anatole France, while the rest of the family enjoyed their enforced leisure as best they could, playing chess, arguing, quarreling, making plans, whispering, for the guards were watching them. It was a strange kind of prison, but they became used to it. At intervals the detached engine would race up and down the line to prevent it from becoming frozen.

When Bulanov had to report some message he had received to Trotsky, he was always kindly and deferential. A tall, fair-haired man, he would attempt to argue with Trotsky, to cajole him, to make him realize the one thing he refused to realize: that Stalin had long ago made up his mind and there was no appeal from his decisions. On February 8, 1929, he announced that there would be no further delays. "I have been given final instructions to take you to Constantinople," he said.

"I refuse to go voluntarily," Trotsky replied. "I will say so at the Turkish frontier."

"It won't make any difference," Bulanov replied. "You will be taken there, whatever happens."

"You must have made a deal with the Turkish police for my forcible deportation to Turkey."

Bulanov shrugged his shoulders.

"We are only carrying out our orders," he said.

There had been no deal with the Turkish police. These matters had been decided on a much higher level. There had been a deal between Stalin and Kemal Ataturk, the dictator of Turkey.

The train sped south at full speed, rarely stopping except to take on fuel and water at small wayside stations. On the night of February 10 they reached Odessa. Sergey and Anya had decided to return to Moscow, Sergey because he wanted to pursue his career in science, Anya because she was no longer in love with her husband. As the automobile raced from the railroad station through the dark streets of Odessa, Trotsky recognized places he had known when he was a young student. He had only a fleeting glimpse of the city, but it was long enough to set him dreaming of the past: the film was being run backward so that the past could be reconciled with the present. He liked to say that he came to conscious life in Odessa; and in a sense it was in Odessa that his life came to an end.

He did not know, though he might have guessed, that all the remaining days of his life would be only a wandering and at every moment he would be in danger of death.

It is only a short distance from the railroad station in Odessa to the docks. The Black Sea was covered with ice. The ship waiting to take him to Constantinople was an empty cargo ship called the *Ilyich*, which was Lenin's patronymic. The irony of the name did not fail to provide Trotsky with some bitter amusement; nor did he fail to observe the armed soldiers who cordoned off the dockside, as though at this very last moment the government was afraid he would burst out of his cage and lead the Opposition to victory.

At one'oclock in the morning, preceded by an ice-breaker, the *Ilyich* cast its moorings and steamed out into the Black Sea. It was a stormy night, but the storm dealt them only a glancing blow. For about sixty miles the sea was icebound; the next morning the icebreaker returned to Odessa. Then Trotsky, Natalie, and Lyova were alone at last on a treacherous sea. The only comfort was that the books, manuscripts, and archives were still in their possession.

Off Buyuk Dere the Turkish police boarded the *Ilyich* to check the ship's manifest. They discovered that there were only three passengers. To the most senior of the police officers Trotsky presented a brief note addressed to Kemal Ataturk:

At the gate of Constantinople I have arrived at the Turkish frontier against my will and I will cross this frontier only by submitting to force. I request you, Mr. President, to accept my appropriate sentiments.

L. Trotsky

As they were entering the harbor, Natalie decided to go up on the bridge to have a better view of Constantinople. Bulanov warned her that it would be cold up there.

"You should put on a shawl," he suggested. "I know you have one."

Natalie was a little surprised by his solicitude and by the fact that he knew she had a shawl. He was a senior G.P.U. officer; he knew everything. In the years to come the G.P.U., sometimes secretly, sometimes openly, would continue to know everything. Spies were planted in the Trotsky household, agents would become their intimate friends, their correspondence was read, their friends were shadowed, and their plans were thwarted. The shadow of the G.P.U. lay over them to the end of their days.

GRANDEURS AND MISERIES OF EXILE

PART SEVEN

She, poor soul, began to reproach me, saying: "How long, archpriest, is this suffering to be?" And I said: "Markovna, unto our very death." And she, with a sigh, answered: "So be it, Petrovich, let us be going on our way."

THE ISLAND 20 OF PRINCES

At first there was only a long silence, a sense of weariness and loneliness in a strange land. Sometimes the silence was broken by the echoes of rumors; telephones were ringing at the end of far distant corridors; Moscow was demanding reports of his behavior; the officials in the Russian Consulate in Constantinople spoke to him deferentially, knowing that he was exiled for being a counterrevolutionary, for preparing an armed struggle against the Soviet Power. Surprisingly they were holding on to him for a little while longer. When the *Ilyich* steamed into the harbor at Constantinople, the consular automobile was waiting for him. He was living now in a wing of the Consulate, and he was in prison again.

He was mortally tired and in need of a long rest. The long journey across Russia, the meeting with Sergey at Ryazhsk and the separation from him in Odessa, the knowledge that he was surgically separated from Russia and that all his followers were being hounded to death by Stalin—all these things had drained him emotionally, spiritually, and mentally. The last stage of the journey in the small black ship on the icy sea was almost too symbolic. He spent a lot of time standing by the ship's rail and gazing out upon emptiness in a state of total numbness, remote from the world as in a grave.

There was no safety in the Consulate, formerly the Imperial Russian Embassy, filled with Persian carpets and heavy dark furniture. He was watched closely while he stood guard over his archives, the most precious of his possessions. They had survived miraculously; it seemed never to have occurred to the G.P.U. to sequester them on the grounds that they could be used very effectively against Stalin. Just as there was no safety in the Consulate, so there was no safety outside it. There were thousands of White Russians in Constantinople who regarded him as a man of the utmost evil, Antichrist and Mephistopheles combined, creator of the Red Army, wielder of the revolutionary power. Memories of the civil war were still fresh in 1929. There were many White Russians who would have given their right arms for the opportunity to put a bullet into his brain.

Natalie and Lyova went out and did the shopping. There was a little money. It consisted of $1,500 given to them when they landed by one of the consular officials. Trotsky, who studied money carefully, regarded it as a derisory reward for his services to the Revolution and spoke bitterly of this paltry gift. This was "going away" money, such as a servant receives after being dismissed, to help him find another job. Nevertheless, it was useful, and he accepted it with as much grace as he could muster.

Inevitably affairs went badly at the Consulate. Even though the consular officials went out of their way to be polite and respectful to the man who had wielded such vast power in Russia, and though Trotsky himself maintained a studious dignity, quarrels flared up. Lyova got in trouble with the police and was briefly arrested. Natalie appeared to be on the verge of a nervous breakdown. The consul, who was oppressed by his new responsibilities, began to wonder how long he would be compelled to remain host to this restless guest, all the more restless because he was sitting quietly in a wing of the palatial Consulate. The consul applied to Moscow for permission to evict him three weeks after he arrived. Permission was readily given. A surprised Trotsky thereupon wrote one of these legalistic letters for the record, in which he explained that the G.P.U. had made many promises and had not kept them. They had promised to find him an apartment in a private house with some minimum guarantees of safety; they had promised that his friends Sermuks and Poznansky would be allowed to share his exile; they had promised or half-promised that he could live in the Consulate as long as he liked. In any case, none of the five or six apartments they had suggested for him could be made ready for him immediately. It would take another three weeks to put them in order. He proposed therefore to remain in the Consulate come what may. The consul threatened to have him "physically isolated," which probably meant that the wing would be cut off from the rest of the house—not the worst of punishments, but it had the unfortunate effect of suggesting an "isolator" in one of the Soviet prison camps. Trotsky replied angrily that he reserved full freedom of action and the Central Committee would have to bear the consequences. Since the Central Committee was dominated by Stalin and since "full freedom of action" gave him very limited choices, Trotsky gained little or nothing from this outburst.

What he was really hoping for was to get out of Constantinople altogether. He applied for permission to live in Germany, England, Norway, and France. The president of the Reichstag announced that he would probably be given the right of asylum; his hopes rose, only to be dashed when a report came from the German Embassy in Moscow that the government absolutely refused to grant him a visa. The Norwegian government refused on the grounds that it could not be responsible for his safety. The French government remembered that the expulsion order of 1916 had not been rescinded. The British government showed no interest, and when the subject was raised in Parliament there was an outburst of laughter, which only confirmed Trotsky in his detestation of the British people generally and their government in particular. "I have studied what appears to be the joke for some time," he commented, "but I still cannot see the point of it."

Some of the bitterest pages ever written by Trotsky are devoted to a recital of his lasting quarrels with governments that refused to grant him a visa. He remembered that many European dignitaries had been his guests in the Kremlin. He had welcomed them, though coldly. Now, in his despair, he wondered why they did not welcome him or at least grant him the right of asylum. He was particularly incensed by Philip Snowden, the former Labour M.P. who was now Chancellor of the Exchequer. In 1920 Snowden visited Moscow as an official guest, he was given a box at the Bolshoy Theater, he had applauded Trotsky for his victories against the White armies, and now this contemptible man refused to lift a finger to help Trotsky find asylum, refused even to contemplate the thought that Trotsky deserved to be assisted. This rankled, not only because Snowden maintained a stubborn silence. When Lenin learned that Trotsky had sat in a box at the Bolshoy with Snowden, he had looked up in that sharp quizzical way of his and said in effect: "What on earth were you doing, sitting in the box with that swine?"

Trotsky vented his anger on the European socialists who refused him asylum with the same anguished hatred that he vented on Stalin. The cutting edge of the knife was sharp but the blade was rusted. It never seems to have occurred to him that he had insulted European socialists time after time, and most bitterly when they voted for war credits at the beginning of World War I. He had no love for them, and they had no love for him. Also, they feared him. In their eyes he was a demoniac force who had hurled himself upon the stage of Russian history, maintained himself in power by extraordinary virtuosity, and burned himself out, and they knew he could burst into flame again. They did not underestimate his power. Imagine Tamerlane defeated in battle and seeking asylum at the court of the Byzantine emperor. How long would it be before Tamerlane founded his own Byzantine dynasty?

So they rejected him, and he cursed them because they treated him as a pariah. Yet, as he knew, it was not simply a question of black and white. The right of asylum had a long history going back to pagan times. Once a man reached a shrine or an altar, he was *provisionally* safe, depending on the crime he had committed: the right of asylum was never absolute. Technically, it did not mean the right of the fugitive to demand protection but the right of a state to grant it. Asylum has many faces, which are traditionally turned more favorably toward slaves and soldiers fleeing from the battlefield. Napoleon sought asylum in England; it was not granted to him; he was too large for England to hold, and so he was kept a prisoner on a small and inaccessible island.

Trotsky, too, found sanctuary on an island. Ironically, his place of refuge was found for him by a G.P.U. man in the Soviet Consulate, a former airman, whom he had befriended long before. The G.P.U. man had visited Prinkipo, the Island of Princes, where in the not too distant past the relatives of the sultans of Turkey were sometimes exiled. The island had a few down-at-heel villas, usually empty except in summer, with a small permanent population of shepherds and fishermen. It was inhospitable in winter and not especially inviting at any time, but it possessed a certain lowly grandeur. Max Eastman, who visited Trotsky at Prinkipo, called it "this bright red-cliffed island that crouches in the sea like a prehistoric animal drinking," but this was to give it more grandeur than it possessed. There was something very ordinary and vulgar about the island, it was made to be a holiday resort, and unlike the Greek islands of the Aegean, it had no character of its own.

The G.P.U. man found a villa belonging to a bankrupt pasha on the very edge of the Sea of Marmora. The pasha had long since abandoned it; the floorboards were rotting, birds nested in the house, spiders spun huge cobwebs. Trotsky visited the villa, liked it, and immediately settled in it, grateful that he no longer had to deal with an obdurate Soviet Consulate. Here he could write in peace, guarded by the two policemen the

Turkish government placed at his service. Here, too, he could fish—it was his one form of exercise and he became a relentless fisherman, never happier than when he was hauling in the nets in his fishing boat with its prow painted bright red, in the company of a gnarled old Greek fisherman who spoke no language he understood but who nevertheless contrived to be perfectly intelligible. This fisherman was his anchor: a man of the earth who helped to keep him sane.

The villa stood at a short distance from the tiny village of Buyuk Ada and was set in a wild garden which no one tended. Neither Natalie nor Trotsky had any gift for gardening. Hedges and trees surrounded the house on three sides, and there were a few trees on the narrow strip of land sloping down to the sea. In the center of the house there was a hall opening on a verandah facing the sea. The hall was sometimes described as "vast," but was in fact only twenty-four feet by fifteen feet, and seemed vast only by comparison with the small closet-sized rooms on either side. There was a tiny dining room downstairs and a tiny kitchen. Upstairs, immediately above the hall, was Trotsky's study with an unvarnished wooden table stretching halfway across the room. It was very simply furnished, spartan in its simplicity. The french windows opened onto a balcony and a breathtaking view of the Sea of Marmora, all royal blue, the same deep blue laced with gold that can be seen around the Greek islands.

The first task was to set the house in order, to whitewash the walls, repair the floorboards, and paint the floors. Trotsky had borrowed twenty thousand French francs from his friend Maurice Paz, a lawyer who had been expelled from the Communist Party, even while he was staying at the Soviet Consulate. He soon discovered that his living expenses on the Island of Princes were minimal. He caught his own fish, hunted his own rabbits, and if he had troubled to transform the wilderness around his house into a vegetable garden, he would have been nearly self-sufficient. He visited Constantinople only once and this

was to see Santa Sophia, a friend having promised him
that he would be overwhelmed by its beauty. He was
not in the least impressed with it. He saw no films,
never went to a restaurant, neither smoked nor drank.
The ordinary expenditures of ordinary people were
quite foreign to him. In a few months he was able to
return the money he had borrowed from Maurice Paz
and was independently wealthy, for publishers were
clamoring for his works, first his autobiography and
then his *History of the Russian Revolution*. Both these
works would appear in many languages. Soon he
would be living on a scale of $10,000 to $15,000 a year, a
considerable sum in those days, but he was not spending the money on himself. The money was being spent
on stenographers, secretaries, guards, the publication
of his *Bulletin of the Opposition*, and gifts-in-aid to
groups of his followers in half the countries of Europe.
Clothes and laundry were his only luxuries, for he
insisted on being impeccably dressed on all occasions.

When Max Eastman visited the house, he was struck
by the lack of either comfort or beauty. "A man and
woman must be almost dead aesthetically to live in
that bare barrack, which a few dollars could convert
into a charming house." He was placing some of the
blame on Natalie, which was unfair, for she had a
highly developed aesthetic sense. But she lived in her
husband's shadow, did what he wanted, and had long
ago surrendered her individuality. When she told Max
Eastman that she had allowed the garden to run to seed
"to save money," it is more likely that a proper translation should read: "My husband could not be bothered
with it."

There were a surprisingly large number of things he
could not be bothered with. He paid very little attention
to food, to money, to entertainment, to sex, to safety.
The two Turkish guards were rarely in their little hut
near the garden gate; they were continually being sent
off on errands or asked to perform small services in the
house. They became members of the family. Trotsky
himself always had a revolver within reach. Lyova,
living downstairs in one of those tiny rooms off the

main hall, constituted himself the chief guard, and he too continually had a revolver within reach. Nevertheless the house was virtually unprotected. A fast motorboat could have raked the house with machine-gun fire and got away without the slightest difficulty. At Prinkipo there were none of the elaborate defenses that were installed in later years in Trotsky's villa in Mexico: no watchtowers, no booby traps, no armored gates and windows. Here he lived openly, quietly, and contentedly, and he made no secret of the fact that he was still working toward world revolution, and against Stalin, while he was under the protection of the G.P.U. In this anomalous position he remained for the four and a half years of his stay on the island.

There was something almost too perfect about Prinkipo as a place of refuge. He called it "an island of peace and forgetfulness," and so it was. News of the world came late, hushed by time and distance, like flotsam drifting to the Sea of Marmora. He had no radio. Newspapers sometimes failed to arrive; French papers took three or four days, Russian newspapers more than a week. There were two French newspapers published in Constantinople and an English newspaper called *The Orient News*, but they were newspapers only in name, full of advertisements and local news with perhaps half a page of international news provided by the telegraphic agencies. These came on the ferryboat, which took an hour and a half to make the journey to the island from Constantinople.

There were no automobiles on the island, and the loudest noise came from the braying of the asses. There was scarcely anything on the island which had not been there a thousand or two thousand years ago. In its loneliness and remoteness Prinkipo was an ideal place for a man who had retired from the world, and a very odd place for a man who still aspired to be a revolutionary leader, who had dominated two violent revolutions and hoped to dominate a third. He was only forty-nine years old when he was exiled from Russia, and he was at the height of his powers.

His day began early, before dawn. He washed and

dressed and padded around the house in his fisherman's uniform, a thick sweater, heavy trousers, sandals or sea boots. Then he would go down to his small wharf where the boat was tied up, and his friend, the Greek fisherman Karolambos, was waiting for him. Karolambos was a small wiry man whose son was a fisherman and whose ancestors as far back as he could remember, to the fourth or fifth generation, were also fishermen. He was a lobsterman as well as a fisherman. Trotsky was a little in awe of him, for though uneducated he had a deep and precise knowledge of the weather and the sea, and like all Greeks he could talk voluminously without opening his mouth, in gestures. Together they invented a new language out of Turkish, Greek, Russian, and French words sometimes taken at random and provided with new definitions. Trotsky provided the motive force; he was the rower. Karolambos was in charge, and Trotsky willingly conceded that his Greek friend knew more about fishing than he would ever know.

Nearly every day there were these fishing expeditions, and sometimes they went out even in winter when unexpected storms swept over the Sea of Marmora. But mostly the sea was calm, as smooth as a mirror, drenched in the heavy sunlight of the Levant; to row smoothly over it was a paradise for lotus-eaters. Trotsky, determined not to become a lotus-eater, expended a vast amount of energy in rowing. The boat was weighed down with heavy stones. The stratagem was to discover where the fish were lurking, arrange the nets in exactly the right position, and then hurl the stones into the water in such a way as to drive the fish into the nets. Trotsky was the stone thrower, while Karolambos cunningly manipulated the nets. Peering into the water he would give the signal for the first stone to be thrown, and where the other stones should be thrown, for there was an art in stone throwing. The idea was to make the fish bunch together, and then with the last stone they would find themselves streaming into the net. The fish were bombarded with stones and led into an ambush. It looked simple but was in fact complicated. Trotsky noted that different kinds of stones were needed at different times of the year and for different configurations of the sea bottom. There were also two very large stones attached to ropes, and it was necessary to learn how to throw them with great force for maximum effect and this had to be done at exactly the right moment.

But it was in lobster hunting that Karolambos showed the greatest resourcefulness. Trotsky described admiringly how the lobsterman went to work:

> The old man peered down into the water to a depth of fifteen or twenty feet until he discovered the lobster's hiding place under a rock. Then with a very long pole tipped with iron he pushed the rock over and the lobster scuttled away. The old man gave an order to the oarsman and pursued the lobster with a second long pole to which a square-framed net bag was attached, and when he had overtaken the lobster, the net descended on the lobster, which was hauled out of the water. And when the sea was disturbed with small waves, the old man sprinkled oil on it with his fingers and peered through the fatty mirror. In this way, on a good day, he catches thirty or forty lobsters.

Unfortunately there was such a glut of lobsters in the Sea of Marmora that the price had fallen long ago, and he made little money out of them.

After the fishing expedition came the morning's work: reading of newspapers, answering letters, dictation, a conference with Lyova or with one of his visitors. Letters from some of his followers were often written in invisible ink or in code, and Natalie would busy herself decoding them. A surprisingly large amount of mail came from Americans who implored him to convert to Christianity. Later there was a frugal dinner downstairs in the tiny whitewashed dining room—Trotsky ate *kasha*, a kind of buckwheat porridge, and very little else, because his stomach had been ruined during the civil war—and there followed a rather ceremonial washing up, from which Trotsky was generally excluded on the grounds that he was inclined to regard washing up as a military exercise and was altogether too dominating. Natalie, Lyova, and the visitors would crowd into the narrow kitchen and do the work in about five minutes.

There was more work in the afternoon. This began immediately after dinner, for Trotsky had never known the advantages of a siesta. The siesta came after supper, when he and Natalie sat on the study balcony and gazed out over the Sea of Marmora with its flaring sunsets, the clouds continually changing color, and the sea turning to a hundred shades of blue until it vanished in the darkness. If there were visitors, they would be invited to see the sunset. At such times Trotsky was likely to be in a bantering mood, gay and lively, having swept most of his problems out of his mind. Outwardly he seemed composed, while the demons of anxiety lay just below the surface.

There was anxiety for his friends in Russia, for his family in Russia, for Russia itself now more than ever at the mercy of a Byzantine dictator. He believed that Europe was on the verge of revolution, but this caused him no anxiety at all: the revolution would come about inexorably according to Marxist theory and he believed he had a role to play in this revolution which should inevitably be the prelude of the world revolution. History moved in inexorable and inevitable ways. He did not know and could not guess that the greatest revolution on European soil would take place in Germany under the command of a man who also hoped to bring about a world revolution by bringing the entire world under German domination. Trotsky had very little understanding of Hitler, perhaps because he despised him, as he despised Stalin. History rarely followed the path of his prophecies.

As a prophet Trotsky proved to be curiously prone to error, but as a historian he was a brilliant, if somewhat ambiguous, interpreter of the past. He saw himself too brightly as a historical figure not to be a little dazzled by his own eminence. He was a victim of hubris, the pride that seeks and almost glories in a downfall. Nevertheless, in his long exile on the Island of Princes he acted and thought more soberly than at any other time. By nature he was a student: the island gave him the leisure to study.

Among the objects left in the villa by its owner, the old pasha, was a lifesize bronze peacock, a familiar ornament in many Turkish houses. No one knew what to do with it; it seemed too valuable to throw away; it was inoffensive, and was allowed to remain on the ground floor, where it was sometimes used as a doorstop. As far as we know, Trotsky never gave it a moment's thought, for he disliked ornaments, and if they were present he avoided looking at them.

Although Trotsky avoided looking at it, the historian is under an obligation to look at the bronze peacock more carefully, for it was the sole object in the villa that descended from an earlier age. It had a venerable ancestry, deriving from the classic period of Mameluke art, when the pride and power of the peacock were depicted by great artists. But this particular peacock, deriving at a long distance from a Mameluke original, was no work of art; it was simply a household object, commonplace, darkened with age. If anyone in the villa had taken the trouble to polish it, he would have discovered that underneath the black grime it shone like gold.

There were moral lessons to be derived from the shadowy peacock that haunted the villa on the island of Prinkipo, that was present and not present, visible and invisible, useful and useless. No one had thrown it on the trash heap because no one was sufficiently interested to do anything about it. So it remained there on sufferance, a dark object discarded in a dark corner, a little like Trotsky, himself a peacock who had once blazed so brilliantly and was now old and vulnerable, living in hiding.

THE REWARDS OF EXILE 21

The months and the years passed, and it seemed as though Trotsky was destined to live on this island for the rest of his life. If he had possessed the power to foresee the future, he might have elected to stay there indefinitely; never, in his later years, would he enjoy so much calm or do so much work. His writings during this period have a broad spaciousness that reflects his style of living. Prinkipo provided him with essential comforts and as much fishing as he could reasonably desire; the old pasha's house suited him perfectly; his secretaries and guards were few in number; he was enjoying a sense of his own power and importance as the one man who had the strength of mind to stand against Stalin; and every evening, as a reward for the day's work, he would sit in a chaise lounge and admire the spectacular sunsets. He wrote once that in prison with a book or pen in his hand he experienced the same sense of deep satisfaction that he did during the Revolution. He told himself that he did not need action as a spur; it was enough to be able to dream, to think, to ponder.

But of course this was not the whole truth. He needed stimulation, travel, adventure, drama. He had gloried in the drama of the revolution and the civil war; he was not made for the sedentary life. Prinkipo suffered from two quite remarkable disadvantages: it provided very little intellectual stimulation, and it was a place from which it was impossible to launch a revolution. He still regarded himself as an active revolutionary and still believed or half-believed that it was in his power at this late date to launch a world revolution. Only on this premise did his life have any meaning. His overwhelming desire was therefore to break out of the island and take command of a revolutionary army.

There were six hundred inhabitants on the island; he knew scarcely any of them. He rarely walked across the island except to shoot small animals. He had walled himself in the old pasha's house among his books and archives, and his empire consisted of the house, the wild garden, a few square yards of foreshore, and the sea. He also possessed an invisible empire which consisted of a small community of followers, numbering two or three hundred people, mostly in France and Germany, consisting of Communists who were disenchanted by the Soviet Union under Stalin and who believed that Trotsky had inherited the mantle of Lenin and was the rightful dictator of the world Communist movement. Occasionally, and not as often as he wished, there would come emissaries from abroad. Thus, early in May 1929, he was visited by Mr. and Mrs. Sidney Webb, the Fabian socialists, who rather foolishly told him that he would certainly be allowed to live in England if the Labour Party won the election. The Webbs were over-optimistic, and Trotsky never forgave them.

It is generally believed that he spent the whole of his Turkish exile on the island of Prinkipo, but it was not so. In February 1931, about an hour before dawn, a fire broke out in the pasha's house. They were all roused from their beds, and Trotsky took command of the rescue operations. It was a fierce fire which apparently began in the kitchen, and there was a very real danger that the whole house might be consumed. The first task was to see that everyone was accounted for; the second was to see that the archives were preserved intact; the third was to salvage the books in the large library. Only the first two tasks were successfully accomplished; most of the library went up in flames. Trotsky directed the operations as though he was commanding a small army, and it was noted that he was unusually calm. At dawn there was a gutted house on the edge of the sea, and all around it, in disorderly piles, were the possessions they had snatched from the flames.

Characteristically Trotsky refused to allow the fire to interfere with the day's program. He went straight from the fire to a nearby hotel, accompanied by his stenographer. In the hotel bedroom he laid papers and documents on the table and began dictating from where he left off the previous day.

There was talk of arson; an inquiry was held; nothing was proved. Trotsky himself seems to have thought the fire was an attempt to burn him in his bed, but whether the arsonist came from Russia or from among the White Guards was beyond his understanding. Although he appeared to be serene, he was depressed and worried.

The task of finding a new house fell to Natalie. A week later she found a suitable house at Kodikoy (Kadikeui) on the Asiatic side of the Sea of Marmora, about twenty minutes by boat from the Galata Bridge. The town of Kodikoy stood on a small promontory, and most of the houses belonged to members of the large British colony. It was a respectable, upper middle-class town with a very small permanent population, for the British came during the summer to avoid the heat of Constantinople and only spent occasional weekends there during the spring and autumn. In the winter it was virtually empty.

Natalie chose a house that was completely undistinguished, unlike the house on Prinkipo, which had some small claim to distinction. It was a simple two-story wooden frame house surrounded by a high picket fence reinforced with barbed wire. As usual, the house was crowded. Two policemen, a cook, Trotsky, Natalie, Zina and her son Seva, the secretary Jan Frankel, and a stenographer all lived in the house. Sometimes there were two or three secretaries and extra guards; important visitors stayed overnight; there was always a fisherman attached to the house. Trotsky's study was upstairs, while most of the bedrooms, the kitchen, and the tiny dining room were downstairs. There was no comfort: only a hard Spartan living together with everyone treading on each other's toes.

From the study window there was a wonderful view of the Sea of Marmora with its islands and ships, and the European shore fading in the blue misty distance. The house was on a high bluff, rather ugly and somewhat dilapidated, and while it lacked distinction, it possessed character.

Winston Churchill, in a jeering essay called "The Ogre of Europe," wrote that "Trotsky, whose frown meted death to thousands, sits disconsolate, a bundle of old rags, stranded on the shores of the Black Sea." It was not the happiest way to describe him. He was not living on the shores of the Black Sea, he was not disconsolate, he was not a bundle of old rags. He was superbly hopeful. Europe in 1931 was in a state of violent crisis, and he believed he had a revolutionary role to play. He was not being blindly self-indulgent in his hopes. Churchill was being somewhat more perceptive when, a few years after writing the article, he incorporated it with some additions in a series of political portraits called *Great Contemporaries* and observed: "No one could wish him a better punishment than that his life should be prolonged, and that his keen intelligence and restless spirit should corrode each other in impotence and stultification." Impotence and stultification were the terrible beasts lurking at the bottom of the pool, waiting to devour him.

To keep the beasts at bay, Trotsky poured himself into his work, writing an impressive number of articles both for his private propaganda sheet called the *Bulletin of the Opposition* and for the bourgeois press, and an even more impressive number of letters to his followers, pleading, warning, excoriating, and sometimes, but very rarely, praising them for their efforts. Trotskyism, like Communism, suffered from an inherent tendency to instability. A group had no sooner been started than there would be a series of convulsions, warring factions would come into being, these in turn would split into their component parts. His followers Maurice Paz, Pierre Naville, and Raymond Molinier in France all headed Trotskyist groups and quarreled violently among themselves. Trotsky did his best to calm these storms and he was well aware that they were damaging him. If his followers were always at each other's throats, what hope was there for a Trotskyist revolution?

The same thing was happening in Germany, where Trotsky went to great pains to set up his own revolutionary organization. Trotsky understood Russian affairs very well, but he appeared to suffer a fatal blindness whenever he wrote upon German affairs. A stream of letters, articles and pamphlets on Germany show that he totally misunderstood the mind of Hitler and misinterpreted Hitler's aims and motives. He wrote in April 1932, less than a year before Hitler achieved power:

> If Hitler overcomes all obstacles and achieves power, he will be compelled, in order to get a free hand in his own country, to begin with an oath of loyalty to Versailles. Nobody on the Quai d'Orsay has any doubt of that. Moreover, it is well understood there that a military dictatorship of Hitler, once it was firmly established in Germany, might become a considerably more reliable element in the French hegemony over Europe than the present German governmental system, whose mathematical formula consists largely of unknown quantities. Hitler in power would mean war, not against Poland, not against France, but against the Soviet Union.

Too many of his political articles are of this kind: ill written, strident, categorical. His prophecies are balloons that float away in the wind, and he knows no more than the next man what will happen tomorrow. It was the same when he met journalists: he would assert the most extraordinary things without the slightest evidence as though he had received a message from the Delphic oracle. Yet he would talk quite sensibly about his personal plans, his personal hopes, his ideas about books, and all the books he hoped to write.

An Associated Press reporter came to visit him when he was living at Kodikoy. The reporter had seen him shortly after he settled in the pasha's house on Prinkipo. Now, some three years later, Trotsky seemed a different man, no longer heavy and sallow, but lithe and ruddy faced. He wore an open-neck white shirt, white trousers, and blue jacket; his thin, pointed face was sunburned from hours spent fishing on the Sea of Marmora; his bristling hair and pointed beard were almost white. Although he had been suffering from recurrent attacks of malaria, the air was alive with his own vitality. There was no bitterness in him. It was almost incredible that a man who had played such a dramatic role in world history should be living in this crumbling wooden house overlooking a peaceful garden and a tranquil sea.

During the interview Trotsky alternately defended and attacked Stalin. The Five Year Plan was a sweepstake; Stalin should have been more cautious. All those who said that Stalin was attempting to revive the private ownership of the means of production were obviously wrong, for such a change could only be brought about by a counterrevolution. He described the Opposition as though it consisted merely of an advisory body made up of critical politicians, but then he went on to say that the bureaucratic regime of Stalin had suppressed the independent political activity of the masses, which was now being revived, leaving to the reporter's imagination how it was being revived, and by whom, and at what cost. He was impressive, but not believable. The reporter caught a glimpse of his daughter Zina, suntanned, wearing large round spectacles. He was told that the young woman was suffering from throat trouble and would soon be sent to Europe for an operation. He learned too that Natalie was ill, and did not see her.

A new government had come into power in Spain, and Trotsky was hoping the Spanish Republican au-

thorities would give him a visa. He was restless. He
wanted to see with his own eyes what was happening
in Europe. He wanted to talk with politicians and
political commentators. He wanted to knit together
those pathetically small organizations that claimed to
follow him and were already threatening to split up like
cancer cells, were already penetrated by Stalinist
agents, and were perhaps incapable of any real revolutionary action. He wanted to make speeches to young
workmen and students, and rouse them to revolutionary action. He wanted to escape from his isolation, and
he did not know that for the rest of his life he would
remain isolated because he was feared and because
governments would do everything in their power to
keep him isolated.

Early in November 1932 Socialist students in Copenhagen invited him to address them in honor of the
fifteenth anniversary of the Russian Revolution. The
Socialist government of Denmark had agreed to grant
him an eight-day visa: Trotsky hoped it would be
extended. He hoped, too, to address more gatherings of
students in Norway and Sweden and perhaps even in
Germany, which was on the eve of being conquered by
Hitler. He eagerly accepted the invitation, and on
November 14 he sailed to France, accompanied by
Natalie and three secretaries, Jan Frankel, Pierre
Frank, and Otto Schussler. The grandson Seva had to
be left behind because it was impossible to obtain
travel papers for him. Trotsky traveled under the name
of Lev Sedov. This was his legal name, for it was the
name written in his Soviet passport when he entered
Turkey.

The journey was a study in frustrations and the art of
applying them. Nearly everything he desired was denied to him. The police watched him closely, the Stalinists spied on him, the bureaucrats took pleasure in
rejecting his requests. He was regarded as a source of
contagion, a walking pestilence, and the governments
were determined to keep him at a distance. Since he
was much less innocent than he appeared to be, since
in fact he had declared war on all existing govern-

ments, there was some irony in his repeated claim that he was being treated unfairly.

The first pettifogging restriction occurred when the ship put in at Piraeus. He was not allowed to go ashore and see the Acropolis for fear that he might spread his revolutionary ideas in Greece. Mussolini's police were less troublesome; at Naples he was allowed to disembark and to visit the ruins of Pompeii under a strong police escort. The French police ordered him, his wife, and the three secretaries off the ship near Marseilles and brought them by motor launch to an abandoned jetty along the coast. Then his party was driven to Lyons by car, put on the train to Paris, rushed from the Gare du Lyon to the Gare du Nord, and put on the train to Dunkirk. *L'Ami du peuple*, the right-wing newspaper, asked why France was playing host to Trotsky, "known in the ghetto as Bronstein, the greatest assassin the world has ever known." *Pravda* wrote: "The lion has escaped," and looked forward to the time when he was once more behind bars. In fact, throughout his journey, Trotsky was accompanied by his cage. Sometimes it was a double cage, with the inner ring formed by his followers and pretended followers, the outer ring formed by the police. Sometimes there was a third ring interposed between the other two, and this consisted of Stalinist agents. Correspondents who caught up with Trotsky at Dunkirk were a little puzzled to find him hidden away behind his guards, who were surprisingly numerous and nervous, attempting to look in all directions at once. Trotsky was well aware that there might be an attempt to assassinate him during the journey.

He traveled by ship from Dunkirk to the Danish port of Esbjerg and then by train to Copenhagen. There were no incidents on the train, but at all the stations they passed through there were small gangs of Stalinists shouting abuse. Trotsky's friends concluded that this was probably a warning of worse things to come, and almost immediately after arriving in Copenhagen Trotsky dispatched Gérard Rosenthal to the headquarters of the Danish Communist Party to ask them point-blank whether they intended to disrupt the speech that would be delivered in the stadium. "I am speaking," said Rosenthal, who was Trotsky's lawyer, "about Leon Trotsky, the man who organized the October Revolution—" This was a very odd confrontation; it was difficult to know what could be gained by it. If we imagine Kerensky dispatching an officer to Trotsky in October 1917 and saying: "I have come to learn whether you intend to disrupt the Provisional Government. I am speaking on behalf of Alexander Kerensky, the prime minister of Russia," what would we expect Trotsky to say? Rosenthal tells us that the youthful-looking Communist leaders of Denmark looked surprised when they heard the question and answered "in their calm Scandinavian way" that the idea of disrupting Trotsky's speech had never once entered their minds.

The house rented for Trotsky's brief visit belonged to a Danish ballerina who was on tour. It was like a doll's house with three small rooms downstairs and three more upstairs. Guards maintained a perpetual vigil downstairs. There were photographs of the ballerina everywhere; the frilly decorations reflected the taste of the young woman, who drenched all her possessions in perfume. Trotsky stayed here for two or three days. When a Danish newspaper published a photograph of the house, he fled to another house in the suburbs. The decision to change his residence came in the evening. Trotsky had scarcely settled into the new house when he turned to his lawyer and said: "It's not worth going to sleep, Comrade Rosenthal. Let's go out and enjoy ourselves in the woods." Together they walked into the nearby birch woods, Trotsky gesticulating and talking loudly, enjoying his freedom and sometimes pausing to assume the posture of a boxer engaged in imaginary fisticuffs. He was in a combative mood but took care that the combat should take place in the dark in a stretch of woodland in the outskirts of Copenhagen. Trotsky and Rosenthal slipped back into the house without being observed, thus demonstrating that the guards—there were at least twenty of them—and the detachment of police deputed to keep watch on the dangerous revolutionary from abroad were equally useless.

Trotsky was given a Danish visa on condition that he stayed for only eight days, engaged in no political activities, and did not advertise his presence except when he made the speech in the Stadium to the Socialist students, and this speech too must be devoid of political content. Predictably Trotsky engaged in a good deal of political activity, presided over secret meetings with his followers, and arranged with the assistance of Harry Wicks, an Englishman in touch with Russian sailors in London, to distribute his underground writings in the Soviet Union. Trotsky had spent much of his life in conspiratorial activity, and could not stop.

The Danish press appeared to be mildly excited by his presence on Danish soil. A correspondent of *Politiken* interviewed him on the train from Esbjerg to Copenhagen, while he talked rather blandly about a previous visit to Denmark in 1910 to attend an international Socialist congress. Lenin, Bebel, Rosa Luxemburg, and Jean Jaurès had also attended. "Who," he asked, "could possibly have guessed what would happen in the future?" He confessed that his days in Copenhagen were among the happiest in his life and that he had nothing but admiration for the Danes who had welcomed him with their traditional gentleness and friendliness. He was asked whether he intended to return to Russia and answered: "Now you are talking politics, and I cannot answer that."

The Soviet ambassador to Denmark objected vigorously to Trotsky's presence on Danish soil. The royal family, through Prince Aage, objected equally vigorously and reminded the Danes that the mother of the murdered Tsar was a Danish princess. All the right-wing newspapers fumed, and the Communist newspaper depicted him as an ogre. Never had there been such unanimity among the monarchy, the capitalists, and the Communists.

At last, on November 27, came the great day of the

speech, or rather the many speeches. On the same day he delivered a radio message to the United States in English, made a short propaganda film for French consumption in French, and addressed the Socialist students in the Copenhagen Stadium in German. It was a remarkable tour de force made a little easier by the fact that his arguments were the same in all three speeches.

The best was the speech broadcast to America by CBS. "My English, my poor English," he complained, but in fact he spoke very simply and concisely, with a terrible accent. He quoted his 1905 prophecy about the coming revolution and how it would come to birth but otherwise had very little to say about his own role in the Revolution. He addressed himself to two questions: How and why did the Revolution take place? Had it stood the test? It came into existence, he explained, because, in Lenin's words, "the chain broke at its weakest link," and because Marxist theory together with his own theory of the permanent revolution had demonstrated the theoretical factors by which an economically backward country could achieve a proletarian revolution earlier than an advanced capitalist country.

In September, Lenin, who was compelled to keep in hiding, gave the signal: "The crisis is ripe, the hour of the insurrection has approached." He was right. The bourgeoisie finally lost its head. The democratic parties, the Mensheviks and the Social Revolutionaries, wanted the remains of the confidence of the masses in them. The awakened army no longer wanted to fight for the foreign aims of imperialism. Disregarding democratic advice, the peasantry smoked the landowners out of their estates. The oppressed nationalities at the periphery rose up against the bureaucracy of Petrograd. In the most important Workers' and Soldiers' Soviets the Bolsheviki were dominant. The workers and soldiers demanded action. The ulcer was ripe. It needed the cut of the lancet.

Although he was exerting the historian's privilege to rewrite history at his pleasure, Trotsky was being reasonably accurate. When he described the peasants burning down the mansions of the landowners, he must have known that these bonfires, "the crowing of the red cock," had little enough to do with the Revolution and had been going on for a hundred years, and when he spoke of the oppressed nationalities on the periphery rising up against the bureaucracy of Petrograd, he forgot to add that they continued to rise up against the bureaucracy of the Bolsheviks, and in this way Finland, Latvia, Estonia, and Lithuania acquired their independence. Nor was it true that the Mensheviks and the Social Revolutionaries lacked the confidence of the masses—these two parties of the left were outmaneuvered, infiltrated from within and without, and summarily destroyed by mass deportations and executions.

When Trotsky asked himself whether the October Revolution had stood the test, he was in a dilemma. Every fiber of his being told him that under Stalin the revolution had failed, that it had been perverted, that it was being hopelessly mismanaged, and that Stalin's triumph was a betrayal of the work of Lenin. Nevertheless, he extolled the Soviet Union. In his view all the sacrifices, all the unnecessary deaths, were justified. Half a million men died in the American Civil War, but surely the war was justified in its fruits! There had been terrible mistakes, collectivization had been introduced with inadequate preparation and understanding, there were errors all along the line, but a beginning of communist society had been attempted, and it could not fail. The "slow, passive, melancholy-mystical Russian people" were becoming a new people, forged in steel. As though haunted by Stalin (*Stal* = steel), Trotsky again and again celebrated the Russians as steel-like. He concluded his speech with the hope that the American people would be sympathetic toward this new society that was raising the Russians to a higher historical level.

Trotsky's broadcast to the United States, with all its ambiguities and subterfuges, was far more than a casual propaganda statement. He was attempting to hammer out a new, more up-to-date interpretation of the Russian Revolution and its aims. He was for the Revolution because he was one of its founders, and he was for the Soviet Union in spite of Stalin's destructive follies. "I was more at the center of the Russian Revolution than any other living person," he declared in an interview given to the newspaper *Social-Demokraten* during the train journey to Copenhagen. This was no more than the truth, but it was also a dangerous truth, since Stalin had already rewritten the history of the Revolution in such a way that Trotsky had no part in it. But in the broadcast, without appearing to do so, he was attempting to heal the breach with Stalin and to look beyond the present murderous struggle with Stalin toward happier times. The newspaper commentators who wondered whether Trotsky had come to Europe for a secret meeting with one of Stalin's agents were wide of the mark, but they were not wholly wrong. Trotsky's broadcast contained at least one coded message to Stalin. It remained to see whether Stalin cared to decode the message.

The speech to the students, which covers twenty-five closely written pages, was to be the last public speech he would ever deliver. It was an elaboration of the same themes he discussed in the broadcast. Once again he presented himself, as he had a perfect right to do, as one of the founding fathers of the Revolution. There was an element of self-glorification only slightly veiled. There was nothing about the labor camps, the torture chambers, the G.P.U., Stalin, and very little about Lenin. He celebrated the October Revolution which was carried out "with cold calculation and flaming determination" as the central event in modern history and poured scorn on those who believed that it was brought about at too great a cost in lives and human hopes. On what scales could the cost be measured? Those who complained of the cost should think of the World War and how little the imperialists cared about the number of men who fell in battle. They easily accommodated themselves to their losses. "It is now our turn to ask: 'Has the war justified itself? What has it given us? What has it taught us?'"

Trotsky kept more or less strictly to his agreement with the Danish government promising that he would deliver a "theoretical" speech rather than a propaganda speech. The theory was embedded in the propaganda; the propaganda threw out cobwebs of theory. And if it was one of his least convincing speeches, it was because he was still bemused by his own fate and uncertain about the future of the revolution he had brought into being, a revolution which was certainly not advancing in the way he had anticipated. "The historical task of our epoch," he declared, "consists in replacing the uncontrolled play of the market by reasonable planning, in disciplining the forces of production, compelling them to work together in harmony and obediently serve the needs of mankind." Here discipline, compulsion, and obedience seemed to have the upper hand, while reasonable planning and harmony seemed to be no more than sops to make the meal more palatable. He went on: "Only on this new social basis will man be able to stretch his weary limbs and—every man and every women, not only the select few—become a full citizen in the realm of thought." This was dogmatism of the worst kind. He was like the religious leader who chooses among the many roads to paradise and says: "This road, and only this road, will lead you there. All other roads are anathema!" There are powerful arguments for socialism, but Trotsky was not presenting arguments. Instead, he was laying down the law.

He was on firmer ground when he described the eight reasons which brought about the success of the October Revolution. They were: (1) the rotting away of the old ruling classes, (2) the political weakness of the bourgeoisie, which had no roots in the masses of the people, (3) the revolutionary character of the peasants, (4) the revolutionary character of the oppressed nations, (5) the significant social weight of the proletariat, (6) the revolution of 1905 regarded as a dress rehearsal for the revolution of 1917, (7) the contradictions brought into play by the war, which "tore the backward masses out of their immobility and thereby prepared the grandiose scale of the catastrophe," (8) the Bolshevik Party. In his view the last was by no means least.

He ended the speech curiously with an invocation of Sigmund Freud who was among those creative spirits who shed light on the mysterious driving forces of the soul and subjected them to reason and to will. Marx's socialism and Freud's psychoanalysis would henceforth go hand in hand to resolve the perplexities of mankind, and together they would bring about a happier future for the human race.

There was applause when he had finished, and he was seen there beaming quietly, looking tired and lonely on the podium, all spent now that he had delivered the speech which had been written with so much care and so many revisions that it seemed to be many speeches. But the applause was not so much for the speech, which added nothing to his stature, as it was a tribute to a brave man who had played a tumultuous role in history and was now in exile and in danger of assassination. Death seemed to hover over him, and men saw him as one of those who are doomed.

The journey to Denmark came to an end abruptly, silently, without fanfare. Trotsky begged the Danish government to permit him to stay a few days or weeks longer; he needed medical attention for himself and his wife. To an American reporter he said wistfully that he could think of nothing better than to be allowed to live in New York so that he could work in its vast libraries. But no country wanted him. The Danes ordered him curtly to leave even before his visa expired; the French kept close watch on him; the Italian Foreign Ministry permitted him to cross northern Italy by train and would allow him only a brief glimpse of Venice. The governments wanted it to be known that they regarded him as a pariah, and were afraid of him, and were glad to see him gone.

He returned to Turkey on December 10, 1932. Earlier in the year he had left the house in Kodikoy and returned to the old pasha's house in Prinkipo. This house, damaged in the fire, had been renovated and improved. He preferred the island in the Sea of Marmora to the

Asiatic mainland, and so he returned willingly, pleased to see the familiar faces of the villagers, feeling more at home on Prinkipo than anywhere else in the world. But he had scarcely settled into the house when two huge shocks struck him: first, his daughter Zina committed suicide in Berlin, and secondly, Hitler came to power in Germany, crushing the well-organized German Communist Party with the greatest of ease, using the weapons of murder and terror which Trotsky had once defended as the essential instruments of power.

The two blows coming so quickly one upon another—Zina committed suicide at the beginning of January and Hitler achieved power at the end of the month—left him numb and dispirited, without strength, almost without hope. Zina had been sickly, mentally unbalanced, given to sudden rages, hopelessly in love with her father. Her suicide could perhaps have been predicted; this did not make it any more tolerable. Hitler's rise to power could also have been predicted, but the poor showing of the German Communists was totally inexplicable. They had crumbled in what Trotsky described as "the greatest defeat of the working class in history." There had been sabotage from Moscow, poor leadership, programs and policies that exasperated too many of the workers; there had been mistakes all along the line, but Hitler too had made mistakes; it seemed incredible that the German Communists should have been defeated so quickly and decisively. Moscow consoled itself with the belief that a Communist "underground" would flourish under Hitler, having been purified by disaster. Trotsky found no such consolation.

His monumental *History of the Russian Revolution* was completed in June 1932, but he was still busily at work supervising the translations, correcting errors, and conducting a considerable correspondence with his many publishers. Vastly successful in Germany, it was banned when Hitler came to power. The *Saturday Evening Post* paid him $45,000 for the serialization rights and thus put an end to his financial problems. In

1933 this was a formidable and splendid sum of money;
he had become a capitalist. He rejoiced in being able to
put the greater part of this money into a fund for
supporting the *Bulletin of the Opposition*, which was
now being published in Paris by Lyova, who had
previously published it in Berlin. He escaped from
Germany only just in time.

Read at the age of twenty, *The History of the Russian
Revolution* can still set the brain on fire. As Trotsky tells
it, it is the story of a wild and improbable adventure
with the heroes and villains clearly indicated, and the
book ends, as all good adventures end, with the
triumph of the heroes and the rout of the villains. It is
the story of the year 1917, and it takes him more than a
thousand pages before he reaches the capture of the
Winter Palace, the turning point of the revolution. He
writes brilliantly and incisively but with an underlying
tone of sarcasm, and he seems to be continually reminding the reader: "What poor fools our enemies are!
How stupid! How infantile!" so that one begins to
wonder why the Revolution was not won more easily.
Too often the sarcasm seems to be an oratorical trick,
effective when spoken aloud, less effective on the
written page. There are long essays on every aspect of
Russian society, disquisitions on the imperial family
and the state of the peasantry and the proletariat, so
that we have the impression that he is determined to
get everything in, to write a history of the Revolution so
comprehensive that no one again would ever attempt it.
Yet, curiously, when he writes about historical events,
even those events in which he took part, we are sometimes aware that he is not so much speaking about the
individual people taking part in a revolution as of
converging lines of force, abstractions of power and
dogmas on the march. He tends to abstractions. We do
not see faces; instead we see huge masses or blocks of
people caught up in the general excitement, and it
is one of the virtues of his prose that he can convey the
excitement of the masses, although we are never completely convinced that the masses have any existence.

Nevertheless the passion remains and is dominant. It

holds the huge edifice together. Even though his descriptions of events tends to be "schematic" and far too often there is the sense that he is administering history for his own purposes, he pours so much passion into the work that, while we are reading it, we are totally convinced. Although he sometimes speaks humbly of himself, we are rarely left in any doubt about who is in command. He strides through his own history of the revolution like a colossus, and only Caesar rivals him as an historian of his own battles.

In the spring of 1933 there came rumors of long-hoped-for relief. The Spanish Republican government had turned down his request for a visa, but there were signs that the French government would be more receptive. Maurice Parijanine, his French translator, had friends in high places and was able to influence so many of them in favor of Trotsky's right of asylum that in the end the French government agreed to grant him a visa, on condition that he lived quietly and attracted no attention to himself. Trotsky rejoiced. For four and a half years he had lived on a small island, remote from the world. He spoke of once more "seeing the world at close quarters" and of "breaking out of my isolation." In the following years he would learn that it would have been better for him if he had remained on the Island of Princes.

A
WANDERER 22
IN
FRANCE

When Trotsky left the island of Prinkipo to live
in France, he exhibited symptoms that invariably plagued him when he made a change of residence: a profound uneasiness, fever, sickness, psychological disturbance. He hated breaking his habits, his
daily rituals. He found it difficult to write while traveling, and he was also aware that travel meant increased
danger. He did not travel like ordinary men but like a
king in exile; reporters were waiting for him whenever
he stopped for the night, police functionaries escorted
him, his route was prescribed for him, assassins were
waiting for him. During the journey from Prinkipo to
France he suffered acute attacks of lumbago, which
appear to have been psychological in origin.

On July 17, 1933, Trotsky sailed on the S.S. *Bulgaria*,
an Italian steamship, bound for Marseilles. In his party
were Natalie, his American friend Max Shachtman,
and three secretaries, Jan van Heijenoort, Rudolf Klement, and Sara Weber, a young American woman. The
journey took them a week. They hoped they could travel
secretly, but when the ship put in at Piraeus, the secret
was already out, the reporters demanded interviews,

and Trotsky was forced to meet them. He told them that his journey had been brought about by the need of medical treatment for himself and his wife, and he hoped the reporters would pay more attention to the critical affairs in Europe—Hitler had been in power for six months and most of the lands bordering on Germany were already in a state of panic fear—than to his own unremarkable travels. His evasiveness, however, only made the reporters more suspicious. It was widely believed that he was traveling to Paris for a secret meeting with Maxim Litvinov, the Soviet commissar of foreign affairs, and that there would be a momentous announcement about his return to high government office in the Soviet Union. The rumor showed that there is no limit to the political imagination. In his own mind he was about to embark on something far more significant than a return to power. He hoped that in France he would be able to found the Fourth International, a worldwide society of Bolshevik-Leninist Communists that would eventually supplant the Third International ruling from Moscow, and he hoped to do this without attracting the attention of French officials.

Meanwhile, the lumbago was getting worse, and by the time they came in sight of the shores of France he was in intolerable pain, had difficulty breathing, and was forced to take to his bed. The French police were in radio communication with the ship. Some miles out of Marseilles the *Bulgaria* was met by a small tugboat, and police officers clambered abroad. Trotsky and Natalie were ordered off the ship into the tugboat. They thought they were under arrest, but in fact all this was being done for their own safety. Lyova, his son, and Raymond Molinier were both on the tugboat to receive them and to explain the reason for the change of plans. The tugboat brought them to the beautiful little town of Cassis, where an officer of the *Sûreté Générale* officially presented Trotsky with a document revoking the order of perpetual banishment issued in 1916. "It is a long time," Trotsky commented, "since I acknowledged the receipt of any official document with so much pleasure."

A few minutes later Max Shachtman and the three secretaries were landed at Marseilles. They made their way to Paris, and some days passed before they were able to reach Trotsky in his hiding place.

This hiding place had been chosen by Lyova and Raymond Molinier with the approval of the French authorities. It was a very small town called St. Palais-sur-Mer, near Royan, between Bordeaux and La Rochelle on the west coast of France, at the mouth of the Gironde River. Atlantic breakers roared against the crumbling coast. It is sometimes described as a bathing resort, but guidebooks warn the traveler: "The sea is very rough here and bathing is dangerous." A secluded place, not very well known, sweet-smelling because there were nearby pine woods, St. Palais-sur-Mer offered an almost perfect refuge. A pleasant villa, large enough to house Trotsky, Natalie, and a small staff, had been rented, and it was expected that it would be guarded unobtrusively by the police.

Trotsky was in continual pain throughout the journey by car to St. Palais-sur-Mer, his lumbago being exasperated by the suffocating heat. He arrived in the afternoon of July 25 and promptly went to bed with a high fever. An hour later he was catapulted out of bed, for the villa had caught fire. It had been a long dry summer, the woods were tinder, other villas had also caught fire. At first Trotsky thought the fire was deliberate and that this was one more heavy burden to bear. Crowds gathered, and he took refuge in Raymond Molinier's car on the other side of the road, and whenever he was approached he spoke in execrable English, saying he was an American tourist. His luck was with him; his presence in St. Palais-sur-Mer remained a secret; soon the fire was put out, and he returned limping to the villa, where he remained for nine weeks, spending much of the time in bed.

The villa, which was called *Les Embruns*, meaning "Spindrift" or "Sea spray," was on the very edge of the sea. It was not badly damaged, but the summerhouse and some of the trees in the garden had gone up in flames. It was learned later that the fire was caused by a spark from a locomotive. The smell of burning hung over the villa throughout his stay.

Visitors came, sometimes in circuitous ways. They were put on trains, kept in ignorance of their destination, taken off the train, driven across country and put onto other trains, given passwords, while a small network of friends and secret agents kept guard over them. The most distinguished of his visitors was André Malraux, who was driven to the villa at night a few days after Trotsky's arrival. Malraux had corresponded with Trotsky, who admired his novel *The Conquerors* with some small and sharp reservations. Malraux had an unlimited admiration for Trotsky as an audacious intelligence, as the war minister who fought a dozen invasions during the Civil War, and as the conqueror of Petrograd on the first day of the Revolution. In his eyes Trotsky belonged to the small number of legendary figures who have changed the course of history; he was therefore excited by the prospect of seeing him. Everything happened exactly as he had hoped. A dark night, the sea roaring only a few feet away. A young man was coming down a road and waving a flashlight, followed by a much older man who could be seen only in the light of the flashlight—at first the white shoes, then white trousers, then a kind of pajama suit, and then at last, as Trotsky moved into the glare of the headlights, a white face, a shock of white hair, the small wide-apart teeth forming the pleasantest of smiles. Trotsky, all in white and bathed in light, was an apparition to be conjured with. Malraux was not startled; he had expected something of the kind, but he was a little surprised to hear the booming of the sea. And as they walked together to the villa, Malraux, searching for the single feature of Trotsky that reveals the whole, concluded that it lay in his sculptured lips which were like those on an Oriental statue.

As they came to know each other, talking half way through the night, and again the next day, Malraux concluded that he liked everything about Trotsky except his ideas. Trotsky had no regard for the works of the poet Boris Pasternak, whom Malraux revered. He confessed never to have seen the great early Soviet films like *Potemkin* and *Mother*, which Malraux justifiably regarded as the supreme artistic creations of the Russian Revolution. Trotsky said he had not seen them because he was at the front when they were first released and in exile when they were revived. He was contemptuous of Christianity and disdainful of liberty. What then, Malraux asked, was the purpose of living? It appeared that the purpose of living was to obey the Marxist laws of society. It was not very satisfactory, and Trotsky was growing tired, losing his grip on the French language, inventing new words to express ideas that seemed to be growing increasingly hazy.

On the next day Trotsky filled up some gaps in history for Malraux. Shortly after the Revolution the Soviet army under Tukhachevsky invaded Poland, expecting the Polish proletariat to welcome them. Instead, all the Poles, from the wealthiest aristocrats to the lowliest workmen, rose up against the invaders, and with the help of a small group of French officers who acted as military advisers, they hurled the Soviet army back beyond the borders of Russia. Stalin, a political commissar with the Soviet army outside Lemberg, distinguished himself by ordering that the attack on the city should be postponed at a time when nearly everyone else knew that postponement was fatal. What was Trotsky's responsibility in this failure? "I had no responsibility for it," Trotsky replied. "I went along with it because Lenin wanted it. There were all kinds of unresolved problems. It was difficult to grasp the situation and disposition of the Polish proletariat. Then there was the fact that a revolutionary army is always exceedingly nervous when it is separated from its supply base and the slightest defeat demoralizes it, especially after there has been a series of victories."

It was not an especially illuminating reply but it served to illuminate Trotsky's weaknesses. "I went along with it because Lenin wanted it." The truth was that Trotsky had left the preparations for the Polish campaign to others, but he was nonetheless responsible for the disaster; there was no excuse, and he, and

Lenin, were morally and intellectually guilty of planning a senseless campaign that brought no credit to the Soviet Union.

Trotsky enjoyed making prophecies. When the subject turned to the United States and China, he prophesied that the United States would soon make China into a colony. By what means? Simply by conquering it. Who could stop them? "Nobody." Then Trotsky added: "When China becomes an American colony, war with Japan will be inevitable."

Malraux, the perennial student of the world's arts, was also a close student of death. The subject absorbed and fascinated him; he liked to examine the philosophical ambiguities of death at enormous length. For Trotsky there were no ambiguities. "I believe that death is, above all, a product of use. First, the use of the body; then the use of the spirit. If the using of the body and the spirit could be carried out harmoniously, death would be a very simple phenomenon. *Death would meet with no resistance.*"

With all the force of his intelligence Malraux was unable to penetrate Trotsky's mind. Whenever they discussed a serious subject the answers were curiously inadequate and unconvincing. Trotsky wore his prophetic robes and against all the evidence prophesied an American invasion of China, and although he was deadly right in his prophecy of war between America and Japan, he was right for the wrong reasons; nor was it particularly difficult in 1933 to arrive at the conclusion that America and Japan were on a collision course.

Malraux's admiration for Trotsky remained unimpaired. It was not so much admiration for his ideas as for his actions, his impatience, his nobility in defeat. In private conversation Malraux sometimes spoke of Trotsky as he would later speak of General de Gaulle, as a man who accomplished impossible things by identifying himself with the forces of history, and just as De Gaulle identified himself with France, Trotsky identified himself with revolution. The man seen on a lonely seashore in western France, all white in the glare of the headlights, was revolution incarnate.

But this was the outward Trotsky: the inner man was at the mercy of his demons which in France and later in Norway took full possession of him. In Prinkipo he had felt unthreatened; the world was far away; the Turkish authorities showed very little interest in him; he was his own master. In France he was dogged by the police and by bureaucrats sent down by the Ministry of the Interior. The international situation was far more dangerous, and he therefore had to be watched more closely. His health was bad; the old fevers returned; Natalie was also ill; and there were financial troubles. In Prinkipo he was buoyed up by the writing of his autobiography and *The History of the Russian Revolution*. Now his chief concern was to see that the *Bulletin of the Opposition* appeared regularly and that the intellectual war against Stalin should continue unabated. It was a hopeless task, and only a sudden turn of events would bring him into prominence again.

St. Palais exhausted him: there were too many visitors, too many problems. Suddenly he vanished. For two weeks he stayed quietly with Natalie in a little watering place called Bagnères-de-Bigorre in the foothills of the Pyrenees. Here they lived in almost complete solitude.

Natalie went to Paris for medical treatment, which she could ill afford. Lyova brought some friends to meet his father for a long discussion, planning to return with them to Paris on the night train. Trotsky wrote to his wife: "I watched Lyovik. His eyes were shining. He was radiant." He went on to describe how Lyova came into the bedroom to say farewell. His face alive with excitement, he approached his father's bed and "like a child" dropped his head on his father's breast. The ocean was stormy and spray was dashing against the windowpane, while Lyova pressed closer and said: "Papa, I love you very much." Then they embraced in tears.

Because the Atlantic air did not seem to agree with him, Trotsky hoped to move into the interior. The French authorities raised no objection and permitted him to live in Barbizon, where Corot, Rousseau, and Millet had lived and painted, celebrating the sunlight on the edge of the Forest of Fontainebleau. There, in a house set in a small park, guarded by a Greek mastiff called "Molosse" and two German shepherd dogs, "Benno" and "Stella," he lived very quietly. He claimed that no one in the village knew who he was, and since he had shaved off his goatee and was rarely seen in the village, it was probably true. He was working half-heartedly on a biography of Lenin, which he never completed, and he was editing the *Bulletin of the Opposition*, and twice or three times a week there came a messenger from Paris with proofs of the *Bulletin* and a pile of books. Life had become orderly again, chiefly because his health was improving. He rose at six in the morning and worked until noon with only a brief interruption for breakfast. After lunch and an hour-long siesta, he worked and studied until suppertime. After supper, having worked for nearly twelve hours during the day, he usually gathered his secretaries and friends around him and engaged in a lengthy discussion on one of the subjects he had been writing about. The times were out of joint, Hitler was in the ascendant, Stalin was punishing the Russian people with renewed vigor, Fascist parties had emerged in France, and in Trotsky's eyes all Europe seemed to be on the verge of war or revolution or both. There was therefore much to discuss, and Trotsky's articles for the *Bulletin* were shrill with warnings of imminent danger.

Still fresh from his timeless, idyllic life on the island of Prinkipo where he spent the greater part of his days living in the past and writing his two autobiographical works, *My Life* and *The History of the Russian Revolution*, he seemed during these early months of his stay in France to have lost his bearings. His judgments of people and events seem strangely erratic. He detested and despised all the Socialist leaders in Europe without exception, and it is possible that his detestation blinded him from making any true judgments; he regarded them as knaves and criminals. They were incapable, in his view, of making accurate formulations of existing political conditions, but instead worked "to pacify the bourgeoisie and to bluff the workers." In a pamphlet called *War and the Fourth International*, which he completed in Barbizon in January 1934, he outlines the course of the coming war: there will be an imperialist (German) attack on the Soviet Union, and in the general upheaval no country, not even Switzerland, will be spared. For some reason the idea that Switzerland will be involved gives him pleasure, for he discusses it at considerably more length than it would seem to deserve. Once the war has broken out, it is the task of the proletariat in all countries to seize power and to go to the aid of the Soviet Union. How will the proletariat seize power? By taking arms from the soldiers. Admittedly this will be difficult, and admittedly this will lead in many countries to civil war, but this is a danger that must be faced. Had not Karl Liebknecht stated the fundamental fact concerning the proletariat in war: "The chief enemy of the people in wartime is to be found in their own country"? And suddenly, as one reads this pamphlet written in 1934, one realizes that he is writing about an imaginary world which has no relation to the world of his time but is very closely related to the world of 1914–1917. He speaks of a small revolutionary party that will once again establish itself in power and bring a proletarian peace to the world, but whereas in 1914–1917 the revolutionaries acted at first very slowly and indecisively, this time "the shift of the masses to the road of revolution will occur much faster, more decisively, and more relentlessly."

But all this was wishful thinking, for he clearly imagined himself at the head of the small revolutionary party, deciding the fate of the world after the nations of the earth have been locked in a titanic struggle. He insists that even though the revolutionaries are very few, they can have an influence out of all proportion to their numbers. The new revolutionary party would constitute itself the Fourth International. Before the decade was over, Trotsky would inaugurate a political party that called itself the Fourth International.

The pamphlet was unsigned, like nearly all his other writings in France, for the government had specifically demanded that he take no part in political affairs. He wrote another pamphlet called *Whither France?* later in the year, calling upon the workers to arm themselves and to form workers' militias. Although it was unsigned, there was no mistaking the harsh, truculent style of Trotsky when he was writing at his very worst.

It was one of Trotsky's perennial themes that a revolution can be brought about by a small number of absolutely dedicated men. He was therefore not dismayed when he realized that he had no more than sixty or seventy dedicated followers in France, including refugees from Germany and the Soviet Union. Among those who claimed to be his followers were agents of the G.P.U.

The unforseeable and the unpredictable play a large role in revolutions and in life. In the middle of April 1934 the idyllic life in Barbizon was to be changed abruptly by the merest accident. Rudolf Klement, one of his secretaries, was riding his motor-bicycle from Paris, bringing Trotsky his mail, when the headlight failed. The police arrested him for riding without lights, handcuffed him, threw him in jail for thirty-six hours, examined Trotsky's mail, notified the newspapers, and in their own good time advanced in a small army on the secluded villa. With the police came the chief prosecuting attorney from nearby Melun, together with a magistrate and a court reporter, and various gendarmes, detectives, and hangers-on. The villagers of Barbizon poured out into the streets to see the spectacle, and Trotsky's dogs, alarmed by the presence of so many people and so many cars, barked and howled throughout the long enquiry which took place in the crowded living room.

Asked what he was doing in Barbizon, Trotsky answered that he was a writer in need of seclusion, grateful to the traditional French liberties which permitted foreigners to live untroubled lives in France. Asked for his passport, he produced one in the name of Lev Sedov issued in the Soviet Union. Was he not Monsieur Trotsky? Yes, he was. Then how to explain that he was both Trotsky and Sedov? Trotsky explained patiently that such things were permissible in the Soviet Union, and he pointed out that his passport was stamped with a visa by the *Sûreté Générale*. And what about the stolen motor-bicycle? It came as a surprise that the motor-bicycle had been stolen, for Trotsky had well and truly paid for it, but it was necessary to prove the obvious and this is always difficult. Rudolf Klement was brought into the living room. He looked distraught after thirty-six hours in police custody. Trotsky offered him a chair, and the prosecuting attorney shouted: "No, he must stand up!" as though Klement was a prisoner in the dock. When at last the delegation from the local police and the prosecutor's office in Melun departed, Trotsky was exhausted and full of foreboding. He was justified in his fears, for the government, bowing to the French Communists and the right-wing newspapers, ordered him to be expelled from France.

It was not however easy to expel him, for no other country was prepared to have him. The *Sûreté Générale* therefore laid down the conditions for his further stay in France. He must live in strict incognito; he must remain at a distance of three hundred kilometers from Paris; he must not live on the frontier; he must show an exquisite discretion. What this meant was clear: he could go on living in France only on condition that he conceal himself in some remote provincial town and vanish from sight. In the company of one of his secretaries, Jan van Heijenoort, a Dutchman of impeccable manners and considerable charm, he set out for southeastern France and quickly realized that simply to become a boarder in a second-rate *pension* demanded strategical gifts worthy of a better cause. Van Heijenoort posed as his nephew; Trotsky and Natalie pretended to be in mourning, eating their meals in their bedroom and rarely emerging except to go to Mass on Sundays—the walk to the church gave them much needed exercise. Meanwhile there was an officer of the *Sûreté* nearby to report on their behavior, though there was nothing to report. In this way they went from one *pension* to another, feeling exhausted and helpless, until at last, early in July 1934, after three months of fruitless wandering, they came to the small village of Domène, a few miles from Grenoble, and found lodging in the house of the village schoolmaster Laurent Beau and his wife Marguerite, where they remained in almost total seclusion, without guards, for nearly a year.

It was the most improbable and the most humble of all their hiding places. There were two pleasant rooms, a bed, a writing table, a radio, a shelf of books, little else. Trotsky's work suffered; the biography of Lenin came to a halt; he appears to have spent most of his time listening to the radio and going for walks in the countryside. Once or twice Laurent Beau was able to arrange clandestine meetings with Socialist teachers from the neighborhood. Soon the loneliness and the silence became oppressive. He missed his friends, his admirers, the sharp cutting edge of debate and discussion. Once a week Natalie went to Grenoble to go shopping, and even this pleasure was denied him. More and more Domène came to resemble a prison, and the daily thirty-minute walk along a pathway behind the village houses at the foot of the mountains resembled the daily walk permitted to prisoners. "Life goes on, as before, in a modified prison style: between four walls, without people."

So he wrote in the diary he began to keep in winter, when life flowed at its lowest ebb, when he felt defeated, aimless, imprisoned by the mountains, the police, and society. He was a reluctant diarist. As usual, his verdicts on politicians were morose and uncharitable. He blasts Leon Blum, soon to become the first Socialist premier of France, for having "set for himself the aim in life of uttering nothing but parlor trivialities and pretentious nonsense." "His minuscule talents," Trotsky continues, "are suitable for parliamentary lobbying but seem wretched and paltry in the awesome whirlpool of our days." Edouard Herriot, a lifelong Socialist, receives shorter shrift. "Herriot," Trotsky announces in his oracular way, "is yesterday." But it is not only Blum and Herriot who are castigated and swept into the dustbin of history. Trotsky in his despair and misery has scarcely a good word to say about anyone.

The real horror was the knowledge that he was dispensable, that he was forgotten, that he was getting old, that very few people cared whether he was alive or dead. Destiny had granted him a life of danger and ferocious activity interspersed with long periods of boredom, and now there stretched in front of him the promise of endless years of imprisonment in a God-forsaken corner of France. He was accustomed to being at the center of things; he was now outside. He had enjoyed his fame, and now it seemed that it amounted to nothing. He knew he was one of the shapers of the modern world and there was scarcely anyone in Europe or Asia who had not in some way been affected by his two greatest achievements—the conquest of Petrograd for the Bolsheviks and the conquest of vast areas of Russian territory from the White armies. Without any military training at all he had shown himself the most brilliant of generals. He derived pleasure from these achievements, but he derived even more pleasure from his theoretical contributions to Marxism. Unfortunately only a very small band of followers listened to them or understood them. Theoretically, he believed, it was still possible to reconquer the Soviet Union for true Marxism from the man he called Cain-Stalin. It would need a small number of dedicated men, acting at exactly the right historical occasion, and he felt that he alone, out of his vast experience, was capable of leading and commanding the reconquest of Russia. In fact, he was sitting at his table in the elementary school teacher's house, brooding and doing nothing.

He wrote in his diary:

It is hard now to work at my book on Lenin: my thoughts simply do not want to concentrate on the year 1893! The weather has changed sharply in the last few days. Although the gardens are in bloom, it has been snowing today since early morning. Everything was covered with a white shroud, and then it melted, and now it is snowing again, but the snow immediately melts. The sky is gray. From the mountains the fog creeps into the valley, and in the house it is chilly and damp. N. is fussing over the housework with a heavy weight on her heart. Life is not an easy matter.

You cannot live through it without falling into prostration and cynicism unless you have before you a great idea which raises you above personal misery, above weakness, above all kinds of perfidy and baseness.

The copybook maxims did not help him very much: he was in despair. He was learning very late that life is full of excruciating sorrow. He learned in April that his first wife, Alexandra Sokolovskaya, had been deported to Siberia, that Platon Volkov, the husband of Zina, had been arrested, and that his younger son, Sergey, who had never shown any interest in politics, was almost certainly under arrest. Natalie was crushed, and imagined the worst. Once arrested, he would be tortured to death not for any crimes he had committed but simply because he was their son. It was as though Stalin had waved his hand and said: "We shall now destroy all the members of Trotsky's family one by one."

The thought of his own tragedy set him thinking about another tragedy altogether—the murder of Nicholas II and the entire imperial family in Ekaterinburg in the summer of 1918. In the spring of that year he had imagined that Nicholas II would be placed on trial for his life and that he, Trotsky, would be the chief prosecutor. The trial would take place in the Kremlin and would be broadcast all over Russia, and Lenin had remarked that these broadcasts would serve an admirable purpose. But the murder of the imperial family took place while he was at the front, and he was not consulted. He wrote in his diary in April, shortly after learning about the punishments inflicted on his former wife, son, and son-in-law:

My next visit to Moscow took place after the fall of Ekaterinburg. Talking to Sverdlov, I asked in passing: "Oh yes, and where is the Tsar?" "It's all over," he answered. "He has been shot." "And where is the family?" "And the family along with him." "All of them?" I asked, apparently with a touch of surprise. "All of them!" replied Sverdlov. "What about it?" He was waiting to see my reaction. I made no reply. "And who made the decision?" I asked. "We decided it here. Ilyich believed we should not leave the Whites a live banner to rally around, especially under the present difficult circumstances . . ." I did not ask any further questions, and considered the matter closed.

The story as told by Trotsky is not entirely credible and leaves too many questions unanswered as he seeks to absolve himself of all responsibility. Yet he was not in the least innocent, for he had expected to be the chief prosecutor and to win a death sentence for the Tsar. The trial would have been a charade like the trials that were taking place under Stalin. He was saved by the merest accident from the necessity of taking part in the trial and execution of the Tsar.

So the empty days passed, and sometimes memories of his former grandeur would rise up to torment him. He remembered the armored train, and the "love look" in Lenin's eyes, and sometimes he dreamed vividly of Lenin and whole conversations heard in the dreams were afterward remembered. Once the scene was the third-class deck of a ship. Lenin was saying: "You seem to have accumulated nervous fatigue—you must rest!" and Trotsky answered that he usually recovered quickly from fatigue thanks to his native resilience, but this time the trouble lay deeper. Lenin said: "Then you must *seriously* consult the doctors," and gave some doctors' names. Trotsky began to talk about his consultations with doctors during his visit to Berlin, and suddenly he looked at Lenin and recalled that he was dead and it was therefore useless to recount these consultations which took place after Lenin's death. Nevertheless he went on discussing these consultations for a while until it occurred to him to add: "This was after your death," but checked himself in time and said: "After you fell ill . . ."

It was a strange dream and a revealing one, and it could be interpreted on many levels. Trotsky saw in his dream that there was no medicine for his new sickness, no doctor could diagnose it or prescribe for it, and there was no hope for him except in the continuing presence of Lenin dead or alive. This time the trouble lay deeper. As he peered into the future, there was no hope anywhere in sight.

In the seventeenth century the schismatic Archpriest Avvakum led his flock according to the ancient rites. For this he was punished by exile in Siberia, the deaths of his children, and finally burning at the stake. Today he is remembered chiefly because he was a prodigious writer of Russian prose, among the greatest Russia has ever known. Trotsky was reading Avvakum's autobiography when it occurred to him that his own fate was very similar. He wrote in his diary:

> Concerning the blows that have fallen to our lot, I reminded Natasha the other day of the life of the Archpriest Avvakum. They were stumbling on together in Siberia, the rebellious priest and his faithful spouse. Their feet sank into the snow, and the poor exhausted woman kept falling into the snowdrifts. Avvakum relates: "And I came up, and she, poor soul, began to reproach me, saying: 'How long, archpriest, is this suffering to be?' And I said: 'Markovna, unto our very death.' And she, with a sigh, answered: 'So be it, Petrovich, let us be going on our way.'"

In the diary the words "How long" are heavily underlined. But he had scarcely finished writing these words when news came that the long exile in Domène was about to come to an end. His son Lyova and his lawyer Gérard Rosenthal had for some time been busily working to find another country that would accept him. A new Labour government had just come to power in Norway; it promised, or half-promised, to grant Trotsky and his wife a visa and a residence permit under the usual condition that he must not engage in any political activity that affected Norway. Trotsky agreed to this condition and traveled to Paris, expecting or half-expecting that a visa would be waiting for them in the Norwegian Consulate-General. It was not waiting there. There were inexplicable delays. Evidently there were people within the Norwegian government determined to prevent Trotsky from living in Norway. Trotsky was desperate. From Paris, where he was staying in the house of a well-known doctor who happened to be the father of Gérard Rosenthal, he sent a pathetic telegram: "The French government believes that I have deceived it, and demands that I leave France in twenty-four hours. I am sick and my wife is sick. Situation is desperate. I solicit immediate favorable decision." The telephones kept ringing. There were urgent requests for "clarification" and still more urgent requests for "the exact date of departure." Old friends came to see him in the doctor's apartment; impromptu discussions on Socialist strategy and tactics filled the hours of waiting, and once again Trotsky was a figure of importance. After the long months of silence in Domène, Paris came as a rich orchestra of voices. And when at last the visa came, he was overjoyed and immediately set out for Oslo—by train to Antwerp and then by ship to the Norwegian capital. If he had known what lay before him, he would have remained in Domène.

23 INTERLUDE IN NORWAY

At first Trotsky genuinely admired the Norwegians and was happy in their country, admiring the beauty of the women and the handsome, rugged features of the men. The landscape delighted him, the freshness of the air quickened his spirits, and the directness and forthrightness of the Norwegians seemed infinitely preferable to the devious politeness of the French. It was arranged that he should live in the house of Konrad Knudsen, a member of parliament and also the editor of a local Socialist newspaper, at Vexhall, a village thirty-five miles from Oslo. Knudsen owned a large and spacious house overlooking the village. He was a man of broad culture, kindly, sympathetic, generous; and if he had any failing, it was that he was too generous, too kind, too sympathetic. He placed two large rooms—a bedroom and a study—at the disposal of the Trotskys, who shared the Knudsens' meals and became part of the family. There were no guards, the street doors were left open, anyone could enter the house, but Trotsky and Natalie felt supremely safe. It was inconceivable that anyone would come to disturb this quiet clapboard house or these sturdy villagers.

And then gradually and almost imperceptibly everything began to go wrong again: his health grew worse, money began to dwindle away, there were quarrels with his Paris office and the small coteries of his followers, each protesting that it was the true inheritor of the doctrine, and once again the work went slowly. He would lie on a chaise longue in the garden, reading desultorily or listening to the radio, or else he would put in a day's hard work, attending to mountains of correspondence, only to suffer a relapse the following day. Norway bored him; it was too bland, too bourgeois, too antirevolutionary. Konrad Knudsen invited some leftist friends to meet Trotsky. They told him that fascism was impossible in Norway because everyone in the country was literate and because capitalism in the strict sense no longer existed. "What if fascism conquers in France and England?" Trotsky asked, and they answered contentedly that they would hold out. Trotsky wrote in his diary after he had met Knudsen's friends: "They have learned nothing. Essentially, these people do not suspect that such men as Marx, Engels and Lenin have lived in this world. The war and the October Revolution, the upheavals of fascism, have passed them by without a trace. For them, the future holds hot and cold showers."

It was brilliant, but it was not true. "They have learned nothing" was one more of those sweeping, condemnatory generalizations which exuded from Trotsky like a foul breath; and the Norwegians knew many things that Trotsky had never known.

Misfortunes crowded upon him like swarms of blackbirds. A doctor came from Czechoslovakia to treat him. The doctor stayed for two weeks, took exhaustive tests, and concluded that he needed more exercise. Trotsky was soon in a state of near collapse. On September 7 he received two letters: one from Alexandra Sokolovskaya, the other from Platon Volkov. They were like letters from the dying or the dead, full of hopelessness and despair. Twelve days later Trotsky was rushed to the Municipal Hospital in Oslo, suffering from high fever and debility, and once again the doctors were unable to discover the cause of those illnesses that waxed and waned like the phases of the moon. When he was released from the hospital, Knudsen thought a change of air might benefit him and suggested a trip to a mountain cabin north of Vexhall. In spite of the intense cold, the trip seemed to do him some good, but when he returned he was ill again. He remained in bed during most of December, proclaiming that he had never spent a worse month in his life.

He abandoned the diary shortly after he arrived in Norway; he abandoned his life of Lenin; he told Lyova in Paris that he would be unable to conduct the affairs of the Fourth International for some weeks; and one day in January or February he walked with Natalie in the deep snow outside the house and said: "I am tired of it all—all of it—do you understand?" Natalie understood very well, for she had many more reasons for despair; but she was braver than her husband and never complained.

Spring came, the warm air came to the frozen mountains, his spirits revived, and the work began again. This time he decided to write a book called *The Revolution Betrayed*, intended to demonstrate with mathematical precision exactly how the corruption of the world's first Socialist state took place, not because there were any flaws in the Marxist argument but because an overwhelming bureaucracy took command and set about deliberately betraying Socialist principles. The bureaucracy enjoyed the rich fruit of the orchard; the people were given the bruised apples and the dry grass. Instead of socialism there was its exact opposite—the dictatorship of the bureaucracy. Significantly he has very little to say about the G.P.U., the most formidable of the many bureaucracies in the state, very little about Stalin, and nothing at all about his own involvement in the creation of the Soviet Union. On a high abstract plane he demonstrates that when the bureaucracy is given complete independence and freedom from control, the people are reduced to obedience and silence, and he forgets to add the inevitable corollary that every dictatorship by its very nature demands obedience and silence from the people and complete independence and freedom for itself. "The prohibition of opposition parties brought after it the prohibition of factions," he wrote. "The prohibition of factions ended in a prohibition to think otherwise than the infallible leaders." But he had himself been one of those infallible leaders who charted the course of the dictatorship; he had exulted in the physical destruction of all other parties in Russia; and he was now caught in the trap he had himself prepared.

The Revolution Betrayed is not one of Trotsky's best books. The fox, caught in the steel trap, too loudly proclaims his innocence. In the maturity of middle age, all his depredations forgotten, he announces with the air of a man who has known it all along that a state must give the people the utmost freedom. He wrote:

> Spiritual creativeness demands freedom. The very purpose of communism is to subject nature to technique and technique to plan, and to compel the raw material to give unstintingly to man everything that he needs. And far more than that, its highest purpose is to free finally and once for all the creative forces of mankind from all pressure, limitation and humiliating dependence. Personal relations, science and art will not know any externally imposed "plan," nor even any shadow of compulsion. To what degree spiritual creativeness shall be individual or collective will depend entirely upon its creators.

For a man who had never shown much respect for freedom, it was a strange volte-face but not entirely unexpected. He was to learn very soon that Stalin's monolithic police state was preparing some unpleasant surprises for him.

On August 5, 1936, he sent the first copies of the finished manuscript to his American and French translators, and on the same day he set off with Konrad Knudsen and his wife Hilda for a holiday on a small island in one of the southern fjords. Some followers of Major Vidkun Quisling, the Norwegian fascist leader, had been keeping watch on the house, and the next morning, while it was still dark, five young fascists forced their way into the house in search of documents which they hoped would incriminate Trotsky by showing that he was engaged in conspiratorial activity in Norway; that at least was the explanation they offered when they were arrested. They also hoped to steal his archives, but these had been removed a few days earlier to the safety of a bank vault.

Nevertheless there were hundreds of books and thousands of pages of written material in his study and they could very easily have got away with them if it had not been for Jordis Knudsen, who was Konrad Knudsen's daughter. She hurled herself on them, shouted to her brother, Borgar Knudsen, who slipped out of the house and summoned the neighbors, and prevented them from taking anything except a single letter and a single article. The young woman and the fifteen-year-old boy kept them at bay. They behaved very bravely, for the young fascists were determined to find what they were searching for, and there was no way of knowing whether they were armed. They had in fact kept the house under surveillance for several days and they had been tapping Knudsen's telephone. They appeared to know the layout of the house, and there was some evidence that the attack was organized by a German who appeared mysteriously in the village, wearing Tyrolean costume. One day the German found his way into Knudsen's courtyard, saw Trotsky, and immediately turned around, as though he wanted to avoid being recognized. Someone asked him what he wanted. He said: "I want to buy some bread." It was not a very satisfactory answer. An Austrian who was a guest in the house engaged him in conversation. The man said he was an Austrian on holiday, but spoke with a pronounced north German accent. Later it was learned that the five fascist youths who invaded Knudsen's house had met this man in a neighboring hotel. This time it was not Stalin but Quisling and Hitler who were causing all the trouble.

Knudsen learned about the intruders by telephone a few hours later. He discussed the matter with Trotsky, and they both concluded that since the five fascist youths had been arrested, and since Jordis and Borgar could be relied upon to guard the house, they might as well continue their journey to the south. While they were on their way, they suddenly discovered they were being closely followed by another car. Knudsen stopped his car, got out, questioned the young people in the other car and received confused answers, which strongly suggested that they were up to mischief, but he could not tell whether they were Stalinists or followers of Quisling.

Finally, they reached the island, hoping for a lazy vacation of rock climbing, fishing, and sitting in the sun. Natalie complained of the cold, but the others enjoyed themselves. It was summer, the air was wonderfully clear, and there was a general feeling that Trotsky had earned a twelve-day rest.

A little more than a week after they arrived on the island, there came the first rumbling of distant thunder. The chief of the Oslo police arrived by airplane and took a deposition from Trotsky about the five fascists who had attempted to raid the house. Since he knew very little about the raid, Trotsky's testimony was necessarily brief. The police chief was good humored and said that the evidence clearly demonstrated their guilt and there was therefore nothing for Trotsky to worry about.

During the night Knudsen heard on his battery-operated radio news that shocked him and was later to shock the whole world. Radio Moscow announced the forthcoming trial of thirteen highly placed government officials charged with conspiring together to form a "Trotskyist-Zinovievist bloc" in league with the Gestapo to overthrow the Soviet government by acts of terrorism. The accused were all Old Bolsheviks, and two of them, Zinoviev and Kamenev, were major historical figures, who could accurately describe themselves as Lenin's comrades in arms, though they had both believed that an uprising in November 1917 would be premature and perhaps disastrous. Nevertheless they had been given high and outstanding positions by Lenin, for Zinoviev became chairman of the Petrograd

Soviet and Kamenev chairman of the Moscow Soviet. In effect Zinoviev was governor of Petrograd and Kamenev governor of Moscow. Among the others arrested were Ivan Smirnov, who headed the Fifth Army during the civil war and was especially close to Trotsky, Grigory Yevdokimov, who mobilized the masses in Petrograd at the time of the revolution and had been head of the Petrograd Tcheka, and Yefim Dreitser, a hero of the Civil War, many times decorated for his military services, and a close friend of Trotsky, who often invited him on the armored train. It was beyond all reason that any one of the accused would embark on a program of terrorism. Even Trotsky, accustomed to the ways of Stalin, was astounded. When Knudsen woke him up and told him the news, he exclaimed: "A trial! Terrorism? Terrorism? Well, I suppose I can understand that! Gestapo? Did they say Gestapo?" "Yes," Knudsen replied, "they said Gestapo."

The theater of the absurd, so often performed in the Kremlin, had now taken full possession of Stalin. The hell-black night was about to descend on Russia, with Stalin parading on a dimly lit stage and giving orders for farcical trials and mass executions according to his whims. Trotsky, with his logical and pedagogical mind, always seeing history as though true cause was invariably followed by true effect, was as puzzled as everyone else by the irruption of the absurd. If Stalin wanted to destroy Zinoviev and Kamenev, there were easier and better ways of doing it than by staging a show trial, which would have to be conducted with extraordinary finesse to be convincing. And as it happened, it was precisely the finesse that was lacking, and no one except the most diehard follower of Stalin was convinced that Trotsky, Zinoviev, and Kamenev had committed any of the crimes for which they were charged.

Once the full horror of the Moscow trial caught hold of him, Trotsky, who was a defendant *in absentia*, took action. He immediately began to write articles, grant interviews, and appeal to world opinion. He hurried back from the south, a perplexed and bitter man, suffering from a high fever, his ears glued to the radio.

In Knudsen's house he sat at the table with an army of red, blue and black pencils, studying the newspapers and attempting to unravel the grotesque absurdities in the courtroom in Moscow, where Vyshinsky, the state prosecutor, displayed ferocious venom against the dazed prisoners in the dock and recited with the help of willing witnesses events that not only did not happen but could not possibly have happened. Trotsky learned, for example, that he and his son Lyova had been meeting Soviet officials in secret and giving them orders to commit terrorist acts. A certain Holtzmann described how during Trotsky's brief visit to Copenhagen in November 1932 he had stayed at the Hotel Bristol and had a secret meeting with Lyova in the hotel vestibule. Holtzmann, or the G.P.U. which drew up the scenario, apparently did not know that the Hotel Bristol had been torn down in 1917 and that Lyova had not accompanied his father to the Danish capital and had in fact never been there. Nearly all the evidence produced at the trial was of this kind. Secret meetings, secret documents, a secret "Center," secret instructions, an entire whispering gallery of secrets was brought on stage to prove that Trotsky, Zinoviev, and Kamenev had conspired to assassinate the rulers of Russia and assume power. Zinoviev and Kamenev admitted everything. Yes, they had organized the conspiracy, held secret meetings, issued secret instructions, received and obeyed orders from Trotsky, engaged in treacherous activities throughout most of their political lives, and were therefore unworthy to live in the Soviet Union and deserved to die. But the evidence brought forward to convict them was such that not even a child would believe it. A certain Berman-Yurin claimed on the witness stand that he had two separate conversations with Trotsky in Copenhagen:

BERMAN-YURIN   I asked him the question of how individual terror could be harmonized with Marxism. To this Trotsky declared: The question cannot be approached dogmatically. He stated that a situation had been produced in the Soviet Union which Marx couldn't foresee. Trotsky also said that in addition to Stalin, Kaganovich and Voroshilov must be murdered.

VYSHINSKY Did he convince you?

BERMAN-YURIN During the conversation he walked nervously round the room and spoke of Stalin with exceptional hatred.

VYSHINSKY You expressed your agreement?

BERMAN-YURIN Yes.

After this, Berman-Yurin was supposedly sent off to Russia with instructions to kill Trotsky's enemies. Stalin was to be shot during one of the Congresses "so that the sound of the shot will ring out through a large assembly," and he must do this alone without help from anyone. According to his own statement during the trial he was unable to obtain a ticket to enter the Congress of the Comintern and the assassination of Stalin was therefore postponed indefinitely.

Berman-Yurin was one of seven men who confessed to having received orders from Trotsky. These seven emissaries had only the most tenuous connection with Zinoviev and Kamenev, who confessed they attended many secret meetings; they had discussed assassinations; they had reviled Stalin and were therefore traitors to the party; they had sat down with the agents of foreign powers planning the overthrow of the Soviet state and were therefore traitors to their country. Everything they said was totally out of character and had obviously been learned by rote following a scenario which had clearly been dictated by Stalin, who wanted only to submit the prisoners to the utmost degradation and humiliation. His purpose was very simple: he wanted to destroy one by one all the Old Bolsheviks until he alone remained of those who had been in commanding positions during the October Revolution.

On August 25, 1936, Zinoviev, Kamenev, Smirnov, and all the other defendants were shot in the nape of the neck in the cellars of the Lubyanka Prison in Moscow. Kamenev died with dignity, Zinoviev died screaming with fear. At the last moment he cried out to his executioners: "Think what you are doing! You are executing the revolution, the party of Lenin!" The officer in charge of the executions, who knew it was no longer the party of Lenin but the party of Stalin, took Zinoviev by the hair with his left hand, forced his head down, and fired a bullet into his neck.

Stalin killed them with no more compunction than he would have killed the flies that settled on his wineglass on a hot summer's day.

When the verdict condemning all the prisoners to death was announced, it included a warning directed at Trotsky and Lyova, who were subject "in the event of their being discovered on the territory of the U.S.S.R., to immediate arrest and trial by the Military Collegium of the Supreme Court of the U.S.S.R." Trotsky feared the Norwegian government would extradite him to Russia. Indeed, he had feared this even before the sudden announcement of the Moscow trial. The Norwegian minister of foreign affairs went to Moscow and was well received. It occurred to Trotsky that one of the subjects the foreign minister was discussing in Moscow was his own fate.

"They are bargaining over my head," he told Konrad Knudsen.

"How do you know that?"

"Moscow is hinting—or saying outright—'We will charter your ships, we will buy your herrings, but on one condition: that you sell us Trotsky.'"

"So you think our principles are for sale?" Knudsen answered with annoyance.

"My dear Knudsen," Trotsky replied, "I am not saying the Norwegian government is getting ready to sell me. I am only saying that the Kremlin would like to buy me."

In fact, as Trotsky learned later, the Soviet government was not asking for his extradition, but it demanded that Trotsky should be silenced and at the earliest possible date expelled from Norway. At a time when Trotsky most needed the freedom to speak out—about the trials, about the monolithic corruption of Stalin, about his own ideas concerning the proper form of government in the Soviet Union—he was effectively prevented from speaking by order of Trygve Lie, the Norwegian minister of justice. On August 26, only a few hours after the execution of Zinoviev, Kamenev, and the rest, he was informed by two senior police officers that he had offended by his writings and interviews against the terms of his residence permit. It was explained to him that if he signed a promise to limit himself to historical commentary and theoretical works "not directed toward any specific country," he would be permitted to remain free; otherwise he would be interned. He refused indignantly to sign a document that would reduce him to being merely a spectator of events.

Two days later, on August 28, he was driven to Oslo for a preliminary interrogation by the examining magistrate concerning the raid of the five fascists on Knudsen's house. Very little was said about the raid. The magistrate interrogated Trotsky for two hours, demanding a full recital of his political activities, his connections, and his visitors. Who were they? Why had they come? Why had he written letters to his friends? Had he at any time criticized foreign governments? It appeared that he had transgressed the law by giving interviews and writing letters. Trotsky asked what kind of country he was living in. Democratic regimes do not consider criticism of a government as an attack against the state. In totalitarian states criticism of the government is treachery and high treason, but Norway was not a totalitarian state. According to his original agreement with the Norwegian government he had promised not to engage in any conspiratorial activity, but surely he could not be prevented from writing articles which appeared abroad. The magistrate thought he could be prevented, and said so. He could be prevented by force or by some other means, which were not spelled out. Trotsky left the magistrate's office in a flaming temper.

A police guard then took him to Trygve Lie's office in the Ministry of Justice. The minister stood behind the table, surrounded by high ministry officials. Trotsky was told that he must sign the agreement previously presented to him, or face the consequences; in addition he must agree to constant police surveillance. Trygve Lie was one of those heavy, pompous, bull-headed, garrulous men whose rough geniality concealed an ice-cold ambition, and it pleased him to have an eminent revolutionary in his power. The new agreement was placed before Trotsky. He refused to sign it, because it meant that henceforth he would be under house arrest, and if he walked to the post office a policeman would walk behind him. He said: "If you want to arrest me, why do you also want my authorization for my arrest?"

Trygve Lie was prepared for this question.

"You must know that between arrest and freedom there is an intermediary situation," he said with an air of profundity, well aware that politics is full of halfway houses.

"This can only be an equivocation—or a trap," Trotsky replied defiantly.

This was the signal for the minister to give orders according to a prepared plan. Trotsky had been accompanied by one of his secretaries, Erwin Wolf, who had married Knudsen's daughter. Wolf was immediately placed under arrest. Trotsky was sent back to Vexhall, guarded by four uniformed policemen, and as they arrived in the courtyard of the house Trotsky saw that his other secretary Jan van Heijenoort was being manhandled and dragged out of the house. Trotsky, locked in the car, watched it all with horror: the Norwegian police were behaving like storm troopers, and indeed many of them were followers of Major Quisling. At first the government planned to intern him in Knudsen's house. The police set up their headquarters in the dining room. Trotsky, released from the car, was allowed to enter the house on condition that he did nothing except think and eat and sleep. Meals were provided by Hilda Knudsen under the surveillance of two policemen, and the bedroom door was kept ajar so that the policemen could be sure Trotsky and Natalie were in bed and not actively conspiring against the government.

Quite obviously the Norwegian government was taking its orders from Moscow. Stalin had ordered that Trotsky must be silenced, and the Norwegian government obeyed on the grounds that the business interests of a country are vastly more important than the rights of a foreigner, an exiled revolutionary who had, it appeared, been admitted to Norway by mistake. And just as obviously the situation could not be permitted to continue. Trygve Lie was determined to silence Trotsky and this could only be done by placing him in prison, beyond the reach of anyone except his lawyer. But placing Trotsky in prison also presented problems. It was therefore decided to provide him with his own private prison, his own private concentration camp. On September 2, under close guard, he and Natalie were taken to Sundby, a village some twenty-two miles from Oslo, at the edge of a fjord. In a large house overlooking the sea they spent the next three and a half months, living on the second floor, while thirteen policemen kept guard on the ground floor. They were never allowed to leave the house, their correspondence was censored, they were permitted no visitors except for a Danish lawyer, who was allowed to come rarely, and during the first days of their internment they were allowed no newspapers, no letters, no telephone calls, no radio. Total silence descended on them. In order to bring this silence about it had been necessary for Trygve Lie to present a special executive order to the King of Norway, who promptly signed it.

A few days later Trotsky was permitted a radio and for a while he luxuriated in Beethoven. When he listened to news or propaganda broadcasts from Moscow or Berlin, he discovered without too much surprise that he was still being denounced in Moscow and reviled in Berlin, as though he were a man with armies at his command, still powerful and still threatening, when in fact he was a prisoner in two small, low-ceilinged rooms in a God-forsaken corner of Norway, with thirteen pipe-smoking and card-playing policemen watching over him. It was worse than Alma-Ata, where at least he had the illusion that his massive correspondence was being distributed all over the Soviet Union, that he was still leading the Opposition, and was still in command of his destiny. The worst indignity, silence, had been inflicted on him, but there were other indignities. All his requests—for newspapers, telephone privileges, visits from his lawyer, permission to mail letters—all these had to be submitted to the police, who in turn submitted them to the minister of justice, who in turn submitted them to the cabinet. Days, sometimes weeks, passed before there was a reply. Meanwhile the mist came in from the sea, the rain fell, the damp wooden house became more and more like a torture chamber, and the sight of the heavyset policemen who held his life in their hands gave him nausea.

Because he was by training a revolutionary and a conspirator, he was sometimes able to outwit his guards. Innocuous letters were sent out, with the real message being written in invisible ink. A visit to a local dentist enabled him to smuggle letters to his followers; a letter was smuggled to him in a cake. Unfortunately for Trotsky most of these ruses became known to the police and to the minister of justice, who threatened to remove Trotsky to a guarded house far in the north, thus bringing him much closer to the Soviet Union. In Paris, Lyova was working twenty-four hours a day to discover another country that would accept his father and simultaneously he was producing the *Red Book of the Moscow Trial* in which he effectively demonstrated that the evidence produced to send Zinoviev, Kamenev, and the others to their deaths was totally false. Moscow claimed that there existed thirty-six volumes devoted to the preliminary examination of the defendants, but no one was permitted to see them. Instead the official government printing press produced a bowdlerized transcript of the trial which included perhaps a quarter of the original transcript.

Among those who were assisting Lyova was a certain Mark Zborowski, known as Etienne. He worked with Lyova on the *Red Book of the Moscow Trial* and the *Bulletin of the Opposition*, and was the custodian of Lyova's most secret correspondence. He was also one of Stalin's secret agents and had been ordered to infiltrate

Trotsky's pathetically small organization. He became Lyova's closest friend and reported directly to the Kremlin. On the night of November 6, Zborowski, for reasons that never became clear, organized the theft of part of Trotsky's archives from the Paris branch of the Institute for Social History on the Rue Michelet. The theft was expertly arranged, the thieves being provided with acetylene torches to cut through a service door. Lyova and Trotsky said later that eighty-six kilograms of documents, consisting mostly of press cuttings, were stolen, and Lyova went out of his way to declare that his friend Zborowski could not possibly have committed the crime, which was evidently the work of the G.P.U. It is unlikely that the documents consisted only of press cuttings, and the mysterious burglary was only one more of those inexplicable events that from time to time darkened Trotsky's life.

A month later, on December 11, Trotsky attended the trial of the five fascist youths who had attempted but failed to steal his archive at Vexhall. The trial was held in camera, and he was merely a witness. But he succeeded during the course of a two-hour speech in transforming himself into judge, jury, and chief prosecutor. Although no transcript was made available to him, he was able to reconstruct the forty-page speech from memory. It was a dazzling feat. He attacked Stalin, Trygve Lie, the five fascist youths, the Norwegian shipowners who had urged the government to do nothing that would disturb Stalin's peace of mind, and all those who were now obstructing him from telling the truth about the Moscow trial. He said in conclusion:

> I accuse the Norwegian government of trampling underfoot the most elementary principles of law. The Moscow trial is the first of a series of similar trials in which not only my honor and my life and those of my family, but the honor and lives of hundreds of people are at stake. Under these circumstances how can they forbid me, the main defendant and the most informed witness—how can they forbid me from making known what I know? To do that is consciously and deliberately to obstruct the march of truth. Whoever by threat or by violence prevents a witness from telling the

truth commits a grave crime, severely punishable by Norwegian law. Of this I am convinced. It is indeed possible that the Minister of Justice will take new measures against me—after my present deposition. The resources of arbitrary power are inexhaustible. But I have promised to tell you the truth, the whole truth, and I have kept my word.

Two days later, when he was back in the wooden house at Sundby, Trotsky had a visitor. It was Trygve Lie, who had come to exact full punishment. Within a matter of days Trotsky was to leave Sundby, where in spite of all police precautions he had found ways to communicate with the outside world, and he would be sent to a remote and inaccessible place in the far north. In effect Trotsky was to be sentenced to political death and perhaps to his real death. In his speech in the courtroom Trotsky had said he expected the minister of justice to take new measures against him; he had not however expected them so quickly. Trotsky told the minister that his friends were hoping with the help of the painter Diego Rivera to obtain a residence permit in Mexico, which would be preferable to enforced exile beyond the Arctic Circle. Suddenly Trygve Lie saw Ibsen's *Works* lying on a table, and there followed a short and spirited discussion of Ibsen in relation to the present problems:

LIE   I see you are reading Ibsen here.

TROTSKY   Yes, I am re-reading him. Ibsen used to be the love of my youth, and so I have come back to him. I have been reading *An Enemy of the People*, and it occurs to me that the situation in the play somewhat resembles the situation we find ourselves in.

LIE   Ibsen can be interpreted in different ways.

TROTSKY   No doubt, but whatever interpretation you give him, he will always testify against you. Remember Burgomaster Stockmann?

LIE   You are not proposing to compare me with that villainous creature, are you?

TROTSKY   Yes, indeed—at best, Burgomaster Stockmann.

Your government has the vices of a bourgeois government without any of its virtues.

LIE *(hotly)* Then I consider you totally lacking in gratitude. We permitted you to remain here under certain clearly specified conditions—you refused to obey them. Letting you into the country was a stupid mistake.

TROTSKY And this stupid mistake, as you call it, will now be rectified by the commission of a crime. Permit me to read to you, Mr. Minister, the words of Dr. Stockmann to his brother. "We shall yet see whether meanness and cowardice are strong enough to close the mouth of a free and honest man."

At this moment Trygve Lie turned on his heels in anger, but then remembered himself and turned to Trotsky to shake hands. Trotsky refused to shake hands and glared at the minister as though he was observing a venomous beast. In this way he rebuked the most powerful man in Norway, in whose power he remained.

Three or four days later Trygve Lie appeared again at the house with news that astounded Trotsky: the Mexican government had granted him permission to live and work in Mexico. He had known through his own secret sources that Diego Rivera had appealed to President Lázaro Cárdenas on his behalf; he had not guessed or known that permission would come so soon. He distrusted Trygve Lie and wondered whether a trap was being set, and he distrusted the minister still more when he heard that he and his wife would be sent across the Atlantic on a Norwegian freighter under armed escort. Trotsky was deeply troubled. Why all this secrecy? He wanted to see his son in Paris. Why could he not leave Norway for Paris? He needed time to see friends, to arrange his affairs, to write letters, to collect his thoughts. The minister was implacable. Trotsky feared the worst: that arrangements had been made for a Soviet ship to overtake the tanker. "They do not know you will be on the ship," the minister replied. "Only I and the owner of the ship know that you will be on it." He was told that he had twenty-four hours to prepare for the journey, he would be taken to the ship in the greatest secrecy, and throughout the journey he would be guarded by Jonas Lie, the police officer in charge of the guards at Sundby, a man whom Trotsky particularly detested. He would be interned until the moment when, a free man, he set foot on the soil of Mexico.

There were so many unanswered questions that Trotsky lost count of them. It was like stepping into an abyss: perhaps after falling a certain number of miles he would reach safety. As usual Trygve Lie had acted without any generosity, without any grace of mind. The haste seemed sinister, and there was something repulsive in the minister's assumption of bureaucratic power: he could break the law, send men where he pleased, summon ships to do his bidding. "Of course, you can take your revenge on us physically," Trotsky said. "But morally you will pay for it dearly, just as the German Social Democrats paid dearly for the assassination of Karl Liebknecht and Rosa Luxemburg. I warn you, if the workers permit you to follow these policies of yours, in three to five years you and all your ministers will be émigrés." This time the prophecy was deadly accurate: four years later the Norwegian government fled to England.

On December 19 the tanker *Ruth* left a Norwegian port bound for Tampico in Mexico with only two passengers on board and a policeman to watch over them. The policeman, Jonas Lie, amused himself by hinting that very strange and unexpected things might happen on the journey. Natalie, close to the breaking point, remained in her cabin, while Trotsky strode the deck, half expecting at any moment to see a Soviet ship bearing down on them. For three weeks the tanker zigzagged across the Atlantic, while Trotsky played the role of the Ancient Mariner, wondering how long he would be forced to carry the albatross round his neck.

THE
FORTRESS
IN
COYOACAN

Part Eight

One more, the final story, and the tale is told.

THE BLUE HOUSE 24

At first, when the tanker *Ruth* sailed into the great harbor of Tampico, Natalie was overcome with a sense of unreasoning dread, as though now at last the long-expected trap would be sprung, as though Mexico would be the grave of all her hopes. She told the captain she would not leave the ship unless she saw the faces of friends. Jonas Lie, the efficient policeman, threatened to use physical force if she refused to leave the ship. Happily friends arrived, but she was still nervous. She was like a frightened bird, startled by every policeman, panicking when she lost sight of her friends.

President Lázaro Cárdenas had sent the presidential train to bring them to Mexico City. Diego Rivera had not come to Tampico to welcome them, but he had sent his wife, Frida Kahlo, a woman of great beauty and a certain indifference to the affairs of this world, for her paintings were mostly concerned with death. On this day she was brimming with kindness and good humor, and became their chief adviser, escort, and protector. Natalie, after her fog-shrouded winter in southern Norway, could scarcely believe the scenery around her: the

391

fierce sunlight on the parched plains, palm trees, cactuses, and superb volcanic mountains. Her fears vanished. Everything pleased her: it was like entering a new and unexpectedly beautiful world. But when the train, according to a prearranged plan, stopped at a small station on the outskirts of Mexico City, Natalie panicked again on being told that she must enter one of the waiting cars filled with policemen. It suddenly occurred to her, remembering her experiences in Norway, that she was about to be taken to prison or to internment. She did not realize that this was a sensible precaution in a country with a growing Communist Party whose members believed that their highest duty was to carry out Stalin's orders.

Instead of prison they were taken to 127 Avenida de Londres in the part of Mexico City called Coyoacan, where Cortés had set up his headquarters before the conquest of the city. It was a low house, painted blue, with large airy rooms, built around a patio with flowering plants. Here Rivera lived in majestic and expensive simplicity surrounded by an impressive collection of Aztec and Mayan sculpture and by his own paintings which crowded the walls. He rejoiced in his genius, his wealth, his gargantuan appetites and his gaucheries. A founding member of the Mexican Communist Party, he had grown weary of the self-righteousness and dogmatism of the Communists and was no longer a member of the party. He was not a Trotskyist. What delighted him in Trotsky was what delighted him in himself—his courage, his bravado, his artistry. He regarded Trotsky as an equal, an attitude that did not always commend itself to Trotsky. He was a good host and did everything possible to put Trotsky at ease.

Trotsky proved to be a difficult guest, for the Blue House was turned upside down to accommodate him. Vicious attacks and lampoons against him were being printed in the Communist press in Mexico, and the atmosphere became so charged with half-concealed threats that President Cárdenas ordered a police guard outside the house, which was annoying to Rivera. Within two weeks of his arrival in Mexico Trotsky became absorbed in the second of the great trials which Stalin staged against the Old Bolsheviks. This trial was, if possible, even more ludicrous and terrifying than the first. This time the defendants included Karl Radek, who accompanied Lenin on the train from Switzerland through Germany and was generally regarded as the Bolsheviks' most brilliant propagandist, and Yuri Pyatakov, once Trotsky's friend, and a former deputy commissar for Heavy Industry. Radek was a caricaturist's delight with his monkey face and fringe of red beard. Pyatakov was a tall, lean, handsome man with a high forehead and an air of brooding intelligence. His head and beard were blond touched with red. Both men were highly intelligent and were notable for a rather ruthless honesty. The trial was staged in order to prove that they were members of "the parallel Trotskyist Center," one more of the many Centers which Stalin invented out of whole cloth.

This time the Soviet government published a lengthy and fairly accurate transcript of the trial, omitting various sections of the trial held in camera. Once again we hear of Trotsky's secret instructions to the Center. According to Pyatakov, Trotsky had made a secret agreement with Rudolf Hess, offering to cede to Germany the whole of the Ukraine and to Japan the Maritime Provinces and the Amur region in return for his own elevation to power in the Soviet Union. Pyatakov declared that he flew to Oslo in December 1935 to receive Trotsky's personal instructions, a fact that bewildered the Norwegian Ministry of Foreign Affairs when they learned that not a single airplane from Berlin had touched down at the Oslo airport during the entire month of December. Everything about the trial was of this order. Orchestrated lies, suicidal admissions, the unfolding of a vast conspiracy which could not possibly have existed and which was elaborated in court with so many inconsistencies that it became wholly unbelievable: the trial seemed to wander away into a kind of prolonged hysteria. Pyatakov said in his final plea: "Here I stand before you in filth, crushed by my own crimes, bereft of everything through my own fault, a man who has lost his party, who has no friends, who has lost his family, who has lost his very self." Radek spoke brilliantly, as though he was someone else commenting on the guilt of someone called Radek. Pyatakov and twelve others were sentenced to death, Radek was sentenced to imprisonment for ten years, and the remaining three prisoners to varying terms of imprisonment.

Once again Trotsky, the prisoner *in absentia*, was informed that if he appeared on Soviet soil, he was subject to arrest and trial by the Military Collegium of the Supreme Court of the U.S.S.R. This threat against his life was incorporated in the verdict.

Trotsky had scarcely settled in the Blue House when he felt bound to use all his energies in an attempt to prove the trial was a murderous farce with profound implications for the future of Stalin's rule. Too many people, too many governments were prepared to accept the evidence at the trial as demonstrating the existence of a worldwide Trotskyist conspiracy. He wanted to show that the evidence was a tangle of organized falsehoods uttered by prisoners who had been tortured or threatened with the liquidation of their entire families; that evil was abroad and must be stopped; that Stalin was executing the Old Bolsheviks and would go on to execute millions of other Russians because they opposed his rule or might oppose his rule or simply because he believed it salutary to murder millions of Russians or to send them to the living death of labor camps, where they perished like flies and a few survived. Trotsky hoped an international commission could be set up to examine impartially Stalin's charges against the "Trotskyist-Zinovievist Center" and the equally imaginary parallel Center and he hoped they would examine his own countercharges.

The idea of an international commission had first occurred to him in Norway, and it was immediately revived when he came to Mexico. His son Lyova was urged to accumulate all the necessary documentation, and sometimes Trotsky snapped at him for being too slow, too lazy, too disinterested, when in fact he was working under terrible strain to bring out the *Bulletin of the Opposition* and to uncover the documents his father needed. Lyova had been told that his tiny organization included a Soviet agent. He refused to believe it, and continued to work steadily and soberly in his father's service.

In an extraordinarily short space of time, arrangements for the international commission were completed. If it was not in any strict sense international, it was certainly a commission composed of responsible citizens. It was headed by John Dewey, the venerable educator and philosopher, the author of *Impressions of Soviet Russia and the Revolutionary World* and countless other books, still vigorous and lucid at the age of seventy-six. There were six members of the commission besides the chairman: Carleton Beals, an authority on revolutions all over the world; Suzanne La Follette, an anti-Marxist American writer and editor of *The Freeman*; Otto Ruehle, a former member of the German Reichstag and the author of a famous *Life of Karl Marx*; Benjamin Stolberg, a well-known journalist; John F. Finerty, who had been a counsel for Sacco and Vanzetti; and Albert Goldman, a labor attorney of some eminence. On April 10, 1937, the commission met for the first time in the large study set aside for Trotsky in the Blue House.

The house had been transformed for the occasion. A heavy police guard stood outside; reporters and others who attended the commission's sessions were searched for concealed weapons; a six-foot barricade of bricks and sandbags rose overnight to protect the room where the sessions were being held; and one of Trotsky's armed guards checked on everyone who entered the room. Diego Rivera attended the sessions wearing a sombrero with a peacock feather, and Frida Kahlo sat as close as possible to Trotsky, wearing Tarascan jewelry and vivid Indian costumes, flaunting her beauty in the presence of Natalie who, after the experience in Norway, had begun to look old and worn.

These sessions took the form of a trial with John Dewey as the judge and the commissioners serving as independent counsel, asking questions, attempting to find explanations for the inexplicable. There was no prosecuting counsel and there were very few sharp questions. Trotsky produced documents which showed that he could not have met the Trotskyists he was alleged to have met, and he replied with dignity to the accusations made against him by Zinoviev, Pyatakov, Radek, and the others. Angrily and contemptuously he dismissed the charge that he had been ordering people to commit acts of terrorism. He was convincing when he pointed out the inconsistencies of the evidence, but he was less convincing when he painted himself in the colors of outraged innocence. He had answers for everything. Had he not, all his life, been on the side of the downtrodden? Had he not served the revolution throughout his life with vigor and intelligence? He was a man of the utmost integrity, and it was therefore inconceivable that he should have been in contact with Rudolf Hess and the Japanese government in an effort to destroy the Soviet state, which he had helped to build. He spoke of his own purity of intention too often to be entirely convincing. This was not entirely his fault. Though he spoke English before the commission, he still thought in Russian, and Russian rhetoric goes badly into English and in addition his English was sometimes difficult and convoluted. He spoke in the grand manner, with grave courtesy and absolute assurance, but sometimes he was so cold and precise that his words came with a chilling effect. He talked about matters of principle and very rarely about people; about his rightness and Stalin's wrongness; about revolutionary movements, not about revolutionaries. "My English is the weakest part of my defense," he told the commissioners, and this was true. His English made him cautious, for he did not always understand the questions of his interrogators. Though nearly all the commissioners obviously admired him and felt honored by being in his presence, he appeared to be acutely aware that none of them, except perhaps John Dewey, was his peer. His pride, which had always been his greatest sin, shone with a fierce light, blinding everyone in the room.

The "bad boy" among the commissioners was Carleton Beals, who had spent a lifetime studying revolutions and the dictators who emerge from them. He sometimes asked sharp questions and observed that Trotsky answered them evasively; nor was he satisfied with the choice of commissioners; nor, as the inquiry continued, did he feel that anything could be gained by Trotsky in his search for vindication. Trotsky had no difficulty convincing the audience that he was innocent of most of the charges leveled against him by Stalin, perhaps all of them. It was much more difficult to prove that he was innocence personified, that he was, as he claimed, a man of impeccable revolutionary virtue. He insisted that he had no contacts except for half a dozen letters with people in the Soviet Union since about 1930. On the face of it this seemed to be highly improbable; it was equally improbable that he could have built up a massive network of informants inside the Soviet Union. Carleton Beals decided to raise the question of his previous secret relations with revolutionary groups, especially in Mexico. In 1919 Mikhail Borodin, who later played an important role in revolutionary China, was sent to Mexico to foment revolution, bringing with him a considerable treasure of Tsarist jewelry to pay his expenses and to bribe Mexican officials. The following exchange began quietly and innocently, and ended in flaring tempers:

BEALS	Do you know Mr. Borodin?
TROTSKY	Personally, no.
BEALS	He was in China.
TROTSKY	Maybe I met him one or two times, but I didn't know he was Borodin. I knew him as a political personality.
BEALS	He came secretly to Mexico toward the end of 1919 or toward the early part of 1920.
TROTSKY	Yes?
BEALS	He founded the first Communist Party in Mexico. He at that time made the statement that he was an emissary of yours.
TROTSKY	Of mine? At that time I was in my military train. I forgot all the world geogra-

phy except the geography of the front. . . . May I ask the source of this sensational communication? It is published—no?

BEALS   It is not published.

TROTSKY   I can only give the advice to the Commissioner to say to his informant that he is a liar.

BEALS   Thank you, Mr. Trotsky. Mr. Borodin is the liar.

TROTSKY *(coldly)*   Yes, it is very possible.

As so often in cases of this kind, something quite extraneous to the main subject of inquiry was throwing light on it. Trotsky's abrupt manner when confronted with an unexpected question was revealing; he would deny everything, even unimportant things, if they affected his interests. If the accusations were true, he would still deny them, and if they were untrue, he could dismiss them just as cavalierly. Above all, he wanted to remain in Mexico, and he felt that the question had been raised to embarrass him with the Mexican government. Carleton Beals felt that it was necessary to distinguish Trotsky's public attitude from his secret acts. In his view the commission had become a public whitewash and was not doing the work it was intended to do. He therefore resigned immediately from the commission, which continued to feed Trotsky the questions he wanted asked. In his final peroration Trotsky held the floor for many hours, demolishing the arguments of Stalin one by one with remarkable effectiveness while leaving many other problems unresolved. In September 1937 the remaining commissioners handed down their verdict, saying that Trotsky had demonstrated his innocence beyond the least suspicion of doubt.

For most of the time during the commission hearings Trotsky showed extraordinary self-possession. Immediately afterward he collapsed. All the old complaints returned to torment him: nervous prostration, stomach cramps, headaches, dizziness. He insisted that his own work for the commission had only just begun, more documents and more proofs must be acquired, and urgent letters were sent off to Lyova in Paris ordering him to redouble his efforts to find the evidence necessary to prove that the Moscow trials were a frame-up. Lyova complained of the extra work, and Trotsky in his vehement fashion accused his son of disloyalty to his father and to the Revolution. Lyova understandably resented the accusation but worked all the harder. He was his father's slave, exhausted by his servitude. He had a highly strung mistress, Jeanne Martin des Pallières, who was legally married to Raymond Molinier, one of Trotsky's early French followers who had since been expelled from the party. She was a dominating woman and sometimes drove Lyova close to madness; she was also tender and loving. His life was inordinately difficult at home and even more difficult in his tiny office where, with the aid of Mark Zborowski, he edited the *Bulletin of the Opposition*, that pathetic sheet that alone had the courage to say that Stalin was a murderer who had betrayed the Revolution.

In the summer of 1937 Trotsky spent a short holiday in the mountains, alone except for a bodyguard, vainly attempting to shake off his illness and to placate Natalie, who had long suspected that her husband was falling under the influence of Frida Kahlo. In a long series of letters Trotsky pleaded that he loved only Natalie, that she was his "eternal wife," and that he was wholly innocent of any wrongdoing. When he came down from the mountain he was still afflicted with dizziness, cramps, and nausea, which were perhaps caused by the fear that the commission might hand down a verdict not entirely favorable to him. When it handed down a verdict that could not have been more favorable, he was elated and some of his nervousness vanished.

Soon after the new year he engaged in some long talks with André Breton, the French surrealist poet, who had come to Mexico in an unusually worshipful mood to sit at the feet of the master. The subject of their conversations was "Art and the Revolution." It was not a subject to which Trotsky had given much thought, but

Breton for a while succeeded in convincing Trotsky that it was important, worth discussing, and perhaps deserving of a manifesto. Breton was quick witted and charming, and looked more like a lumberman than a poet. To show Breton some of the glories of the Mexican countryside, Trotsky took him on excursions in the neighborhood of Mexico City, and these outings became progressively more dangerous even though they were usually accompanied by a Mexican policeman, and sometimes Diego Rivera and the exotic Frida Kahlo were present. Many photographs taken during these excursions show Natalie next to Frida, as though she was keeping close watch on the woman she regarded as an adversary. Breton's visit was not wasted. A manifesto, largely written by Trotsky, affirmed that the artist must be given the utmost liberty, the only limitation being that the artist must never use his liberty to attack the proletarian revolution. The manifesto entitled *For an Independent Revolutionary Art* demanded that the artist should wage war against the false arts of Fascist Germany and the Soviet Union under the slogan:

> The independence of art for the revolution. The revolution—for the definitive liberation of art.

If the slogan was not particularly helpful, it at least showed that Trotsky was attempting to think out, however inadequately, a new aesthetic for a time of revolution.

Breton left Mexico in a somewhat exalted state of mind, pleased with the document which was signed by himself, Trotsky, and Diego Rivera, who had almost nothing to do with it. A few days later Trotsky suffered the most terrible blow of his life—Lyova was murdered.

From the beginning of the year Lyova was convinced that the net was tightening around him. He wrote an article announcing that, if he was found dead, it would be because Stalin had sentenced him to death; that he was of sound mind and in good spirits and had not the slightest intention of committing suicide. Toward the end of January he suffered some stomach pains which grew progressively worse. A doctor diagnosed appendicitis and he was taken by ambulance to a clinic run by White Russians on the rue Narcisse-Diaz; and in the clinic records he was described as M. Martin, an engineer of French nationality. His mistress Jeanne and his friend Mark Zborowski alone were permitted to visit him. The operation, which took place on the night of February 8, 1938, was successful and he appeared to recover in a normal fashion, his temperature remaining stable and his mind alert. Suddenly during the evening of February 13 he began to hallucinate, he threw off his clothes, raved deliriously in Russian, staggered through the clinic, and finally collapsed on a sofa in the director's office. The doctors could do nothing for him except to give him repeated blood transfusions and to attempt in a last desperate operation to clear up what appeared to be an abdominal occlusion. On February 16, after spending his last hours in a coma, he died. He was only thirty-two.

The news reached Mexico City on the following day. Diego Rivera heard it and immediately went in search of Trotsky, who was spending a few days in the house of Antonio Hidalgo, an old Mexican revolutionary who lived near Chapultepec Park in the heart of the city. He was living there because Diego Rivera had observed some strange people prowling around the Blue House. Hidalgo owned a pleasant house, the sun flooded the rooms, and Trotsky was writing a strangely vitriolic pamphlet called *Their Morals and Ours* in which he justified with extraordinary violence the morality of the revolutionary Bolsheviks against the "rotten and obscene" morality of the bourgeoisie. "Only that which prepares the complete and final overthrow of imperialist bestiality is moral, and nothing else," he wrote. "The welfare of the revolution—that is the supreme law." These words could just as easily have been written by Stalin to justify the murder of Lyova Sedov.

To tell a father that his son is dead is a terrible task, to be undertaken with the utmost care. Diego Rivera burst into Trotsky's room and blurted out: "Lyova Sedov is dead!"

"What is this you are saying?" Trotsky shouted, and immediately afterward, in a towering rage, he roared at his friend and protector: "Get out of here!"

Somehow Trotsky made his way back to the Blue House to confront Natalie with the news. He found her busy sorting old photographs of her sons. She looked up and saw an old man with bent shoulders and a lined, ashen face. She asked him whether he was ill, and he answered: "Lyova is ill, our little Lyova . . ."

They were both so shattered with grief that they remained in their room together for eight days, seeing no one. They gave themselves up wholly to their grief, wept uncontrollably, saw no one, and attempted to comfort one another when no comfort was possible. When Trotsky finally emerged from his room, his eyes were swollen, his beard overgrown, and he looked like a haggard, quivering ghost of himself. What had been young in him now died, and the bright memory of Lyova haunted him throughout the remaining months of his life. A few days later he wrote a brief account of his son's life, ending with these words:

Goodbye, Lyova, goodbye dear and incomparable friend. Your mother and I never thought, never expected that destiny would impose on us this terrible task of writing your obituary. We lived in firm conviction that long after we were gone you would be the continuer of our common cause. But we were not able to protect you. Goodbye, Lyova! We bequeath your irreproachable memory to the younger generation of the workers of the world. You will rightly live in the hearts of all those who work, suffer and struggle for a better world revolutionary youth of all countries! Accept from us the memory of our Lyova, adopt him as your son—he is worthy of it—and let him henceforth participate invisibly in your battles, since destiny has denied him the happiness of participating in your final victory.

In 1956, Mark Zborowski, having reached the United

States, was brought before a Senate judiciary committee, which was interested in his relations with Lyova. Zborowski admitted that he was a G.P.U. agent who had wormed his way into Lyova's confidence, that he had summoned the ambulance that took Lyova to the clinic, and that he had informed the G.P.U. of Lyova's whereabouts. In this way he was able to set up the murder.

Stalin had decided to punish Trotsky according to a method of his own choice. He was a connoisseur of murder, its subtleties and refinements, and he was a close student of the tortured reign of Ivan the Terrible. It was related of Ivan the Terrible that he suspected a certain Prince Afanasy Viazemsky of treachery. Every day the prince attended the Tsar's court and every evening he returned to his house. One evening he found some of his servants lying dead in his courtyard. The next evening there were more servants lying dead. The following evening he found his brother lying dead, and there was another dead brother the next day. At last, unable to bear the strain of seeing so many of his servants and relatives dead and fearing for his own life, Prince Viazemsky fled. The Tsar's police caught up with him, and he was brought back in chains and thrown into prison where he died.

Like Ivan the Terrible, Stalin was utterly indifferent to the number of people he killed. In 1937 he had almost his entire general staff shot by firing squads. After his death there were found long lists of names, sometimes amounting to two thousand names, of people to be executed, and he had only to put his initials to these documents and they were immediately executed without trial, without ever learning what crime they were supposed to have committed. These lists were compiled weekly. These were the mechanical deaths that followed Stalin's whims or the whims of his secret police. With Trotsky something less mechanical was required. He was to suffer the Viazemsky death; he was to see his servants and his relatives killed one by one and only when he had savored the full horror of their deaths would he be permitted to be killed.

Trotsky's first wife, Alexandra Sokolovskaya, vanished into a prison camp. His friends, all those who had worked closely with him, were executed after purge trials or their names appeared in those lengthy lists which Stalin sometimes reviewed two or three times a week. Trotsky's son, Sergey, the engineer who showed no interest in politics, also vanished into the labor camps. Seven of Trotsky's secretaries were killed—one, Erwin Wolf, was murdered by the G.P.U. while fighting for the Republican army in Spain; another, Rudolf Klement, was later murdered in Paris and his headless body was found floating in the Seine. Everyone around Trotsky was under sentence of death.

On March 2, 1938, two weeks after the murder of Lyova, there opened in the October Hall in the Kremlin the last of the great purge trials which Stalin inflicted on his country. Five of the men on trial were famous, while the others were relatively unknown. The five included a former premier, two well-known diplomats, a man who had spent twenty years at the side of Lenin and was loved and respected by him as a revolutionary and a theoretician, and one of history's most infamous murderers. The man loved by Lenin was Nikolay Bukharin, the murderer was Genrikh Yagoda, a dwarf who headed the secret police until Stalin grew weary of him.

According to the scenario drawn up by Stalin, all the defendants had been in some way connected with Trotsky and had taken part in antistate activities. The trial would show that they had all confessed their crimes, that they were well aware of their enormity, and desired only to make amends according to the law. Of the twenty-one men on trial, eighteen were condemned to death and promptly executed, and three received long prison terms. All the defendants expected to be executed, and the trial therefore assumed the appearance of a dance of death, a macabre exhibition of doomed men who with one eminent exception accepted the roles assigned to them because death was preferable to torture. All the defendants and all the witnesses had been broken by the G.P.U. and admitted to criminal acts they either did not perform or, as in the case of Yagoda, obviously did not perform in the way described by them.

Although the main outlines of the scenario were simple, there were many intricate and confused subdivisions, minor plots and subplots that threatened to get out of hand, and some of the characters in these plots were given roles to play for which they were obviously unfitted. The scenario had been constructed over more than a year and had been so changed, amended, added to and subtracted from that it resembled a patchwork quilt with many holes in it. The puzzling thing was why Stalin troubled to hold the trial at all: the victims were in his power, he could have shot them in the cellars of the Lubyanka, and nothing more would ever have been heard of them. Instead he chose to put on a show trial in which the prisoners were threatened with torture and death unless they faithfully followed the approved script. Few of them were able to follow it with the precision demanded of them with the result that the trial records, even after they were carefully edited, resemble nothing so much as a surrealist nightmare. After the death of Stalin, all the victims were posthumously rehabilitated.

Two of the prisoners, Christian Rakovsky and Arkady Rosengoltz, had been very close to Trotsky. Rakovsky had been a lifelong friend and a participant in the Left Opposition until he was exiled from Moscow in 1927. Seven years later he recanted and was reinstated in a high position. Rosengoltz had been one of Trotsky's most brilliant commanders during the Civil War, a man of great charm and ferocious tenacity. Rakovsky was almost excessively cultivated, Rosengoltz all fire and energy. Together they represented the two complementary sides of Trotsky's character.

The only man who came out of the trial with dignity was Bukharin, who invented a kind of Aesopian language which permitted him to communicate his total innocence while admitting his crimes. He would admit everything without exception until his admissions assumed the form of preposterous nonsense, and be-

tween these admissions he would offhandedly accuse
the accusers, reminding them that he was not a criminal, that he had never in his life plotted to assassinate
anybody, spied on anyone, taken part in wrecking
activities, or worked on behalf of foreign powers. When
Vyshinsky reminded him of his detailed confessions, he
answered dryly: "The confession of the accused is a
mediaeval principle of jurisprudence." Asked whether
he pleaded guilty, he answered: "I plead guilty to the
sum total of crimes committed by this counterrevolutionary organization, irrespective of whether or
not I knew of, whether or not I took a direct part in, any
particular act." In this way he confused the issue of his
guilt, and in the course of the trial he showed sometimes directly, sometimes indirectly, that he knew nothing at all about the various Trotskyist plots, blocs and
Centers, while admitting an excessive responsibility
for all of them. The ugly, piercing voice of the prosecutor was met by the dry, subdued voice of Bukharin, who
was speaking not to the court but to history.

With the murder of Bukharin in the cellars of the
Lubyanka prison, the Old Bolsheviks passed from the
scene. There remained only Trotsky and Stalin, who
had always been a little apart from Lenin even though
they worked beside him. They were born to be enemies
and they would fight to the death.

Trotsky's comments on the trial of Bukharin and
twenty others show signs of exhaustion. He imagined
that Stalin's rule was a throwback to Tsarist autocracy,
and in the order of historical events the execution of
Bukharin could be likened to the assassination of
Rasputin, and in this way it became a signal for the
new revolution that would overthrow Stalin. If the
comparison was ludicrous, it could be explained by the
fact that the trial was ludicrous, irrational, and absurd.
Just as in the previous year he had murdered his
generals, so now Stalin was murdering the wisest and
best of the Old Bolsheviks not because he feared them
but because he could not tolerate their presence, because they irritated him, and because he was preparing for the inevitable confrontation with Hitler and

Trotsky in his study five months before his death.

Snapshots of Trotsky taken in Mexico in 1938.

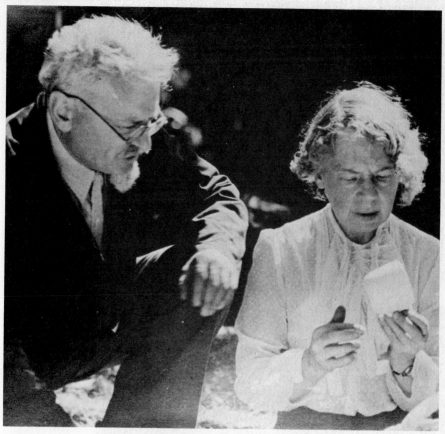

Trotsky and Natalie in 1939.   *(Pathfinder Press)*

IDENTIDAD DE:

RAMON MERCADER DEL RIO   CON   JAQUES MORNARD

DIRECCION GENERAL DE SEGURIDAD

JEFATURA SUPERIOR DE POLICIA

Barcelona 12-VI-1935
Clisé n.º 20888
Iris 2   Talla 1.780
Nació el 7-11-1914

INDICE DERECHO

SECCION DE IDENTIFICACION

AT.   SERIE C-2-40 FOT. 98079. EXP.

OMBRE MONARD VAN DENDRESHED JAQUES ó
) JACKSON N. FRANK.

OTIVO Homicidio, At. Pel. y Port Arm. Proh.
Juez 16/o ó/a C. P. Formal pris. decre
BSERVACIONES tada por el C. Juez 1/a Instanci
de Coyoacan 28 de Agosto de
1940.

FORM. V-3333 V-2222 3233
3333

1935 EN ESPAÑA   MEXICO 1940

A composite made in 1950 identifying the photograph and fingerprint of Ramon Mercader taken in 1935 with photograph and
fingerprint of Jaques (Jacson) Mornard taken in 1940.

(Isaac Don Levine)

Top photograph: Ramon Mercader at fifteen, *middle* shows him in jail in Barcelona at twenty-one, *lower* shows him in jail in Mexico City at forty-four. At right (B.5.d) is Guadalupe Gómez, the friend who accompanied him to Russia after his release. The photograph was taken in 1957. *(All from Isaac Don Levine)*

The fortress in Coyoacan where Trotsky was murdered.

(U.P.I.)

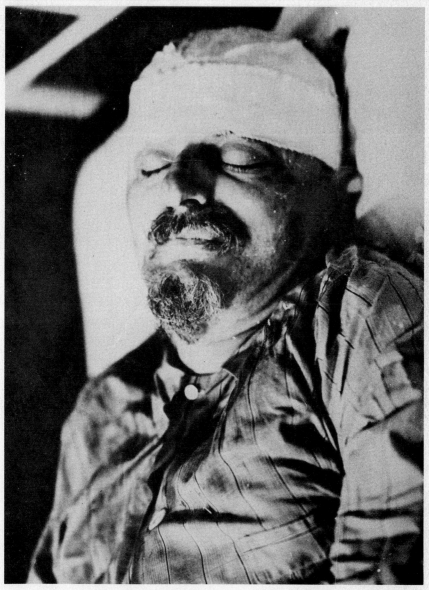

Shortly after death.   (Wide World)

The ashes of Trotsky and his wife lie under the memorial in the garden at
Coyoacan.

wanted complete freedom of action without the necessity of consulting anyone. He was drunk with power and more than half-mad. Hitler, too, was drunk with power and more than half-mad. Between them they would throw the world into convulsions.

Trotsky believed he still had one powerful card to play. He would inaugurate and preside over the Fourth International, which would unite the working classes of the world against their overlords—the capitalists, the bourgeoisie, Stalin. The Third International had been one of the playthings of the rulers of the Soviet Union, permitting them to maintain control of Communists all over the world while pretending that the organization was wholly independent of the government. Trotsky had once offered excellent reasons for believing that a Fourth International was futile; he now changed his mind; it became the one hope of humanity and the only possible way in which he could dominate events.

Because he was always a conspirator, he went about the inauguration of the Fourth International conspiratorially. He became the secret president, the inaugural meeting took place in great secrecy in the small village of Perigny outside Paris, the delegates were chosen by him, the leader of the Russian section was Mark Zborowski, who was in the pay of Stalin, while Lyova, Erwin Wolf, and Rudolf Klement, all killed by Stalin, were honorary presidents. Max Shachtman, an American Trotskyist who later quarreled violently with Trotsky, was appointed acting president. Altogether twenty-two delegates attended in order to proclaim the existence of the new World Party of Socialist Revolution. Many of those who attended, like Alfred Rosmer, in whose house the conference took place, were tired and dispirited and did so out of loyalty to Trotsky. The secret conference lasted only one day, September 3, 1938. Later a communiqué was issued, stating that the Founding Conference had met in Lausanne, which was not true, and henceforth the Fourth International alone would represent the true interests of the toiling masses.

One of the interpreters at Perigny was Sylvia Ageloff, a young woman of Russian-Jewish ancestry born in

New York. Her lover, who called himself variously Jacson or Jacques Mornard, spent the day waiting patiently outside Alfred Rosmer's house so that he could drive her back to Paris. He was one of four or five people who had received orders to assassinate Trotsky.

THE PROPHET'S ROBES 25

Diego Rivera was a man of sudden enthusiasms and unpredictable temper. He was squat and heavyset, well aware of his fame, devoted to his art, and equally devoted to the world's toiling masses who were portrayed in his immense canvases. Intellectually he was an anarchist, who approved of communism only because he believed in revolution and thought that the communists had the muscle and intelligence to bring the revolution about. He believed, like Trotsky, that Stalin had betrayed the Russian Revolution and at the beginning of 1939 he had convinced himself that President Lázaro Cárdenas was "an accomplice of Stalin." He was also completely disenchanted by Trotsky's Fourth International, which he regarded as a futile and vainglorious gesture. Toward Trotsky he showed a continual politeness, but it was clear that their relations were at breaking point. In the spring of 1939 Trotsky moved out of the Blue House and set up his establishment in a large rambling house with a wild garden on the Avenida Viena in another part of Coyoacan. The house was surrounded by a high wall, which afforded him a minimum of security. Here he worked on his books and articles, presided over the Fourth International, kept rabbits, collected strange varieties of cactus, conducted a vast correspondence, and awaited the coming of his grandson Seva (Vsevolod), the son of his dead daughter Zina, for he possessed a grandfather's affection for his grandchild.

As the months passed, the house on the Avenida Viena was transformed into a small fortress. The Mexican government provided him with a police box; policemen were permanently on duty outside the house. Theoretically they were supposed to challenge all comers to the house but in fact they merely added moral support. Young Americans and occasionally young Mexicans acted as guards. There was a large and pleasant living room, a kitchen, study, library, and two bedrooms. There were rather spartan living quarters for the guards built against one of the surrounding walls. There were usually eight or nine people in the house, including a Russian secretary who came nearly every day from Mexico City, and the servants.

The war which had become inevitable since Hitler seized power in 1933 was coming closer. Increasingly in his articles Trotsky assumed the role of a prophet. Prophecies spilled out like jewels from a queen's robe. There was a pattern in his prophecies. He saw the world ceaselessly moving toward revolution. He was sure an anti-Stalinist revolution would break out in the Soviet Union. He believed that Stalin was about to be dethroned and his own concept of the organization of revolutionary power in Russia would prevail. He prophesied that England, France, the United States, and Japan would soon erupt in violent revolution, and sometimes he would say sadly that the United States was inexplicably slow and cumbrous in its movement toward revolution. Sometimes he couched his prophecies in epigrammatic form, giving them a finality which was awesome and uncompromising, as when he prophesied that "the Soviet Union will be Americanized technically, Europe will either be Sovietized or descend to barbarism, the United States will be Europeanized politically." Only the first of these prophecies came true, and this was the easiest prophecy to make, for it was already in the process of coming about.

Early in 1939, Sybil Vincent, a correspondent for the London *Daily Herald*, interviewed Trotsky at Coyoacan and asked him a series of questions, all of them involving the gift of prophecy. She asked him about the growing power of Japan, which had already devoured large areas of China, and whether it represented a menace to the Soviet Union, England, and the United States. He replied:

> Japan is not capable of war on a great scale, partly for economic reasons but above all for social reasons. Not having emancipated itself up to now from the heritage of feudalism, Japan represents the reservoir of a gigantic revolutionary explosion. In many ways it calls to mind the Tsarist empire on the eve of 1905.

That, of course, was the trouble—prophecy by analogy is too easy. He equated Hirohito's Japan in 1939 with Nicholas II's Russia of 1905 and drew the inevitable conclusions. Knowing very little about the social and economic conditions of Japan, he was able to arrive at a conclusion that was profoundly satisfying. Earlier, at the time of the Japanese invasion of Manchuria, he had prophesied that the Japanese people would inevitably rise up against the militarists in a bloody revolution. It had not happened. This prophecy, like so many others, was abandoned by the wayside.

She asked him whether a world war was inevitable. If so, would it mean the end of the capitalist system? He answered:

> Yes, a world war is inevitable, if a revolution does not forestall it. The inevitability of the war flows, first, from the incurable crisis of the capitalist system; secondly, from the fact that the present partition of our planet, that is to say above all, of the colonies, no longer corresponds to the economic specific weight of the imperialist states. Looking for an escape out of the mortal crisis, the parvenu states aspire, and cannot fail to aspire, to new partitioning of the world. Only children at the breast and professional "paci-

fists" to whom even the experience of the unfortunate League of Nations has taught nothing, can suppose that a more "equitable" repartition of the territorial surface can be realized around the green tables of diplomacy.

This was not a very convincing prophecy. Marx, too, had talked about the incurable crisis of the capitalist system and prophesied its downfall. It was true that the parvenu states, by which he meant Germany, Italy, and Japan, were attempting to repartition the earth, but this was a fact known to every schoolboy. Trotsky's statement, offered with the finality of a papal edict, suggests that he was suffering from a great weariness. The only important phrase, the one closest to his heart, is: "if a revolution does not forestall it." A revolution where? Led by whom? For what purpose? These were mysteries he was not prepared to divulge. But if sometimes the prophetic impulse seemed to be aroused by ignorance alone, there were occasions when he could be deadly accurate, and this happened when prophesying about people he knew well. Speaking on March 18, 1939, he could say that to his certain knowledge Stalin was now ripe for an alliance with Hitler. There were very few people at the time who could speak on this subject so authoritatively.

He told Sybil Vincent that he was finishing a book on Stalin that would soon appear in the United States, England, and other places. He explained that it was a political biography which "has as its objective an explanation of how a second or third rank revolutionary can appear at the head of a country when the Thermidorian reaction begins." He believed that Stalin was on the verge of his downfall. He also believed that "if it is not liquidated in time by socialist revolution, fascism will inevitably conquer in France, England and the United States with the aid of Mussolini and Hitler, or without them."

The chief danger of the prophet is that he is always tempted to draw the long bow and rarely knows when to stop. He uses the word "inevitably" when it would be wiser to use "perhaps" or "if I am not mistaken."

Trotsky enjoyed "inevitably" and "with absolute certainty." He had assumed the role of prophet very early in life and suffered from the fact that he believed too often in his own infallibility. He was right in 1917, but he may have been right for the wrong reasons.

Just as his prophecies were sometimes hopelessly wrong, so his political judgments were sometimes wide of the mark. To the end of his life he believed that Hitler was the prisoner of the landowners and industrialists. Shortly after Hitler came to power, he wrote: "The investiture of Hitler with power served a two-fold purpose: first, to decorate the camarilla of property-owners with the leaders of 'a national movement'; and secondly to place the fighting forces of Fascism at the direct disposal of the property-owners." There were others writing at the time who recognized that Hitler was no man's prisoner and that "the camarilla of property-owners" was among the least of his tribute bearers.

Trotsky's powers of prophecy seemed to weaken on Mexican soil, perhaps because he was becoming more and more isolated from world affairs. When the war broke out in September 1939 he was recuperating from one of his bouts of illness in a remote Mexican village and did not hear the news. When he returned to Coyoacan, he seemed almost disinterested. "Whichever camp is victorious," he said, "humanity will be left far behind." The war, in his view, was merely a continuation of World War I, "a reactionary war on both sides." "The nations will come out of this war different than when they went into it, and will reconstruct our planet according to the laws of reason." In this way, with a wave of his prophetic hand, he abandoned the war to the reasonable victors.

One day in October 1939 there occurred a strange incident which would have seriously alarmed him if he had realized its implications. A man who called himself Manuel Fernandez Barrechena attempted to enter the house in Coyoacan. He told the guards that he had an urgent message for Trotsky, and was a refugee from Spain, a former pilot in the Republican Air Force, and a member of the Communist Party. He looked as though he was a mischief maker and the guards sent him away after asking him where he lived. He said he was living at the Hotel Moderno in Mexico City. On the following day, before any further inquiries were made, Trotsky received a telephone call from a man who represented himself to be General José Miaja, the general who had been in charge of the defense of Madrid during the Spanish Civil War. According to the "general," Manuel Fernandez Barrechena was a man of sterling quality and considerable wealth whose greatest desire in life was to present Trotsky with an automobile. Trotsky thanked him and telephoned the real General Miaja, who was also living in exile in Mexico. The real general had never heard of Barrechena or his automobile. One of Trotsky's secretaries then went to the Hotel Moderno to discover more about Barrechena and especially his real motive for coming to Coyoacan. Barrechena was nervous, had little to say for himself, and evaded all questions. He was not a refugee from Spain but appeared to come from South America. He had no documents of any kind. He appeared to be one more of those hapless people recruited by the G.P.U. to spy out the house on the Avenida Viena. Since he had not yet committed any crime, the police let him go.

There were two or three other incidents of this kind, and Trotsky took them in his stride. He had rarely been afraid, and it was too late to learn fear. More and more in the new house he behaved as he had behaved on the island of Prinkipo. He made excursions into the countryside and paid visits to people in Mexico City, taking only the most elementary precautions. In July 1939 Alfred Rosmer came to stay with him, bringing his wife Marguerite and the boy Seva, who was the apple of his grandfather's eye. Marguerite had found him hidden away in an obscure orphanage in Alsace; Gérard Rosenthal, Trotsky's Paris lawyer, had torn through mountains of red tape in order to unite the boy with his only living relatives.

Trotsky was now working on a life of Stalin which had been commissioned by Harper and Brothers in New York. He found little pleasure in contemplating Stalin.

He was working against the grain, for he despised Stalin, knowing full well that it was dangerous to despise him. For some reason he had abandoned his life of Lenin after completing an account of his childhood and youth. Stalin presented special problems. How does one describe a monster who killed everyone in his path? Trotsky needed time to ponder, to contemplate, to revise. He was mortally tired, and the death of Lyova had left a wound still bleeding. As he surveyed his small estate, the high-walled fortress, the muscular young Americans who guarded him, the garden, the cactuses, the rabbit hutch full of black and white rabbits resembling miniature giant pandas, the watchtowers, the alarm systems, the machine guns in the guard room and the revolver on his desk and all the complex engineering that went into defending him from a hostile world, he was well aware that he was not safe from Stalin. Even if the entire fortress was covered with an enormous bubbletop of armor plating and if he was protected underneath the earth by a twenty-foot-thick floor of reinforced concrete, Stalin would find a way to him. He was writing a long and detailed book about Stalin while being hunted by Stalin. It was an extraordinary situation, and the irony of it sometimes filled him with a kind of sardonic amusement.

The book was going slowly, and badly. Like many writers, he wrote out of sequence. As an idea occurred to him he would write it down, and then a totally new idea, about another aspect of Stalin or another incident in his life, occurred to him and he would enlarge on this, forgetting the first idea. In this way he constructed pieces of a mosaic which would later have to be filled out. The danger of this way of writing is that the author later has to join together in cold blood pieces originally composed in the fire of inspiration or at least in a state of excitement. Trotsky's bridge passages are sometimes almost too evident. Also, as Boris Souvarine had discovered when he was writing his own monumental life of Stalin, there are special difficulties and dangers in writing about a man whose character never changes and who is always murderous.

One day, early in 1940, Trotsky was visited by his publisher, Cass Canfield, the head of Harper and Brothers, who was holidaying with his wife in Mexico City. He had no difficulty finding Trotsky's address and telephone number in the telephone book and soon drove out to the house on the Avenida Viena. There were some soldiers or more probably policemen patrolling outside the house. Canfield was amused. He turned to his wife and said: "This is a bit of musical comedy. I can't imagine that Trotsky's life would be in any particular danger in Mexico City." In this, of course, he was wrong: Trotsky had lived dangerously all his life, but his life was never in greater danger than during this year.

They came to the big iron gate which was opened by an armed guard. Some yards further on they encountered another armed guard. Finally they were taken to Trotsky's study, where to their surprise they saw galley proofs of the finished part of the book on Stalin hanging on a kind of clothesline. Trotsky was "rosy-cheeked and bouncy," in the best of health. He wore a white Russian smock and gray trousers. With his strong face and white shock of hair, his good color and quick movements, he looked like a man who did a great deal of exercise. Canfield asked him how he kept in such fine physical condition, and he answered in English: "Oh, I go to the neighboring mountains and hunt game." Canfield was reminded of an Austrian aristocrat saying that he got his exercise by chamois hunting. He was not the first to see the aristocrat in Trotsky.

Affable, courteous, and high-spirited, Trotsky was the perfect host. Once he complained of the difficulty of obtaining source material for the life of Stalin: some books came, but very slowly, and sometimes they were smuggled out through friends in the Soviet Union. Canfield was beginning to think of him as a kind of political Voltaire, maintaining a vast correspondence, happy in exile, and in command of his destiny. This was an impression Trotsky liked to convey, but it was far from being the whole truth.

The Soviet Union and Nazi Germany were in alliance; Poland, torn apart, had vanished from the map; the Finns were still fighting the Red Army and inflicting heavy damage on it. Trotsky characteristically explained these defeats away by saying that the Soviet troops fighting in Finland were recruited from the Ukraine and southern parts of Russia, which was not true. He was profoundly nationalistic, very much on the side of the Soviet Union against the Finns, and he was sure Stalin would win the battle in spite of the army purges which had removed so many capable generals and officers, and in spite of the political commissars who wielded overwhelming power over the career officers. He spoke in the same vein to many people and in many articles. Implicit in his argument was an acceptance of Stalin as war leader and a kind of admiration for Stalin's cleverness in making an alliance with Hitler.

Trotsky had not the least doubt in the outcome of the war. He was sure Germany would lose the war after a great struggle. He was also quite sure that America would be compelled to intervene. And when Canfield asked him how he foresaw the end of the war, Trotsky answered: "A ruined planet under American hegemony. There will be a revolution in the United States, and presumably elsewhere, coming at a time of profound economic dislocation." He added that the war would be the death blow of the British Empire, the colonies would split away, and Britain would become a second-rate power.

Trotsky's prophecies, always vigorously advanced, often involve extraordinary contradictions. As always he believed that war was the mother of revolution. He believed that America, exhausted by the war, would be ripe for revolution, and simultaneously he believed that American industrial power would enable her to acquire hegemony over the rest of the world, forgetting that a country in a state of revolution is by the very nature of things so engrossed in its own turmoil that hegemony is the last thing it can think about. In 1917, after the Revolution, he had dreamed that Russia would acquire a kind of hegemony over the world. So now in the first year of the Second World War he dreamed of revolution and hegemony, but this time America would dominate the rest of the world.

When Canfield asked him whether he would like to visit the United States, Trotsky answered quickly: "Indeed I would, and I would be there now except for the Man in the White House. Mr. Roosevelt knows enough about me so that he wouldn't consider letting me into the country. If you had a Republican President he would have been less well informed and I would have been able to cross your border." And when he was asked what he would do if he was allowed to enter America, he answered: "Start a revolution, of course."

This was taken as a joke, but in fact he was deadly serious. The idea of somehow bringing about a revolution in the United States had occurred to him almost from the time he arrived in Mexico. The greater number of his followers were young Americans; most of his financial support came from the United States; he was convinced by the logic of his own theories that America would soon be ripe for revolution and it was a question merely of giving history an extra push. In 1917 there were people in the Social Democratic organizations in Brooklyn who regarded Trotsky as the preordained revolutionary dictator of the United States, the one man who could speak with authority, inflame the masses, and lead the revolution to a successful conclusion. Now, twenty-three years later, he was groping toward the same end. The words spoken to Canfield in an offhand manner expressed his real intentions. We shall see later that he was gradually building up the machinery of revolution in the United States and was preparing to take an active role. From our own perspective of history the attempt appears almost ludicrous, so small were his forces against the power of the established order, but when he had arrived in Petrograd in 1917 his forces were even smaller. In his own mind he remained the revolutionist and life had no meaning for him except as a revolutionist. The last supreme effort of his life was to be devoted to bringing about a revolution in the United States.

Canfield had no particular interest in Trotsky, except as one more of those writers whose manuscripts are interminably delayed. He was therefore in a position to see Trotsky freshly, without illusions. He was one of the very few American visitors to the house on the Avenida Viena who was not under Trotsky's spell.

Trotsky believed he could finish the book on Stalin by August 1940. Circumstances intervened, and it was never finished. A Russian scholar, Charles Malamuth, was given the task of assembling seven completed chapters, five uncompleted chapters, and a mass of notes, and the book was printed and ready for publication early in December 1941. On December 5 the advance copies were sent out; three days later, the same day the United States declared war on Germany and Japan, the books were recalled. Canfield had come to the conclusion that the publication of the book would be deeply resented by Stalin, that representations would be made by the Soviet Foreign Ministry to ban the book, and there would be all kinds of trouble. He therefore withdrew the book, which was not published until 1946. The decision weighed heavily on him: he was not certain then and is still uncertain whether he did the right thing.

We can see now that he did the wrong thing. Trotsky's book, with all its faults of disorganization, provided for the first time a long steady look at Stalin by one who had known him well. It was well documented and authoritative; it was evidently biased but there was a plenitude of evidence to support the portrait of a man who was treacherous to his friends and insanely cruel to his imagined enemies. The kindly "Uncle Joe" of wartime propaganda never appears. Instead he shows a Stalin who took a savage delight in compromising people, leading them carefully and cautiously into the center of the maze, and then when they were hopelessly bewildered, unable to find the exit, he would say: "I will show you the way out. It is very simple, but first you must promise to obey me always, you must promise to submit to me always, you, your wife, your family, everything you own and everything you hope for."

When they have promised all this he shows them the exit—a bullet in the nape of the neck.

By long experience Trotsky had become aware that Stalin was possessed of a medieval cunning of a very intricate kind. Lenin described Stalin as "coarse." Trotsky, who had the opportunity to study Stalin at greater length, was more impressed by the intricacy of his mind. It was true that the intricate machinery was rarely renewed, that the young Stalin was scarcely to be distinguished from the old General Secretary, and that what was most terrible about the machine was that it did nothing but grind people up: nevertheless the machine was complex. There was a certain art in it. Not everyone is capable of leading men into the maze, forcing them to commit heinous and unforgivable crimes, and then when he has no further use for them shooting them in cold blood. Trotsky showed how the same processes were repeated endlessly. They were habitual and perhaps instinctive. He did not act; he reacted, always with cruelty and with a blind, calculated rage against mankind.

Trotsky's book on Stalin is among the least widely read of all his works, but in its own time it was one of the most necessary. It was one of the few books that could stand up against the heavy weight of Soviet propaganda. It was a corrective and a warning. If Roosevelt or Churchill or Truman had read it and understood it, they might not have fallen into the many traps Stalin laid for them. For Stalin allies were always expendable: they were permitted to suffer the same fate as his enemies.

When the book could have been most useful, it was lying in Harper and Brothers' warehouse, printed, bound, and ready for distribution. It had been reduced to a nonbook. It was not banned but was placed deep in limbo. And perhaps, after all, it made little difference whether it was published or not, for Churchill, Roosevelt and Truman were men who rarely read books and preferred their own judgment on Stalin to that of anyone else. They found Stalin hard but endearing, warm, jovial, expansive. They did not know until it was too late that he was a consummate actor.

Trotsky tells chilling stories about Stalin's behavior. Once, when Stalin was in prison in Baku, he heard a fellow prisoner talking about the coming of revolution. "Then you must have a craving for blood!" Stalin exclaimed, and saying this, he took the knife hidden in his boot, pulled up one of his own trouser legs, and inflicted a deep gash on himself. "There's blood for you!" he said. He was pleased with what he was done. In future the craving for blood was directed toward the wounds of others.

Although Trotsky recognized the complexity of Stalin's cruelty, its deviousness, its cunning, and its vast knowledge of all the weaknesses of people, especially government officials, who only needed a little prodding to betray themselves, there was another element in Stalin which Trotsky found almost incomprehensible: his piglike buffoonery, his stage-managing of meetings of the Central Committee so that they resembled "obscene and rowdy bar-room burlesques." In the role of stage manager Stalin walked up and down at the back of the hall where they met, and having learned the scenario by heart, he looked ironically at the performers, pleased when they carried out their assignments and still more pleased when they hurled shameless threats at everyone who disagreed with the scenario as Stalin had written it. He pulled all the strings. In retrospect Trotsky found him uninteresting. In Stalin he found no intellectual distinction, no grace of mind. Stalin had betrayed the Revolution, perverted Marxism for his own purposes, destroyed millions of innocent people, and left on Russia a claw mark that would endure for centuries. All this was true, but it was not the whole truth. Stalin was one of those men who create enemies so that they can have the pleasure of killing them.

In the midst of a war with Finland and on the eve of a war with Germany, Stalin finally decided to kill Trotsky.

26 THE FIRST ATTACK

In February 1940, Trotsky appears to have had a premonition that his life would soon be coming to an end. He was alarmed by his rising blood pressure, his fainting spells, his lassitude, and an increasing debility. The doctors could do nothing for him, perhaps because he did not trust them and refused to obey them. He was also acutely aware of the coming of old age and was terrified by the thought of senility. Outwardly he gave every impression of good health; he had a ruddy complexion; walked jauntily; worked well, though not at the height of his powers. He was not afraid of death and had long ago come to the conclusion that life was an inexorable archway between birth and the grave: there could be no beautiful youth without old age and death. He was satisfied that he had lived fully, having spent by far the greater part of his life as a Marxist revolutionary. He was fifty-nine years old.

He felt that the time had come for him to write his testament, his farewell to the world. It was a carefully considered document, brief and succinct, paying tribute where it was due, without claiming for himself any achievements except that he had fought throughout his life under the banner of Marxism. He said nothing about his services in the creation of the Soviet Union, or about the great days in his life when he had changed the course of history. Lenin wrote his testament in a conscious effort to lead the Communist Party along the path he had chosen for it. His testament was a political document which failed in its purpose. Trotsky's testament was far from being a political document. Instead, he wrote a deeply personal confession of faith in the ultimate victory of the proletariat, ending the document very simply with a curiously moving account of his wife walking across the patio to open his window wider so that more sunlight could enter his study; and in the opening of the window he saw a kind of promise of a future free of oppression and violence.

Testament

My high (and still rising) blood pressure is deceiving those near me about my actual condition. I am active and able to work, but the end is evidently near. These lines will be made public after my death.

I have no need to refute here once more the stupid and vile slander of Stalin and his agents: there is not a single spot on my revolutionary honor. I have never entered, either directly or indirectly, into any behind-the-scenes agreements or even negotiations with the enemies of the working class. Thousands of Stalin's opponents have fallen victim to similar false accusations. The new revolutionary generations will rehabilitate their political honor and deal with the Kremlin executioners according to their deserts.

I thank warmly the friends who remained loyal to me through the most difficult hours of my life. I do not name anyone in particular because I cannot name them all.

However, I consider myself justified in making an exception in the case of my companion, Natalya Ivanovna Sedova. In addition to the joy of being a fighter for the cause of socialism, fate gave me the happiness of being her husband. During the almost forty years of our life together she remained an inexhaustible source of love, magnanimity, and tenderness. She underwent great sufferings, especially during the last period of our lives. But I find some comfort in the fact that she also knew days of happiness.

For forty-three years of my conscious life I have
remained a revolutionist; for forty-two of them I have
fought under the banner of Marxism. If I had to begin it all
over again I would of course try to avoid this or that
mistake, but the main course of my life would remain
unchanged. I shall die a proletarian revolutionary, a Marxist, a dialectical materialist, and consequently an irrecon-
cilable atheist. My faith in the communist future of mankind is not less ardent, indeed it is firmer today, than it was
in the days of my youth.

Natasha has just come up to the window from the
courtyard and opened it wider so that the air may enter
more freely into my room. I can see the bright green strip of
grass beneath the wall, and the clear blue sky above the
wall, and sunlight everywhere. Life is beautiful. Let the
future generations cleanse it of all evil, oppression and
violence, and enjoy it to the full.

L. Trotsky

February 27, 1940
Coyoacan

This was the personal testament; there remained the
more formal testament concerning the disposition of his
possessions and particularly the royalties from his
books. He drew another sheet of paper toward him and
wrote:

Testament

All the possessions remaining after my death, all my
literary rights (income from my books, articles, etc) are to
be placed at the disposal of my wife, Natalya Ivanovna
Sedova. February 27, 1940, L. Trotsky.

In case we both die—

He wrote nothing more on the page, perhaps because
the thought of her death was intolerable to him and he
wanted more time to ponder it. There was perhaps also
another reason: he had long ago come to the conclusion
that a man had a perfect right to commit suicide if he
was suffering from a painful and lingering illness, and
Natalie agreed with him. We can therefore translate the
words: "In case we both die" into "In case we are both

destroyed by Stalin" or "In case we commit suicide together."

Five days after writing this brief testament he wrote a statement on what he believed to be his medical condition and added an apologia for suicide.

March 3, 1940.

The nature of my illness (high and rising blood pressure) is such—as I understand it—that the end will most likely come suddenly—again, this is my personal hypothesis—through a brain hemorrhage. This is the best possible end I can wish for. It is possible, however, that I am mistaken (I have no desire to read special books on the subject and the physicians naturally will not tell the truth). If the sclerosis should assume a protracted character and I should be threatened with the prospect of being an invalid over a long period (at present I feel on the contrary rather a surge of spiritual energy because of the high blood pressure, but this will not last long), then I reserve the right to determine for myself the time of my death. The "suicide" (if such a term is appropriate in this connection) will not in any respect be an expression of an outburst of despair or hopelessness. Natasha and I have often said that we may be in such a physical condition that it would be better to cut short our own lives or, more accurately, the too slow process of dying. . . . But whatever may be the circumstances of my death I shall die with unshaken faith in the communist future. This faith in man and in his future gives me even now such power of resistance as cannot be given by any religion.

L. Trotsky

All these documents were placed in an envelope and sealed. No one in the house on the Avenida Viena had the faintest suspicion that Trotsky and his wife were contemplating suicide, and if they had known they would have been dumbfounded.

Outwardly Trotsky showed no signs that he was breaking. He still commanded his small fortress as he had once commanded his armored train. He gave orders, received reports, wrote articles and manifestos with what appeared to be his customary energy, and held fast to the belief that the Fourth International would provide a rallying point for proletarian revolutionaries in the coming war which would inevitably involve Nazi Germany and the Soviet Union. He still believed he had an important role to play in the world. But when Natalie was alone with him in his study, she would sometimes look up to see his face grown suddenly careworn and there would come from him a deep sigh, as he said: "I am so tired, so tired. I can't take it any more." Sometimes, too, when he thought he was alone, she heard him whispering the names of his friends, Rakovsky, Smirnov, Muralov, Sosnovsky, Kamenev, and many more, all dead, having died violently at the hands of executioners. At such times the wounds opened, for there was no comfort, only excruciating pain, to be derived from the long litany of the dead.

On the night of May 24, 1940, Trotsky took a sleeping powder before he went to bed. He slept soundly until about four o'clock in the morning when he was awakened by what he thought were fireworks celebrating a national holiday. The sleeping powder was slowing down his responses. Natalie whispered urgently: "They're shooting—they're shooting into the room—" They rolled off the bed onto the floor, lying between the bed and the wall, Natalie trying to shield her husband with her body until he was able to convince her to lie flat, and all this happened in two or three seconds, while the bullets ripped through the door. Lights flashed through the bedroom, machine-gun fire seemed to be coming from all directions, and suddenly the door of the other bedroom, where Seva, their grandson, was sleeping, burst open, and Natalie saw or thought she saw a man standing there in the fiery glow, silhouetted against flames, the metal buttons of his coat gleaming red, and she remembered that the face under the helmet was contorted. He was like an apparition; he was doing something but exactly what he was doing she did not know. Later, when they were able to examine the bulletholes, it became clear that he was firing with a Thomson machine gun at their bed and especially at their pillows.

Trotsky's logical mind, moving from the particular to the general, attempted to grapple with the problem. The bullets were very close, there was the sharp smell of gunpowder growing sharper, at least one hand grenade had exploded, there were many people moving about in the patio, fires were burning, and the bedroom was being attacked from all directions. What, then, had happened to their lines of defense, the iron doors, the trip wires that would start jangling when the pigeons brushed them with their wings, the policemen outside, the armed guards inside the twelve-foot-high walls? Had all their defenses suddenly broken down? It was inconceivable that the enemy was able to walk into the house and shoot from three sides into the bedroom. Had all the guards been kidnapped or killed? In a daze, lying close to the wall, while chips of plaster and splinters of glass flew around the room, Trotsky tried to make sense of what was happening and gave up in despair, thinking that his grandson, the Rosmers, and the American guards must all be dead, and Natalie and he would soon be dead, and the whole fortress would go up in flames, and soon there would be only the blackened walls.

Suddenly there was a shrill scream from Seva's bedroom, where a wardrobe was on fire. It was Seva shouting: "Grandpa!" Trotsky thought it was a cry for help. He was sure the boy was being kidnapped, and at this thought the life seemed to go out of him. The shooting had stopped. There was an unearthly silence. Seva ran out of his bedroom and across the courtyard to the outhouses where the guards who were not on duty spent the night, saw that they were still alive, and then ran back into the house by way of the door leading to the dining room, where he found Alfred and Marguerite Rosmer. He was so delighted to find them alive that he screamed again at the top of his lungs: "Al-fred! Marguer-ite!" About five minutes had passed since the enemy broke into the fortress.

Natalie went into the boy's bedroom, where the floor was smoldering and the wardrobe was on fire. She threw rugs and blankets over them and put out the flames. Then she turned her attention to the study, which was the room next door to the bedroom, and found the door locked. Through the bullet holes in the door she could see the wooden table where her husband worked, the shaded lamp which had been turned on, the books and papers in order. Whoever had been standing in the room and pumping bullets into the bedroom had no time to disarrange the room, but he had taken the trouble to lock the door. Why? This too might become clear in time. Meanwhile both Natalie and Trotsky marveled at the room's immaculate calm in contrast with the two bedrooms torn by about two hundred bullets. The door of the study was opened by Otto Schussler, who was small, blond and Jewish. He told them that one of the raiders had stood under the eucalyptus tree in the patio between the outhouses and the house, firing off bursts from a machine gun and thus preventing the guards from coming to their rescue. Otto Schussler was thirty-five years old, had worked for Trotsky on the island of Prinkipo, and was now occasionally employed as a secretary. Charles Cornell, twenty-nine years old, a Californian from Fresno, also served as a secretary-guard. There were four other guards, all Americans: Harold Robins from Detroit, Walter O'Rourke from New York, Jake Cooper from Minneapolis, and Robert Sheldon Harte from New York. They were all young, and Robert Sheldon Harte was the youngest, being only twenty-five years old.

By this time dawn was coming up and they could see the extent of the damage: the walls pockmarked with bullet holes, an incendiary bomb flung down in the patio, where the grass was still burning, the garage doors wide open, and the two cars belonging to Trotsky gone. Robert Sheldon Harte had also vanished. He had been on guard duty during the night. When last seen he was wearing khaki riding breeches, brown riding boots, a sweater under a brown coat, and over his shoulders a Mexican *serape*. The *serape* lay on the floor of the garage, and so did his revolver. It was easy to understand why he might have removed the *serape* but it was difficult to understand why he had abandoned the revolver. It was still more difficult to understand why he had permitted the well-armed raiding party to enter the patio by way of the heavy armored door which he alone could open. For some reason the guard stationed with a machine gun on the watchtower was absent that night. It was as though the raiders had simply ignored the formidable defenses of the fortress and burst through the walls as though they were paper.

Soon they discovered that the police guards outside the house had vanished, except two or three who were trussed up. The captain of the guard had spent the night at home; two policemen had slipped away with two girls sent to seduce them. Trotsky's cars were found abandoned not far away; the raiders had escaped in still another car. Other things were found: a dynamite bomb with a time fuse which had failed to explode. Packed with three pounds of dynamite, it would have blown up the whole house with everyone and everything in it. Clearly the chief purpose of entering the house was to plant the bomb, destroy Trotsky, his family, his guards, and his archives, leaving nothing behind. The police also found a rope ladder, grappling irons, an ordinary wooden ladder, an electric saw, several detonators, fuse wire, an ax, seventy-five .45-caliber cartridges, hundreds of spent cartridge cases, two Mausers, submachine-gun clips, and a particularly ugly and brutal iron bar known in the underground as a "holy child." There were also pieces of clothing, cartridge belts, and caps. Everything went to show that the raiders had rushed into the patio with extraordinary speed and within seconds had fired their submachine guns, planted their large bomb, and afterward there was a kind of lull, while they kept the guards quiet and surveyed the damage they had caused. Surprisingly, considering their careful planning, they had caused very little. Trotsky, Natalie, and Seva had all been hit by bullets but very lightly. Trotsky received two grazing bullet wounds in the right leg, Natalie received a grazing wound in the arm, and Seva received a wound in his big toe. This was the most serious wound, for as he ran out into the patio he left a trail of blood. Although he had always lived dangerously, Trotsky had never been wounded before, and these wounds were so slight that they scarcely counted.

There is exhilaration in danger, and Trotsky was unable to conceal his exhilaration at the thought that so many men had planned to assassinate him and failed. All the advantages were on the side of the raiders who must have thought when they left the house that they had killed Trotsky, his wife, and grandson, and soon there would be nothing left of the archives. Colonel Sanchez Salazar, the chief of the Presidential Police, came to the house in Coyoacan, examined the patio, marched through the house, counted the bullet holes, made a few superficial inquiries, and concluded that Trotsky could not possibly have lived through that hail of fire and therefore the attack was a hoax. It seemed to the colonel that Trotsky must have stage-managed the whole affair. He came to this conclusion without too much difficulty. First, Trotsky was very calm, and a man who has been under intense and concentrated fire is not expected to be calm. Second, he had examined the bedroom and observed the pattern made by the bullets. Third, he completely failed to see how a large number of men could break into the house and not kill him, if that was their purpose. Fourth, when he asked Trotsky whom he thought responsible for the raid, there occurred what seemed to be a few moments of conspiratorial play acting. Instead of answering immediately, Trotsky took him by the arm and led him in silence to a secluded part of the garden. Then Trotsky whispered with great intensity: "Joseph Stalin!" Apparently it was a kind of conspiratorial stage whisper and Salazar felt alarmed, as though he was dealing with a madman. He wrote later that he was "stupefied" by Trotsky's reply. By this time he had convinced himself that Trotsky or his guards had fired the bullets, and he ordered the arrest of the two guards who seemed most suspicious to him and also the servants.

That Trotsky should have appeared so calm and even

disinterested would not have surprised anyone who knew him well. In emergencies he was nearly always calm. That he should have taken Salazar by the arm and led him away to a quiet corner to announce dramatically that it was the work of Stalin was even less surprising, since Trotsky had a gift for drama and enjoyed playing a dramatic role. Salazar misinterpreted the nature of the attack and misunderstood Trotsky's character. He also knew very little about the workings of the Mexican Communist Party.

By mid-morning all the various pieces of the puzzle were beginning to fit together. The raiders had been provided with the layout of the house; they knew there would be no guard in the watchtower and their only problem was to ensure that the guard stationed at the entrance would open the heavy iron gate. Probably they came over the wall, surprised Robert Sheldon Harte, gagged him, held him at pistol point, and made him open the gate. One of the policemen trussed outside the house remembered that he saw Harte walking between two of the raiders toward a waiting car. The policeman noted particularly that Harte was not struggling but the raiders were walking very close to him. You do not struggle when two gangsters descend on you, hold their pistols close to your side, and march you off to a car. The alternative theory was that he knew one of the raiders and was himself a part of the conspiracy. This theory gained some credence when it was learned that Harte kept a picture of Stalin on the wall of his New York apartment. Both Trotsky and Natalie were firmly convinced that Harte was loyal to them. He was tall and handsome, red haired, with an easy smile and a rather shy manner, and Natalie was touched by the fact that he liked to take walks near the house to gather bouquets of field flowers. Nevertheless they knew very little about him; he had been there only a few weeks; he was not especially intelligent and he was sometimes dangerously careless. Natalie told the story of how, when a workman with a wheelbarrow came off the street every fifteen or twenty minutes while the house was being strengthened with concrete reinforcements, Harte tossed the keys of the gate to the workman so that he could continue building a bird-cage. It was an act of incredible stupidity. When Trotsky heard about it, he warned Harte that such carelessness might lead him to be the first victim. Strangely he made no effort to have Harte sent back to New York.

And in fact Harte *was* the first victim, for he was killed by his abductors five days later in an abandoned farmhouse in the hills near Tlalminalco in the Deserto de los Leones. The house had been taken over by two brothers, Leopoldo and Luis Arenal, both members of the Mexican Communist Party, some days before the attack on Trotsky. The house was made of adobe, had three small rooms, a basement with a kitchen, and two storerooms. To some Indians who saw a truck coming up to the house with pieces of furniture and asked what these strangers were doing there, one of the Arenals answered that a painter would soon be coming to paint the scenery. In fact the farmhouse was to be a hideout for one of the most famous Mexican painters of modern times, David Alfaro Siqueiros, who was married to Angelica, the sister of Leopoldo and Luis Arenal. Si-queiros was a founding member of the Mexican Com-munist Party, fanatically pro-Stalin, and a man who delighted in conspiracies. He had organized the raiding party. Trotsky, who had made a minute study of the Mexican Communist Party and its leaders, said very early in the investigation that he saw the hand of Siqueiros in it.

Harte was taken to the farmhouse and kept under guard until the conspirators decided what to do with him. Clearly he was a nuisance to them, for he was an American and might talk. Even if he was working with the Communists, he could not be completely relied upon. On the night of May 29 Leopoldo and Luis had a pleasant conversation with him before he went to sleep. Later in the night they crept into his bedroom and shot him twice, once in the head and once in the nape of the neck, in the approved G.P.U. manner. Then they carried the body into the kitchen in the basement, where a grave had already been dug. Quicklime was poured over the body, the grave was filled, and a day or two later the Arenal brothers fled to New York.

One of the reasons why they killed him may have been that the Mexican police were on the trail of the conspirators. Colonel Salazar abandoned his theory of self-assault two days after the attempted assassination. Like Trotsky he became convinced that Siqueiros had masterminded the attack. The fact that Trotsky had immediately accused Stalin was no longer suspicious. The Communist newspaper in Mexico City was proclaiming the virtues of the self-assault theory at great length; they protested too much. Siqueiros could not be found; he had gone into hiding. The two guards arrested by the police, Otto Schussler and Charles Cornell, had given a satisfactory account of themselves; so had the two female servants arrested at the same time. The police wanted to keep them in jail a little longer, but Trotsky sent off an angry letter to President Lázaro Cárdenas demanding their release. The President saw the logic of the demand and ordered them released immediately. They were more useful guarding Trotsky's life than languishing in jail.

Gradually the police were able to identify nearly all the attackers. Siqueiros was still in hiding, the Arenal brothers still in New York, but all the minor figures were rounded up, including the chauffeurs of the four cars that brought the attackers to Coyoacan, and a certain Mariano Vasquez, an unemployed laborer who guarded Harte while he was a prisoner in the lonely farmhouse in the Deserto de los Leones. On the night of June 25, the police, accompanied by Vasquez, climbed up the hill to the farmhouse and found it deserted, as they had suspected it would be. They found an easel, paints, canned food, clothing. There was a folding cot which the Arenals had attempted to burn because there were bloodstains, but they had done their work hurriedly and the bloodstains remained. There was also a bloodstained quilt, half burned. In the basement kitchen the police found signs of recent digging. They summoned a neighboring peasant, gave him a spade and told him to start digging. It was not long before the spade uncovered a human stomach from which there came an overwhelming stench of putrefaction. At this point they covered the body with earth and sent off to the nearest fire station for gas masks and a fire engine. It was raining in torrents. There were long delays. The fire engine was needed because it had powerful lights and they had been working in the half-dark, with flashlights. In the early hours of the morning they recovered the body of a tall man with red hair. It had been covered with quicklime, and the flesh for some reason, perhaps because of a chemical reaction between the lime and the acids of the earth, had turned to the color of reddish-bronze. His features were still recognizable, his expression was one of great calm, and there was little doubt that he was shot while asleep and died instantly.

The next morning Colonel Salazar accompanied Trotsky to the mortuary to identify the body. There was not the least doubt that it was Robert Sheldon Harte. Trotsky said: "Yes, this is Bob," and wept. Photographs taken of the body give him an immense dignity; he seems to have aged by thirty years and to be not so much a dead man as a sculpture hammered out of bronze.

Later in the day Trotsky composed a telegram to be sent to Jesse Harte, the boy's father, who lived in New York.

> My wife, my collaborators, I, bow in deep mourning before the grief of the mother and father of our dear Bob. Only consolation in these bitter hours is that the wild slander against Bob through which the assassins tried to conceal the assassination is now unmasked. As a hero, Bob perished for ideas he believed in.

The telegram was signed by Natalie and Leon Trotsky, and all the surviving guards.

For the rest of his life Trotsky refused to believe any arguments concerning Harte's complicity in the assassination attempt. Rightly or wrongly he trusted his guards implicitly. He felt close to them as though they were his sons, and this feeling was all the stronger because he had lost his sons. The raiders had employed an arsenal of modern weaponry—high explosives, bombs, machine guns and submachine guns—in order to destroy him, and in their haste and excitement, even though all their moves were carefully planned beforehand, they had failed completely. There were too many of them; they got in each other's way; they fired blindly; they panicked and fled before they were certain they had accomplished their mission. Siqueiros was arrested. He seems to have regarded the raid as a joyous spree, delighted with the noise and commotion in the patio. He insisted against all the evidence that he had not intended to kill Trotsky but to frighten him. The Communist press in Mexico City spread the story that Trotsky had not been in his bed but had been hiding in his cellar. Trotsky replied scornfully that he might just as well have been hiding in the henhouse. There are few things that are absolutely certain about the raid, but the accounts given by Trotsky and Natalie of what they saw when they were lying on that bedroom floor possess a psychological truth that seems to be unchallengeable. They were telling the truth as they knew it, nor was there anything to be gained by telling lies.

Yet there were many mysteries about the raid. How did the raiders come to know the layout of the house? How did they know that Robert Sheldon Harte would come off duty at exactly 4 A.M.? How were they able to cow the guards who lived together in a single room, so that not a single shot was fired by them? The two maidservants, Belem Estrada and Carmen Palma, dictated to the police accounts of the affair that were obviously false. Why? Were they faked by the police to justify a self-assault? Trotsky was given copies of their depositions on July 5 and flew into a justified rage, for it was quite clear that the police had put words into the servants' mouths. He was inclined to think that Carmen Palma may have been implicated in some way with the conspirators, but he could not prove it. She may have given them the layout of the house and she evidently knew the times when the guards went on duty. She was the cook and would scarcely be noticed as she moved about the house. Trotsky was more inclined to blame the interrogators than the servants. And then there were the workmen who were continually entering the house to build new installations to shore up its pathetic defenses. There was no way of knowing whether they were Communist agents. And what did all this matter compared with the fact that the Mexican Communist Party was mobilized against him?

Robert Sheldon Harte was demonstrably careless but he was not a traitor. So Trotsky refused to listen to anyone who cast any suspicion on him, and whenever his name was mentioned, Trotsky had to fight back his tears. Although by this time thousands and perhaps hundreds of thousands of men had been sent to their deaths for being his followers, or even on suspicion of being his followers, Trotsky reserved a special place in his heart for seven men who had been close to him—and who had died for him. One of them was Nikolay Sermuks, who had been in command of the armored train in 1918 and later worked on Trotsky's secretarial staff. Israel Poznansky had once been in charge of the bureau concerning Red Cavalry affairs, and he too became a member of the secretarial staff. Both of them attempted to follow Trotsky to Alma-Ata but were deported to the north, and they died miserably, probably of a bullet in the nape of the neck. There was Georgy Butov, who worked with Trotsky in the Revolutionary Military Council and died in prison in 1927. Mikhailo Glazman was another secretary during the time of the civil war. Erwin Wolf, who had been his secretary in Norway, joined the International Brigade to fight against Franco. He never reached Madrid, for the G.P.U. caught up with him in Barcelona, and nothing more was ever heard of him. Then there was Jacob Blumkin, who helped Trotsky to write a book called *How the Revolution Armed Itself*, secretly visited Prinkipo, and was betrayed when he returned to Russia. Finally there was Rudolf Klement, a German émigré who had been Trotsky's secretary at Barbizon and was the secretary of the Fourth International Bureau in Paris. In July 1938 he was abducted from his hotel room, and his headless body was found some days later in the Seine. To these seven Trotsky now added an eighth—Robert Sheldon Harte. In the garden of his house he set up a bronze plaque with the inscription:

IN MEMORY
OF
ROBERT SHELDON HARTE
1915–1940
MURDERED BY STALIN

27 CONVERSATIONS WITH LUND

The hot Mexican summer dragged on while Trotsky attempted to set his bullet-riddled fortress in order. He continued to work according to his inflexible schedule; he worked throughout the morning, took a short siesta, worked again, fed the rabbits, held conferences, worked again. He was absorbed by his life of Stalin commissioned by Harper and Brothers, but progress was slow and he was having much more difficulty with it than he had expected. He usually wrote easily—only his *History of the Russian Revolution* had proved difficult, perhaps because everything had happened so suddenly and violently and sometimes so mysteriously that it was almost impossible to see the revolution in perspective. And now there was the man he called Cain-Stalin, moving like a heavy brooding shadow, ruling Russia as Tamerlane once ruled Central Asia, majestic in his absolute tyranny, and it was difficult to write about him while waiting to be killed by him.

Trotsky knew there would be more attacks: he expected them, and was ready for them. He appears to have thought that Stalin would eventually kill him. Yet, in spite of his many defeats and the loss of so many of his followers, he was able to convince himself that his own truth would prevail. He did not give the impression of a man who was doomed; on the contrary he gave an impression of ebullience, as though he was enjoying the fight against a man who was immensely powerful, as though he felt there was still one chance in a thousand that he might rouse the workers to overthrow Stalin.

Meanwhile he surveyed his defenses and made them stronger. Steel shutters were placed over the bedroom windows; the doors were lined with steel, the roof reinforced with concrete, and three new bulletproof towers were erected. The entrance now was a double steel door operated by electric controls. American friends sent him a siren which could be heard a mile away and a bulletproof vest which he rarely wore. The number of guards was increased and they were more heavily armed, while the number of police guards outside the house was tripled, from five to fifteen, by order of the Mexican government. The cost of protecting Trotsky was very nearly prohibitive. Most of the cost was paid for by his American followers.

Every morning, when he woke up, he would say to Natalie: "We've slept through a whole night and nothing has happened to us," or he would say: "You see, Natasha, we have been given a reprieve." Natalie would smile at him encouragingly, but she had noted that after the raid he suffered more frequently from fainting spells—always an ominous sign. There were long periods of lassitude, and too often for his own health he took double doses of sleeping powder.

A good deal of his time was spent in consultation with the police, reviewing their reports, writing commentaries about them, arguing, debating with them. The Communist newspaper in Mexico City was toying with a new theory: Trotsky, an agent of American capitalism, had conceived of a plot in which he would appear to have been blown up by raiders while in fact he had been spirited away to the United States where he would go into hiding until the time when the Americans could make use of him. The theory depended upon the fiction that Trotsky was a tool of American imperialism. The theory was ludicrous and was soon replaced by other and even more improbable theories. Trotsky was not amused by these inventions, patiently examined them, wrote sensible replies, and marveled at the inventiveness of newspaper correspondents.

He reasoned that the next attack would come soon, for the G.P.U. would attempt to wipe out the disgrace of failure in the shortest possible time. Hence all the added fortifications to the fortress. Long ago he had come to believe that the greatest danger would come from visitors who claimed to be his followers and wormed their way into his confidence. He was not a quick judge of men; he had to know men well before he was able to give a proper judgment of them. By nature he was not suspicious, and like Robert Sheldon Harte he was sometimes careless.

Four days after the attempted assassination Trotsky met his murderer for the first time. His name was Jacson-Mornard—it was one of many names. He carried a passport in the name of Frank Jacson. This name was invented by the G.P.U. which had come into the possession of a Canadian passport belonging to a Yugoslav-Canadian called Tony Babich, a name that could be changed by a forger to produce an English-sounding name with the minimum of trouble. The *T* of Tony could easily be transformed into an *F*, the *o* could be changed to an *a*, and an *r* could be inserted after the *F*. Only one letter—the y—had to be refashioned with the aid of vanishing ink. Similarly the *h* in Babich could be reduced to an *n*, the *c* could easily be made into an o, and there remained only three letters to be redrawn. What the forger did not know was that the name Jacson does not exist in the English-speaking world.

Babich's passport had been taken from him when he arrived in Spain to fight against Franco. When he was killed in battle, it was added to the stockpile of passports used by G.P.U. agents all over the world. Armed with these passports the agents were able to enter any country at will.

Jacson-Mornard, alias Frank Jacson, owner of a

Canadian passport saying he was born in Lovinac, Yugoslavia, on June 13, 1905, and naturalized as a Canadian citizen in 1929, alias Jacson-Mornard Vandendreschd, born in Teheran in 1904, the son of a Belgian diplomat and writer, was in fact Jaime Ramon Mercader del Rio, born in Barcelona on February 7, 1913, the son of a young woman who had once entered a nunnery and who later married the respectable Don Pablo Mercader Marina, the scion of a well-known Catalan family, and later still abandoned her husband and became the mistress of many members of the French Communist Party, living a wild and dangerous high-flying life in Paris. Her children, for there were two more sons and a daughter, lived with her.

The confusing aliases of Mornard were easily explained away. He told Sylvia Ageloff, who was his mistress, that as a Belgian citizen he would have been drafted into the army if he had not possessed a false Canadian passport, which enabled him to travel at will in the United States and Mexico. She believed him. She was a rather plain young woman; he was dashing and handsome, and apparently very rich; and she was hopelessly in love with him.

Although Trotsky met him face to face for the first time on May 28, 1940, he was not a stranger to the house on the Avenida Viena. The guards knew him as "Sylvia's boy-friend," a personable young man who on the days when Sylvia worked as one of Trotsky's secretarial assistants drove her to the house gates in his expensive automobile in the morning and came to collect her again in the evening. He rarely ventured through the gates and made no effort to see Trotsky. He did, however, meet the Rosmers and came to know them well, going out of his way to be obliging to them. Because they were cooped up in the fortress, he sometimes invited them to dinner in Mexico City, performed small services for them, and took them on occasional rides through the countryside. He was a master of the small service.

On this day, four days after the attack, the Rosmers were leaving Coyoacan to go to Vera Cruz to catch a ship for France. Mornard had offered to take them in his automobile, telling them that he had often driven to Vera Cruz on business and it was no trouble at all. It was a big car; Natalie and Riba Hansen, the wife of one of Trotsky's guards, decided to accompany the Rosmers to the coast; and for the first time Mornard walked into the garden, found Trotsky busy at the rabbit hutch, and shook hands with him. It was a very brief first meeting, for Trotsky was absorbed in feeding the rabbits. Mornard withdrew and talked to Seva and was next seen in Seva's bedroom, which could easily be reached from the garden. Mornard had brought a toy glider and was explaining how it worked. While Mornard and the boy were playing with the glider, Trotsky and Natalie invited him to the dining-room table for a cup of coffee. For the first time he was sitting down with the man he was determined to kill.

The journey to Vera Cruz took place without incident. Natalie was a little surprised when she discovered that he was having difficulty making his way about the city and kept stopping to make inquiries, since he had assured her that he had often driven there on business, but she was too polite to ask any questions. Natalie thought him a kindly and personable man and she had no suspicions about him because he was so obviously on good terms with the Rosmers, who were her closest friends.

A few days later, in the second week of June, some American Trotskyists from Minneapolis came to Coyoacan to take part in a general discussion on the work of the Fourth International, with special reference to the war in Europe and America's inevitable involvement in it. The conference was being held after the German breakthrough, while the British were evacuating Dunkirk and France was about to fall. Mornard learned about the coming of the small delegation from Minneapolis and offered to take them on a sightseeing trip to the ancient city of Toluca, an offer which was gratefully accepted. During the trip, on a winding mountain road, Mornard swerved the car to the edge of a precipice and swerved back to the road just in time, commenting: "In that way everything would be finished." No one paid very much attention to the remark; he was nervous, highly strung, and enjoyed taking risks. What the delegates did not realize until later was that he was learning a great deal about Trotsky from their conversations.

The conference, later printed from a stenographic report under the title "Discussions with Lund"—"Lund" being one of Trotsky's pseudonyms—was far more than a simple survey on the operations of the Fourth International. It was a seminar on the art of revolution and the art of transforming a war into a civil war. It was a pathetically small group for so large a subject, for only seven people sat round the table with Trotsky. Three of them were Trotsky's guards, Joseph Hansen, Charles Cornell, and Harold Robins. The others who attended were James Cannon, Farrell Dobbs, Sam Gordon, and Antoinette Konikow. Trotsky was discussing nothing less than the seizure of power in the United States.

Twenty-three years before, in Brooklyn, during his brief visit to the United States, some of his excited followers had spoken of him as a future dictator of America. Now once again, in Mexico, he was speaking as though the vast military power of America might one day soon fall into his hands. Such miracles had happened before. When he returned to Russia in 1917, it never occurred to him that he would capture Petrograd from the Provisional Government and six months later, as minister of war, would command armies so powerful that they were able to hurl the soldiers of eight nations out of Russia. He thought it natural to command; the world crisis was deepening; war would break out, and once again he would be ready to lead the proletariat to victory.

It was astonishing—it was absurd—but there was no doubt that he was thinking in this way. He firmly believed that the Fourth International would change the world, was already changing it. He spoke of an organization with millions of members, especially among young workers, and very soon most of these young workers would be going through military training. The Fourth International would teach them how to turn their guns against their enemies. They would be under the control of "our own organizations." They would fight for socialism under the government, against the bourgeoisie. He imagined a Senator introducing a bill in the Congress for training camps for workers; it would cost $500 million; and this money would be a pure gift to the revolution. He said: "Our military transitional program is an agitational program." "We must make the most categoric predictions in the darkest colors," he went on. "We must come out categorically for the dictatorship of the proletariat. We prepare the new arena to overthrow the militarists. We must learn the art of handling arms." From time to time James Cannon interjected a remark about the weakness of the organization in the United States and about the absence of any tradition among the young workers of entering the army and turning their guns against their officers. Trotsky brushed these arguments aside. He suggested that the workers could be reeducated "at an extremely rapid tempo." It might be necessary to test them with a small experiment in Minneapolis or St. Paul, and it was clear that he meant an armed uprising. He said nothing about the cost in human lives of such an uprising, or about its inevitable failure, or about the fact that even if his arguments were sound, which they were not, a premature uprising would only advertise the existence of a revolutionary plot and lead to the arrest and execution of the plotters, while the chief conspirator remained secure in his small fortress in Mexico, but for how long?

Trotsky envisaged a workers' militia in the United States, made possible by compulsory military training. He knew very little about the history of the United States. He believed, or pretended to believe, that the New Deal under President Roosevelt had "exhausted all the reformist and democratic possibilities and created incomparably more favorable possibilities for revolution." He appeared to imagine that the United States in 1940 was in the same position as Russia at the beginning of 1917, but it was not true and he must have known it was not true, or else he was profoundly ignorant.

It occurred to him that simply by writing a manifesto to the Communists in America he would be able to draw them away from their loyalty to Stalin, and even if he drew only a few of them away, the disintegration of the Communist Party would begin. According to the stenographic report, he said: "They have been terribly poisoned. If we show that we understand, that we have a common language, we can turn them against their leaders. If we win five per cent, the party will be doomed." His mathematics were at fault, and he had lost touch with reality.

For four days the three guards and the four delegates from Minneapolis seriously discussed the overthrow of the American government. Trotsky showed how it could come about: the sudden growth of the movement among the workers, the establishment of a central committee with full powers, a period when the party members would be allowed to engage in free discussion followed by a period when all discussion would be forbidden. Centralism, by which he meant dictatorship, would be imposed by "the leadership which is based by and large on the experience of the past." In a revealing passage he spoke about freedom of speech during the Civil War in Russia. "Even at the front we had closed party meetings, where all party members discussed with complete freedom, criticized orders, etc. But when we left the room, the orders became a strict discipline, for the breaking of which a commander could be shot." He was implying that he made his own decisions but allowed people to talk a little if it made them feel better.

Even now, in these last weeks of his life, he was seeing himself in a commanding position, changing the destiny of nations. The revolution would break out in Minneapolis and he would be summoned to take charge of it. He was not dismayed by the fact that his followers were very few and at odds among themselves. He enjoyed the company of the delegates from Minneapolis and later he would describe them as "active, optimistic, sure of themselves and thoroughly revolutionary."

Revolutions! Always revolutions! One day he was contemplating the revolution in the United States, on the following day a revolution in the Soviet Union to overthrow Stalin, and there was also the revolution in Germany which would keep Hitler so busy that he would have no time "to fulfill the role of executioner in Paris, Brussels or London." None of these imaginary revolutions took place. He was a prophet who had lost the gift of prophecy.

He kept on working, continued to conduct his interminable correspondence, continued to study the evidence produced by the assassination attempt in May, and sometimes for part of a day he would busy himself with the new fortifications that were being installed with the help of gifts from his United States followers. Once he complained to Joseph Hansen: "It reminds me of the first prison I was in at Kherson. The doors made the same sound when they shut. It is not a home; it is a mediaeval prison." At another time he was discussing the fortifications with Hansen, Cornell, and Jacson-Mornard, who had arrived to take Sylvia Ageloff back to their apartment. Mornard was asked what he thought of all these protective measures. He thought they were well done, and added: "Of course, in the next attack the G.P.U. will use other methods."

"What methods?" Hansen asked.

Mornard shrugged his shoulders.

DEATH BLOW 28

On the last day of his conscious life Trotsky woke up feeling wonderfully refreshed, having taken two sleeping powders and enjoyed an unusually sound sleep. "I feel very well," he said. "I haven't felt so good for a long while. These sleeping tablets do me good."

Natalie in her wifely way pointed out that it was not the drugs but the sound sleep that did him good. "You used to say the same thing when we were in Norway," she went on. "Then, of course, you were more often depressed than you are now."

"Yes," he said, and went to open the heavy steel shutters over the windows. This was the daily ritual. As he opened them he would say: "Siqueiros did not kill us last night, and you are still dissatisfied." It was a kind of joke, and she trained herself to fight against his graveyard humor with a gentle remark that would put him at his ease. She had first heard that particular note when they were on the train leaving Moscow for Alma-Ata. They were both in a state of terrible subdued excitement, unable to sleep, suffering a kind of nervous exaltation, afraid of what awaited them in the east. Trotsky said: "It is better to go into exile. I never liked the idea of dying in my bed in the Kremlin."

Then, brimming with energy, he washed and dressed quickly, and then marched out into the patio to inspect the rabbits and chickens. He enjoyed feeding them and he enjoyed watching them, becoming completely absorbed in them. Then he would return to his study. Sometimes he could be heard speaking or muttering to himself, and sometimes, too, when an idea occurred to him he would talk into his dictaphone. He had breakfast with Natalie and again spoke of his feeling of well-being. He told her he was going to dictate to his secretary an article about conscription in America, presumably his recent reflections on the possibility that the conscripts might be induced to turn their guns against their officers and the government. He intended to work on another article about the war and if there was any time left he proposed to do a few pages of *Stalin*. He worked steadily through the morning. At one o'clock Rigault, the lawyer who represented him on all matters to do with the attempted assassination, came with some documents concerning the Communist newspaper *El Popular*, which had been strenuously attacking Trotsky and provoking him into long and detailed rebuttals. This time *El Popular* claimed that Trotsky had defamed Mexico and the Mexican police and should be put on trial for defamation or booted out of the country. This was a serious matter, and Trotsky was in no mood to let them get away with it. His rebuttal would be added to the many other rebuttals against charges leveled by *El Popular*. But now it was no longer a question of answering the charges. He proposed to take them to court.

"I intend to take the offensive," he told Natalie. "I am going to accuse them of outright slander."

He must have known that nothing was to be gained by bringing *El Popular* to court and much might be lost. There was nothing that *El Popular* would have liked more, for in court they would be able to taunt him mercilessly, and even if he delivered the most brilliant speech in the most fluent Spanish and showed himself to be the destined leader of the working class all over the world, they would be able to make him dance to their tune. They were goading him; their continual attacks were designed to circumscribe his movements and to waste his time; and his continual rebuttals resembled those exhaustive lawyers' briefs which prove too much and send the judge and the jury to sleep.

"What a pity you are going to do that!" Natalie said. "You won't be able to finish your article on conscription."

"I can't help it—I'll postpone it for two or three days. I have asked for all the available documents to be placed on my desk. After dinner I'll go over them."

Then, for the fourth or fifth time that day, he remarked that he was feeling well.

Natalie was not altogether satisfied with these constant reminders of his good health. Those strange fainting spells which had dogged his life apparently since he was a young student were now much less severe. His eyes were bright, he had a good color, he worked exceedingly hard without ill effects, while the attempted assassination had not affected his spirits but on the contrary exhilarated him, as a brush with danger often exhilarates a man. Yet she was worried by something in his appearance that had not yet received a name. After lunch and a brief siesta he went to his study to work on his perfectly useless refutation of the article in *El Popular*, which claimed that he had defamed Mexico. He turned from this to his own article on conscription in the United States, dictating some disjointed paragraphs into the dictaphone which he intended to polish later. The juices were flowing free. He was doing what he liked to do, and as Natalie wrote later, he was enjoying a day of physical and spiritual equanimity.

Yet the nagging doubts persisted. All through the afternoon Natalie kept coming to the door, opening it a crack, and peering in. She would watch him for a moment as he worked at his long desk, his head bent and his pen in his hand, an absorbed expression on his face. Then she would turn away, closing the door silently. Once, as she peered into his study, the thought occurred to her that he was living in a self-imposed prison, like a cloistered monk, but one dedicated to a great struggle. This same thought must have occurred to her innumerable times before. Later, while she was watching through the doorway, a line of Pushkin entered her mind. It came from Pushkin's poetic drama *Boris Godunov*, and was spoken in his cell by Father Pimen, a monk and chronicler, as he completed his history of his times with an account of the murder of the Tsarevich Dmitry, the youngest child of Ivan the Terrible, by Boris Godunov. Natalie remembered the opening line of the scene: "One more, the final story, and the tale is told." The words in the original are very sonorous and memorable, and to an educated Russian they suggest the whole scene, the final story, the murder of the Tsarevich. The old lame monk writes and talks in the dark, with a single candle beside him, the shadows wheeling across the cell, and death is everywhere. It is a one-line threnody on the deaths of princes and kings.

At five o'clock in the afternoon Natalie, Trotsky, and one or two members of the staff took tea, according to their habit. Natalie could never remember what they talked about: probably the inconsequential things one talks about at teatime. She took the tea things back to the kitchen, and at about half-past five she stepped out on the balcony and saw Trotsky standing beside the open rabbit hutch, feeding the rabbits. Beside him was an unfamiliar figure wearing a hat, with an overcoat over his arm. It was a bright, sunny afternoon, and she was puzzled that the man should be carrying an overcoat. When he turned, she recognized the person she knew as Jacson or Jacson-Mornard. She asked herself why he had come—it was the fourth time he had visited the house in Coyoacan during the month of August. She told herself he was coming too often, but she was not suspicious. When he came up to her, he said: "I'm terribly thirsty. May I have a glass of water?"

She asked him whether he would like a glass of tea instead.

"No," he replied. "I had lunch too late, and the food is up to here—" His hand pointed to his throat. "It's choking me."

He looked very nervous, very ill. His face was gray-green. He was distraught and evidently under great pressure.

Natalie observed that his overcoat was hanging over his left arm, pressed close to his body. Her critical senses revived. She said: "Why are you wearing your hat and your overcoat on such a sunny day?"

"It won't last long," he answered. "It might rain."

This seemed to be an inadequate answer and she found herself wanting to argue with him. She remembered that he had once said he never wore a hat or coat even when the weather was bad. Because she was a solicitous host and wanted always to put people at their ease, she decided not to argue with him. She felt depressed. She said: "How is Sylvia feeling?"

At this question a completely blank look came over Jacson's face. He did not understand her and for some moments remained silent. His train of thoughts had been interrupted. Natalie remembered that he seemed to be rousing himself from a deep sleep when he finally collected himself and said: "Sylvia? Sylvia?" as though he had never heard the name before. Then, in a casual tone he said: "She is always well."

Natalie gave him a glass of water, and after he drank it, he began to walk back to the rabbit hutches.

He did not get very far, for Natalie called after him: "Is your article ready?"

He turned toward her.

"Yes, it is ready."

"Is it typed?"

"Yes," he said, and with an awkward movement, still pressing his overcoat against his body, he removed from the overcoat pocket what appeared to be some typed pages of manuscript. He pulled them out with some difficulty and showed them to her.

"It's a good thing that you did not write it out by

hand," she said, glancing at the manuscript. "Lev Davidovich dislikes illegible manuscripts."

She was being like a schoolmistress, taking him to task, and she had good reason to act in this way. Two days earlier Jacson Mornard had called at the house, wearing a hat, with an overcoat over his arm. Natalie was not in the house. Her husband told her he had behaved very strangely. Still wearing his hat and carrying his overcoat, he entered Trotsky's study and promptly sat on the desk and showed Trotsky some pages of a manuscript—ill-written, dreary, badly composed, scarcely more than an outline for an article or a brief sketch.

Trotsky, standing in the sunlight, took a long time to close the rabbit hutches. Jacson was standing at his side. They were talking as they walked toward the house. Seeing Natalie, Trotsky said: "Sylvia will be coming here. They are leaving for New York tomorrow." Natalie said: "I gave Jacson a glass of water. I offered him tea, but he said he was not feeling well." Trotsky peered intently at Jacson. "You don't look well," he said. "That's not good. Well, you were going to show me the article." Saying this, he removed his gardening gloves and with Jacson beside him he climbed the few steps that led to a small balcony and his study.

At that moment in the late afternoon at least four guards were on duty, but they were not guarding Trotsky. Three of them, Joseph Hansen, Charles Cornell, and Melquiades Benitez were working on one of the watchtowers, installing the powerful siren that had been sent from America, connecting it up with the existing alarm system. They had seen Jacson's Buick sedan coming along the road, and they had watched it as it made a complete turn so that it was pointed in the direction of Mexico City. Usually the Buick would be parked with the nose pointed at the wall of the house. The three guards attached no importance to this change in his usual way of parking his car, nor were they surprised by his coming, although they had received no advance warning. They knew him as Sylvia

Ageloff's boy friend; they had heard Trotsky speaking highly of Sylvia, and they had assumed that her friend was in good standing. Getting out of the car, Jacson had waved to the men on the roof and shouted: "Has Sylvia arrived yet?"

"No," Joseph Hansen shouted back. "Wait a moment."

Charles Cornell had pressed the button that operated the electrical controls of the double doors opening on the patio. As the doors opened, Jacson crossed the first hurdle. There remained another. This was Harold Robins, gaunt and longfaced, armed with a pistol, who stood just inside the patio to examine and receive the visitor. This was the fourth time he had come to the fortress in the month of August. According to the record of visitors kept in the guardhouse, he visited the fortress on the 8th, 10th and 17th.

Robins observed that Jacson was wearing a hat and was carrying an overcoat on his arm. This did not disturb him in the least, for although the sun was shining strongly, there were heavy clouds over the mountains in the southwest, and he expected a rainstorm before the evening was over.

Now that they were coming to the end of their plans to strengthen the fortress, the guards were making slow progress. The original plan called for barbed wire to impede the progress of attackers and sandbags to strengthen the walls. None of these had yet arrived, and it was not felt that there was any urgent need for them. Hansen spent the next ten minutes in the tower with Cornell and Benitez, copying out on white labels the names of all the guards, and these would later be affixed to the switches connecting them with the alarm system. Robins had remained in the patio.

All the guards saw Jacson talking with Trotsky near the rabbit hutches. Accustomed to the man's presence, awaiting the arrival of Sylvia Ageloff, and seeing that Trotsky was completely relaxed, they thought nothing was amiss. It was a lazy summer afternoon, like all the other summer afternoons.

In fact, all of them had been given warning. Jacson's

behavior and appearance called for careful examination. He should have been frisked for weapons but was not. In the lining of his overcoat he was carrying a dagger, a short-handled ice pick, and a revolver. The bulkiness of the overcoat should have attracted attention. Only Natalie seemed to be obscurely aware that something was wrong, terribly wrong, but she was incapable of making the leap from suspicion to action. It was as though everyone, even Jacson, was caught up in a lingering stupor. Natalie, Trotsky, and Robins were all strangely inattentive; they had failed to take the most elementary precautions and at the same time they were all dimly aware that they were in the presence of a destructive agent who had been admitted into the house only because they were genuinely fond of Sylvia Ageloff, who at that precise moment was sitting down to an evening supper with Otto Schussler somewhere in Mexico City.

Trotsky had not the slightest interest in Jacson's manuscript. He neither liked nor disliked Jacson. In his mind Jacson was a neuter, one of those shadowy creatures without charm or intelligence who exist, as it were, at second hand by virtue of being attached to other people. Over the last few moments of his life there hovered, like an angel of death, the image of Sylvia Ageloff.

Jacson followed Trotsky into the whitewashed study with the map of Mexico on the wall, the simple cane-bottomed chairs, the long table piled neatly with books and manuscripts. There was a gluepot, a telephone, pens and pencils in a jar, a pair of scissors, an ivory paper cutter, an old-fashioned dictaphone with disks that resembled black tubes, and a long-stemmed lamp that could be bent forward or backward. Under the table there was a switch which, when pressed, would immediately activate the alarm system. In a drawer there was a Colt .38 automatic, and on the table itself, serving as a paperweight, there was a small .25 automatic. Both weapons had been recently oiled and loaded. There were no ornaments in the room, no photographs, no paintings, no figurines. Everything about the room was severely plain and practical, as befitted a man who hated to be distracted when he was at work and admired plainness for its own sake.

Jacson had been in the room before. He knew where the switch was, and as Trotsky sat down to read the typewritten article, Jacson deftly threw his overcoat on the table in such a way that Trotsky would be unable to reach for the switch. Almost at the same moment he made the decision to strike with the short-handled ice pick rather than the dagger: the revolver was the weapon of last resort, for at all costs he wanted to kill Trotsky in silence and then make his escape. His hat, a trilby with a thin black band, also lay on the table. Jacson himself was sitting on the edge of the table, looking down at Trotsky's bare head with the thinning white hair.

About thirty seconds after Trotsky sat down at the table, Jacson struck with the ice pick. He was physically strong and broad shouldered; he knew exactly what had to be done and he had practiced the necessary movements many times; it was inconceivable that he would make an error. He made two errors. Because he was terrified by what he was about to do, he closed his eyes when he brought the ice pick down on Trotsky's skull. The second error was to bring the flattened end, not the needle-sharp pointed end, down on the skull. If he had aimed accurately at the crown of the skull, the pick would have entered four or five inches into the brain and remained there, and Trotsky would have died instantly without making any sound. Instead the slightly curved, two-inch-wide blade penetrated the side of Trotsky's head, making a wound about two and a half inches deep. There was a brief period when Trotsky's motor reflexes remained unimpaired. In spite of the wound and the great damage done to his brain, Trotsky was able to rise from his chair and grapple with Jacson, a much taller and stronger man. He hurled himself on his adversary with extraordinary strength and determination. In the struggle his glasses were smashed and he could scarcely see. He caught Jacson's hand and bit into it deeply. As they fought he gave out a wild unearthly scream which could be heard all over the house. Natalie, who was some distance away, had not heard the sounds of the fighting. She had not heard the lamp, the books, and half the objects on the table crashing to the floor. But she heard the scream and came rushing into the study. Trotsky was standing on his feet, breathing hard, blood streaming down his face, his blue eyes looking naked without his spectacles. His hands hung limp at his side.

"What happened?" Natalie asked, throwing her arms around him.

There was no answer.

"What happened?" she said again.

Natalie imagined that some plaster had fallen from the ceiling and wounded him. She had forgotten that Jacson was still there and at first she did not see him.

Trotsky wanted time to put his thoughts in order. At last he said without any bitterness: "Jacson." It was as though he was stating a fact of some importance that needed to be stated calmly. Together they took a few steps, and as he grew weaker he fell to the floor, his falling made easier because Natalie was holding him.

Melquiades Benitez, Charles Cornell, and Joseph Hansen all heard that long-drawn wavering scream from the watchtower. Hansen, from the guardpost high up on the wall, caught a glimpse of Trotsky in his familiar blue work jacket fighting with an intruder. Benitez seized his gun and aimed at the study windows. Hansen shouted: "Don't shoot! You might hit the Old Man!" Then he raced to the ladder and slid down it, reaching the patio near the library. The siren had been switched on, the high-pitched wailing sound arousing the whole neighborhood. Trotsky had somehow raised himself and was staggering toward the balcony of his study. Harold Robins, who had been guarding the gate, came running into the house. Robins and Hansen reached the study about the same time. Jacson was standing there, gasping for breath, his face contorted, his arms limp, his revolver dangling in his hand. Natalie was grappling with him. Robins leaped on him, wrested the revolver from him, and brought him to the floor. Everything was happening very quickly and no one was making an accurate account of events. Somehow Trotsky seems to have made his way along the balcony and down the steps into the patio. He lay there resting, with a pillow under his head, while Natalie put ice on his wound and wiped the blood from his face. His voice was surprisingly firm. He said: "Natasha, I love you." He was attempting to comfort her, and she was so moved by the grave and firm voice that, while she was kneeling beside him, she swayed and was in danger of falling over him. He went on: "Promise that everyone who comes to see you is first searched. You must take Seva away from all this. You know, while I was in there, I knew—I sensed what he wanted to do. I knew he would strike again, but I didn't let him!"

His voice was breaking, trailing away. He was speaking with great difficulty. "I didn't let him!" was spoken with a note of triumph. Joseph Hansen was kneeling on the other side. The wound did not look very deep. He said: "What happened'"

"Jacson shot me with a revolver. I am seriously wounded. I feel that it is the end this time."

"No, it is only a surface wound. You will recover."

Trotsky was less interested in the wound than in Jacson.

"We talked about French statistics—" he said, and once more the voice trailed away.

Hansen suddenly realized that nothing was being done about getting an ambulance. He scrambled up the ladder to the roof and shouted to the police guard outside: "Get an ambulance." But that meant an ambulance in the city, and when he was once more in the patio it occurred to him that there was a doctor nearer at hand. He looked at his watch. It was ten minutes to six, and about a quarter of an hour had elapsed since Trotsky was felled with the ice pick. He turned to Charles Cornell who was beside him and told him to summon the doctor. At about this time there were sounds of renewed struggle in the study; clearly there was a good deal of life in Jacson. Trotsky understood what was happening and said: "It is not permissible to kill him. He must be made to talk." Only Trotsky appeared to be completely in command of himself; everyone else seemed to be sleepwalking.

Jacson was a skilled mountaineer with an agile brain, extraordinary strength, and a well-trained capacity to deceive. Harold Robins had brought him to the floor and apparently stunned him, but had failed to tie him up. Hansen was stronger than Robins; the two of them together were more powerful than Jacson, who now received his just punishment. He was badly beaten up, with Hansen hitting him in the mouth and on the jaw below the ear, while Robins struck him on the head with a hard instrument until he fell unconscious. Hansen broke his hand in the fight. When Jacson recovered consciousness, he moaned: "They put my mother in prison. Sylvia Ageloff has nothing to do with it. No, it was *not* the G.P.U. I have *nothing* to do with the G.P.U."

Later it was learned that his mother and a G.P.U. officer were in a getaway car about half a mile away, waiting to take him to an airplane and out of Mexico.

Hansen remembered these words exactly as they were uttered in English. Robins remembered that when he first brought Jacson down, when Jacson must have thought he was about to suffer the same fate as Trotsky, he said: "They *made* me do it!" Neither Hansen nor Robins had the least doubt who "they" were.

Many things were still going wrong. Charles Cornell had run out to Jacson's car, hoping to use it to find the local doctor and to bring him back to the house. But there were no keys in the car, nor could they find any keys in Jacson's pockets. Hansen ran out to open the garage door; Cornell jumped into one of Trotsky's cars, and was on his way.

Natalie was still kneeling beside Trotsky, holding his hands, trying to bring him back to life while he was slipping away from her. His voice was rough now. When Hansen said: "He did not shoot you—it is only a surface wound," Trotsky's hand went to his heart and he said: "No, this time they succeeded," and smiled faintly, as men sometimes smile in the certain knowledge of approaching death. His words were growing indistinct. Turning to Hansen, he said: "Take care of Natalie. She has been with me many, many years."

Toward Natalie he had behaved all his life with deliberate courtesy. He was trying to comfort her, and at the same time he was drinking in her features, knowing that he was dying.

At last the doctor came, a brisk, cheerful, matter-of-fact man, who announced that the wound was not grave even though the whole left side of the body was succumbing to paralysis. The ambulance came a little later. Altogether it had taken half an hour for Trotsky to receive any medical attention. At least the ambulance men from the Green Cross Emergency Hospital in Mexico City were efficient. They bandaged him, asked who would accompany him—Natalie was terrified of the thought of a hospital, knowing that her son Lyova had been killed in a hospital in Paris—and then she and Hansen climbed into the ambulance to sit beside him while he lay on the stretcher.

The ambulance drivers in Mexico are among the most reckless in the world. Led by an escort of motorcycle police, the ambulance with its screaming siren sped through the streets of the city at seventy miles an hour. At the Green Cross Emergency Hospital five doctors examined him and concluded that a trepanning operation was essential: four square inches of his skull were removed. In their first report they announced: "The following lesions were discovered: fracture of the right parietal bone with bone splinters projecting into the brain substance; damaging of the meninges and destruction of the brain substance, and hernia of same. The prognosis is very grave, although the immediate results of the operation are satisfactory."

In fact, considering the extent of the wound, the operation was useless and did nothing to prolong his life. He was in a coma when he entered the hospital, but his powerful heart continued to beat all night and throughout the next day. He died at 7:25 P.M. on the following evening. A few minutes before the end his breathing, which had been deep and regular, suddenly became very fast, as though in these last moments he was racing to complete the journey.

He lay there on the white hospital bed, looking as he had looked in life, proud and defiant, with no trace of suffering, so calm that he seemed to be alive and about to rise from the bed, and so sure of himself that he seemed even now to be in command of his destiny. He wore his white bandage like a helmet, and on his lips there was the faintest of smiles.

All over the world, except in the Soviet Union, there were headlines: TROTSKY IS DEAD. People who had no reason to like him, people who feared or admired him, and the ordinary people who simply watched the unfolding of history at a distance saw in his death the last act of a tragic drama, and they knew, if the Russians had forgotten, that he had been one of the great pivotal figures of history, the man who had brought the Russian Revolution into existence. And there were some, the unforgiving ones, who thought the cold and slender ice pick wielded by an assassin was a more human weapon than the bullet in the nape of the neck which was all the Kronstadt sailors were given.

In Europe the war was raging; France and Poland had fallen; England was fighting for her life against massive bomber attacks; Stalin, at the head of the Soviet Union, was the uncomprehending ally of Hitler, whose announced purpose was the destruction and annihilation of the Soviet Union. It was a strange moment to kill Trotsky. No one doubted that Stalin had given the order, for he alone could benefit by it, but there were some doubts about whether he had weighed the consequences. The long arm of the G.P.U. had reached Trotsky in a small Mexican fortress, and from the fortress ripples of fear spread out like the concentric ripples formed when a stone is flung into a pool. Stalin calculated that these ripples of fear could do no harm in a world convulsed with fear. Presidents and politicians all over the world were being taught a lesson. If Stalin could reach Trotsky, he could reach anyone.

On the day after his death the funeral cortège wound through the streets of Mexico City watched by three hundred thousand people. When the cortège paused outside the Pantheon, there were speeches in his honor which sounded strangely inadequate. For five days the body lay in state in the Alcazar Mortuary, guarded by leather-coated stalwarts of his party. Finally, a week after the attack on his life, he was removed to a crematorium, head and hands bare, the rest of his body clothed in a shapeless black sack. As the furnace door flew open, the body slid head-foremost into the flames.

Outside in the streets the people were still singing a song called the *grand corrido de Leon Trotsky* written by an anonymous balladeer:

> Murdered Trotsky lay dying
> Through a night and a day,
> For they had carefully planned
> Vengeance sooner or later.
>
> He believed that in Mexico
> On this great and hospitable soil
> He would live very happily
> Under the roof of this sky.
>
> Finally destiny conquered him
> In his own house,
> When a cowardly assassin
> Snatched away his life.
>
> The assassin was carrying
> An Alpine pickax,
> And being alone with Trotsky
> He struck without danger to himself.
>
> On a Tuesday afternoon
> Came the fatal tragedy
> Which has stirred the nation
> And the entire city.

The *grand corrido* told the complicated story in its simplest form, but was no less true for being simple. "The cowardly assassin"—*el cobarde asesino*—assumes the shape of legend, and Trotsky, murdered and dying, dead and yet living, also assumes the shape of legend. There was the danger that he would vanish into legend and escape out of history altogether. In the Soviet Union his name had been scrubbed out of the history books and history was rewritten in such a way that he was given only a small, sneaking part in the October Revolution.

All that remained of him, a handful of ashes, was buried in the garden of the fortress at Coyoacan. Over the ashes, in due course, there was erected a stone stele on which there was engraved his name above a huge hammer and sickle carved in relief. Natalie continued to live in the fortress with young Seva, who grew up, married, and fathered four daughters; but life was difficult for her, she grew old and deaf, and went to live with friends in Corbeil, a suburb of Paris. She outlived her husband by more than twenty-one years, dying on January 23, 1962, at the age of seventy-nine. A few weeks later some workmen gathered in the garden at Coyoacan to carry out the wishes of the indomitable old lady. They lifted up the stele, found the concrete box containing the ashes, and mingled her ashes with them. Then they replaced the stele, and did not add her name to it, for they knew she would not have wanted it.

She was the heroine of the story. Sweet-tempered, uncomplaining even though terrified by the rigors of a revolutionary's life, she was the perfect wife. She worked very close to him, encouraged him, and knew all his ideas and all his secrets. After the October Revolution she asked one favor of him: to be allowed to work in a museum. After her husband and her children, art gave her the greatest pleasure. She was a devoted curator, a devoted student of the arts of Russia and Europe. Of the last moments of her husband's life she wrote: "They lifted him up. His head drooped on one shoulder. His arms dangled like the arms in Titian's *Descent from the Cross*. Instead of a crown of thorns the dying man wore a bandage. The features of his face retained their purity and pride."

STRANGE ASSASSIN 29

The man who had murdered Trotsky and who was so easily apprehended was a mystery to the police and has remained something of a mystery ever since. He was not in the least a typical G.P.U. agent, who murders habitually and precisely like a skilled artisan working on a machine belt. A pathological liar, without any central core to his being, he resembled those thieves who instinctively try to open every door in the knowledge that sometimes a door will remain unlocked, and then blunders into the house, kills the first person he meets, and then out of fear and shock runs away without stealing anything. Almost he was mindless. Yet he accomplished an assassination which had profound consequences and elevated Trotsky to the role of a martyr. He was an unlikely candidate for killer of one of the world's most famous revolutionaries.

In the history of assassinations Jacson-Mornard occupies a comparatively small place perhaps because he was so completely without a recognizable character, because his motives were so obscure, and because he vanished from sight after serving a long prison sentence. We now know a great number of facts concerning his life but we are not very much closer to knowing how and why he embarked on an assassination that appears in a curious way to be fortuitous and almost accidental. There is evidence of design and purpose, but they are not the design and purpose of Jacson-Mornard. To a quite extraordinary degree he appears as a manipulated man, blindly obeying orders, very unsure of himself, and almost incapable of making decisions when he is on his own; and in the life of an assassin there comes at least one moment when he must make his own decisions. We do not know, though we can guess, the names of the men who held him on their leading strings and there is no mystery about the reasons why they wanted Trotsky killed. The mystery lies in the killer, the pathological liar who would seem to have been incapable of any useful work, who surrendered to his fantasies and dreamed his life away.

While Jacson-Mornard was lying in Green Cross hospital suffering from nervous prostration and some minor head wounds inflicted on him by Trotsky's guards, there was found on him a long, neatly typed letter written in French and signed in pencil: JAC. The letter, which was probably written in its final form on the morning of the assassination but had evidently been prepared many days beforehand, should be quoted at some length because it reveals indirectly a great deal about the man:

Gentlemen,

In writing this letter I have no other object, in case of accident, than to explain to the public the motives that have forced me to commit the act of justice I propose to carry out.

I belong to an old Belgian family. In Paris, where I studied journalism, I made the acquaintance of some young people of my own age who belonged to various left-wing organizations and who little by little converted me to their ideas. I was pleased to find in journalism a means of livelihood, for I was thus able to fight more effectively against the present system of social injustice. It was then that I came to know the Trotskyists who convinced me of the justice of their ideology and I willingly entered their organization. From then on I applied all my energy and all my faith to the revolutionary cause. I became a devoted follower of Leon Trotsky and would have given the last drop of blood in his service. I began to study all that had been written on the revolutionary movements in order to better instruct myself, and in this way to be more useful to the movement.

At this time I made the acquaintance of a member of the Fourth International who, after several conversations, proposed that I take a trip to Mexico, so that I could meet Leon Trotsky. Naturally the journey greatly appealed to me, for it was the realization of my dreams, and I accepted wholeheartedly. This comrade arranged everything for me: all the expenses of the journey, papers, etc. It should not be forgotten that, because of mobilization, it would have been impossible for me to go with my own papers.

Before leaving, I came to understand through the course of many conversations with this comrade that something more was expected of me than from an ordinary member of the party, though no precise details were given to me. I made the journey first to the United States and then to Mexico.

When I arrived, I was told that I must remain for some time at a distance from the house in Coyoacan, so as not to draw attention to myself, and some time passed before I began to visit the house at the request of Leon Trotsky, who little by little began to give me some indication of what was expected of me.

This was a great disillusionment for me, for instead of finding myself face to face with a political leader who was directing the struggle for the liberation of the working class, I found myself before a man who wished only to satisfy his desire for vengeance and hatred, and who used the workers' struggles only as a means of hiding his own paltriness and selfish motives.

From that moment I remained chilled by his skill in sowing discord in our own party, setting some against others, the leaders of yesterday against those of today, which brought into our ranks discord and confusion, so that the majority of the party members wasted time discussing among themselves questions of a secondary and personal order relating to a secondary plane all the problems of the working class, and this ended by dispiriting many of the members who, like me, joined the movement in order to consecrate their lives to the cause.

After several conversations he at last explained to me what was expected of me. It was then that there were sown in me the seeds of a profound disillusionment and the greatest contempt for the man in whom I had previously felt confidence and trust.

It was proposed that I should go to Russia and organize a series of attempts against various persons, and in the first place against Stalin. This was contrary to all the principles of a struggle which until then I had considered frank and open, and contrary to all my principles. However, I said nothing, for I wished to know the full extent of this man's hatred and baseness.

I began to ask, among other things, the means I must employ to enter Russia. I was told not to worry about this, for all means were justifiable to secure such an end, and he hoped for and relied upon the support of a great nation and also on the support of a certain foreign parliamentary committee.

This, for me, was the drop of water that overflowed the glass and from that moment there was no doubt in my mind that Trotsky had no other object in life than to use his followers in order to satisfy his personal ends. Above all I was distressed to discover his close ties with certain leaders of capitalist countries and came to the conclusion that the Stalinists were not far from the truth when they accused Trotsky of looking at the working class as if it were a dirty sock.

After my conversations with him I was astonished to hear with what contempt he spoke of the Mexican Revolution and of everything Mexican. Naturally all his sympathies were with Almazán, but apart from him and one or two of his followers, he puts them all in the same bag, criticizing the policies of Cárdenas and the Mexican police, which he said is absolutely corrupt. And I will not mention what he said about Lombardo Toledano and Avila Camacha, whom he hoped would soon be assassinated, thus leaving a free field for Almazán (and, knowing him as I do, I am sure he knows something about a plot designed to bring this about, otherwise he would not speak in this way, for he is very fond of proclaiming himself a prophet. It would be wise not to trust him).

This is not to be wondered at when you consider that he feels the same hatred for the members of his own party who are not absolutely in agreement with him. It is for this reason that, when speaking of the minority in the party, he always insinuates that there may come into existence a battle of another political order, and when he says the minority will wish to attack one of these days, he means that they will be confronted with a bloody struggle.

One day, speaking about the fact that his house had been transformed into a fortress, he said: "It is not only to defend myself against the Stalinists, but also against the minority." And this meant he wanted to expel many members of the party. Regarding the house, which as he very well says he has transformed into a fortress, I often asked myself where the money comes from for such a work, since in reality the party is very poor and in many countries cannot even afford to publish a party paper, an indispensable tool in the struggle. From where does this money come? Perhaps the consul of a great foreign nation who frequently visited him could answer this question.

Finally, in order to demonstrate what little interest he shows towards everything that does not touch him personally, I add that, being engaged to a young woman I love with all my soul because she is good and loyal, when I told him that I could not go to Russia because I wished to marry first and after that would go only with my wife, he became upset and told me I must break with her because I could not marry someone who "supported the minority rabble." If, as is possible, after what I am going to do, she may not want to see me any more, nevertheless it is also because of her that I have decided to sacrifice myself utterly in order to rid the labor movement of a leader who has done nothing but harm it. And I am sure that later not only the party, but history itself will vindicate me when it is seen that the implacable enemy of the working class has disappeared.

In case anything unfortunate should happen to me, I demand the publication of this letter.

JAC   20.8.1940

This letter is worth examining not only because it is full of lies that point directly to the truth, and because it shows signs of being composed originally by several hands, but because it fails dismally to be what it sets out to be—a document of historical and psychological importance. It is intended to explain the mind of the assassin and to make a claim on history, and does neither of these things.

The modern jury system involves direct confrontation

of the prisoner with the jury, who can thus observe whether he is telling the truth or lying. The jury observes, when he is lying, his confusions, repetitions, sudden alterations of pace, of emphasis, of timbre; it watches for the broken links in the chain of argument and seeks out the pattern of the self-defending mechanism, watching especially for the moment when the new self-defending mechanism takes over after the first has proved untenable, for people generally defend themselves in depth, throwing up one barricade after another. Jacson-Mornard's letter is a series of replies from the dock: we do not hear the questions but they are not difficult to imagine. The letter has been composed with great care, many times, in many conferences, but too often it answers the wrong questions, falls into confusion, is tentative where one would expect an outright answer, and loses itself in vague accusations intended to ward off the accusations of the prosecuting counsel.

Jacson-Mornard repeats three times in slightly different contexts his disillusionment with Trotsky. The repetition is not demanded by the logic or the emotion conveyed in the letter. Three times he approaches Trotsky and three times he is disillusioned. He suggests that after a long period of being held at arm's reach he suddenly became intimate with Trotsky and is given secret orders to assassinate Stalin with the promise of help from a great foreign power, obviously the United States. Jacson-Mornard rejects the order only after Trotsky rejects his future wife. The question of money arises only at the point where Trotsky announces that the fortress has been erected not only against Stalin but also against dissident Trotskyists. The party is very poor and cannot afford to publish a newspaper "in many countries." He dwells briefly on Trotsky's poverty, and then asks where all the money is coming from. Obviously it is coming from the United States, whose consul "frequently visited him," which is indisputably untrue. In the letter Jacson-Mornard presents himself as a man charged with a crime and defends himself in the appropriate manner—by attacking. But the attack is terribly ill organized. We can almost hear the words of the G.P.U. officials: "Now write it down in your own words."

If we accept the possibility that the letter is a ghost version or mirror image of the truth, everything begins to fall into place. The Trotsky of the letter has become curiously identified with the G.P.U. official who has taken Jacson-Mornard in charge. The man he approaches with such trepidation and hesitation, and who is so obviously corrupt and intimidating is close at hand. The man who gives orders to kill is not Trotsky. The man who orders him to give up his mistress is not Trotsky. The man who is contemptuous of the Mexican Revolution is not Trotsky. The man who talks about the split in the party is not Trotsky. It is not that Jacson-Mornard is necessarily lying: he is using what he knows. He knows little about Trotsky, whom he met rarely and briefly, but he knows a good deal about the G.P.U. official who dominated him, confused him, and made him an almost mindless tool of the Stalinist secret police.

Jacson-Mornard went on lying: there was nothing else he could do, and he did it badly. He retreated from one defensive position to another. The Mexican police suspected he was neither Jacson nor Mornard: he explained that his real name was Jacques Mornard Vandendreschd, that he was born on February 17, 1904, in Teheran, where his father, Robert Mornard, the husband of Henriette Vandendreschd, was the Belgian ambassador. He attended the St. Ignatius of Loyola College at Brussels on the Waterloo Embankment and the Military School at Dixmude at a time when he was simultaneously attending lectures at the University of Brussels and the School of Journalism in the Sorbonne. His father died in 1926, leaving a fortune of between three and four million Belgian francs. During the last few years he had supported himself by journalism in Paris while receiving an allowance from his mother.

It did not take long for the Mexican police to discover that every single one of these statements was untrue. For example, there was no Belgian ambassador to

Persia in 1904, the St. Ignatius of Loyola College was not on the Waterloo Embankment in Brussels, and there was no Military School at Dixmude. It became evident that Jacson-Mornard was a fabrication, a straw figure, put together from odds and ends of half-remembered information, without logic and without order. The figure he had invented so carelessly had neither weight nor substance; it was not so much a parcel of lies as a collection of random statements based on a haphazard knowledge of Belgium. It was even doubtful whether he had ever been in Belgium, and it was certain that he spoke no Flemish, for when the Belgian *chargé d'affaires* in Mexico City visited him in prison and reminded him that Flemish was spoken in Dixmude, and went on to speak a few words in this language, he understood nothing. The *chargé d'affaires* concluded: "He is not a Belgian, and has no knowledge of Belgium."

There was one revealing moment during the interview. Jacson-Mornard had said that his mother lived for a long time at No. 1 Havre Embankment in Brussels. There is no Havre Embankment, but there is a Wavre Embankment, which is occupied entirely by large stores. When he was told this, Jacson-Mornard said: "No, my mother did not live in the store—she lived above it." It was not convincing, but it showed how his mind worked—he was lying as a child lies.

The Mexican government went to extreme lengths to attempt to identify him. Inquiries were made all over the world, massive dossiers were compiled, three separate police organizations were set to work, and a team of psychologists interviewed him for six hours every day, for a period of six months. Their completed report was 1,359 pages long. At the first meeting with the psychologists he announced: "You are not going to get anything out of me." They got very little.

Nevertheless, being a gregarious man, he welcomed the psychologists, answered their questions with amused contempt, submitted willingly to tests, and built up still another persona to add to the two he had already constructed. An extensive, six-month examination was bound to reveal some things about him. It revealed for example that he was an expert mountain climber, a skilled athlete, and had obviously had some military training, for he could take a Mauser rifle apart in the dark and put it together in the dark in a little less than four minutes. He loved clothes and collected an expensive wardrobe. He was hypersensitive to pain, possessed exceptionally good night vision, was short-sighted, showed no physical abnormalities except a lack of body hair, his heart was strong and his pulse was steady, and though he affected deafness on occasion, there was nothing wrong with his hearing. Since he claimed to be born on February 17, 1904, which would make him thirty-six years old in 1940, the psychologists and the doctors who examined him were puzzled by the fact that he had the body of a much younger man. In fact, he was born on February 7, 1913, and was only twenty-seven when he committed the murder.

All the discoveries of the psychologists, all the massive documentation accumulated with so much care and industry, all the word games and loaded conversations intended to trap him into various admissions amounted to very little. The final document resembled an autopsy report: the body of the man had been examined, the convolutions of his brain were known, but the real man remained concealed. More puzzling than anything else was the fact that in the twentieth century with all the resources of the Mexican government at its disposal the examining magistrates and the police were unable to identify the killer. He lay in bed for a large part of the day with the sheet drawn over his face, lived on warm milk and bread, and defied everyone to discover who he was. He still called himself Jacson-Mornard, but it was already known that this was not his real name. He had no antecedents, no biography.

Yet there were some clues. Once, while the psychologists were examining him, he wrote down the word "Lenin" then drew a box around the word, and within the box inserted in large letters the word "Kamo." The psychologists could make nothing of "Kamo." Yet students of Russian revolutionary history know a great deal about Kamo, and what they know helps to identify the kind of man Jacson-Mornard was. Among the thousands of words he was induced to write or say during the long months of his imprisonment, this word was the one that reveals something about the essential core of the man.

Kamo was an Armenian, his real name being Semyon Arshakovich Ter-Petrosian. It was said that his revolutionary name was given to him by Stalin. He was the son of a rich contractor, who once advertised for a tutor for the boy, who was doing badly at school. Stalin answered the advertisement, but instead of teaching him the subjects demanded by the school, he taught him to become a revolutionary. Kamo was not a very successful revolutionary, but he was remembered for his style, his immense courage, and his total devotion to the revolutionary cause. He was a consummate actor. Given some revolutionary pamphlets to deliver, he would disguise himself as a *kinto*, a street peddler, balancing a basket of vegetables on his head, pushing his way through the crowd under the eyes of the police; the next day he would be disguised as an elegant young officer traveling by train to another city in a carriage full of young women, with whom he flirted ostentatiously, and no policeman on the train would think of looking at his luggage. On the return journey he would assume the role of a peasant carrying an enormous basket of eggs and he would even appeal to the police to help him preserve the eggs because there were so many people on the train and he wanted to prevent them from being broken. He was an excellent gun runner, he carried bombs from one end of European Russia to the other without the police ever suspecting him, and he was a capable expropriator of money from the state banks. The first raid on a bank in Kutais brought in 15,000 rubles. In a second raid on a bank in Tiflis a bomb blew up prematurely. He was badly wounded, lost the sight of his left eye, and was within an inch of being arrested. A third raid on the State Bank in Tiflis was the most spectacular: two mailbags full of bank notes were captured by the revolutionaries, but the bank had taken the precaution of noting down the serial numbers and they proved to be non-negotiable. Kamo was a capable bank robber but he was more successful as a courier. His fame rested on an attempted "expropriation" in the house of a millionaire banker in Berlin. He was caught red-handed with explosives and a bomb packed in his suitcase. The Russian government demanded his extradition. Kamo pretended that he had gone mad. He screamed for hours on end, remained mute for weeks, refused to eat, tore out his hair, attacked his jailors so that they became mortally afraid of him, and simulated insanity so well that he probably became insane. Finally the Germans felt that they might as well surrender him to the Russians and he was handed over to them in a strait jacket. The Russians placed him in the psychopathic ward of a mental hospital, from which he escaped. For a while he took refuge with Lenin, whose wife, Nadezhda, remembered with affection the hours when Kamo regaled her with stories of how he had outwitted the German and Russian police.

Kamo's example was held up to the young Bolshevik revolutionaries as something to be followed. When arrested, they must resist even to madness. The life of Kamo was included in prescribed courses in the training of G.P.U. officers. By writing one word, "Kamo," Jacson-Mornard confirmed what nearly everyone had suspected: that he had been trained by the G.P.U. to remain mute on every subject concerning the murder of Trotsky, while being permitted to speak of other matters to his heart's content. He was a more gentlemanly version of Kamo.

The psychologists were in the habit of asking him to tell them his dreams. To amuse them, he invented dreams which would be of interest to psychologists. In one of these dreams he described how he had been racing in an outboard motorboat off Royan and in the mysterious way of dreams the outboard motorboat was suddenly transformed into a 15-meter sailboat with high sails taking part in a regatta. One boat sank, and the sailors swam away. Then he saw his own boat sailing in a circle, and the men swimming away from the sunken boat refused to come on board. It was strange that he had chosen to invent a dream that began at Royan, where Trotsky had taken refuge when he came to France in 1933, and stranger still that the dream should lend itself so easily to a classical statement of rejection, the sailboat (himself) circling aimlessly, the swimmers (those who might have helped him) refusing to come on board. Sometimes, as he wrote down his made-up dreams, free associations permitted him to reveal some portions of the truth.

By the time the psychologists had completed their work, they had come to the conclusion that he was probably a Spaniard trained in the Soviet Union, with an overmastering mother and a weak father, at the mercy of an overriding passion to prove himself stronger than his father. "He wanted to sacrifice himself for a great cause and yet at the same time build up an inner world which would protect him," they wrote. "He was weak and at the same time determined, and he showed no remorse."

Early in the spring of 1943 Jacson-Mornard was finally brought to trial. Contemptuous of the proceedings, he made almost no defense, although he changed the story told in his typewritten letter. This time he said he had been suddenly enraged when Trotsky said: "You are nothing but a military idiot!" while reading his article. Trotsky then jumped up from the table and attacked him physically. Mornard used the ice pick because he was afraid of being murdered, for Trotsky had a revolver within reach. This improbable account of the murder carried little conviction. The court could not bring itself to believe that he had acted in self-defense and sentenced him to twenty years imprisonment, nineteen years and six months for premeditated murder and six months for illegal possession of arms. He appealed but the verdict was upheld.

Not until September 1950, ten years after the crime was committed, was his real identity discovered. Dr. Alfonso Quiroz Cuaron, one of the psychologists who had interviewed the prisoner at such length, visited Spain with copies of Jacson-Mornard's fingerprints. He gave them to the fingerprint expert at the headquarters of the Madrid police and in a surprisingly short time he was told that they matched those of a certain Jaime Ramon Mercader del Rio arrested in Barcelona on June 12, 1935. In the police file there were photographs of Ramon Mercader full face and in profile, and there was not the least doubt that this was the same person as Jacson-Mornard.

With the discovery of the fingerprints and the photographs it became possible to fill in the family background. The most resourceful searchers were Dr. Alfonso Quiroz Cuaron and the American writer Isaac Don Levine, who succeeded in tracking down and talking with Don Pablo Mercader, the murderer's father, in his apartment just off the Plaza de España in Barcelona. He was then seventy-five years old, very tall and straight, with the bearing of an elderly nobleman. In 1911 he had married Caridad del Rio, a Cuban woman of considerable beauty, after an impassioned three-year courtship. At the time of the marriage he was twenty-seven, the bride was nineteen. She gave him three sons and one daughter. Ramon was the second son. For about ten years the marriage was uneventful, and suddenly Caridad began to take lovers, talked wildly about communism, rejected her husband, and became emotionally disturbed. To save his family, Don Pablo took them all to live in Toulouse. In 1929 Caridad made her third suicide attempt. Don Pablo decided that while she was in hospital he would make one last effort to keep some part of his family together and removed his children to Barcelona while leaving their mother in Toulouse. It was no use. The children escaped from their father and went to live with their mother. Ramon had little education. He studied briefly at a training school for hotel workers in Lyons, became a bellboy in a Barcelona hotel, and then an assistant to the chef in the Ritz Hotel, the most prestigious hotel in Barcelona. He became one of the organizers of an underground communist cell which had its headquarters in a bar in the

Calle Wilfredo, and it was there that he was arrested with seventeen others on June 12, 1935. Photographed, fingerprinted, placed on trial, he was sentenced to an indeterminate term of imprisonment in the prison of San Miguel de los Reyes in Valencia. In the following year he was released following the amnesty for political prisoners proclaimed by the Popular Front Government. When Franco launched his attack on Republican Spain in July 1936, Ramon was a communist in good standing and became a political commissar with the rank of a lieutenant in the 27th Division on the Aragon front. While serving in the Republican army he was recruited into Soviet intelligence by General Kotov, whose real name was Leonid Eitingon. With the defeat of the Republican army he went to the Soviet Union and received training in an G.P.U. training school. Long before this Caridad had become the mistress of General Kotov.

Such were the facts that the psychologists and prosecutors in Mexico City had vainly been attempting to discover during their long investigation, and yet surprisingly they tell us very little. From bellboy and assistant chef and youthful political commissar he rose through his mother's influence with General Kotov to become an agent of the G.P.U., a Spaniard in the service of the Soviet Union who traveled on a forged Canadian passport. He was a man without roots, without a nation, existing at the center of a moral and emotional vacuum. Emotionally he was dead; perhaps he had always been dead. It was easy for the G.P.U. to capture him, to flatter him, to write on his brain that he was capable of a heroic deed that would benefit the Soviet fatherland. Having no will of his own, he submitted to the will of his mother and the general, reserving for himself only the satisfaction of performing an act of heroism. His chief object when murdering Trotsky was to persuade himself that he had a place in history, that he was triumphantly alive, that he was Jacson-Mornard, that is to say that he was "someone else."

The awful thing is that it was so easy. Anyone could have done what he did, because anyone can go up to an

STRANGE
ASSASSIN

old man and shoot him dead or split open his skull with an ice pick. Siqueiros had mounted a small invasion force complete with machine guns, hand grenades and sticks of dynamite, and failed. Ramon Mercader, scarcely knowing what he was doing, terrified out of his wits, succeeded only because Trotsky was remarkably trusting. There was no glory in it.

Ramon Mercader went on living in the Mexican jail in considerable comfort. He was given a large room and permitted to have a mistress. He was treated with respect as an important and indeed famous prisoner, and the prison guards were discreetly deferential. When the President of Mexico announced that prisoners who taught their illiterate comrades to read and write would receive a remission of their sentences, he was among the first to enlist in the literacy campaign. In December 1952, when he had served half of his sentence, he found work in the radio and television repair shop of the prison. For his work as an electrical engineer he received extra pay, and soon he was permitted to accept outside jobs, which brought him more income. He was placed in charge of the entire electrical system in the prison. He read technical manuals and wrote articles for electrical journals. He hoped that his services inside the prison would lead to a remission of his sentence, but the parole board refused, chiefly on the ground that he had never shown the slightest remorse and was "proud of his status as an enigmatic man."

On May 6, 1960, Ramon Mercader walked out of jail. Everything had been arranged for him, and the most minute details of his travel plans were already worked out. Accompanied by two guards from the Czechoslovak Embassy in Mexico City, and bearing a diplomatic passport bearing the name Jacques Vandendreschd, he flew on a Cuban passenger plane to Havana, where he stopped for only a few hours and was then flown to Prague. He disappeared beyond the Iron Curtain and nothing more has ever been heard of him.

In this way the man who had wanted to be a part of history and accomplished his aim with fatal ease, escaped out of history altogether. The man he killed brought about the greatest single revolutionary movement in our time, commanded armies that fought from Riga to Vladivostok and from the Crimea to Murmansk, wrote brilliantly, spoke with extraordinary oratorical skill, and remained to the end of his life a strenuous agitator for his beliefs. His virtues, which were many, were flawed by a towering pride; he possessed very little feeling for human suffering. His defeat and ultimate destruction by Stalin was a Shakespearean drama: he played his role with grace, courage, and magnanimity, fighting to the last. He saw the evil in Stalin before others saw it. In an age without heroes he showed a heroic temper. On a bitterly cold night in November 1917 he issued the order to capture the Winter Palace, and the world is still shuddering from the consequences of that order.

He was one of the giants of our time. He was utterly ruthless in his search for power and contemptuous of all those he destroyed. There is a certain magnificence in the revolutionary as he claws his way to power, and Trotsky possessed magnificence. But once in power he was inevitably corrupted by it, and he was one of those who lived long enough to be corrupted by defeat.

Lenin and Trotsky failed, and Stalin failed more dreadfully. In human terms they were all failures because they produced an inhuman form of government based on the powers of the secret police. They were not in the least concerned with the dignity of the individual; they were concerned to reduce him to a statistic, to a number, to something that could be ordered about with impunity; and they succeeded beyond their wildest hopes.

All the works of revolution must begin again. The Russians have not found the way.

APPENDICES

SELECT
BIBLIOGRAPHY

Balabanoff, Angelica. *My Life as a Rebel.* New York: Harper & Brothers, 1938.

Bittelman, Alex. *Trotsky the Traitor.* New York: Workers' Library, 1937.

Bunyan, James. *The Origin of Forced Labor in the Soviet State, 1917–1921.* Baltimore: Johns Hopkins Press, 1967.

Canfield, Cass. *Up & Down & Around.* New York: Harper & Row, 1971.

Carr, E. H. *A History of Soviet Russia.* Harmondsworth: Penguin Books, 1973.

Chamberlin, William Henry. *The Russian Revolution, 1917–1921.* New York: Grosset & Dunlap, 1965.

Churchill, Winston S. *Great Contemporaries.* New York: G. P. Putnam's Sons, 1937.

Daniels, Robert V. *A Documentary History of Communism.* New York: Random House, 1960.

Deutscher, Isaac. (Ed.) *The Age of Permanent Revolution: A Trotsky Anthology.* New York: Dell, 1973.

———. *The Prophet Armed: Trotsky 1879–1921, The Prophet Unarmed: Trotsky 1921–1929, The Prophet Outcast: Trotsky 1929–1940.* London: Oxford University Press, 1954–1969.

———. *Stalin: A Political Biography.* New York: Oxford University Press, 1949.

Draper, Theodore. *The Roots of American Communism.* New York: Viking Press, 1957.

Eastman, Max. *Great Companions.* London: Museum Press, 1959.

————. *Leon Trotsky: The Portrait of a Youth*. New York: Greenberg, 1925.

————. *Love and Revolution*. New York: Random House, 1964.

————. *Since Lenin Died*. New York: Boni and Liveright, 1925.

Fischer, Louis. *The Life of Lenin*. New York: Harper & Row, 1965.

————. *The Soviets in World Affairs*. Princeton: Princeton University Press, 1960.

Goldman, Albert. *The Assassination of Leon Trotsky*. New York: Pioneer Publishers, 1940.

Goldman, Emma. *My Disillusionment in Russia*. New York: Thomas Y. Crowell, 1970.

Gorky, Maxim. *Untimely Thoughts*. New York: Paul S. Eriksson, 1968.

Hansen, Joseph, and others. *Leon Trotsky: The Man and His Work*. New York: Merit Publishers, 1969.

Hare, Richard. *Maxim Gorky*. London: Oxford University Press, 1962.

Harris, Frank. *Contemporary Portraits*. Fourth series. New York: Brentano, 1923.

International Committee of the Fourth International (ed.). *How the GPU Murdered Trotsky*. London: New Park Publications, 1976.

————. *Security and the Fourth International*. New York: Labor Publications, 1976.

Jewish Daily Forward. Articles by Trotsky on January 30, February 1, February 15, February 23, 1917.

Kerensky, Alexander. *Russia and History's Turning Point*. New York: Duell, Sloan & Pearce, 1965.

Lademacher, Horst. (Ed.) *Die Zimmerwalder Bewegung*. The Hague: Mouton, 1967.

Lenin, N., and Leon Trotsky. *The Proletarian Revolution in Russia*. New York: The Communist Press, 1918.

Lenin, V. I., and Leon Trotsky. *Lenin's Fight against Stalinism*. New York: Pathfinder Press, 1975.

Levine, Isaac Don. *Eyewitness to History*. New York: Hawthorn Books, 1973.

————. *The Mind of an Assassin*. New York: Farrar, Straus & Cudahy, 1959.

————. *The Mind of an Assassin*. (Rev. ed.) New York: Signet Books, 1960.

Liebman, Marcel. *The Russian Revolution*. New York: Random House, 1972.

Lunacharsky, Anatoly. *Revolutionary Silhouettes*. London: Penguin Press, 1967.

Medvedev, Roy A. *Let History Judge*. New York: Alfred A. Knopf, 1972.

Meijer, Jan M. *The Trotsky Papers*. The Hague: Mouton, 1964.

Mett, Ida. *La Commune de Cronstadt*. Paris, Spartacus: René Lefeuvre, n.d.

Morizet, André. *Chez Lénine et Trotski.* Paris, La Renaissance du Livre, 1922.

Mosley, Nicholas. *The Assassination of Trotsky.* London: Michael Joseph, 1972.

Nedava, Joseph. *Trotsky and the Jews.* Philadelphia: Jewish Publication Society of America, 1971.

Novack, George. (Ed.) *The Case of Leon Trotsky.* New York: Merit Publishers, 1969.

Olgin, M. J. *Trotskyism: Counter-Revolution in Disguise.* San Francisco: Proletarian Publishers, 1935.

Payne, Robert. *The Fortress.* New York: Simon and Schuster, 1967.

———. *The Life and Death of Lenin.* New York: Simon & Schuster, 1964.

———. *The Rise and Fall of Stalin.* New York: Simon & Schuster, 1965.

Pollack, Emanuel. *The Kronstadt Rebellion.* New York: Philosophical Library, 1959.

Reed, John. *Ten Days that Shook the World.* New York: Random House, 1960.

Report in the Case of the Anti-Soviet Trotskyite Centre. Moscow: People's Commissariat of Justice, 1937.

Reswick, William. *I Dreamed Revolution.* Chicago: Henry Regnery, 1952.

Rosenthal, Gérard. *Avocat de Trotsky.* Paris: Robert Laffont, 1975.

Rosmer, Alfred. *Moscow under Lenin.* New York: Monthly Review Press, 1972.

Sanchez Salazar, Leandro. *Murder in Mexico.* London: Secker & Warburg, 1950.

Schapiro, Leonard, and Peter Reddaway. *Lenin: The Man, the Theorist, the Leader.* New York: Frederick A. Praeger, 1968.

Serge, Victor. *From Lenin to Stalin.* New York: Monad Press, 1973.

———. *Year One of the Russian Revolution.* New York: Holt, Rinehart and Winston, 1977.

Serge, Victor, and Natalia Sedova Trotsky. *The Life and Death of Leon Trotsky.* New York: Basic Books, 1975.

Shachtman, Max. *Behind the Moscow Trial.* New York: Pioneer Publishers, 1936.

Shub, David. *Lenin: A Biography.* Harmondsworth: Penguin Books, 1966.

Smith, Irving H. *Trotsky: Great Lives Observed.* Englewood Cliffs, N.J.: Prentice-Hall, 1973.

Souvarine, Boris. *Stalin.* New York: Longmans, Green, 1939.

Stalin, J. V. *On the Opposition.* Peking: Foreign Languages Press, 1974.

Steinberg, I. N. *In the Workshop of the Revolution.* New York: Rinehart and Company, 1953.

Sukhanov, N. N. *The Russian Revolution.* New York: Harper and Brothers, 1962.

Against Individual Terrorism. New York: Pathfinder Press, 1974.
Against Social Patriotism. Colombo: Lanka Samasamaja, 1952.
The Bolsheviki and World Peace. New York: Boni and Liveright, 1918.
Diary in Exile. London: Faber & Faber, 1959.
The Essential Trotsky. New York: Barnes & Noble, 1963.
Flight from Siberia. Colombo: Young Socialist Publications, 1969.
The History of the Russian Revolution. Ann Arbor: University of Michigan Press, 1960.
In Defence of Insurrection. Maradana: Lanka Samasamaja, 1954.
In Defence of Marxism. New York: Pathfinder Press, 1973.
Lenin: Notes for a Biographer. New York: Capricorn Books, 1971.
Lenin's Fight against Stalinism. New York: Pathfinder Press, 1975.
Leon Sedov: Son, Friend, Fighter. London: Plough Press, n.d.
Leon Trotsky on Britain. New York: Pathfinder Press, 1973.
Leon Trotsky Speaks. New York: Pathfinder Press, 1972.
Lessons of October. London: New Park Publications, 1971.
Literature and Revolution. New York: Russell and Russell, 1957.
Military Writings. New York: Pathfinder Press, 1971.
Mis Peripecias en España. Madrid: Editorial España, 1929.
My Flight from Siberia. Colombo: Young Socialist Publications, 1969.
My Life. New York: Grosset & Dunlap, 1960.
1905. New York: Random House, 1972.
On Literature and Art. New York: Pathfinder Press, 1970.
Our Revolution. New York: Henry Holt, 1918.
The Permanent Revolution. New York: Pathfinder Press, 1968.
Political Profiles. London: New Park Publications, 1972.
Problems of the Chinese Revolution. Ann Arbor: University of Michigan Press, 1967.
Problems of Civil War. New York: Pathfinder Press, 1970.
Problems of Life. London: Methuen, 1924.
The Real Situation in Russia. New York: Harcourt, Brace, 1928.
The Revolution Betrayed. New York: Pathfinder Press, 1974.
Stalin: An Appraisal of the Man and His Influence. London: Hollis and Carter, 1947.
The Stalin School of Falsification. New York: Pathfinder Press, 1971.
The Struggle for State Power. Colombo: Young Socialist Publications, 1966.
The Suppressed Testament of Lenin. New York: Pioneer Publishers, 1946.
Terrorism and Communism. Ann Arbor: University of Michigan Press, 1972.
Their Morals and Ours. New York: Pathfinder Press, 1973.
War and the 4th International. New York: Pioneer Publishers, 1934.

War and the International. Wellewatt: Wesley Press, 1971.

Whither France? New York: Merit Publishers, 1968.

Women and the Family. New York: Pathfinder Press, 1973.

Writings of Leon Trotsky. 12 vols. covering 1929–1940. New York: Pathfinder Press, 1969–1975.

The Young Lenin. Harmondsworth: Penguin Books, 1974.

The Zimmerwald Manifesto. Colombo: Lanka Samasamaja, 1951.

Tucker, Robert C. (Ed.) *The Great Purge Trial.* New York: Grosset & Dunlap, 1965.

Wheeler-Bennett, Sir John W. *Brest-Litovsk: The Forgotten Peace.* New York: St. Martin's Press, 1966.

Wilson, Edmund. *To the Finland Station.* Garden City: Doubleday, 1953.

Wolfe, Bertram D. *Three Who Made a Revolution.* New York: Dell, 1964.

Wolfenstein, E. Victor. *The Revolutionary Personality: Lenin, Trotsky, Gandhi.* Princeton: Princeton University Press, 1973.

Wyndham, Francis, and David King. *Trotsky: A Documentary.* Harmondsworth: Penguin Books, 1972.

Zeman, Z. A. B., and W. B. Scharlau. *The Merchant of Revolution: The Life of Alexander Israel Helphand.* London: Oxford University Press, 1965.

Zinoviev, Grigory. *History of the Bolshevik Party.* London: New Park Publications, 1973.

Ziv, Grigory. *Trotsky—Kharakteristika po Lichnym Vospominaniam.* New York: Narodopravstvo, 1921.

I have also consulted the files of *The Militant, Socialist Appeal,* and *The New York Times.*

CHAPTER
NOTES

A few abbreviations have been used in the chapter notes. Trotsky's *My Life* is given as "Life," Max Eastman's *Leon Trotsky, The Portrait of a Youth* is given as "Portrait," and in general the reference is given in its shortest form. Thus Grigory Ziv's *Trotsky—Kharakteristika po Lichnym Vospominaniam* is described simply as "Ziv."

page

13	At such times . . .	*Life*, p. 21
15	"Come, write this . . .	Id., p. 7
27	"He was only ten . . .	*Portrait*, p. 17
28	"Those golden buttons . . .	Id., p. 19
30	He was a lean . . .	*Life*, p. 30
42	"Don't tell me that . . .	*Portrait*, p. 66
45	I was walking along . . .	*Life*, p. 104
45	"It's very simple . . .	Id., p. 105
49	Neumann climbed . . .	*Portrait*, p. 83
50	Do not believe anyone . . .	Id., p. 85
60	Oh, little oak club . . .	Id., p. 109
62	"Uninterrupted noise . . .	Id., p. 112
62	"May you explode . . .	Id., p. 115
65	In March 1898 . . .	Ziv, p. 25
71	"You were wrong about . . .	Id., p. 32
77	I run out there . . .	*Portrait*, p. 137
89	A tremendous amount . . .	Trotsky, *Our Revolution*, p. 41

94	Sire! We the workers . . .	Payne, *Lenin*, p. 184
96	"bombs and dynamite . . .	Id., p. 185
97	The prestige of the Tsar's . . .	Id., p. 185
97	The Revolution has come . . .	Trotsky, *Our Revolution*, p. 53
98	"The hero, Gapon . . .	Id., p. 56
98	"clear revolutionary thinking . . .	Id., p. 60
98	"our organization . . .	Id., p. 61
99	"our fight for a revolution . . .	Id., p. 55
107	"Citizens . . .	Deutscher, *Prophet Armed*, p. 129
108	Khrustalov's star . . .	Lunacharsky, p. 60
109	"Please do not interrupt . . .	Deutscher, *Prophet Armed*, p. 143
113	"The influence of the Russian . . .	Trotsky, *Our Revolution*, p. 143
114	The proletariat can . . .	Id., p. 102
118	The domination of the . . .	Id., p. 98
120	What is an uprising . . .	Trotsky, *In Defence of Insurrection*, p. 7
121	The autocracy . . .	Id., p. 9
122	I ask you . . .	Id., p. 16
125	Forest, forest, endless . . .	Trotsky, *My Flight*, p. 46
127	Whether a terrorist . . .	Trotsky, *Against Individual Terrorism*, p. 6
129	"with those youngsters . . .	*Jewish Daily Forward*, January 30, 1917
134	"a case of an ulcer . . .	Trotsky, *Bolsheviki*, p. 117
135	"The epoch into which . . .	Id., p. 232
139	*Workers of Europe!* . . .	Trotsky, *Zimmerwald*, p. 1
142	Vladimir Ilyich suddenly . . .	Trotsky, *Lenin*, p. 171
145	*To the Minister of State* . . .	Trotsky, *Against Social Patriotism*, p. 1
148	This chapter is based entirely on Trotsky, *Mis Peripecias en España.*
167	"Twenty-four hours . . .	Draper, p. 241
171	All the European . . .	*Jewish Daily Forward*, January 30, 1917
172	In America the popularity . . .	Ziv, p. 68
176	"Good God . . .	Harris, p. 199
178	"Prisoners of War . . .	Wyndham, p. 35
190	"You want to take the road . . .	Payne, *Fortress*, p. 411
191	I usually spoke . . .	*Life*, p. 293
192	"under the influence . . .	Lunacharsky, p. 64
208	We shall withdraw . . .	Trotsky, *Lenin*, p. 109
209	"Fortunately we were . . .	Id., p. 109

212	"It is the most comic war . . .	Deutscher, *Prophet Armed*, 363
213	"I am not sure . . .	Id., p. 391
219	I learn that . . .	Serge, *Year One*, p. 291
220	"The game is won . . .	Trotsky, *Diary*, p. 83
225	"The foundations of the militarization . . .	Trotsky, *Terrorism and Communism*, p. 141
226	Transportation must be . . .	Id., p. 157
227	There is no doubt . . .	Meijer, *Trotsky Papers*, I, p. 623
231	"The attraction of hunting . . .	*Life*, p. 470
236	*Resolution of the General* . . .	Emma Goldman, p. 194
239	The Workers' and Peasants' . . .	Steinberg, p. 285
240	Field-Marshal Trotsky . . .	Chamberlin, II, p. 444
242	March 17. Kronstadt . . .	Id., p. 444
243	"Suffice it to say . . .	Trotsky, *Stalin*, p. 337
243	The truth of the matter . . .	Trotsky, *Writings, 1937–1938*, p. 367
251	During the war . . .	*Life*, p. 467
254	"The machine tears itself . . .	Fischer, *Lenin*, p. 585
257	Comrade Stalin, having . . .	Payne, *Lenin*, p. 564
259	Stalin is too rough . . .	Id., p. 571
262	Lenin is no more . . .	Id., p. 612
263	Dear Lev Davidovich . . .	*Life*, p. 510
268	Man will become immeasurably . . .	Trotsky, *Literature and Revolution*, p. 256
270	"The Revolution is strong . . .	Id., p. 88
271	The Christian myth . . .	Id., p. 240
271	"Mediaeval society . . .	Id., p. 240
273	The workers' State . . .	Trotsky, *Problems of Life*, p. 60
274	The Revolution is . . .	Id., p. 79
278	"Lenin," wrote Trotsky . . .	Trotsky, *Lenin*, p. 123
278	"Here are those . . .	Id., p. 123
280	From the moment . . .	Trotsky, *Lessons of October*, p. 47
282	"a professional exploiter" . . .	Stalin, p. 130
283	British pigeon-fanciers . . .	*Leon Trotsky on Britain*, p. 74
284	"Why, why did he say . . .	Trotsky, *Diary*, p. 69
286	"To choose a victim . . .	Id., p. 64
288	Dear Lev Davidovich . . .	Payne, *Stalin*, p. 363
302	"Shoot me, Comrade . . .	*Life*, p. 541
304	"Comrade workers . . .	Reswick, p. 228
310	The work of your political . . .	*Life*, p. 559
311	The greatest historical strength . . .	*Militant*, April 1, 1929
312	To demand that I renounce . . .	Id.
313	"To each his own . . .	*Life*, p. 562

314	Since the end of October . . .	*Militant*, February 2, 1929
315	*Considered* . . .	*Life*, p. 562
318	"I have been . . .	Id., p. 564
319	At the gate of Constantinople . . .	Id., p. 565
332	The old man peered down . . .	*Leon Trotsky Speaks*, p. 272
338	"No one could wish . . .	Churchill, p. 174
339	If Hitler overcomes . . .	Trotsky, *Writings, 1932*, p. 79
340	The interview is given in the *New York Times*, July 13, 1931.	
345	In September, Lenin . . .	Trotsky, *Writings, 1932*, p. 322
347	"It is now our turn . . .	*Leon Trotsky Speaks*, p. 261
348	"The historical task . . .	Id., p. 268
357	"I had no responsibility . . .	Trotsky, *Writings, 1933–1934*, p. 334
358	"I believe that death is . . .	Id., p. 336
359	"I watched Lyovik . . .	Trotsky, *Leon Sedov*, p. 38
361	"the shift of the masses . . .	Trotsky, *War and the 4th International*, p. 35
364	"Life goes on . . .	Trotsky, *Diary*, p. 99
365	It is hard now . . .	Id., p. 66
366	My visit to Moscow . . .	Id., p. 81
368	Concerning the blows . . .	Id., p. 135
371	They have learned . . .	Id., p. 153
373	"The prohibition of opposition . . .	Trotsky, *Revolution Betrayed*, p. 104
373	Spiritual creativeness . . .	Id., p. 180
377	Berman–Yurin . . .	Shachtman, p. 87
379	"Think what you are doing . . .	Serge, *From Lenin to Stalin*, p. 85
379	"They are bargaining . . .	Trotsky, *Writings, 1935–1936*, p. 145
381	"You must know that . . .	Id., p. 126
384	I accuse the Norwegian . . .	Id., p. 146
385	"I see you are reading . . .	Deutscher, *Prophet Outcast*, p. 351
387	"Of course, you can take . . .	Id., p. 353
393	"Here I stand before you . . .	*Report of the Anti-Soviet Trotskyite Centre*, p. 541
397	Beals . . .	Novack, *Case*, p. 412
401	"The welfare of the revolution . . .	Trotsky, *Their Morals*, p. 7

402	"Lyova Sedov is dead . . .	Serge, *Life and Death*, p. 228
402	Goodbye, Lyova, goodbye . . .	Trotsky, *Leon Sedov*, p. 21
410	"the Soviet Union will be . . .	*Militant*, March 12, 1932
411	Japan is not capable . . .	*Socialist Appeal*, April 4, 1939
411	Yes, a world war . . .	Id.
413	"The investiture of Hitler . . .	*Militant*, February 24, 1933
413	"Whichever camp is victorious . . .	Trotsky, *Writings, 1939–1940*, p. 85
416	"This is a bit of . . .	Canfield, p. 147
418	"Indeed I would . . .	Id., p. 149
421	"Then you must have . . .	Trotsky, *Stalin*, p. 414
423	Testament . . .	Trotsky, *Diary*, p. 162
425	March 3, 1940 . . .	Id., p. 163
426	"They're shooting . . .	Serge, *Life and Death*, p. 256
434	My wife, my collaborators . . .	Trotsky, *Writings, 1939–1940*, p. 295
443	"In that way everything . . .	Levine, *Mind* (revised), p. 91
444	"Our military transitional . . .	Trotsky, *Writings, 1939–1940*, p. 256
445	"They have been terribly poisoned . . .	Id., p. 282
445	"Even at the front . . .	Id., p. 288
446	"It reminds me of the first . . .	Levine, *Mind* (revised), p. 93
447	"I feel very well . . .	Hansen, p. 35
449	"What a pity . . .	Id., p. 35
450	"I'm terribly thirsty . . .	Serge, *Life and Death*, p. 267
456	"What happened . . .	Id., p. 267
457	"Jacson shot me with a revolver . . .	Hansen, p. 16
458	"They put mother in prison . . .	Id., p. 17
461	Murdered Trotsky lay dying . . .	Sanchez, p. 110
462	"They lifted him up . . .	Hansen, p. 39
464	Gentlemen . . .	Albert Goldman, p. 5
470	"No, my mother did not . . .	Sanchez, p. 174
474	"You are nothing but . . .	Levine, *Mind*, p. 192

ACKNOWLEDGMENTS

I would like especially to thank Mr. Isaac Don Levine and his wife Ruth Levine for much kindness and help during the writing of this book, for the loan of many photographs, for his sketch-map of the fortress at Coyoacan, and for unpublished material concerning the early life of Natalie Sedova Trotsky. His booming voice electrified me when I first met him many years ago and it still reverberates merrily in my ears.

I am also grateful to Mr. Harold Robins who in a brief conversation answered three questions which seemed to me to be of capital importance, and to Mr. Louis Falstein who tracked down and kindly translated for me Trotsky's articles in the *Jewish Daily Forward* written in 1917.

I am indebted to Mrs. Bertha Klausner for innumerable kindnesses, to Miss Patricia Ellsworth for correcting my spelling, to Mr. Carleton Beals for his friendship and for many illuminating comments on Trotsky's life and works, to Dr. Alexandra Adler and her brother, Dr. Kurt Adler, for their reminiscences of Trotsky and Natalie in Vienna, and to Miss Gladys Carr, my editor, for her insight and understanding.

INDEX

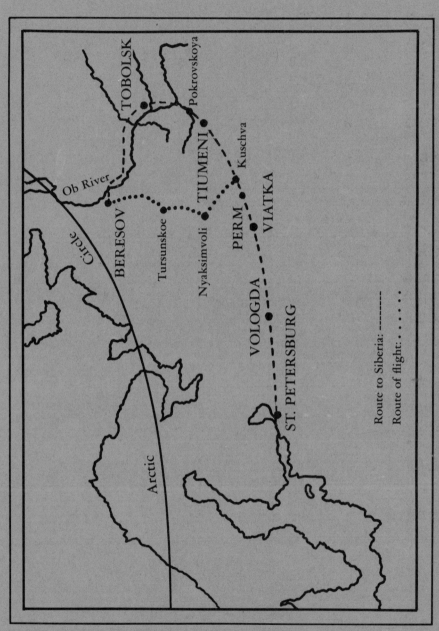

Map showing Trotsky's second flight from Siberia.

TOBOLSK

BERESOV

Ob River

Tursunskoe

Nyaksimvoli

TIUMENI

Pokrovskoya

Kuschva

PERM

VIATKA

VOLOGDA

ST. PETERSBURG

Circle

Arctic

Route to Siberia: ———
Route of flight: • • • • • •